Elizabeth Wurtzel's
BITCH: IN PRAISE OF DIFFICULT WOMEN

Bitch Gets People Talking . . .

The Good

"One of the more honest, insightful, and witty books on the subject of women to have come along in a while." —*The New York Times Book Review*

"The Courtney Love of letters . . . extraordinarily thought-provoking, absorbing, wise, often poignant. You can disagree with Wurtzel, but at least she always has a definite point of view." —*Entertainment Weekly*

"Wurtzel . . . is truly a *Wunderkind*. She's brilliant, original, outspoken . . . This is a big, brash, and bountiful book." —*Booklist* (starred review)

"It's got the preposterous energy of a great, drunken tantrum, and a voluptuous, sprawling style, with lots of good, zinging jokes . . ." —*The Village Voice Literary Supplement*

"This promiscuous rampage through the raw stuff of popular culture . . . is as outrageous, suggestive and difficult as the post-feminist role-model it takes as its subject. A vastly entertaining, at times virtuosic rant . . ." —*Esquire* (U.K.)

"The history of female manipulation as told by the baddest, brainiest babe from Generation X . . . for all her bitchy poses and sassy one-liners, she still comes across as someone who is generous, fun, thoughtful and—irony of ironies—nice." —*The Express* (London)

"Wurtzel is an intelligent writer . . . fast-paced and convincing."
—*The Daily Telegraph* (London)

"*Bitch* is a brilliant feminist manifesto in the great tradition that stretches from Mary Wollstonecraft to Germaine Greer." —Elaine Showalter in *The Guardian* (London)

"[Wurtzel] drops phrases that are surgically funny in their incisiveness. Depending on the occasion, Wurtzel can be catty, opinionated, empathetic or scurrilous, but always with a backbone of solid research." —*Publishers Weekly*

"*Bitch* is a show-stopping, name-dropping, gossip-dishing, wild rock-n-roll performance . . . [Wurtzel's] analogies, similes and metaphors are wildly exuberant, and exciting . . . This is a bitch of a book."
—*Washington Post*

"Thoughtful analysis, a lot of entertaining information, and a good deal of clever writing . . . Wurtzel's talent for provocative prose and sexy subjects perfectly lends itself to a screed on female power."
—*Kirkus Reviews*

"Certainly, Wurtzel has her finger, even her middle one, on something here." —*USA Today*

The Bad

" 'The Blonde in the Bleachers' takes Hillary Clinton over the sticks for underachieving. A tiring read." —*Time Out* (London)

"It is unclear why Wurtzel, a prodigiously gifted, if outrageously self-involved, writer, believes that this tawdry story, which has long since been picked clean of any insights, merits yet more parsing." —*The Globe and Mail* (Toronto)

"Her aggressively chatty book reads like a dorm-room bull session, rambling from Delilah to Anne Sexton to Courtney Love to Nicole Brown Simpson—all difficult women 'of extremely different sorts'—without really presenting a definition or an argument . . . Along with the old feminism she has so gladly jettisoned, she has abandoned any attempt at polite sisterhood." —*San Francisco Chronicle*

"The next installment in The World According to Liz . . . puts Wurtzel in serious contention to usurp Camille Paglia as the loud-mouthed loose cannon of pseudo-intellectual, quasi-feminist cultural criticism." —*New Times Los Angeles*

"Wurtzel's reductive theorizing, coupled with her penchant for posing in half-naked states of repose, established her mainly as hot damaged goods . . . self-flagellation, as Wurtzel can attest, is a hell of a career move." —*Spin*

"*Prozac Nation* established Wurtzel as the voice of all self-centered, self-pitying own-worst-enemies. Her new book is that much more proof that she's the right woman for the job." —*Fort Worth Star-Telegram*

"*Bitch* is, more or less, a meandering lamentation on the fate of irrepressible women, those too angry, too tormented, too selfish . . . While Wurtzel's plaint is heartfelt, it isn't more than that. The book is all shapeless feeling." —*Time*

"One wants to say: Please shut up, because Wurtzel rambles endlessly, making points and then abandoning them, piling up plots and song lyrics and media detritus, pausing now and then to opine on various things . . . These struttings and preenings suggest that she prefers her audience prone, passive and awestruck. When I finally put this book down, my overwhelming feeling was one of relief at having been released from such a confining role." —*The Nation*

"The book's glimpses of truth are unnerving, mostly because they close the distance between themselves and *Bitch*'s exceedingly distraught author." —*Time Out New York*

"Wurtzel's second book, *Bitch,* is not a good book . . . After the introduction, *Bitch* disintegrates quickly into a rant. In most of the book there is no method to Wurtzel's affected madness." —*New York Press*

"Hip turns of phrase frequently replace logic in this often smug and overwritten screed. In her defense, Wurtzel has taken on a huge project, and every now and again she introduces a startling insight about how women manipulate situations to control their lives . . . Recommended only as catalyst for debate." —*Library Journal*

The Bitchy

"What follows can ultimately be judged by its cover: saucy, sassy, but ultimately rather silly . . . Wow—what a bitch." —*The Wall Street Journal*

"One wants to scream at the cover picture, 'Damn, honey, no one's gonna confuse you with a beauty queen, either.' *Bitch* begets bitchiness." —*Salon*

"Ostensibly a book about bitchy women throughout history, it is really a bitchy book about one woman: the author herself." —*Swing*

"Bottom line: Rambling, self-important dog of a book." —*People*

"I find myself flip-flopping between sympathizing with and wanting to muzzle the mercurial Wurtzel." —Louisa Kamps, *Mirabella*

The Bottom Line

"Like demanding women, pathbreaking and impossible to dismiss." —*Ms.*

"It will absolutely make you furious. Yet while you may want to bash *Bitch* or burn it, I dare you to put it down for long. There's something about it—so bold, so bald?—that's just so good." —*Hartford Courant*

"Wurtzel is insouciant. And that's the reason many loathe and others like her book." —*Boston Globe*

Bitch

Also by Elizabeth Wurtzel

Prozac Nation

Bitch

In Praise of Difficult Women

Elizabeth Wurtzel

ANCHOR BOOKS
DOUBLEDAY
NEW YORK LONDON TORONTO SYDNEY AUCKLAND

For Betsy Lerner and Lydia Wills, without whom . . .

AN ANCHOR BOOK
PUBLISHED BY DOUBLEDAY
a division of Random House, Inc.
1540 Broadway, New York, New York 10036

ANCHOR BOOKS, DOUBLEDAY, and the portrayal of an anchor are trademarks of Doubleday, a division of Random House, Inc.

Book design by Brian Mulligan

Bitch was originally published in hardcover by Doubleday in 1998.

The Library of Congress has cataloged the Doubleday hardcover edition as follows:
Wurtzel, Elizabeth.
  Bitch : in praise of difficult women / Elizabeth Wurtzel. —1st ed.
    p. cm.
  Includes bibliographical references.
  1. Women—Biography. 2. Femmes fatales—Biography. I. Title.
 HQ1123.W87 1998
 920.72—dc21   97-52106
                 CIP

ISBN 0-385-48401-1

Copyright © 1998 by Elizabeth Wurtzel

All Rights Reserved

Printed in the United States of America

First Anchor Books Edition: June 1999

10 9 8 7 6 5 4 3 2 1

Down with a world in which the guarantee that we will not die of starvation has been purchased with the guarantee that we will die of boredom.

—Situationist graffiti
Paris 1968

Contents

Manufacturing Fascination

The chief glory of a woman is not to be talked of, said
Pericles, himself a much-talked-of man.

VIRGINIA WOOLF
A Room of One's Own

In the November 1996 issue of *Allure,* editor-in-chief Linda Wells
writes a column about how she wants to be dark and bad. This is a
woman so blonde and light-eyed and white as the driven snow that for
her to imagine herself as lush, in torrents, a smoky volcano of gushing
feminine lava, is preposterous. As it is, Ms. Wells runs a makeup magazine and doesn't even wear much makeup. But still, when a man in
the gym flirts with her by saying, "Hey, Ivory Girl, can I walk you
back to work?" she is deeply offended. "In my mind, I'm the last
person who'd . . . wash my face with a soap billed as $99\,^{44}/_{100}\%$
pure," Wells writes. "I may look blond and corn-fed, I may come from
a long line of Iowa farmers, but in my heart I am dark and cynical and
dangerous . . . So humor me. Tell me I'm Catherine Deneuve, Anna
Magnani, Dominique Sanda, just don't tell me the truth."

This true confession is, of course, much less alarming than any
woman admitting that, in her secret life, she wishes she were Sandra
Dee or Doris Day or Tipper Gore. Unless she wanted to take on these
roles in order to prove—in a fantasy within a fantasy—that these girl-

next-door types, these natural blondes in shapeless Lilly Pulitzer garden shifts and white gloves, are actually, really and truly, bad girls too. Because bad is where it's at: bad is such a good thing that in the Orwellian terms of hip-hop speak, *bad* means *good*. Consider the metamorphosis that unfurls within that multiplex touchstone of feminist bad-goodness (good-badness?), *Thelma & Louise*. Consider, in particular, the way Geena Davis' ditsy Thelma butterflies from a mothy, frothy microwave-meal homemaker into an Amazon avenger who chooses death over drudgery, who refuses to be stuck between a rape and a hard place. "You better be nice to your wife," Thelma warns a highway patrolman as she holds a gun to his head and leads him to be locked into the trunk of a car. "My husband wasn't nice to me, and look how I turned out." To be a do-right woman, the movie's moral assures us, sometimes you have to do wrong.

And now that Mother Teresa is finally dead, it is safe to say that the Goody Two-Shoes as real, live girl has so thoroughly fallen from grace in recent years that those branded with virtue—perhaps with a scarlet letter "V" on their foreheads, like two fingers signing for peace—will go as far as taking off their clothes just to change the label. Really: Mary Poppins, also known as Julie Andrews, actually pulled off her top and triumphantly bared her breasts in the 1981 movie *S.O.B.*, seemingly for no reason other than to let the world know that she actually *has* breasts. Judy Norton, best-known as eldest daughter Mary Ellen on *The Waltons*, felt locked in the role of Depression-era daddy's girl—where she will stay forever if the Family channel has anything to say about it—and tried to remedy this in 1982 by posing nude in *Playboy*. Of course, Miss America 1984 was not trying to prove anything when she turned up nude and sapphically engaged in the pages of *Penthouse*. And while Vanessa Williams may not have wished for the unsanctioned exposure, she is the only Miss America to have a real, infomercial-free show business career—Phyllis George, Lee Meriwether and Mary Anne Mobley are examples of title holders who have not-real not-quite-careers—and it's probably in no small part thanks to the photographic revelations of her raunchy un-American activities. But if Ms. Williams let down Bert Parks and America, Jessica Hahn betrayed God, the church and Jim Bakker—of course,

Jim Bakker was also betraying God, the church and probably himself—by posing nude in *Playboy* (before and after extensive cosmetic renovations). La Toya Jackson betrayed her family (which is hard to do) by posing nude in *Playboy*. Of course, some people try to escape their treacly-true pasts in less drastic ways: Debbie Gibson became Deborah Gibson and made sultry videos that involved sheer clothing and wet hair, directed by fashion photographer Matthew Ralston. While Ms. Gibson wasn't able to escape her cheerleader days quite so easily, cute little Gertie from *E.T.* grew up to be Drew Barrymore and showed no sign of her cherubic childhood ever again; she too posed nude in *Playboy*.

Obviously, in the pageantry of public life, in the places where women invent personae, the one statement a girl can make to declare her strength, her surefootedness, her autonomy—her self as a *self*—is to somehow be bad, somehow do something that is surely going to make her parents weep. No one is advocating acting like Marie Antoinette, no one wants to show serious indifference in the face of human suffering, but rebellious and unladylike and occasionally antisocial acts are the obvious statement.

The bitch as role model, as icon and idea, has moments of style and occasions of substance—it at times looks like just the latest mask, a game to play, a chance to dress like something out of a Joan Crawford movie, and to act like something out of *Mommie Dearest;* but quite often it reveals itself to be about genuine anger, disturbance, fear and the kind of female resentment and rage that produce the likes of Jean Harris, Lorena Bobbitt, Amy Fisher, Susan Smith and Aileen Wuornos, among others. But no one in her right mind wants to end up doing time, no one wants to be moved to Medea-like acts or gun-crazy jealousy—no one wants to end up a sex kitten in the slammer. What we all want is to cop the cosmetic attitude, we want to be Olivia Newton-John in the last scene of *Grease,* the girl swiveling her foot like a broken record to put out a cigarette with one of her red Candie's slides, the girl with ratted hair, in slinky shiny black pegged pants, the girl in the blue eye shadow that launched a thousand teenage makeup misfires. Yes, by the end of *Grease,* Sandy has become your basic 1958 model ho: the girl who, after suffering months of rejection for being a party-pooper prude who didn't drink or smoke, has finally realized that you *do* have to pet to be popular, that you *do* have to put out to get the guy, that it isn't the blondes who have more fun—it's the sluts.

These same good girls gone bad of that epoch would linger, languish and finally reemerge at century's end as the full-grown woman in a song by Trisha Yearwood, the Galatea-good Everygirl of country music who is careerist and proud of it, and who sings in "I Want to Go Too Far" about a reliable, steady housewife who wants to fuck up once in a while, who wants to forget to pick up the kids from soccer practice, who wants to wear fishnet stockings. It is the same woman played by Michelle Pfeiffer in *Batman Returns,* the mousy and meek secretary by day who uses leather and lamé to become Catwoman by night, to flip and strut, to scratch and bite, to be the mouse that roared with dangerous curves; and cat-scratch fever, we're meant to understand, is a mild malady compared to what this feline woman can do to you when she's mad. It is the same woman who, way back in the seventies, went from natty housecoat to negligee in a perfume commercial, all the while singing, "I've been sweet and I've been good / I've had a long hard day of motherhood / But I'm gonna have an Aviance night." Presumably, an Aviance night involved all sorts of naughty behavior, though at this point none of us will ever know since the fragrance is either gone or gone into remission. Not that there is any want of new potions and pills and powders, more and more each day, promising Poison and Opium and Tabu and Obsession, meant to induce the same idea, still selling hope in a bottle, still assuring those of us who are cursed with wholesomeness that we can somehow fake it, can somehow be a bad girl—or just look/smell/act like one.

These days the only female role more entrancing than the darkly, distraughtly bad is the small town sweetheart who drips sugar and saccharine for all the world to see but is in fact full of lust and evil (which are one and the same in woman) and malice and bad thoughts in her secret, sinful Jungian shadow life. That was the idea behind the fresh-faced teen-dream doom of Laura Palmer, in the briefly mesmerizing *Twin Peaks,* her busty body the most enchanting corpse ever to grace network television, with eyes of red and lips of blue, purple from bruising and slugs and decay, wrapped like crepe filling in cellophane—this was the homecoming queen by day and the hooker with a heart of dope-pumping ventricles by night. These two Palmer personae seemed to compete for dominance—would sweet sixteen or sordid slut prevail?—with death the *deus ex machina* that allowed the series' creator David Lynch to avoid the impossibility of integrating both, of granting this girl on the edge of womanhood the frankly simple complexity that would allow her to be a sex maniac who also participates in 4-H Club. The fact that our culture seems to swing between sweet spans of preferring perky Debbie Reynolds and sophisticated bouts of embracing the more soignée charms of Elizabeth Taylor—with Eddie Fisher hanging in the balance—is further fomented by the way these contradictory impulses are played out within the woman herself: Laura Palmer was a crude mock-up of the divided girl, and the war of attrition within was seen as more destructive to this character than the murder weapon that killed her. David Lynch could not conjure a woman good and bad at once.

But of course it's not that simple. Calvin Klein's launch of a fragrance called Contradiction in the fall of 1997 was fashionable mass production's first acknowledgment of woman's desire for her warring factions to find peaceful coexistence, for bad and good to show a unified front—and really baffle an unsuspecting world that would prefer to reduce us to all types.

There was a point in the late fifties and early sixties when what was really simple old-fashioned blandness in Doris Day and her cohort could actually be mistaken for virtue and goodness—for actual traits and not a lack thereof. There was even a time, a bit before that, when it almost seemed interesting—and it was surely profitable—to be the good girl. It was a time when Betty Grable's million-dollar legs looked plumply wholesome even photographed from behind, when this St. Louis pinup girl could be the top female box office draw for eleven years straight (1941–52) and could find her Midwestern self, in 1942, earning more money than any woman on earth—raking it in by selling sex appeal that packed no wallop, by representing to our warring men abroad their innocent nonsyphilitic sweethearts at home. But at this point in time, it is no longer possible to fantasize a good girl who's not also a bad girl, it is impossible to think of Mary Magdalene and the Virgin Mary as anything other than one and the same, to understand that good and bad are not opposites, they are both just different forms of intensity. Even good old-fashioned Christianity seems to recognize the slippery slope of sin and saintliness: Saint Augustine was not beatified until after he lived out his *Confessions;* Pope John Paul II did not work his way up the Vatican without first spending his youth among the Warsaw theater crowd—and we all know about those actor types. Likewise, in Mary Magdalene, a whore becomes a devotee of Christ; in the Virgin Mary, an out-of-wedlock birth becomes an immaculate conception. Unless you are running for First Lady, no one wants to seem simply virtuous—of course, we all in fact want to *be* virtuous: We want to use our powers of persuasion to do evil to those who deserve our evil, we want to be Xena and Wonder Woman and Mata Hari and Judith, we want to be the hooker with the heart of gold who elbows the seducer and goes home with the hero. If a woman is good enough to be good, she is also good enough to be bad. The idea is always to tame the shrew, to turn decadence to devotion. Barbara Stanwyck is a murderous wife in *Double Indemnity* and a saintly mother in *Stella Dallas;* Joan Crawford could play both roles in a single film, going back and forth from terrifying to tragic in *Mildred Pierce.*

And with the complexities of the forties film star in mind, the cosmetics industry has helped paint the forbidding face and inviting body of the woman with trouble in mind, creating surface solutions so subtle that you don't have to be cheap or tarty to carry them off, proferring bits of bad detailing to the otherwise well-behaved woman, like silky, sexy, lacy lingerie worn under a corporate, conservative gabardine suit. The trend began with the blood-black Chanel nail polish called Vamp that no store in the country could keep in stock when it debuted in 1994, and which has since been spun off into Metallic Vamp and Very Vamp, as well as Vamp-colored mascara, for that bloodshot, bloodless bad-girl look. In the wake of the Vamp phenomenon, in an effort to satisfy the desire for rouge-noir nails and a matching mouth, Estée Lauder has come up with a color called Midnight, Revlon makes a version called Vixen, Maybelline calls its gash-red varnish Seduction and the manicurists' brand Essie gets right to the point with Wicked. In general, makeup makers, sensing that women may use lipstick to evoke outlaw images that their workaday world won't abide, have taken to naming their shades not after, well, colors, but in suggestion of ideas and concepts: MAC's deepest darkest lipstick is called Diva, Estée Lauder's pure purple is called Naughty, its pinkish purple goes by Racy, its rich mauve is known as Fatale (also the name of a MAC sheer purple). Maybelline just introduced potent red lipstick and nail polish in a color called Rogue Vogue, and a cheap line of nail color called Temptress names its dark shades after legendary bad girls like Circe and Delilah.

But for most of us, there are some obvious associations with the word "bitch": stiletto heels and dark, demimonde eyes on recent runways; the Gorgon-like horror produced by movies like *Fatal Attraction* and *The Hand That Rocks the Cradle,* the evil of bland ambition in *To Die For* and *Disclosure,* the chilly allure of films like *Body Heat* and *Basic Instinct;* the cool badness and icy manipulation of all of Sharon Stone's roles, of her grande dame style, of her refusal to return the diamond necklace to Harry Winston after the Oscars; the calamitous onstage presence and offstage existence of Courtney Love, which have allowed her to realize in real life a character that Madonna in her mock bravado could only dream of; Roseanne's habit of saying things like "All women should kill their husbands"; the icy young blondes of the Grand Old Party; the gabby and acerbic pundits (or "pundettes," as they've been diminutively called) with long legs in short skirts and think-tank or law-clerk credentials, like Ann Coulter, Jennifer Grossman, Kellyanne Fitzpatrick and, arch-Conservative above all, Laura Ingraham, whose leopard-print mini helped get her stints as a commentator on CBS and MSNBC; Shannen Doherty's reckless behavior and brattiness that caused an ex-fiancé to get a restraining order against her and some anti-fans to create the *I Hate Brenda Newsletter;* or the simple fact that the much-maligned model Naomi Campbell, dropped by Elite because "no money or prestige could further justify the abuse that has been imposed on [those she worked with]," simply said in response to her dismissal, "I'm a hardworking bitch. I do what I want to do. Life is too short—you have to go for it."

You have to go for it.

After all, as it says on a needlepoint sampler or throw pillow or the occasional bumper sticker: *Good girls go to heaven, but bad girls go everywhere.* In high heels. Or mules by Manolo Blahnik, the strappy, tangly kind that give you blisters. And when their feet start to hurt, they bitch about it a lot, until someone agrees to carry them home. Bad girls understand that there is no point in being good and suffering in silence. What good has *good* ever done? We women still only make seventy-one cents, on average, for every man's dollar. We still have to listen to studies telling us that a single woman over the age of thirty-five had best avoid airplanes because she is more likely to die in a terrorist attack than get married (and even after Susan Faludi refuted the numbers, we still had to hear Rosie O'Donnell point out in *Sleepless in Seattle* that the study "feels true, even if it isn't"). We still have to endure *The Rules* and learn never to accept a Saturday-night date if it's after Wednesday. And we're still stuck with Clarence Thomas on the Supreme Court. So why be good? Anita Hill, a good girl if there ever was one, uptight and reticent, a woman who chooses to live in Norman, Oklahoma—and probably wanted nothing more than to just be left alone in her Valium-like calm—still had to listen to Orrin Hatch read to her from *The Exorcist,* still had to be asked by Senator Howell Heflin if she was a "scorned woman" and still had to have an entire book written about her by right-wing muckmaker David Brock. Like Anita Hill, Princess Diana behaved with perfect restraint and dignity for years—waving from the royal horse coach and giving her head over to millinery madness, all the while her husband carried on with Camilla Parker Bowles—and what good did it do her?

Women seem to be the repository of aeons of ages of bad blood, beginning with Eve, ending our stay in Eden with her curiosity and lust for strange fruit, and it has started to seem that even if we act like good girls, the world is still quite likely to find us bad. So to hell with dignity. Dignity has got nothing on Rita Hayworth singing "Put the Blame on Mame" in *Gilda,* and absolutely nothing on Mae West in anything. It seems far more exciting to be a Siren beckoning with her song or Calypso captivating on her island than to be Penelope, the archetype of female fidelity, weaving and unweaving at her loom, sending her suitors away, waiting for the errant Odysseus to return, waiting while he luxuriates in lotusland, waiting while, as one correspondent to *The New York Times Book* Review put it, he "commits adultery with various gorgeous, high-class women," waiting for her husband like Lucy waits for Desi at the end of the day, or Alice waits for Ralph at the end of the night. Bad girls don't wait around—one doesn't get to go *everywhere* by sitting by the phone.

* * *

If fascination with fabulous women of great mischief were not a real phenomenon, the media probably would have invented it. In 1993, *People* put Sharon Stone on its cover next to the caption "HOLLY-WOOD'S SEXY REBELS: SHARON STONE, SHANNEN DO-HERTY, KIM BASINGER and a new breed of actress are playing by their own rules and making no apologies for taking charge of their lives." A *Village Voice* "Female Trouble" column titled "Season of the Bitch" mused that Sharon Stone gets to play characters who kill men and say, "I wasn't dating him; I was *fucking* him." Novelist Katherine Dunn weighed in on bad girls in *Vogue* in 1995, pointing out, "It isn't the 'Fuck me' pump anymore. Now it's the 'Fuck you' shoe," and also noted that "women who pay their own rent don't have to be nice." British *Elle* contemplated "The Rise and Rise of the Bad Girl." *Cosmopolitan* covered the "Hollywood Brats." In an article titled "Temper, Temper," the September 1996 *Allure* noted an increase in the unabashed acting-out of celebrity rage, itemizing such incidents as photographer Annie Leibovitz' balling out a cripple whose slow gait was slowing down her taxi, Marla Maples' sidewalk tirade at a snoopy reporter while sapling Tiffany looked on, Lauren Bacall's screaming so loud into her cellular phone that she made the limousine she was riding in shake, Raquel Welch's scissoring a costume and throwing a mirror backstage during her engagement in Broadway's *Victor/Victoria,* and bad book-tour behavior that has earned the best-selling author of *My Mother, Myself* the sobriquet Nancy Friday the Thirteenth. Amazingly, the article did not once mention Roseanne.

In April 1996 *Esquire* gave the subject of dangerous women per-haps the most thoughtful and serious attention when it put Nadja Auermann, sharply and coldly blonde, looking every inch the pinup girl for the Third Reich (the Allies had Betty Grable—I'm sure they must have had *something*), on a black-and-white cover with the head-line "I'M SORRY I RUINED YOUR LIFE." The accompanying essay by Ron Rosenbaum, "In Praise of Difficult Women," seemed a triumph for her kind because it viewed those manipulative, heartbreaking wonders of wile precisely as they would like to see themselves: as trouble, trouble and more trouble—but worth every minute of hell. It did not surprise me when, several issues later, *Esquire* published an article called "The Return of the Alpha Male," which seemed to in some way be about how to arm yourself against predatory women.

At the same time, British writer Julie Burchill came out in the *Sunday Times* of London—after having left her husband for a woman and then left that woman for her brother, all the while engaging in a transatlantic fight by fax with Camille Paglia—with an article titled "I'm a Bitch and I'm Proud." *Glamour* published "22 occasions when you shouldn't hesitate to be a bitch," including the all-encompassing "When reason, negotiation and fury have failed." A 'zine called *Bitch* with the tag line "Feminist Response to Pop Culture" appeared in 1996, and *Bust,* one of the more glossy house organs of female trouble, devoted a whole issue to bad girls, including an essay by Courtney Love called "Bad Like Me," a manifesto that explained, "Bad girls fuck your boyfriends, yeah, but we feel shitty about it, sort of." *Rolling Stone,* a magazine whose coverage of women's music has been lax and late at best (a 1969 issue devoted completely to groupies seemed to indicate that editor-in-chief Jann Wenner advocated a rock and roll derivation of Stokely Carmichael's assertion that "a woman's position in SNCC is prone"), tried to redress a three-decade imbalance by devoting its thirtieth anniversary issue, delivered in autumn of 1997, to rockers of the second sex. The distaff trinity of Tina Turner, Madonna and Courtney Love seemed to float on the photo on the cover. Trumping the competition by a month, *Spin* magazine—which has found its niche as the affirmative-action arm of rock publications—offered "The Girl Issue" in November 1997, with Fiona Apple's mischievous face on the front, highlighted by headlines promising that "SHE'S BEEN A BAD, BAD GIRL." *The New York Times Magazine* gave an all-encompassing nod to womanhood in general by devoting a whole issue to "Heroine Chic," and examining female icons from Gertrude Stein and Eleanor Roosevelt to Elizabeth Taylor and Greta Garbo to Martha Stewart and Coco Chanel. The issue's focus was not on bitches per se, but it is safe to argue that anytime a woman projects the kind of intense personality that all these women do, she is *somebody's* idea of a bitch. That may not actually be true about Eleanor Roosevelt and Gertrude Stein, but that is only because they were not pretty enough.

And these days putting out one's pretty power, one's pussy power, one's sexual energy out there for popular consumption no longer makes you a bimbo—it makes you smart. So now, all of a sudden, actresses and models whose livelihoods aren't in trouble take it all off for *Playboy*. The nude photographs—as likely to appear in *Vanity Fair* as elsewhere, especially if the subject is pregnant—are a career move, not a way to cash in, and it says: I've got it, and goddamnit, I'm gonna flaunt it, because anyone can think I'm a bimbo, but not just anyone can look this good naked. Sharon Stone and Cindy Crawford posed first in arty black-and-white in the late eighties and thereby made it safe for Drew Barrymore and Elle Macpherson to do the same thing in full color in the nineties. Farrah Fawcett, who first got naked for *Playboy* back when the mere sight of her unruly nipple puckering-up beneath an orange swimsuit made her hot stuff in the history of poster art, posed for the magazine once again at age fifty. For this half-century event, Farrah took the opportunity to demonstrate her artistic avocation, a kind of X-rated finger painting that involves covering her body with oil colors and impressing her flesh upon the canvas to produce abstract, amorphous results; a live-action pay-per-view special, with running commentary by Camille Paglia, accompanied the issue's publication. On the forever-young front, Drew Barrymore, who never seems older than eleven to me, even if she is over twenty-one and even if she was already married for a whole twenty-five days, makes a career of kitty-cat sexy roles and stripteases on David Letterman.

Beyond sex, of course, there is violence, though it is better when both are combined, hopefully in a way that is more dignified than, say, female mud wrestling. Toward that end, *Marie Claire* printed an article about criminal women at large, portraying them as clever and comely, and reminding me of two of the most indelible images of American life in the last twenty-five years: the promotional poster for *Bonnie and Clyde,* with Faye Dunaway in beret and thirties maxiskirt, wielding a gun, glamorous and competent all at once, her fashion statement somewhere between Ché Guevara and Edith Head; the other of Patty Hearst, in her Symbionese Liberation Army garb—fatigues and semiautomatic gun are topped off once again with a beret—just before she told the arresting officer, when forced to give an occupation, that she was an "urban guerrilla." I have no idea why it took so long thereafter for *Thelma & Louise,* for *La Femme Nikita,* for Linda Hamilton in *Terminator 2,* for Geena Davis in *The Long Kiss Goodnight* or for the NRA to find a female president in a four-foot-eleven grandmother named Marion Hammer (thus giving the appearance that as many women as men are gun-toting maniacs, an idea that, while interesting in the movies, seems both unlikely and unsavory in real life).

Naturally, the difficult dame has made her presence felt on Madison Avenue as well. When an update of the classic fragrance Ciara was introduced, it was called Ciara Femme Fatale, and is promoted with glamorous black-and-white photo ads of model Yasmeen Ghauri in a seductive pose and a sequined gown with copy that assures us, "Because the female of the species is more dangerous than the male." Van Cleef & Arpels, merchants of diamonds and rubies, played up the importance of giving the goods to the girl who plays hard to get with a series showing an elegantly groomed model coyly posed next to the ornate lettering of phrases like "She is the first woman who refused to take your phone calls" or "She is the woman men always wanted to run away with. You did." And while there is nothing particularly cheeky about the campaigns themselves, when the Duchess of York, Sarah Ferguson, became the spokeswoman for Weight Watchers and Ocean Spray, it prompted a *New York Times* advertising article on the wisdom of employing a controversial person like Fergie to pitch your product (the verdict: only Michael Jackson is absolutely verboten). Levi's for women sell jeans with anti-Cinderella print ads whose swervy yellow background is a wall for graffiti-ish handwriting that reads: "the princess dream. the pony dream. the pretty bride dream. Ready for the kick butt dream?" Nike ads have for a long time implored, even us girls, to just do it. Lingerie, always selling sex anyway, recently decided to sell—what the hell—omnipotence, in a sultry black-and-white ad for Lilyette bras and panties with copy that read: "I'm his nightlight. I'm his heater. I'm his favorite channel. I'm his umbrella. I'm his blanket. I'm his weapon. I'm his little voice. I'm his painkiller. I'm his savior. I'm his pillow. Which I guess could also make me his worst nightmare." Or mine—when, I have to wonder, does this woman find time to actually wear underwear? All this was reminiscent of an old television spot for an evanescent seventies scent called Enjoli, in which the model—who has got it going on in the bedroom and the boardroom—boasted that, among other things, "I can bring home the bacon / Fry it up in a pan / And never ever let you forget you're a man / 'Cause I'm a woman . . ."

Tough and tender—or maybe just plain tough—still has a sufficiently strong hold on women's hopes and dreams that we now, for the first time, appear to have a female boxing star, a West Virginia native named Christy Martin who's already merited a profile in *The New York Times Magazine*. This fledgling professional sport lures pay-per-view subscribers with leather-and-lingerie tournaments, and no doubt *Playboy* would not be covering the women's ring if the catfight fantasy were not part of the draw—but it should not be mistaken for male entertainment along the lines of female mud wrestling. Like the WNBA—whose sales and attendance in its 1997 debut season exceeded expectations by margins so large that the league is swiftly expanding—women's boxing has attracted spectators sickened by the antics of Mike Tyson and millionaire male fighters who have substituted theatrics and hysterics for admirable athleticism. Rene Denfeld, in gloves and gear on the cover of the paperback version of her book *The New Victorians,* became the first woman author to appear on her book jacket in such attire, not as some joke, but because she's a serious amateur contender. In 1997, the magazine *Condé Nast Sports for Women* was launched to serve both participants and observers of the boom in women's athletic activity. At this point in time, it seems a good idea for feminists to bury the hatchet when it comes to Pat Benatar's "Hit Me with Your Best Shot": maybe it inadvertently advocates domestic violence—but maybe it's just about getting in the ring. More and more, I notice women who don't, at least physically, look like they are vulnerable to shit. Angela Bassett may spend most of *Waiting to Exhale* dissolving in tears and scotch, but her muscle tone makes her appearance anything but fragile.

*   *   *

But women have long held a near-monopoly on artistic villainy. Apparently, we come to it by honest means, we seem to be built, or at least bred, for cattiness. "According to psychologist Robert Cairns, girls, at around age ten, develop a powerful, sophisticated technique that, although not physically assertive, uses alienation and rumor-mongering to vanquish a rival," writes Michael Segell in one of *Esquire*'s periodic attempts to remind its readers why women are not to be trusted. "This style of indirect aggression can emotionally devastate the victim, who often has no idea why, or even by whom, she's being attacked. Organizing social intrigues as a way of ganging up on a peer not only prolongs conflict but kindles larger group discord. As girls enter adulthood, they become even more skilled at using gossip, aspersions, and social ostracism to assault their adversaries." This doesn't even touch on the way women either do or are thought to use sex as a weapon, but it suggests the developmental model for the iconic bad girl, for the woman who thinks that bad means sassy, sexually manipulative, intriguing, a woman who knows that her persona is greater than her person. It's a woman who understands that she will achieve her apotheosis when anybody can project any idea, any neurotic impulse or erotic fantasy, onto her person, because she is the parallax view, the human *Rashomon*—because she is either that beguiling or that empty. Doesn't matter which is true.

And men somehow seem less inclined or less amenable to this kind of personality-as-performance thing. The strange idol worship that has attended Elvis since his death (nothing of that magnitude has followed John Lennon, Jim Morrison or Kurt Cobain) would suggest that it is possible for men, at least posthumously, to become mere receptacles for the projectile emotions of the masses. But Elvis is a highly sequined anomaly: for the most part it is famous women, both dead and alive, who become the dustbins for our dreams. This may just be because women are naturally more iconic than men are: there is a female quality, perhaps it is passivity, the ability to be objectified, to be the face that launched a thousand ships without so much as saying a word, that makes women perfect for ongoing and mesmerizing examination, even once they are six feet under. Women are idolized more for what they don't do—for how they look and what they project—while men must be men of action. That's why the female villainess is always more interesting than her male counterparts. In modern cinema, men rarely get to be *villains*—true Iagos—rather, they are just *bad guys*: the wrong sets of Mexicans in Sam Peckinpah films, the savage Indians in Sergio Leone Westerns, the evil cowboys in Kevin Costner movies, the guys Jeremy Irons and Jack Nicholson always play, that Jimmy Cagney and Marlon Brando used to play, the actors epitomized by James Woods, the ones with pockmarked cheeks, deep forehead scars, the ones with steely blue eyes and Indo-European accents. The ones you recognize immediately as Bad Guys. Tom Cruise and Tom Hanks will never play these parts. They are Good Guys always, that's that. Women are granted a bit more complexity. In fact, emotional complexity is the female icon's lot, while heroic simplicity is what works for the men. A female villainess rarely holds up a bank, and she gets to be seductive and sweet until that creepy moment when, suddenly, she just isn't. She is conniving and manipulative and tempting and treacherous. Insofar as a man ever becomes a complex character in old-fashioned film noir roles, it is because of the way the evil woman, the bitch, brings him down. Surely Fred MacMurray would not have done what he did without Barbara Stanwyck, without the way she walked down the stairs in her Los Feliz bungalow, the way he could tell by her ankle bracelet that she was hot.

She was hot, and by the end of *Double Indemnity* she was dead.

I only mention this as a reminder of the typical fate of the usual bad girl. Because it's important to remember that behind all the intrigue, almost like behind the curtain in *The Wizard of Oz,* these bad girls live miserable unfulfilled lives, lives of great style and utter misery. This book is a chronicle of that unhappiness. This book wishes to remind people that though Delilah may have brought Samson down, she went down with him, the temple falling on her head as well as his. Cleopatra may have been the great female ruler of her day, lover of many men and spurner of many more, she may have been the royal romper of the Nile, but she was a fool for love and she fell for Caesar and completely lost her head, and somehow she managed to let her boyfriend burn down the library in Alexandria, the repository of all the world's books and most of its knowledge. Anne Boleyn, of course, literally lost her head, as did Marie Antoinette—and Nicole Brown Simpson. And then there are all those glamorous literary babes: Zelda Fitzgerald as the toast of Montparnasse, Anne Sexton as beautiful blue-eyed Pulitzer Prize poet, who two-timed (and three-timed and four-timed) her husband, Sylvia Plath as sensitive suicidal college girl who married Ted Hughes and made a real-life Catherine and Heathcliff. Well, of course, Zelda died in an institution, Anne Sexton died in a gaseous garage and Sylvia Plath, most famously, stuck her head in the oven. Did Lou Reed write "Femme Fatale" for Edie Sedgwick or for Nico? Not that it much matters since both are dead now, both victims of the needle and the damage done, while Lou, he's clean, he's in love (with Laurie Anderson), he's a serious artist, he composes operas he gives performances at the Brooklyn Academy of Music using a stand for his lyric sheets as if he were a real musician. Eva Duarte Perón, a.k.a. Evita, not only died at thirty-three of ovarian cancer but has had to suffer the indignity of having her life turned into an Andrew Lloyd Weber musical. Of course, it could be worse: She could be Bette Davis, ending her career and her life with the likes of Shari Belafonte and Connie Sellecca (Mrs. John Tesh) on *Hotel*.

Thank God the only Rita Hayworth we know is the one from *Cover Girl* and *Blood and Sand*, the original redheaded pinup (I still wonder what they were thinking when they made Jean Harlow, who had already earned the distinction of being the original platinum blonde, the star of *Red-Headed Woman*), all aflame and ablaze. Let her daughter raise money and throw benefits on behalf of Alzheimer's disease sufferers like her mom—I'd just as soon remember Rita Hayworth the way she was, absolutely fabulous. And speaking of renowned redheads, do you suppose Sarah Ferguson, the Duchess of York, better known as Fergie, really enjoys having to do battle over titles and custody with Buckingham Palace? Don't you suppose that if she knew all this would happen she would have left the toe chomper back in Texas? For that matter, of course, the one bit of gratification Diana might have gotten from all her nasty dealings with Charles is that some of us still remember his telling Camilla Parker Bowles on a tapped telephone that he wished he could be one of her tampons.

Maybe it's me, but I would not want anything to do with any man who wished to be my, much less someone else's, tampon.

But these glamorous, tragic women were legends, such legends. For the sake of her legend alone Diana could have done nothing more graceful than die. A spate of sudden, recent and reissued biographies make for Diana-dominated best-seller lists, books repeating and competing over various versions of events, the godly details of the myth-making machinery retelling the same stories with minor differences, like the gospels of the New Testament. What becomes a legend most? Is it Natalie Wood in blackglama mink or Natalie Wood in a shroud? Put it this way, by the time she was floating like cork or beach glass or maybe just like a corpse, dead and drowned near Catalina Island, it had been years since *Bob and Carol and Ted and Alice,* years since *Marjorie Morningstar,* and married to the star of *Hart to Hart,* how long before she'd have been on bad television, the bitch-matriarch on a nighttime soap, Joan Collins and Jane Wyman and Barbara Bel Geddes all at once? But dead, today, she is still a black-haired beauty, it is still possible to forget that Marni Nixon did her singing in *West Side Story,* it is still possible to remember the sad, straitjacketed girl of *Splendor in the Grass,* still possible to wonder if Robert Wagner did not in fact kill her.

If Cary Grant, Jimmy Stewart, Clark Gable, Rudolph Valentino, Laurence Olivier and the likes of them, the male heartthrobs and matinee idols, have ceased to be fascinating postmortem, the female icons of yore have come alive in their deaths. Sure it's interesting to know that Olivier had an affair with Danny Kaye or that Gable secretly sired a daughter with Loretta Young. But the intrigue with these dead white males, it doesn't take on the quality of an archaeological dig, the longing to understand why Greta Garbo wanted so badly to be alone, why Judy Garland was so damn tragic, why Marilyn Monroe was a demolition derby, destroying nothing so much as herself. Marilyn, about whom so many books have been written that even non–biographer types—like literary lion Norman Mailer and feminist pussycat Gloria Steinem—have weighed in with deconstructing tomes of their own, occasionally seems to broaden the meaning of necrophilia. Thought to be a lot of trouble in her lifetime—in fact, Ms. Monroe's erratic behavior on the set of *The Misfits* was blamed for the death of Gable—Marilyn in the afterlife has become the liveliest corpse of all, a radiant effigy we hang over and over again.

*   *   *

One reason I think many bad girls come to a nasty end is a lack of conviction: they recoil at their own badness and try to be the sweethearts they were raised to be. They revert to type, a tad bit embarrassed that they actually stood up and stood out and demanded and demolished at will—at Nietzschean will—and try to cover their steps, back their tracks and be angelic. It is the mixed message, the ambiguity and ambivalence, that finally destroys them. The strong clear vision that is required to be a woman of heart and mind, of her own free will, is really quite hard. Just ask Madonna or Courtney. Why do you suppose that every so often—say, every third news cycle—those two will do interviews where they speak of their loneliness and vulnerability, where the reporter writes in astonishment about how ladylike they seem. In a recent profile of Donna Hanover in *W* magazine, the First Lady of New York City—who is also an anchorwoman and actress best known for a small part in *The People Vs. Larry Flynt*—allowed that Courtney had been to visit at Gracie Mansion. "She told me, 'I'm really much more conservative than people realize,' " Hanover reported. At this point, Courtney has had an entire makeover—conceding in interviews that she has surrendered her body to several cosmetic surgery procedures—and she appears on the cover of *Harper's Bazaar* and in the pages of *Vogue* as the Versace muse who has left her grunge-girl days behind her. Mademoiselle Love happily plays the part of rich socialite who, *mais oui, sans doute,* flies to Milan for the *alta moda,* to Paris for the *haute couture* collection shows, who has opted for lady instead of tramp.

Even Heather Locklear—who is not a bad girl, but plays one on TV—feels a constant need to distance herself from Amanda Woodward, saying that when the character is called a bitch, "I love it. As long as they don't call *me* a bitch." Blah blah blah. It's not that all this stuff isn't true—I bet it's completely true, but it probably always was. The point is that the world does not have room for women with big strong personalities—it simply will not tolerate their existence past a certain point, so they just kind of have to behave periodically—if they're smart (and the footnotes of the history of Hollywood, of literature and of rock and roll are littered with the names of the ones who weren't smart).

In contemporary cinema, it is not so much the great beauties whose private lives are found to be wanting as the ones who are career women or more generally manipulative. And most of the energy that should be going into creating compelling plots on-screen seems to go into the construction of personae off, so that insofar as films revolve around women at all—and mostly they don't—it doesn't much matter what happens, because the real fantasy is going on in gossip columns and on talk shows and tabloid TV. Put it this way—if people like to see Mel Gibson, Tom Hanks or Tom Cruise on the big screen, it's for what they are doing on-screen. Not that we aren't interested in who they're married to and what countries they are adopting children from and all that, but it is secondary. However, when we watch Julia Roberts, Sharon Stone, Cher or Barbra Streisand it is because of their messy, madcap private lives as much as anything: they are movie stars much more for their entire creation and being than for their talent per se. Actresses who cannot quite manufacture fascination, who don't have that *Vanity Fair* cover-story way about them—like Meryl Streep—can be very successful, but they will never be movie stars. Never. And the ones who do, even if their talent is minimal or unclear—think Drew Barrymore, Elizabeth Hurley, Madonna—will always find work, will always be on our minds, even if by all rights they have no business preoccupying anybody.

Beyond the sad story, this is also one that explores fascination. How is it that certain people become larger than life, it girls, cover girls, dream girls, goddesses, furies? How is it that for a period of time—sometimes just days, and occasionally decades—it does not matter how many stories are printed about some women, you could always stand a few more. Think of the weeks when we could not find out enough about Tonya Harding, distant as they seem now. Think of the months when we were held captive by the latest developments with Marla Maples and Ivana Trump, with Gennifer Flowers or Donna Rice and the political wives who refused to be involved in an imbroglio over infidelity. Or think of the era when Edie Sedgwick was so fully engaged with being a youthquaker that she made it seem like a legitimate job. And think of how long we've had to suffer with the headlines about Elizabeth Taylor and her men, her drugs, her muumuus, her diets, the chicken bones caught in her throat. And, by God, enough already with Jacqueline Kennedy. Ditto Marilyn Monroe. Or any of the fucking Kennedy women—any of the sisters, wives, mothers, mistresses—may they all dry out in the same sanitarium and leave behind no record of their recovery that can be turned into yet another tome.

Somehow there are these certain women who are capable of manufacturing fascination, who just seem so damn interesting, everything they do bespeaks trouble and scandal and a feeling that even when they're home all alone, there is always a party going on. Who can say just what makes it so? A couple of years ago every glossy magazine on earth seemed to be profiling the Miller sisters—Marie Chantal, Alexandra and Pia—because these three heiresses to a duty-free fortune (already this is off the charts for the vast majority of us who don't spend half our lives on the Continent) were all marrying princes and getting titles, or becoming fashion designers or renovating castles, or whatever. Point is, no matter how many pretty pictures there were of them or their elaborate nuptials—flowers by Robert Isabell, music by Peter Duchin, gown by Carolina Herrera, or something like that—it was impossible to care. They were just ciphers. All they did was get married. So what? Likewise, the only thing that actually made Gwyneth Paltrow seem interesting was dumping Brad Pitt, and he is the only reason she seems interesting to some people in the first place. Carolyn Bessette, on the other hand, has managed to hold our attention because there is something dark and unpleasant about her. She seems unhappy. She seems no-nonsense. She keeps her mouth shut. If she just sticks to this program, she may even have a future.

Women, you see, only become interesting if they give you the feeling that something is not quite right. In fact, altogether better if it's clear that things are very, very wrong. Your life may be miserable, but your death will be immortal. After all, Jayne Mansfield became much more interesting when she got involved with the Church of Satan, befriended Anton LeVay and then was rumored to have suffered the diabolical fate of being decapitated in a car accident. In fact, her big blonde wig was simply flung off her scalp when her neck snapped, and when it flew out of the convertible she was driving, tabloid pictures recording the scene turned the hairpiece into a head. This myth of Mansfield's beheading is rarely debunked because what can the truth hold to a story like that? Sure, she's still just a B movie Marilyn (this does not account for the many times when Monroe herself was just a B movie Marilyn) with a figure that defied gravity, but clearly she had her own demons. At any rate, she seems more substantial than Mamie Van Doren . . . but that's another story.

*   *   *

When I was an adolescent, I read *Rolling Stone*—this was back when it wasn't even properly stapled—with the rapt devotion as if it were the Bible and its Apocrypha combined. Probably the first girl rock and roller I got infatuated with who was not already dead was Deborah Harry. Blondie was a breakthrough, far more significant than they are given credit for, and their album *Parallel Line*'s a triumph of the cultural melting pot, where downtown punk met uptown disco. But really for me it was all about Debbie, her status as a junkie, her stint as a Playboy Bunny. All I wanted in life was bleached blonde hair and cheekbones so protuberant that they could seat six. But I really think I finally understood why the magazine had become my Ten Commandments when the first article about the Pretenders ran. *Rolling Stone* hardly ever bothered with girl singers, but Chrissie Hynde was special, a punk who wrote love songs, and she gave me a new possibility of chick, so tough, smoky eyes, boozy lips, but with this utter vulnerability.

And then there was Bernardine Dohrn, La Pasionaria of the sixties left, the smart part of the Weather Underground, the Post Office pinup bomber girl on the FBI's ten-most-wanted list who only surrendered herself to the law in 1980 after the G-men had so thoroughly harassed her and her fugitive family—she was by then the married mother of two, residing peacefully in the quiet post-radical enclave of Nyack, New York—that she negotiated her way above ground with a guarantee that she wouldn't have to serve time. Beautiful Bernardine—*Rolling*

Stone described her as "a stunningly attractive woman—bisque skin, brown eyes, a full figure"—was an attorney who attended the University of Chicago Law School; she knew about writ of *habeas corpus*. And still, Ms. Dohrn's dossier particularly interested me because for all her intellect, she couldn't help her hypersexuality, her need to seduce all the guys in the room. "She used sex to explore and cement political alliances," a friend is quoted in *Rolling Stone*. "Sex for her was a form of ideological activity." The article about her went on and on about how when she lived in a group house in Chicago with her fellow Weathermen, she would expose her breasts at the dinner table, make other outrageous plays for attention, refuse to contain her need to be noticed. "She would be arguing political points at the table with blouse open to the navel," one of her male housemates recalled. "It wasn't a moral thing, just sort of disconcerting. I couldn't concentrate on the arguments. 'Bernadine! Would you please button your blouse!' She just pulled out one of her breasts and, in that cold way of hers, said, 'You like this tit? Take it!' " To my teenage mind this was simply magnificent! What a distracting, dominating female presence she must have been! She was not some simple, easy girl who could be reduced to the stereotype of slut, her sexuality was so clearly her strength and not her weakness. Reading about Bernadine Dohrn made steamy carnality combined with college-girl smartness seem suddenly possible.

I'd had a taste of a different version of this same kind of excitement when I first heard Patti Smith's *Horses* a few years before. After that I stole her book *Babel* from the Lincoln Center Library of the Performing Arts and read it obsessively, especially the poems about rape and Judith and Marianne Faithfull and Edie Sedgwick. I didn't know what it was all about but I knew it was dirty and I thought it had something to do with liberation in a very large sense. *Jesus died for somebody's sins but not mine*—what more do you need to say, really? That's how *Horses* began and it always sounded just like I felt. And I don't think anyone who has not had this experience can really imagine what I mean. Sure, everywhere I looked, all around me, were terrific female role models, women doing amazing things, running for Congress, joining the army, refusing to be excluded from the Oak Room at the Plaza Hotel, having babies at age forty, whatever. But the feeling I got listening to Patti and Chrissie—as Michael Stipe put it in *Spin:* "There was a rawness and energy to *Horses* that I had not heard in any other music, ever. It was really wild and raw; there was an energy and a charisma to that music that set the room on fire. I'd never heard anything like it in my life, like someone had torn my head off and slapped it back on for me. From then on my life was changed." And me, I felt for the first time that I was a world waiting to be born. I felt it. I didn't think it or know it but goddamn I felt it. I felt that way listening to the Velvet Underground, or the first Stooges album or the MC5 doing "Kick Out the Jams." And hearing my true idol, Bruce Springsteen, I felt it also, but my connection with him came later. Patti and Chrissie, they were a wake-up call. I'm convinced that if Liz Phair and Courtney Love and a whole gamut of women in the raw had been around back then, I'd have been invincible. As it was, listening to Patti Smith, listening to the Pretenders, I was certain that if I ever got my hands on the world, I'd be sure to change it because the urgency I felt was that big. THAT BIG.

And I thought to myself: I don't have to live like this. I can be wild and free. I saw whole new ways to be a woman in the pages of *Rolling Stone* magazine, which was good because I didn't have the faintest idea of how to go about it on my own.

To explain it better—civil rights types and Negro leaders could talk about liberation and revolution at every church south of the Mason-Dixon line, but until Rosa Parks said with her actions, *I will not move,* it was all talk. And basically, until Patti Smith, a woman with hairy armpits and dirty hair got onstage and said, *"Can't you show me nothing more than surrender?"* the ERA really didn't mean shit. And that's why all the backpedaling and backstepping that goes on with powerful women today, with Hillary Clinton saying she could have stayed home and baked cookies and blah blah blah, and then offending everybody so that she had to say that she does, in fact, *love* to make cookies, loves it almost as much as she likes to trade agricultural futures. I mean, what is that about? All this I'm really a lady, I'm really a nice girl crap—who needs it? It really is nothing more than surrender.

The vibrancy I got from the women I idolized when I was growing up—I didn't get those feelings because they were giving the world a bunch of lines; I got them because they radiated truth.

*   *   *

For a woman it is never enough to be just an artist, just a talent: our art is our life, carrying on with charisma, all that counts. I don't mean that a woman has to be a great beauty to matter—Janis Joplin was far from anything of the sort, but she had great possession, great élan, she wore lamé and feathers and wiggled a lot, and the intensity of release in her soul singing all adds up to great style, and in that a great fight against the invisibility that would be hers because she is a woman and she is not a beauty. That's how Madonna came to be: she is the triumph of style alone, talent more in mise-en-scène than elsewhere. She reduces the requirements of visible femaleness so that all that is left *is* visible femaleness. And it is not surprising that she is the leap between Patti and Chrissie and eventually Courtney and Liz (in the rock world, there was nothing in between—Quarterflash and Pat Benatar don't count).

But woman's ability to use her sexuality to express liberation—which Madonna's whole career is so stylishly symbolic of—resulted paradoxically in her body's increased availability as an object of oppression. Since the sixties, the commodities of temptation and desire have been put on display in both a blatant and sidelong sense more now than ever: sex lines, the videocassette market that has made pornography a $5 billion a year industry, Victoria's Secret catalogues as a softer substitute, the Playboy channel, the virtual-reality sex sites that are the only real moneymakers on the Internet—all of these things are actually born of women's newfound freedom, and all of them serve mostly the interests of men. There is so much sex available in so many purchasable, perishable, inconsequential and trivial ways, so much that it practically *demands* that men focus on their sexual needs and ignore everything else. This has made for a lonelier world that gives the impression that it is more free. "I had come of age at a time when sexual liberation did not yet mean groupies and massage parlors, when it was still a potent metaphor for liberation in general," wrote Ellen Willis in 1975, in a *Rolling Stone* article about her brother's conversion to fundamentalist Judaism while visiting Israel. "Though I hated the way this vision [of sexual freedom] had been perverted, co-opted and turned against women, I believed no less in the vision it-self."

As feminism has charged forward—and no one can deny the leaps and strides it has made—so has the invention of the overeager hyper-sexualized female body. Nowadays you pay for sex not because you are lonely and miserable and can't get laid, or married and looking for cheap thrills, but because sex as a commodity is not distasteful; it's *interesting*. The recent best-seller by three Hollywood call girls, *You'll Never Make Love in This Town Again,* essentially chronicles the avail-ability for money of just about anything. The women write about their experiences servicing major Hollywood movie stars, men who presum-ably don't "have to" pay for sex, but like to be able to control the action, or like the absence of any emotional involvement, or just plain think it's cool. In the midst of all this, it seems hard to talk about date rape or anything else, because as much as women may try to be seen not as sex objects there is a countervailing force, in which many women collaborate—mostly out of financial need—to turn women into nothing but sex objects.

Which is why the good-time liberated lady whose sexual bravado could be celebrated by Germaine Greer and Helen Gurley Brown alike has metastasized over time into a harsh, hard force of flat, canned sexuality whose most protuberant and pertinent metonymy is the ob-vious and bulbous silicone breast implants that caricature a sexual reality that is already a cartoon, that don't even try to mimic mam-marian nature.

I think the choices become whether you will use it for yourself or against. Look, I think many people have rescued themselves from this game, but pretty girls, girls who learned to manipulate, girls whose hearts always belonged to daddy—they just can't help it. And the world rewards it at the same time it condemns it. On the whole, one lesson of a book like *You'll Never Make Love in This Town Again* is that sex is really not much of a weapon in the end. You need to have some talent and brains or nothing will work. Most men who sleep with some girl won't want to give her a job since they'd prefer never to deal with the situation again. I think that's the main thing that's miss-ing from any discussions of this subject—the complexities of date rape, the way strip clubs have become feminist enterprise zones while ignoring the degrading damaging nature of the work. For a woman to do just as she pleases and dispense with other people's needs, wants, demands and desires continues to be revolutionary. Men pretty much do as they will, and women pretty much continue to pick up the slack. That's why books like *The Rules* and *Men Are from Mars, Women Are from Venus* succeed. It remains to this day, even after feminism, a woman's chore to close the gap. Time is not on our side, our youth and beauty is brief, tick-tock the biological clock, and that message is thrown at us over and over again. In *Manhattan Nocturne,* an unusually perspicacious noir novel with the genre's usual theme of the good man brought down by a beautiful bad girl, the author Colin Harrison muses at one point on what a short shelf life a pretty girl in New York City has. "I would say the most determined people are the young women who arrive in the city from America and around the world to sell, in one way or another, their bodies: the models and strippers and actresses and dancers who know that time is running against them, that they are temporarily credentialed by youth."

Of course, we are meant to understand that this is the lot of glamour girls, that those of us who put brains before beauty need not worry about this stuff. But to paraphrase Rosie O'Donnell once again: It *feels* as if it's true for us all. And while there are commitment-phobic women, the story you always hear when there is a troubled relationship—when the balance of power is off—for the most part it's always the one of women trying to get men to tie the knot. Now, I personally know a number of women who are putting off their boyfriends who are eager to get married—but those relationships are not the ones that seem in constant crisis, they are not the ones where somebody is always complaining, because for any number of reasons, the focus on commitment still only assumes a desperate cast when the woman is the injured party.

And the fact that all this relationship anxiety marks a regression of sorts is not lost on pioneers of the women's movement who thought it would be better by now. London eating disorders expert Susie Orbach, author of *Fat Is a Feminist Issue,* is the founder of the Women's Therapy Centre, where among her patients was Princess Diana. "I see all sorts of young confident women around," she told *Mirabella* in late 1996. "But when they're in my consulting room, they talk about the same bloody issues we had thirty years ago. They're afraid. Women in the most oppressive relationships are trying to manage them rather than get out of them. Only now, with no women's movement, if you have problems you feel like a freak. All the problems are internalized."

That's why *The Rules* is a runaway best-seller and may well be a perennial hit.

But it is wrong to see that book as a setback to feminism in any way, or to be mad at the authoresses for their Aunt Edna-like advice because the book is completely nonideological: feminism is beside the point in a list of what is probably fairly sound advice for learning to behave like a woman who is about to embark on some serious, goal-oriented dating. It tells women how to act so as to compensate for the fact that while feminism has changed the way many of us think and behave, while it has made men change diapers and do dishes and spend quality time with children while women perform neurosurgery and direct movies and trade Eurodollars, it has failed to truly change the way we *feel*. As Ellen Willis put it, most succinctly: "Feminism had transformed women's consciousness without, as yet, transforming society, leaving a gap between what many of us demanded of a relationship and what most men were willing to give." The proof: Go to any bookstore and there are hundreds of titles in the self-help section about how to overcome love addiction and fear of abandonment and the like, and while there are plenty of books for women about how to deal with commitment-resistant, impossible men—*Smart Women, Foolish Choices* and the like—there is not one book addressed to men about how to work out their own damn problems with relationships. No book for men about how to get over fear of commitment, how to learn to open one's heart, how to stop running from emotional involvement—I know, because I searched high and low for such a thing for my last boyfriend and it doesn't exist.

Do you know why?

Because it doesn't need to. Men don't have to change the way they sexually assess women, the way certain triggers and indications of female power or feminine weakness may frighten them off. They don't have to change the psychic messages inculcated into their brains from way back in their preverbal, pre-Oedipal days. They don't have to because we women will learn to behave. We could all enact, by collective will, an emotional *Lysistrata* of sorts, we could all walk out, like Meryl Streep in *Kramer vs. Kramer,* like the woman in Mary-Chapin Carpenter's song "He Thinks He'll Keep Her," like the women in a zillion country songs—we could all say that we abdicate all responsibility for the emotional well-being of our relationships, let the men learn to cope with it all. But we don't. And there's no indication it would do any good anyway. So we'll "adjust"—the word Betty Friedan used over thirty years ago in *The Feminine Mystique* to describe how intelligent Seven Sisters types learned to accept the notion that Mop & Glo was intellectually stimulating—and if we're from Venus and they're from Mars, we'll learn to speak Martian. We'll follow *The Rules:* We won't call them, we won't ask them out, we won't talk about ourselves, we won't make snide comments, we'll be good.

Well, I for one am sick of it. All my life, one person or another has been telling me to behave, saying don't let a guy know you're a depressed maniac on the first date, don't just be yourself, don't show your feelings. And the truth is, this is probably good advice, men probably don't like overbearing, hotheaded women who give blow jobs on the first date. In all likelihood the only man who will ever like me just as I am will probably need to believe I'm somebody else at first. I probably *do* need to learn to behave. But I don't like it. It seems like, all this, all these years of feminism, Mary Wollstonecraft, Charlotte Perkins Gilman, Simone de Beauvoir, Virginia Woolf, Gloria Steinem, Susan Faludi—all that smart writing all so we could learn to behave? Bra burning in Atlantic City—so we could learn to behave? *Roe* v. *Wade*—so we could learn to behave? *Thelma & Louise*—so we could learn to behave? The gender gap—so we could learn to behave? Madonna, Sally Ride, Joycelyn Elders, Golda Meir, Anita Hill, Bette Davis, Leni Riefenstahl—all those strong, indefatigable souls so we could learn to behave? What good really have any of those things done if we still get the feeling that we have to contain our urges and control ourselves in the interest of courtship and love? Did Germaine Greer importune us so long ago with the words "Lady, love your cunt," and did Anka Radikovich regale us with her tales of the sexual picaresque in *The Wild Girls Club* so we could be told never to succumb to sexual abandon on the first date? After all this agitation, along comes *The Rules* to tell us that we're not even allowed to accept a date for a Saturday night after Wednesday.

Here's my point: I have no quarrel with *The Rules* or the advice it gives—it actually seems pretty sound to me—but if we had really come a long way, baby, if men's perceptions of women had transformed fundamentally and intensely so that we were accepted as full-fledged sexual creatures and romantic operatives who were free to chase or be chased, and if this expanded dimension of women's sexual personae were not frightening or overwhelming to them, then we would not need *The Rules*. We would be truly free.

So of course the bitch persona appeals to us. It is the illusion of liberation, of libertine abandon. What if you want to be large in a world that would have you be small, diminished? You don't want to diet, you don't want to say *no, thank you,* and pretend somehow that what is there is enough when always, always, you want more. That has been your defining characteristic: You have appetites, and only if you are truly shameless will you even begin to be sated because nothing is ever really enough. Not because you are greedy or insatiable but because you can't help it, you can't go along with the fiction that the world would have you believe and adhere to: that you ought to settle and be careful and accept the crumbs that are supposed to pass for a life, this minimized self you are supposed to put up with, that feminism and other political theories of woman cannot really begin to address because this is about something else entirely.

This is about what has become the almost monstrous notion of female desire. This is not about making demands of other people or wearing down those who have their own screams for MORE! to address: You'd be amazed at how often we are reluctant to indulge ourselves by our own means. It is amazing that the smallness of the space we've been told to squeeze into has meant that we don't even know how to ask or what to want. Everything tells us to stop, to not talk to that guy first, to not have a thousand lovers if that's what feels right because one husband is supposed to be enough. Everything says we don't need another piece of chocolate cake, we don't need another Gucci bag, another dime-store lipstick, another Big Mac, another night on the town, another spin on the Rainbow Room dance floor.

Well, this is meant to be a story about people who are so beyond need, who want and have figured out that it's never too soon to make demands of this life, this world, this everything. It's about how nice it must be to just decide I will not be nice, I am never sorry, I have no regrets: what is before me belongs to me.

I think for men this attitude is second nature, it's as much in their atmosphere as snow is in an Eskimo's. They don't even *know* how much they assume.

But for a woman, to assume she has to be not nice, it puts her outside of the system, outside of what is acceptable. She can be a deeply depressive Sylvia Plath, a luxuriating decadent Delilah, a homicidal adolescent Amy Fisher, she can be anyone who decides that what she wants and needs and believes and must do is more important than being nice. She may, in fact, be as nice as can be, but as soon as she says *catch me if you can I'm so free this is my life and the rest can fuck off and die*—as soon as she lays down the option of my way or the highway, it's amazing how quickly everyone finds her difficult, crazy, a nightmare: a bitch.

*   *   *

In the meantime, I intend to scream, shout, race the engine, call when I feel like it, throw tantrums in Bloomingdale's if I feel like it and confess intimate details about my life to complete strangers. I intend to do what I want to do and be whom I want to be and answer only to myself: that is, quite simply, the bitch philosophy, and it seems particularly refreshing in the face of all the contortions women are taught to put themselves through. All over the world there are men shouting orders and being impossible, and there are women hewing to these creatures' wills. The few women who manage to completely spit in the face of such an arrangement are naturally heroic. The appeal of films like *The Last Seduction* and *Basic Instinct* and *Thelma & Louise,* the reason the miniseries *Samson and Delilah* was recently made with Elizabeth Hurley, the reason Cher and Barbra Streisand have such staying power, the reason the bad behavior of Shannen Doherty and Naomi Campbell and Courtney Love is so intriguing is that you don't get the feeling these girls are reading *The Rules.* You don't necessarily get the feeling that they are happy, or that they are in healthy relationships, but at least their enslavement (and rest assured, these creatures, fact and fiction, are idolizing something or other or they would not be making so much noise) is not to a stopwatch reminding them to get off a phone with some guy after ten minutes, because they don't want to seem too chatty.

We have willingly accepted courtship terms not invented by us when really we should be insisting that the oppressiveness of this is terrible for all. "Of what materials can the heart be composed which can melt when insulted, and instead of revolting at injustice, kiss the rod?" Mary Wollstonecraft asked in 1791 in *A Vindication of the Rights of Woman,* a question still applicable, with our full realization of double entendre in use. We decide to learn to be the way men want us to be, rather than insisting they change to suit us. That's why we all hate Glenn Close in *Fatal Attraction:* It's not just that Alex is nuts, but also that she reads the situation from her own point of view, from a female perspective. She refuses to accept the idea that married men get a little on the side but are happy with their wives. The time-honored assumptions of the role of the mistress in a civilized society have not been rejected by her—no, it's far worse: they have not occurred to her to begin with. She is like a savage who encounters the affection and lust and electric energy she felt for that one weekend with her married lover and takes it for what it feels like: love. She is unable to mediate that emotion with societal truths, with the rules of engagement, with the demand that she be dignified and cool and know that he is married and that what she felt is therefore false. In our world, Alex is patently nuts for trusting her own experience, her own version of events. All of us, even women—even me—watch that movie and wish she'd get a grip. We don't honor her uncivil disobedience of the rules, even though those rules were written by men and for men. Why, at this late date, are women still playing by their rules?

It was an interesting cultural moment when Alanis Morissette's song "You Oughta Know" became a huge, smash, runaway hit. And besides the enormously appealing energy that is apparent in all aspects of the song, I have no doubt that it was such a marked success as much for the message—the grim, hurt, angry, avenging message—in the lyrics as anything else. It is, above all, a thoroughly desperate and undignified song addressed to a man who has left her—the narrator, the singer, the Alanis persona—for someone else. Of course, the history of the Top 40 is written in songs about this kind of heartbreak, so this isn't really a breakthrough. But Alanis' complete lack of shame about how crazy and bereft she feels—combined with a frightening fury, the kind that *Fatal Attraction* did so much to make the woman scorned feel embarrassed about—is what is so new. Morissette's voice vindicates Alex's actions. When she sings, "Do you remember how you told me that you'd love until you died / But you're still alive," you half expect that the next move will be homicide. And every time I hear that couplet, there is a part of me that thinks: *She* ought to know that people say that kind of thing all the time—"I'll love you forever," "You're the only one," etc.—and when the love dies so does the feeling, so grow up and deal with it. My sentiment, in fact, is a lesson of feminism—no woman should ever lose her mind over a man, a woman needs a man like a fish needs a bicycle—and it is also, strangely, one of the major messages of *The Rules*. "You're a *Rules* girl! Your life is never on the edge because of a man," the authors write. "Either a man is available and in love with you or he's taken and you have nothing to do with him romantically. You are not desperately waiting . . . You have a life of your own."

Of course, what is so refreshing about Alanis' song is its firm refusal to go along with this dictum: I mean, of course she has a life of her own, that's clear enough, she writes and sings songs. But she doesn't feel like any of that much matters, in the context of the situation of "You Oughta Know," because she is, indeed, on the edge because of a man. And she is not going to keep quiet about it. She is raving, she is sad, she is mad, she feels betrayed, and even if every day, all over the world, hearts are breaking like shards of china, she is not going to keep it in perspective, because *her* pain is too important. She is going to scream, she is going to disturb him at inappropriate moments—"I hate to bug you in the middle of dinner"—and she is going to ask him unacceptable questions—"And are you thinking of me when you fuck her?"—and she is even going to throw a voodoo curse his way—"Every time I scratch my nails on someone else's back I hope you feel it." And the funny thing is, by the end of the song, I do get the feeling that Alanis Morissette has achieved a great deal more dignity by being true to herself, her impulses, however idiotic, than any of us are by staying in control. Yes, it's better that you don't call five million times and stalk someone who has broken your heart because these actions genuinely have an incoherent and self-abasing quality, because few of us can be as firm in our convictions about having been wronged as the narrator of the song is. That's why, once again, we're all perhaps better off sticking to *The Rules*.

But let us not deny that this is a form of enslavement meant to please men, not women. "Men love independent women because they leave them alone," insists the book. "They love chasing women who are busy." In other words, that MBA, that PhD, those French lessons, that book contract—it's all so that men think we have better things to do. Which, I suppose, is one approach. But the other one, the Alanis Morissette approach, which has something to do with being true to yourself, with making clear what you need and want rather than concerning yourself with what men like—well, maybe I'm crazy, but I'd prefer her method any day. Because, frankly, I have a tough time feeling that feminism has done a damn bit of good if I can't be the way I am and have the world accommodate it on some level.

And I'm sure lots of people do things for Sharon Stone, Shannen Doherty, Drew Barrymore and the like just because they ask. Of course, people end up feeling put out and put upon, which is why I, like all women who believe the world needs them more than they need the world, am basically doomed, while the girls who live by *The Rules*, or some version thereof, seem happy. And at the same time that I want to celebrate and delight in these women's behavior, I want to always remember that the image that is being dangled before all of us is just another decoy meant to suggest that this is really possible, that wild women are thriving in this world—it is meant to distract us from the truth of the matter, which is that they really are not. And I don't just mean that most of us are not beautiful or talented enough to get away with this—I mean that *no one* is. Perhaps the whole world noticed when Di twisted her hair up and revealed her statuesque neck, but her husband was carrying on with someone else, overwhelmed and threatened by her flair for fascination. In *The House of Mirth*, what good did it do Lily Bart to be so enchanting? What consolation awaited Isabel Archer for her troubles in *Portrait of a Lady?* What happiness was there ever found for Anna Karenina?

The world will adulate the woman lying on the settee with a turban on in silk pajamas asking for the world to do her bidding, but ultimately it will extract a price in failed relationships, in isolated lives. I don't think it's really about being bitchy or demanding or cold or calculating: those characteristics, after all, can be attached to most women with even the paltriest of evidence. I think, quite frankly, that the world simply does not care for the complicated girls, the ones who seem too dark, too deep, too vibrant, too opinionated, the ones who are so intriguing that new men fall in love with them every day, at every meal where there's a waiter, in every taxi and on every train they board, in any instance where someone can get to know them just a little bit, just enough to get completely gone. But most men in the end don't quite have the stomach for that much person. Why do you suppose Arianna Huffington married a complete simpleton? Does anyone know where it is in the state of Tennessee that Dolly Parton keeps her husband hidden? These women knew what they needed to do to make the world work with them. But that's unusual.

Otherwise, the world has not really made room for alternate possibilities. Even Simone de Beauvoir was ultimately a fool for Sartre. No one is making it easier for us to just be free. Everybody loves to watch, whether it is a voyeurism of great anger like Courtney Love or great pain like Janis Joplin, or magnificent vulnerability like Marilyn Monroe, or gorgeous madness like Anne Sexton or stony glamour like Sharon Stone. But up close, up real, real close, it is not terribly accommodating to eccentric personalities. From a distance, we all admire the insane person, the creative genius and colorful type. But up close, no one wants to be bothered. And if this is true for men, it's doubly or trebly true for women. We have always been willing to cannibalize these brilliant creatures who shine, but really and truly we would much prefer that, in our dealings with them, they behave, they play by the rules: We want good girls, really we do.

This is a book about women who wrote and write their own operating manuals, written in the hope that the world may someday be a safer place for them, or for us, for all women.

PART ONE

He Puts Her on a Pedestal and She Goes Down on It

I told myself it was all something in her
But as we drove I knew it was something in me

BRUCE SPRINGSTEEN
"Highway 29"

On a recent Sunday, one of the hints in the *New York Times* crossword puzzle was "Acts like Delilah." I kept thinking that the answer would be "seduces" or "tempts" or "entices."

It was "betrays."

Right there you've got everything you need to know about what's wrong with the way most people read the Bible.

Most people I know who were forced as children to attend Sunday school or to take some extracurricular Bible class when they could have been throwing a Frisbee or—and this really dates me—playing Atari were, naturally, bored by it. In fact, the experience has left them with the sense that the Bible itself is boring. But I always knew better. I always knew that if Jerry Falwell had ever actually read what ought to be called "the good book" only with the greatest of irony, there is no way he would urge his congregation to do so. The Old Testament is a crazy caricaturish catalogue of archetypal stories that rely on random events and the last-minute hand of God—the *deus ex machina* as real event, not literary convention—to make them work out, in which the good and noble suffer endlessly and the naughty often get off scot-free (with promises of hell in the afterlife, which we somehow never see— Hades being a Greek invention of the New Testament epoch). Any attempt to decipher a moral message is wasted. It is a grim view of the world, one where might makes right, where birthright makes right— and if hairy Esau is the firstborn, then it is acceptable for less hirsute and less savage Jacob to steal the blessing of the eldest through deceit and trickery.

Whatever prattling homilies are offered in the more conciliatory gospels that comprise the New Testament (and the book of Revelation pretty much destroys the good intentions of the earlier chapters by offering an anarchist's cookbook of diabolical fare), the unredacted worldview of the Old Testament is a history of families and clans that beget nationalities and wars—it's all Serbs and Croats, Cowboys and Indians, Hatfields and McCoys, Irish Catholics and English Anglicans, Arabs and Jews—in short, the beginnings of what Freud describes as "the narcissism of minor differences." And none of it is very pretty. You barely get into Genesis and out of the Garden of Eden before Cain slays Abel, his own brother, and adds insult to injury by claiming he's not responsible for his actions: "Am I my brother's keeper?" is the natural precursor to the Twinkie defense and the abuse excuse. For the impulsive sin of turning to look back at the funereal pyre of Sodom and Gomorrah, Lot's wife is transmogrified into a pillar of salt as she flees the inferno; such a harsh punishment for such a thoroughly hu- man impulse as looking back longingly—this is just an example of how God makes an example of those who *just don't listen* to Him. After being the dream boy born to a ninety-year-old, presumed-barren Sarah, fair Isaac is saved from sacrifice on Abraham's altar—an inci- dent of God-mandated filicide that set the stage for a world in which the odds that a murdered child was killed by his own parents are twelve to one—by a whimsical Deity's last-minute interference, the rescuing hand of God that other victims of their parents' ill will—the children of Susan Smith, for example—were not granted.

But these acts of atrocity—occasionally alleviated by eleventh-hour episodes of Divine intervention—brought on by an Old Testament imagining of a Creator who is personified as both "jealous" and "vengeful," are small compared with the long, lingering pain that some of God's best-loved seem to endure. No sin can explain why Jeremiah suffered so much that he virtually invented the lament with his Jeremiads, no cinematic stage set of Herman Melville's dreams could justify Jonah doing time in the Leviathan, no bad behavior could be vindicated by forcing the prophet Ezekiel to lead the people through an atonement ritual that involved eating barley cakes mixed with excrement, nor did Daniel need to wrestle the lion to let us know that the Lord is God and what He wants, He gets, so heaven help us all. On a wager with Satan, God—as if heaven and hell were just a game of baccarat in a Las Vegas casino—takes the ever-faithful Job, smites his cattle with disease, decimates his wealth, sends a dust-bowl wind that bashes in his house, and when the roof caves in, it kills all ten of his children at once, all just to prove that nothing—*nothing*—will make this long-suffering servant of the Lord renounce righteousness and embrace the devil. "This man was blameless and upright," says the first sentence of the book of Job, describing the man it was named for. "He feared God and shunned evil."

Every year on Yom Kippur, Jews beg forgiveness, likening themselves to clay in God's sculpturing hands, but Job, it seems to me, was more like putty that was stomped upon by God's foot. You read his story and if you are gullible you may see a parable of faith, of cleaving to belief even as the rug is, almost literally, being pulled out from under your feet; but if you are sensible, you can only see that it's the portrait of an unjust world, and you must derive the anti-Aesop lesson that there is no reason to be good—not because mankind is foul but because the great and good Creator who made us in His image is far fouler. As Virginia Woolf remarked, in that rather dry and wry way of hers: "I read the book of Job last night. I don't think God comes out well in it."

Certainly, with the righteous so downtrodden, a careful reader of any Old Testament book can only conclude that you might as well murder and make mayhem: perhaps crime does not pay, but goodness actually seems to cost. After all, Moses, for all his devotion, is never allowed to see the land of Canaan, and David, the warrior-king, has too much blood on his hands to be the one to build the Holy Temple.

Never mind that these two chosen ones of God are chosen for no reason other than that *they just are:* it is not that they are good and virtuous, but rather because an assortment of Divine whims—along with some previous life experience working as a shepherd, the apprenticeship job for all of God's anointed ones because sympathy for one's woolly flock is meant to be good preparation for leading a group of the human variety—make it so. "See how the mighty crumble": these were David's famed horror-struck words when King Saul fell on his sword to avoid being slain by the enemy in battle. Saul too was one of God's chosen shepherd-monarchs, and his humiliating death is in part a punishment for failing to destroy the enemy's farm animals—God had ordered him to leave no trace of the arch-evil Amalekites—and in part penalty for sacrificing one of the spared ovine creatures to express gratitude for his victory sooner than he was supposed to: essentially, Saul, who was crazy as a loon—a paranoid schizophrenic obsessed with destroying the young David, whom he believed was after his throne, which was actually true (as with Richard Nixon, King Saul's suspicion begot its own cause)—was ultimately killed over scheduling problems.

Aside from the random morality presented by an Old Testament God whose creed is BECAUSE I SAID SO, THAT'S WHY, which prepares us for childlike obedience to forces we can't comprehend (i.e., totalitarian regimes, parents), I am hard pressed to see what anyone can learn from these paragons of life in the time of God. The brute cruelty of the Old Testament is the engine of its own overthrow: despite the 613 laws codified within its text, no actual system of crime and punishment prevails. And when we are done studying up on the fascist ways of the Lord, there are mainly just stories involving rape, incest, whoring, lust, coveting thy neighbor's wife, deflowering one's teenage daughter. Anyone who has taken the time to figure it out knows that the Bible is kind of like a dictionary in the hands of a ten-year-old who can while away the hours looking up "sex" and "prostitute" at an age when just the individual words have the power of vulgar electricity. Find Tamar and Judah, find David and Bathsheba, find Tamar and Amnon—and find the story of sexy stories, Samson and Delilah: stick with these and it is always an entertaining and sacred scandal sheet.

Now I know that this is obviously a massive generalization. Certainly there is moral guidance: the books of Leviticus and Deuteronomy are tedious with tax codes and instruction on dealing with everything from mildew to infectious skin diseases—which is why no one ever reads them. And the Ten Commandments remain the code of civilized nations to this day. But, of course, even they did not come off without a bit of a mess: as Moses walked down the mountain, he saw the weary crowd with the golden calf and threw the two tablets down in frustration (probably not with quite the gusto of Charlton Heston, but still). The previous attempt at laying down the law, the Seven Rules of the Children of Noah—handed down at Mount Ararat after the deluge—actually includes a proscription against taking a bite out of a living being, which should give you an idea of how primitive things were—I mean, even Mike Tyson would have seemed ordinary back then.

Nonetheless, with enough shovels, and the right interpretive skills, one can dig some real lessons out of the many tales of the Torah—the spartan text lends itself to alternative readings, and it is in its terse and diverse chronicles of flawed, miserable humanity that this book continues to compel us over time. When Job pleads with God, the poignancy of his search for the Creator who could do this to him, his desire not to succumb to the belief that "it profits a man nothing when he tries to please God," his wish to make order and sense of a world that has wrecked him recklessly, is poetry itself, philology more than theology. "Why do you hide Your face and consider me Your enemy?" Job asks of the sky above. "Will You torment a driven leaf?" The passages that comprise the book of Job show nothing of a just and good world or of a God worthy of worship by any but the most twisted monotheists, but the portrait of this omnipotent monster who seems like an arsonist who has fled the building he's thrown kerosene and matches at, the picture of God in hiding while imposing all this grief on Job—turning from his responsibility, looking away from his own mess like an absentee father—provides pathos that is unsurpassed.

It was precisely this crazed desperation that seemed omnipresent in the Bible that occupied me through my twelve years of hard-core Orthodox Jewish education. The pursuit of God, of meaning, it was really about a lust for life in the face of the obvious poverty of the world's paltry offerings. The lesson we were supposed to learn was that flawed behavior will take you down; the lesson I in fact learned is that *any kind* of behavior *may* take you down, and on balance, the good suffered more than the bad.

In a world that's basically no-fair and in a time without pity, it was the image of David falling in love with Bathsheba as he gazed at her from the loneliness of his palace roof that felt to me like a picture of longing and need and desperation that would carry the story of this coupling through the ages. This common boy who would be king, this simple shepherd who was the son of a shepherd, the harpist and psalmist who really did not have the constitution of a ruler so much as that of a poet: this was a king who necessarily had to find the love of his life by gazing at her from a distance. He needed a woman from outside the royal court, far from the sycophants and the madding crowd. The insane twists and turns of their courtship: If he was so in love with her, how could he be so willing to give her back to her husband? And, for that matter, why are so many great biblical loves born of adultery and bad behavior that both sullies and intensifies the romance? And the price they paid for their sins—sins against people, not against God—make this love one of the most beautiful and intensely human of the Bible narratives.

In fact, David's story offers rare verisimilitude, perhaps because his own poetry, prayer, philosophy and other writings—combined in the compendia of Psalms and Lamentations—give us insight into a struggling man. Sin and forgiveness and a measure of justice seem to punctuate this story.

If the story of David is sensible and symmetrical by biblical standards, if his character's complexity is developed by a multitude of his own writings and others' chronicles, the minimal approach to the doomed love dance of Samson and Delilah is quite the opposite. While this is one of the most famous of Old Testament pairings, a first-degree fatal attraction that is also the first of its kind, the first episode of a femme fatale—of a woman whose mere existence is a contagious, airborne virus for that certain susceptible sucker of a man—the entire section on Samson amounts to four short chapters in Judges, with Delilah only fitting into the final of those, and of its thirty-one verses, she appears in only sixteen. In her mysterious silence, Delilah becomes the Jackie Kennedy of Philistia—though Oliver Stone doesn't even think that the First Lady was part of any conspiracy to assassinate her husband (though I do think it's a clever new angle for someone to explore), while Delilah was absolutely in cahoots with Samson's enemies. Despite the sorry end, in less than a score of sentences, the saga of Samson and Delilah provides us with enough material to provoke pictures of a great romance, it's got enough to it—and suggests so much more—to make up the treatment for a Cecil B. DeMille epic in grand Hollywood style (starring Victor Mature and Hedy Lamarr, neither of whom was iconic enough to carry it off). It is the archetypal story of cross-cultural love between members of warring nations: this is Romeo and Juliet, if the Capulets were Florence and the Montagues were Siena and the medieval castles of Tuscany were well-fortified fortresses for city-states battling for dominance. To put this in more precise terms: she was a Philistine and he was an Israelite, and in modern terms they would be a Palestinian and an Israeli; it's not just that their respective peoples are natural enemies—it's that, just like today, even back then they were engaged in interminable territorial disputes. This is not, say, the fairly usual act of a German and a Jew marrying in 1998; it is the German and Jew taking their nuptial vows in Nuremberg in 1939—and then refusing to leave the country as a matter of principle. Essentially, the story of Samson and Delilah is one of fatal love, where someone is bound to die, it is not a matter of *if,* only *who* and *when*—and in this case, it winds up being both of them.

From the time I first learned about Delilah when I was ten or eleven years old in elementary school, I wanted to know more. Now, when you're as young as I was, you don't particularly have a feminist consciousness, you don't yet have a notion of what a woman's rights and privileges in the world really are, and a sense of sexual power is only in its nascent phase; that preteen moment marks the age when men look and leer and then catch themselves doing it and feel ashamed at ogling this pretty baby. The power you have as a girl at eleven is to make men uncomfortable; it is not yet to make them feel good. So when I learned about Delilah, curiosity and imagination were all that I had at my disposal. And yet, it seemed to me, I felt in some visceral way that Delilah had the right idea. I also became similarly fascinated with Potiphar's wife, Vashti, Bathsheba—all the girls of scandal provided by the Bible. I liked the women who behaved badly, and I liked the women who made men behave badly. I liked Jael, the warrior woman, who in the book of Judges lured the enemy commander Sisera into her lair, fed him a soporific potion and then hammered a peg through his temple and left him for dead. Jael was a heroine, a seductress in the service of God, but that makes her a minority of one: all the other self-actuating, sexually compelling Bible women were presented as Satan's spawn. The idea that a woman could be *that* dangerous just fascinated me. Who cared about Deborah, Sarah, Esther, all the good girls? It seemed far better to be bad.

And in recent years, I've found myself likewise obsessed with the criminal cases of Pam Smart and other women whose weapon of choice was the stranglehold of sex. Ms. Smart, you may recall, was the pretty, prim school-district employee in New Hampshire (she was often referred to, erroneously, as a teacher) who seduced a fifteen-year-old virgin boy—a seemingly sweet son of a single mother whose bleak trailer-park clam-digger existence was suddenly brightened by sex several times a day with this older woman who liked Motley Crüe and Van Halen as much as he did—and then told him that he couldn't have his source of joy any longer if he didn't kill her husband. Since little inheritance or insurance was involved in this transaction, for the life of me I could not comprehend why this woman did not just get a divorce, and sickening as the situation was, it just fascinated me that she had fucked this teenager into submission. She had literally bartered her body in exchange for her husband's corpse for no clear reason—except perhaps the thrill of causing this much mess. This was so incomprehensible to me that I investigated excessively. And my interest in this subject, in how and why it happens, in the way all those clichés are played out—strong men become weak and oh how the powerful and mighty crumble—has never abated over all this time.

And women who were forcibly adorned with the albatross of voodoo sexual powers preoccupied me even more. So Delilah was instantly heroic to me—perhaps this was misguided, perhaps this was just an attempt to find a God who looked like me—but the rabbis were all telling me that she was a witch, a bitch, a termagant, a whore. There were other problem women in the Bible, the main problem being that their sexual existence could not be denied, and while everything about a woman can be controlled and regulated—right down to whom she is or isn't allowed to sleep with—her elusive, effulgent sexual anima, her ability to project lust and allure, cannot be contained by any set of rules. It just is. Sexual energy, like the warmth of sunshine or the green color of grass, is an indigenous characteristic with exogenous manifestations that can't be stopped, can't be helped, and should not be blamed—though all those things often are (for sunburn, for grass stains, for rape). Nothing the rabbis said had any real impact, but certainly I later noticed that even at this late date, women perceived to be sexual—never mind sexually powerful—are scary.

My fancy for biblical bad girls probably had something to do with a desire to discover or—failing that—invent an image for myself of a powerful sexy woman, the kind who got her way and got around. This was during the late seventies, a funny time to be a preteen girl, perhaps because it was such a strange time to be a woman. The women's movement was still fresh enough that it had not yet come to the point where all the serious and determined types were going to Wall Street to make a fortune—there was still some desire to have female empowerment delivered on female terms, to "feminize" the value system so that traditionally male traits like ambition and money hunger and greed could be displaced by caring and sharing, by creativity and professional fulfillment; so while women, for the most part, had not yet assumed the slick sheen of power and moxie, they no longer had the conventional accouterments of femininity and wily sex appeal at their ready disposal either. That period of American womanhood was dowdy as can be—even with Raquel Welch out there campaigning for the ERA, the measure did not pass, at least in part, I would guess, because no one wanted to sanction that plain, bland model of femaleness it seemed likely to bring in its wake. Feminism simply had not done much in the way of window dressing—which is to say, Bella Abzug's hats did not make equal work for equal pay look terribly grand or glamorous.

On the big screen, the locus of our collective fantasy life, we could have been given updates of Bette Davis and Joan Crawford and Katharine Hepburn, of brash, brassy career women with renegade style in shapely, fitted suits or sporty pants ensembles. We could have been granted the fleshed-out fashionable celluloid rendering of the modern, liberated lady—the hardworking hussy or the well-bred broad to be reckoned with. Instead we got realistic women, single mothers played by Marsha Mason and Meryl Streep. The wispy forbidding beauties of the early seventies and before, the Katharine Ross and Susan Anspach and Carrie Snodgress types—the college girls with hippie hair and elegant, educated diction and ballerina posture that seethed of Seven Sisters schooling and a certainty that they would easily be able to resist even Jack Nicholson's charms—had retired, it seemed, to motherhood in Topanga Canyon or Sonoma Valley, to horse breeding and sheep farming but not to anything like acting. Everybody on the screen was warm and accessible or struggling and stressed out because that unrealistic bitch goddess was understood to be a dream of the prefeminist variety. Even Princess Leia had a foul mouth and earmuffs for hair.

So Delilah to me was a sign of life.

I lived in a world of exhausted, taxed single mothers at the mercy of men who overworked and underpaid them, men who forgot to send child-support checks, men who forgot they had children, men who forgot everything because they knew that women—at some point while crawling around the floors grabbing at what crumbs the world may have left over for them—would remember. I grew up in a world where only John Lennon, who had so completely prostrated himself before Yoko, would have dared to say that woman is the nigger of the world. It took a former Beatle to point out a plain truth. I had never in my life encountered a woman who'd brought a man down. Until Delilah.

Of course, the problem with the Bible is that it suffers from Tom Cruise syndrome, which is to say that it leaves an impression that men are the stars of the story, when anyone reading it knows that the women are the interesting part. Without women entering for the occasional intrigue, it would all be men doing their manly things—men sojourning and men wandering and men battling. It would be the *Iliad*, or one of Hemingway's less interesting novels that contends for all the world to hear that bullfighting or trout fishing is all anybody needs to get through life. Only the periodic presence of women rescues the Bible from battle fatigue and worse. Without them, the whole book would just be men fighting over land in the name of the Lord. Who would supply the glamour? The suspense? The mystery? Women are the whole reason that the book is the all-time best-seller. Actresses of an earlier era understood this. Could you imagine Bette Davis or Barbara Stanwyck or Joan Crawford or Rita Hayworth or Elizabeth Taylor or Marilyn Monroe ceding her star billing to someone as insignificant as a man? Back in their day Tom Hanks or Arnold Schwarzenegger would never be thought of as able to "open" a movie because female movie stars knew how to be stars. They were second billing to none. Bible women were not granted stardom, but they pilfered it with impunity. They snuck in, serpentine, and stole the plot. They were charged sex objects. It would not surprise me at all to discover that Eve started the whole mess with the serpent and the Tree of the Knowledge of Good and Evil and Original Sin just to get attention. And it worked. Though it is not Bette Davis who is referred to in the title *All About Eve,* if ever there was an actress who was meant to lead all of creation out of paradise, it is she.

Just as Delilah, to me, was clearly the star. She was sexy and wild and got her way, even if it did all come crashing down on her head in the end. Even if the desert love concluded with Samson pushing apart a pair of pillars that bolstered the temple of Dagon, pressing these columns as if forcing open a resistant pair of female thighs, with the resulting burst being the death of Samson and Delilah and thousands of present Philistines, even if it all came to naught, Delilah had her sixteen minutes. She was grand and untidy and disturbing and disorderly, and she denied her life the minor-character status it was assigned to. And of course, Delilah's centuries-old superstardom and sex-symbol status has been accorded only because she brought this strong man down. And the lesson I derived from this—and I don't know what the rabbis wanted me to learn—was that whatever power a woman created herself was a direct derivative of her potency to destroy men. Long before film noir, the Bible practically mandated the femme fatale as a feminist model. I mean, if I ever commit some criminal act or some man I'm involved with is mysteriously murdered, I'd have Leslie Abramson represent me, and we'd have to subpoena all these bearded little rabbis to prove that I was the victim of excessive Torah study and a Yeshiva education.

Delilah also represented to me the notion of woman on a pedestal, that quality that is worshipped, that gaga quality. I know, of course, that the problem with that role is how easily you can be knocked off that pedestal, and also that so few of us would qualify, but sometimes I feel like feminism be damned. Wouldn't it be nice if women in daily life were just a bit more mysterious and unattainable and alluring as they apparently once were? That's why there are no glamorous movie stars: our *entire* culture has become dowdy. The episodic interest in recent years in *haute couture*, in red-hot lipstick and glimmery-glowing eyes, in stiletto heels and silky lingerie, seems an attempt to redress this loss of outward indications of style and sensuality. We, as a people, miss playing dress-up. I, personally, am simply tired of the *whatever* and *who cares* and *never mind* of every aspect of culture: though I loved the Seattle grunge stuff to begin with, a few years later I don't think I can stand to listen to one more rock album that doesn't contain a single love song, that is so indifferent to the world outside an angry, bitter adolescent head that even the boy-meets-girl business, the romance and the possibility that it poses for redemption, has no place. I want more love songs like "Do You Want to Know a Secret?" and "I'm a Believer," more songs where the girl is a dream and the guy is in reverie and everything isn't all so goddamned *so what*. In Delilah's world, there seemed no possibility of Samson raging and raving and having terrorist tantrums in his antisocial, antistate stance, because love became more important to him. Her effect on him is as strong as his physical strength—she is a colorful creature of charisma and sex, and she is *undeniable*. She is the temptation and lust story of the Bible, the story of a guy who should have known better but became weak in her presence.

In legend, all of Samson and Delilah's time together is stolen, unsanctioned: they are having an affair, even though they are husband and wife (nowhere in the text does it say they are married, but most interpreters seem to assume that). This is a romantic fable full of forbidden-fruit possibilities, it is as sweet and insane as true love, as intense and sweaty as passion in its purest distillation, because to sleep with the enemy is to live outside the law. Since women traditionally mark this strange area upon which men assert their property rights—like deeded houses or branded cattle—Delilah embodies the failure of this male prerogative when it comes to regulating human emotions: though regarded by law as chattel, women in fact have free will *within* their pre-owned bodies and minds. Delilah can fall in love with Samson and no one can really do much to change that.

And there are many reasons why, if you were a Philistine satrap, you really might want to change that, or at least make advantageous use of a compatriot woman's sway over Samson. Samson is a terrorist stirring up trouble on behalf of the Israelites' struggle to cast off the yoke of the Philistines who rule them. His activities, on behalf of his cause, are the B.C. equivalent of planting a bomb in the public bazaar on a crowded shopping day or hijacking an El Al airplane to some Arabic emirate. Samson does things like take a thousand foxes, attach firebrands to their tails, and set them loose in a large field to set all the crops on fire; or else he makes a bet with thirty Philistine men, and when he loses—albeit unfairly—he makes good on his debt to them by slaying thirty men in another city and giving the garments of the dead to the men he lost to; or he picks up an ass' jawbone that he finds lying at the side of the road and uses it to kill a thousand soldiers, all by himself. Assuming the current Middle East situation reigned back then, Samson would not only be part of the PLO, he would be the leader of Hamas. "He's a man of the moment, he can't see past the moment," says Carol Fontaine, a professor at Andover Newton Theological School. "He is a Danite Terminator." It is in fact his God-ordained duty to behave irrationally—he is meant to get the rebellion started, to "begin the deliverance of Israel," as it is written in Judges; it is not for Samson to see the liberation all the way through. He is supposed to inspire and incite and then leave, he is meant to shout "Fire!" in a crowded theater and watch as everyone scurries in chaos, he is intended to be a nomadic troublemaker, a Che Guevara of the Sinai Peninsula, or perhaps, in his more sanguinary moments, a Robespierre. So naturally, Samson is a wanted man in Philistia, as much a dangerous public menace as the World Trade Center bombers or Timothy McVeigh left loose would be to us today.

To be Delilah, to be in love with this dangerous man whose paranormal, supernatural strength makes him impossible to cage or contain, is to be in love with a deadly weapon. So the sixteen verses that have been passed down over time as a story of passion in the silky

sumptuousness of Delilah's desert tent—that conclude with her betraying Samson with a haircut that saps him of his strength and traps
him, with blinded eyes, in a Philistine labor camp—is actually a great
deal more complicated. That this Bible romance has become the basis
and blueprint for each and every episode when a woman with her
wiles drags down a good man who is just no match for her sexual
trickery—whose mind is basically no match for the demands of his
body—just shows that we are not careful in our examination of what
he did to get into this mess.

When we speak of prostitutes who come forward with their salacious stories and "ruin"—I use quotation marks because in both cases
these men have made comebacks—the careers of Jimmy Swaggart and
Dick Morris, when we attribute the breakup of the Beatles to Yoko
Ono or the suicide of Kurt Cobain to Courtney Love, when we see the
cause of the Profumo Affair to be a young woman named Mandy Rice
Davies (who is now an old woman, living in a council tenancy in
England, obviously not the beneficiary of any of her powerful men),
when we let Henry VIII believe that Anne Boleyn bewitched him into
heresy (if she's got such sorcery, it's hard to figure how she ended up
beheaded), when we let porn star T. T. Boy blame the wife for the
suicide of his fellow on-camera fellatio-recipient Cal Jammer (née
Randy Potes), and refer to Mrs. Jammer as "the wicked bitch" in *The
New Yorker*, when we let any men in colonial-era Massachusetts
blame their infidelities on women who must be witches (once again,
somehow their power to arouse adultery was not adequate when it
came to the hangman): every time we watch men of world events or
minor characters in our own lives as they come completely undone
over some girl, and we assume she manipulated and cajoled and co-
erced him into ruin and disaster, every time we believe that *she
brought him down,* we are really letting him off the hook rather easily.
If women are granted so much responsibility and credit and blame for
the behavior of men that they sleep with, then that means we really do
believe that any guy with a hard-on has truly cut off the blood flow to
his brain—which, I have to say, is pretty much true, but usually men
do come to their senses at some point. If men were truly sexuality's
simple serfs, then Gennifer Flowers would be sitting behind the desk
of the Oval Office and Bill Clinton would be a lounge singer in the

Excelsior Hotel in Little Rock (maybe Hillary would be Vice President). I mean, if pussy power is so potent that it can be the ruin of a British administration, that it can cause John Lennon to make some seriously unlistenable albums and pose for some embarrassingly pale-assed pictures, and if it can make Samson—a man so strong that Samsonite luggage, indestructible even in the hands of a gorilla in a cage, is named for him—weak and wobbly-kneed and a slave to his lust, if men are this easy to manipulate, then why did it take us until 1920 to get the vote? Why are the majority of households with incomes below the poverty line headed by women? Why have they still not found a cure for menstruation? Why does Strom Thurmond continue to be reelected to the Senate? And why is it that they can put a man—*many* men—on the moon but we can't get *one* woman elected into the White House?

Every time somebody says, about any situation of sexual politics, that *she* brought *him* down, the speaker must always be reminded that it's a little like saying *Rebel Without a Cause* is a movie starring Natalie Wood: half of the story is missing. To see Samson as somehow less than complicit in his own destruction and disaster and disarray, to pin it all on Delilah—who may have been a luscious babe, but she was only a woman, and an ignorant Philistine (in the cultural-rube sense of the word), at that—is to give her responsibilities but no rights. It seems important to remember who is meant to be the star of this story, to keep in mind that this section of Judges is about Samson's journey through a life of physical frenzy in which he only achieves maturity as a blinded, bound man, he only lives the life of the mind once he is metaphorically castrated when Delilah cuts off his hair: it is only when Samson is no longer enslaved to his dick or his whimsical muscleman games that he really grows up. This is a morality tale about emotional maturity, and Delilah is just an agent of God's agenda for Samson. She's got a bit part in his life, not unlike Marilyn Monroe, who had a minor role in *The Asphalt Jungle;* and yet she's the only thing anyone remembers about that movie.

Women, you see, like any other group of people obstructed from paths to power, tend to get their action on the sly. And that is precisely why, on certain occasions, it does seem that there is no power like pussy power: men are so comfortably accustomed to being in charge, they forget how drooling and besotted they can become with some woman. It is only because men assume their centrality with the nonchalance and insouciance of those who've never even thought it might be otherwise—and I'm not sure that feminism has been able to make any real headway into this presumed privilege—that they are still able to get all astonished and flustered by the incursion of love into the safety of their sphere. Delilah can sidle from the margin to the center because Samson loved her and he thought that was the whole story; he thought his enemies were the Philistine soldiers who were anywhere but in Delilah's bed. He mistook his will to power, he mistook his wondrous capacity to destroy armies of men with only a jawbone as a weapon, he mistook the command he had over a ferocious lion that he tore apart with his bare hands—he mistook all these displays of dominance over his world for mastery of the whole man-woman thing. He has no notion of the pain that can be caused by a person who loves you very much. Samson is the first man in the Bible—and, by extension, in the canon of the Western world—to discover heartbreak and hurt, to be so infatuated by a woman that it is said "she made him sleep on her knees" (which may well imply the first recorded episode of cunnilingus). His life is so unexamined that he cannot see that his strength guarantees his safety on the battlefield, but nothing can help him if he is careless with his heart: Samson is scared of the wrong thing. The one thing a man can't control—whether the source of his power is his money, his muscle or just being a man in a man's world—has got to be the most frightening thing he can conceive of. And love is surely the wildest card life can deal to you: O. J. Simpson could not get Nicole under his control until he sliced her head off; all the rhinestones in Tennessee could not keep Priscilla at Graceland, even if Elvis was the King; and Bob Dylan could write "You're a Big Girl Now" and "If You See Her, Say Hello" for his wife, Sarah, but the most beautiful and melancholy love songs that he could come up with could not save his marriage.

Love does not respond to the imperatives of the rest of life. Love is a bitch.

*   *   *

Samson and Delilah are the beginning of an ongoing onslaught of bad-woman stories, skimpy, scantily clad portraits that offer little detail, but just enough information for us to attach all kinds of nefarious traits to the woman. "In our culture the story of Samson and Delilah is the paradigmatic case of woman's wickedness," Mieke Bal, a professor at the University of Amsterdam, writes in *Lethal Love: Feminist Literary Readings of Biblical Stories.* "The combination of seduction, unfaithfulness, and treason is an unavoidable and fatal one. However strong a man is, and Samson *was* strong, he will always be helpless against woman's strategies of enchantment. Once seduced, he will be betrayed. This is how the myth of Samson and Delilah is naturalized."

In the rather brief text in the book of Judges, so little information is actually imparted that the assumptions attached to this story tell us far more about ourselves than they do about Samson or Delilah. "The characters have no development, no depth—they are types," writes biblical scholar J. Cheryl Exum in her essay "Samson's Women," from the collection *Fragmented Women: Feminist Subversions of Biblical Narrative.* All we know is that Samson "loved a woman in the Valley of Sorek, and her name was Delilah"—the text says exactly that, though it never tells us if *she* loved him. But in any reading of the story, certain assumptions—mostly about Delilah—are pretty consistent. "Delilah is presented [by commentators] as beautiful at the moment when Samson's falling in love with her is mentioned but as false, unreliable, and greedy when the transaction with the Philistines is concluded," writes Bal in *Lethal Love.* "What interests me here, however, is the reaction of the readers (the authors of the [commentaries]) to events on which the Bible itself makes no comment." In fact, Delilah's looks are just such a thing. Despite a collective conclusion that Delilah was a sexy siren, Rita Hayworth in *Blood and Sand* or the astral, ethereal goldilocks goddess rising, Phoenix-like, from the foam of a half-shell in Botticelli's *Birth of Venus,* the text itself says nothing of the sort. Many times in the Old Testament a woman's looks are sized up simply as "pleasing to the eye" (*yefat mareah* in the Hebrew original), while Rebecca is "fair to look upon," Rachel is "beautiful of form and beautiful to look at," and Bathsheba is described as simply "very good-looking"—but Delilah is not sized up at all. The book of Judges is equally mum on the subject of Delilah's personal probity, though the Old Testament does not shy away from conveying a woman's poor character, usually by calling her a "prostitute" or a "wayward wife," with adjectives like "immoral," "loud and defiant" and "brazen" most commonly applied to the biblical bad girls. (Interestingly, Jezebel is never characterized as evil, though she would be one of those rare incontrovertible instances; although perhaps the report early on that she's made a project of "killing off the Lord's prophets" gets the point across well enough.) In fact, the closest the text comes to commenting on Delilah's morals is in introducing her with the phrase "her name was Delilah," and not "Delilah was her name": the former is the structure that the Bible uses to indicate a righteous person.

But the lack of biographical information given about such a viscerally vivid character has been duly noted. "Scripture is completely silent about Delilah's age. Was she considerably younger than [Samson], or was she perhaps the same age?" asks Rabbi Gershon Weiss in *Samson's Struggle,* an Orthodox Jewish reading of the strongman's life. "It is usually assumed that [Samson] was primarily attracted to Delilah's beauty. If this is true, however, why does Scripture never mention that she was beautiful, as it does in other cases? If Delilah was not beautiful, just what quality of hers did attract [Samson] to her?" But this brief story, free of modifiers, has its own life because, like Sophocles' invention of Oedipus, its themes are those of fear and betrayal, and these are issues not just at the heart of toxic, politically vexed male-female relationships, but even in love that is basically sound and sane. While in previous chapters lust that is presumed to be love drives men to rape the over-ogled object of desire, and jealousy causes murder between two or more men who've gone berserk over one passive little woman, Samson and Delilah are the first couple in which the destruction takes place *within* their relationship, the distrust and desperation generated between their two bodies and minds causes all the trouble: this is the first ever incident of intimate terrorism.

Samson and Delilah earn their age-old romantic resonance by telling the story of a universal and usually unspoken fear, a desperate dread that taints our deepest attachments with a subtle blue shade of sorrow, and a creepy, constant fear that warns us to always watch our backs. Somewhere down deep in even the happiest couples, the stablest of relationships, is the horror of what we don't—*can't*—know about even the closest and most dear, about the lover we wed and the face we will wake up next to forever: all that is hidden and unknown and unpredictable and possible and probable when you join your life to another person's, all the power you relinquish to someone who is that close, who can run amok with it and you any day, all the crimes committed with knives and guns and the teenage babysitter and worse, all the violations not even thought of by the Marquis de Sade—these are intimacy's unmarked land mines. You go into a relationship for safety and security, and it's easy to forget that this irenic quietude may shelter you from the teeming masses, but it also puts you at the mercy of one person. The most likely person to kill you is your wife, but that probably won't happen. What probably will happen is a million little betrayals of varying degrees of pain, brought on by people you love, the only ones who really *can* hurt you. This fact should scare us, but instead it combines to make us panic about crime and build fortresses around our homes, and to avoid relationships altogether, rather than take a chance. Samson and Delilah is only the most crass and obvious case study to illustrate how the ones we love the most can so easily hurt us through abandonment, through a roving eye, through simple betrayal, through any and all of the vicissitudes that conspire to tear the delicate vellum of love apart.

Samson and Delilah offer the first example of what we now call sexual politics, the infant years of a he said/she said situation, the clear establishment of a man who gets in trouble and offers, by way of excuse, the insistence that she made me do it. It happens that in the text Samson never makes such an accusation, nor is there any courtroom drama that might reveal the characters' differing versions of events. But without the benefit of even a bit of disputation, the story has been passed down as one in which a man lost his way while being led by his dick, which was in hot pursuit of some dame—and the presumption at the end of this gander-goose chase is that she made me do it.

In an earlier episode of potential sexual politics, Jacob's daughter Dinah is raped by an uncircumcised heathen he-man sort named Shechem one day when she went out for a walk. In spite of the obvious rebellious forthrightness it took for a teenage virgin to go wandering about the town without a chaperone—despite the fact that this behavior could be seen as asking for trouble, and under the circumstances rightly so—Dinah is never accused of inviting rape. While the case is handled terribly—her twelve brothers view this violation as an affront to their manhood and to the family name, and take it upon themselves to massacre Shechem's people and rape the women, tit for tat for tit—no one ever blames Dinah for it. In fact, Dinah quickly fades into pretext status, merely becoming the passive person that gives the men just cause for mayhem. It is not until Delilah, in her foreign exoticism, that a woman is held responsible for just being sexy. The rare, remote possibility that this facade of physical appeal can house a fatal weapon—like the pretty dolls that the Soviets would leave lying in public spaces in Afghanistan, brightly colored plastic toys that lured the starved, deprived children and blew up faster than their parents' warnings not to touch the bomb—has become the excuse to distrust *all* women.

Evil men in the Bible are as a rule state enemies, known foes in long-standing disputes or grudge matches. Women—who still are prohibited from hand-to-hand combat in the U.S. military—can only serve their country in their natural role as spies in the house of love. But even in the workaday world, women have been deemed more dangerous than the battlefield: at least you know what to expect from a man you are at war with—a woman you are in love with is a tender trap. But it works both ways—men destroy women all the time, in fact it is far more common for a woman to have her life ruined by a man's handiwork—to have it destroyed in tangible, economic ways—than the reverse. Pretty early in Genesis, Abraham casts his maid-mistress Hagar and their illegitimate son Ishmael out of his household to contend for themselves in the desert; the seemingly constant onslaught of celebrity men who are served paternity suits by the women they wish they'd never slept with for the sake of children they would rather not know bears witness to how many men sort-of love and completely leave women behind to contend with their offspring. And despite what is surely horrible conduct on the part of the first patriarch, Abraham, the Bible does not concern itself with the evil of men—in fact, the whole episode is blamed on his wife Sarah's jealousy, even though, until that moment, Abraham was comfortably the head of his house.

If sexual politics is only casually covered throughout the Bible, Samson and Delilah's disarray and disintegration departs from that norm, at least partly because the book of Judges is such a crazy, inconspicuous volume within the context of Old Testament lore. It is the *How the West Was Won* of its era, it encompasses the years of the Israelites settling into Canaan, there is guerrilla warfare, and a lot of mixing and miscegenation between the natives and the new settlers, with many Jews worshipping the God of Moses, but also adopting pagan practices. The story of Samson and Delilah is sandwiched between two strange incidents recalled in Judges: in one, a man abandons his concubine to be gang-raped by a mass of marauders and left for dead on his porch, after which he cuts her body into twelve parts and sends one to each of the tribes; in the other, an army leader named Jephthah vows to sacrifice the first thing that walks out the door of his house upon his safe return from battle, and when he is greeted by his own daughter, he blames her for forcing him to slaughter her upon the altar; Jephthah, in effect, kills his daughter and claims that she made him do it. It is in the book of Judges, with strangers in a strange land that is supposed to be their own, that the chaos of life is constantly countered with "she made me do it." And so has it been ever since. In the sexually charged relationship between father and daughter, who can say what perversity was intended by this accusation, but the Delilah story buttresses the notion that women drag men down with their wiles. Somehow despite the fact that Delilah herself was being manipulated by the Philistine governors and secret police—that, in essence, the CIA was approaching her and demanding that she reveal the secret of Samson's strength—and even though, like all women, sexually sweet or not, she was still at the mercy of the might of men, Delilah is thought to have destroyed a man who was clearly bound to self-destruct. "In popular notions of the tale, women are blamed for Samson's downfall, although in the biblical story both the Timnite woman (Samson's first wife) and Delilah act as they do because they are manipulated by the Philistines," writes Cheryl Exum. "Their power over Samson is appropriated by men, in the interests of an androcentric agenda."

"The man captivated by her charms no longer has will-power, enterprise, future; he is no longer a citizen, but mere flesh enslaved to its desires, cut off from the community, bound to the moment, tossed passively back and forth between torture and pleasure," writes Simone de Beauvoir in *The Second Sex*, explicating the dangerous seduction of Circe, a latter-day Delilah. The poison of her sexual ecstasy is that she makes a man—even goodly, godly Odysseus—believe he has no other cares or concerns. "The perverse sorceress arrays passion against duty, the present moment against all time to come; she detains the traveler far from home, she pours him the drink of forgetfulness."

The danger to the poor man graced with such unearthly delights is that he doesn't realize that the drug will wear off and the world of widgets and wampum and bargains and deals will beckon once more. "For a while, I'll let it make you strong / make your heart lion," the poet Ai writes in "Woman to Man," as she proffers a taste of her pussy power. "Then I'll take it back."

*   *   *

It is wrong to blame anachronistic attitudes for any image of Delilah as dangerous, because feminism or the lack thereof seems to have very little bearing on how the femme fatale is received and perceived. In 1671, John Milton wrote the semi-epic (as compared with the outright epic *Paradise Lost*) poem *Samson Agonistes*, the blind scribe telling the life of the blinded judge. In it, he distributes the blame for disaster and drama quite evenly: while he calls Delilah "That specious monster, my accomplished snare," he also has Samson taking the rap for the relationship, admitting, "Of what now I suffer / She was not the prime cause, but I myself, / Who, vanquished with a peal of words (O weakness!) / Gave up my fort of silence to a woman." Milton's Samson even concedes that he saw the betrayal coming, that he knew Delilah was seeking the source of his strength so that the very thing could be summarily sapped; it is her openness and his inability to resist the nonsubterfuge of her seduction that makes him *really* want to bang his (shorn) head against the wall: "Her importunity, each time perceiving / How openly, and with what impudence, / She purposed to betray me, and (which was worse / Than undissembled hate) with what contempt / She sought to make me traitor to myself." In most interpretations in the Judeo-Christian tradition inhabited by Milton,

Delilah is despised for her sneakiness; here, in Milton's reading of events, Delilah is blamed for not being crafty enough—for having the audacity to know and show what a bird in the hand feels like. She can't win for losing! But while Milton's rendition has the standard elements of a decent guy duped by his lust for a devil woman, the bard is keen to remind us that Samson acted on his own volition until love took away such a will; it is Samson's stupidity, susceptibility and sexual appetite that drive the action, while Delilah, sultry and supine, an amulet of charms, is only driven to reaction.

While Milton gave at least some credence to the notion that it takes two to tango—if, in fact, they did any ballroom dancing of the duo-as-duel variety in Restoration-era England—many more modern thinkers have held far more antiquated views of Delilah and her sexual power. "Delilah is, as it were, a whore at heart aware of the hero's love for her and how his emotions may be manipulated to serve her greed and lust for power," one scholar named John B. Vickery could opine as recently as 1981.

Obviously, if the author of the Bible wanted to invent the possibility of a woman so tempting she'd drag a good man down and throw that out as something to aspire to, He did good. Another view, beyond standard feminist criticism, sees women as oppressed, grasping at what little power is in their reach, ultimately only serving male interests. Of course this is true, but why not also celebrate that power, why not admire the love? In real life, people are more than just forces of history and nature, they have complex feelings and emotions that explain why they do what they do. Love must be a big part of Delilah's motivation. And love really is part of every story like this. What is wrong, however, with the view that boils Delilah down to nothing but betrayer, or says that women bring men down, that love destroys, is that it concludes with the misguided fear of emotional free fall that we all hide from, it occludes—except from our most peripheral and blurry vision—a safe and simple truth: that people are much more resilient than they give themselves credit for. The awesome awfulness of Samson's story is that love turns out to be truly lethal for him; basically, very few of us are going to be murdered as a result of a bad relationship—in fact, mostly we just get the pathetic, prosaic fate of crying and feeling lousy and listening to Linda Ronstadt sing "Long, Long

Time" over and over again. But that is life and that is the beauty of life. People surrender to love—they do it reluctantly and with trepidation, but when they give in it is sweet surrender as well as sweet victory. It is part of life, that potential hurt, that fearsome thrill, but women don't seem to have nearly as hard a time with it. In the end, in the final tally, who knows who has brought the other down more or the most—we only know that this is life's rich pageant, and we all have to take responsibility for our own feelings, for wishing to succumb and letting it happen. It is degrading to put the blame on Mame or anyone else for the chances we all take freely.

One of the more interesting passages of *The Rules* occurs when the authors discuss how to handle rejection: "Just move on." This is, of course, good advice, along the lines of just buck up and snap out of it. It is particularly good advice for the overwrought, the overreacting, the downright hysterical, for the people who feel every heartbeat is a heartache, and every breakup is the end of the world. The types who brood over a one-night stand as if it were the end of a ten-year marriage. It is good advice, but bad philosophy. Bad philosophy because it fails to account for the value of human experience in and of itself. It's not that anyone ought to suffer too many rejections, but the reason *The Rules* is so popular is that it caters to women who have been dating too long and have already had enough philosophical responses to the things men have done to them.

But the thing that the book misses is that most of our emotional triumphs occur on the margins of life, at the moments when we least expect them, at the points when we've been so hardened that our hearts feel like they're made of petrified wood and it seems perfectly possible that we'll simply turn to stone, turn to a pillar of salt like Lot's wife looking back at Sodom and Gomorrah every time we shudder to think about how many ways we've been wronged by love. And for whatever reason—I have very little evidence of it, but I have no evidence of anything happening any other way—it's at those precise times when things could not be worse and it seems like there is no man from here to the southernmost tip of Tasmania who has not already proved disappointing—to put it mildly—that life surprises us, that some nice person comes along and makes us feel four years old and walking in a field of daisies all over again. I think the fear of Delilah and of all of her kind has to do with some desperate desire to avoid that pain, to stay away from the women who are obviously going to be devastating, soul-murdering. And the stupid thing about fearing that kind of exposure is that the worst pain will not necessarily come from the bad girls—the truth is that it can come from anybody you fall for, anybody who has the capacity to bring you down. That's why the fear of Delilah tends to extend to a fear of all women, a fear of all intimacy—all of it is potentially threatening, emasculating.

One of the best movies of recent years—and certainly the best debut film of the late eighties—was Steven Soderbergh's *sex, lies & videotape,* which found its profundity in a message that boils down to: You can run, but you can't hide. Set in Baton Rouge, the movie revolves around characters who, each in his or her own way, are deeply disconnected from feelings—from spouses and family and lovers, and from themselves. Andie MacDowell is Ann, a tightly wound homemaker, probably sixth-generation Bayou belle, who walks around vaguely disturbed all the time, somehow knowing that everything about her life with her corporate lawyer husband is all wrong, all empty, but she's so cut off from any sense of what a full emotional life might entail that she's not quite sure what, if anything, she should do about it. She's never had an orgasm, she—I suppose this is obvious—doesn't much care for sex, and is blithely unaware of the fact that her husband is fucking her hotheaded, oversexed sister during sweltering, smoldering Louisiana afternoons when he should be with clients. Her whole life is an avoidance of her whole life—though that too would not strike her as anything particularly troubling. Meanwhile, James Spader is Graham, an LSU fraternity brother of her husband's who shows up in town after nine years, dressed completely in black like no one in Louisiana ever does if a funeral is not in the offing, and he is obviously far from the beer-guzzling party-hearty guy he'd once been. A traumatic relationship has so shell-shocked him that he's ceased to have sex with anyone, instead making videotapes of women talking about their fantasies, which he then uses for pornographic self-pleasure.

In the course of the movie, the MacDowell and Spader characters become close, the alienation that results from Ann's willful denial somehow a good, safe match for the withdrawal that results from Graham's overexposure and inability to deny anything. It is through this bond that both shed their remoteness and try—tentatively, frightfully, as if life were a first date all over again—to connect, not just with each other, but with the world they've been skimming for so long. As a model of the fears of intimacy that are so common to contemporary life, the film achieves an unusual honesty, mainly because not much happens, the gradual and then sudden pace of emotional motion is somehow honored. And the movie never loses sight of the way nothing happens in a vacuum, the convergence is always harmonic: people don't just swoop down and make a mess of life. There is an order, a drift to things. This could be the classic story of a stranger who comes through town and throws everyone's life into chaos, but Soderbergh never allows his film to reduce itself to such a simple parable: in this case, the stranger changes the people he meets, but they change him too.

Toward the end of the movie, Ann bursts into Graham's apartment and tries to get through to him. "You've got a problem," she says. After much denial, after pointing out that compared with the rest of the cast of characters he is pretty sane, he finally concedes, "You're right. I have a lot of problems. But they belong to me." And this is an assertion that Ann is just not going to let him get away with. She realizes that her marriage and her whole life are a lie because she has refused to be a full participant, has refused to refuse the half-life she is living. And she will not have this man, who has had such a drastic effect on her, whom she's opened up to as she has not with anyone else, get away with telling her that his problems just belong to him. "You think they're yours, but they're not," Ann says. "Everybody that comes in here becomes part of your problem, everybody that comes in contact with you. I didn't want to be part of your problem, but I am. I'm leaving my husband. And you're the reason. Maybe I would have anyway, but the fact is I'm leaving him now, and part of it's because of you. *You've had an effect on my life.*"

Graham feels himself unraveling at the thought of this woman who is getting close to him whether she means to or not—and whether *he* wants her to or not. "When you're with another person, and you're *inside* them, you're so *vulnerable,* you're revealing so much, there's no *protection,*" he says. "And somebody could say or do something to you while you're in this state of nakedness. And they could hurt you without even knowing it. In a way that you couldn't even see. And you would withdraw. To make sure it didn't happen again." This, of course, would be a classic castration complex, the fear that in the sex act a woman will suck a man up, sap him of his motivation, blind him and mute him and deafen him to all but the moment. The man in *sex, lies & videotape* finds the prospect so frightening that he has not had sex in nine years. That's a lot of pleasure to trade in for privation just to keep your private parts and pieces intact. And for what? To what end? What exactly is this man saving himself for? What could have happened to him nine years earlier that was so terrible that it induced him to give up on love—emotional and physical—for so very long? What use is all this self-preservation if you do not expend yourself in some way? "This is what you come up with?" Andie MacDowell taunts him.

By now it is basic Freudian-feminist cant that the socialization process tends to make men flee from women—something about having to learn to separate from the mother and identify with the father, a more radical transition from what girls have to go through since they need only emulate the same person who nurtured them, which in most cases is the mom, and hence they are less inclined to separation and are more comfortable with connection than boys are—and this is meant to explain misogyny and cold feet and all the other male behaviors that make it seem like women need to snare some man by hook or by crook. By feminine wiles. The very thing that makes men scared of women is what also makes women scary, a self-perpetuating process that has been in effect for so many years that who can say it isn't what makes the world go round. The mechanism of this fear in our age is love's officially sanctioned anarchy: no longer do men control marriage in the sense that a girl is given over to her groom by her father. But it's not as if women have gotten the upper hand either. The result is women wishing they could be cool and sassy like Delilah, and men frightened away by a phantom threat of emasculating female power. But if any of us had Delilah's power, men would be too flummoxed to be frightened: we'd all like to be so enchanting that men don't even notice that they're falling in love until they're already there, don't even notice that they need to be afraid, be very afraid.

I'm gone on you: I once heard a guy in a bar band singing that line to some anonymous woman, some girl out there, and I thought that of all the ways a man could tell a woman I want you bad, that had to be the nicest. *I'm gone on you:* You can make my night or ruin my life and I'll take my chances. And if only the fear of falling were not so great, if only the possibility of pain came to seem normal and not extraordinary, we all could stop being so guarded and defensive—and ultimately vulnerable to hurt when we finally do open up.

What scares me so much about books like *The Rules* is not that they promote bad values, because they don't; it's more that it seems bad enough that so many men are so shut up and careful—why turn women into Teflon-coated emotional shell-shock survivors as well? How horrible is it to take a chance on love and to lose it all? Most of the dramatizations, novelizations and scholarly speculations on the relationship between Samson and Delilah suggest that it was gigantic, a big, big love, and I think this characterization of their affair gives Samson his due, grants him a romantic heroism for daring to fall so hard. "One of the main themes of this story is that love is stronger than all the physical ferocity of Samson," says Gregory Mobley of the Harvard Divinity School. I think this story has held up over the centuries more because of the strength of their love than the evil of the betrayal. The story of Samson and Delilah is one about two people who took a chance, who dared to fall in love under rather unpromising conditions and saw their sorry situation end badly, tragically and predictably, like any union that is entangled in war and politics.

The story of Samson and Delilah is also the Bible's first telling of love by choice, unsanctioned by parents, by the demands and definitions of clan and kin. They met somewhere or other, they obeyed their hormones and desires, and set up house the way a couple in contemporary society would. And of course this is naturally a caveat for future generations who would choose to fall in love rather than, I suppose, aspire to love someone who is appropriate: this love of choice that Samson has come up with is, after all, a relationship lost in the wilderness, it has no context, no place to function acceptably except within its private domain. But marriage, and life partnership, are meant to be public because any love allowed to exist solely in a vacuum has no higher authority to answer to. It can end anytime without consequences because the couple is not mingled into a community that cares, that has a stake in their stability. Secret and secreted love is thrilling for its lawlessness, but it can get twisted and self-involved in its isolation, what seems delightfully intoxicating can become horribly suffocating, and the way love plays out in this petri dish, the calamitous conclusion it can come to, can be blamed on nobody. Samson and Delilah chose an unconventional path, and that choice cost them both. Somehow these complexities tend to get tossed into the dustbin of popular history.

Every marriage possesses its own mysteries, which is why the play *Who's Afraid of Virginia Woolf?* by Edward Albee or the novel *Desperate Characters* by Paula Fox and even older works like Tolstoy's *Anna Karenina* or Ibsen's *A Doll's House* are so interesting: through close observation and character study, they try to disinter the deep-down truths of the marriages they portray, but as much as they leave us with a basic picture, a human understanding of what went wrong or why, there is still so much we will never get, never imagine. As outsiders we are in both a better and a worse position to see than those enshrined in the drama. That it is not quite satisfying, that the arrangements and compromises made, the devil's deals struck are never entirely comprehensible to us, and that the dull thud that is the end or sometimes just the continuum of an empty marriage remains curious to the audience, is how we know that these works speak truth. Writes Jouhandeau in his *Chroniques maritales:* "You realize that you are a victim of a poison, but you have become habituated to it. How to renounce it without renouncing yourself? . . . When I think of her I feel that conjugal love has nothing to do with sympathy, nor with sensuality, nor with passion, nor with friendship, nor with love. Sufficient unto itself, reducible to none of these various sentiments, it has its own nature, its particular essence, and its unique character, according to the couple it unites."

One other problem is that this is a great story that actually has no bearing on real life. In reality, many more women have gone overboard over some guy than the opposite. I always feel obligated to point out that *Fatal Attraction* is actually a movie about a woman who is wrecked by a man, not the opposite. More to the point, this whole way of thinking must stop, this notion that women drag men down with sex. It is the basis for too much silliness—it is the reason why rape victims are not named but alleged rapists are—implying that the former, not the latter, should be ashamed because she must have *made him do it*—she drove him to a felonious act. I mean, if our attitude toward female sexuality were normal, rape victims would proudly proclaim their names for all the world to hear because they'd feel good and brave about their decision to prosecute the perpetrator, while the rapist would be cowering in abject shame for being a perverted monster. It is the reason we can't get a woman elected President, the reason Sol Wachtler felt he had a right—was somehow entitled—to stalk Joy Silverman, the reason people still think Yoko Ono broke up the Beatles and the reason that in the 1988 issue of *Esquire* devoted to "Women We Love," a double-page spread of some girls that the editors didn't much love was completely comprised of look-alikes of Donna Rice, Fawn Hall, Jessica Hahn—all the year's scandal girls—posed and presented as women who somehow collectively were bringing down the whole nation. Women don't bring men down; men, for whatever reasons, bring themselves down, and then all of a sudden it's *cherchez la femme*.

Can women use sex as a weapon? Of course. But as Eleanor Roosevelt once said: "No one can make you feel inferior without your consent." Meanwhile, Hillary stands by Bill, Dick Morris' wife stands by him, Lee Hart stands by Gary, Magic Johnson's wife stands by him—I doubt too many men would put up with what they put up with. As Simone de Beauvoir noted: "The misbehavior of a man in more modern societies is only a minor folly, often regarded indulgently; even if he disobeys the laws of the community, man continues to belong to it; he is only an *enfant terrible,* offering no profound menace to the order of society." If you don't understand this point, put it this way: Where exactly is Tonya Harding now? Working as a professional wrestling promoter back home in the Portland area? Getting divorced again? Publicly apologizing to Nancy Kerrigan in another round of publicity fodder? But, of course, we all know exactly where convicted rapist Mike Tyson is. We all know Evander Holyfield beat him out of the title. It is only the fact of his defeat that gives his story a bit of justice. Ah, sweet Pyrrhic victory.

* * *

After thousands of years, it seems like time we buried the hatchet on Delilah and her ilk, which is to say all of us women. The idea that women are predatory is an odd one, since of course our strength is less than men's, which is why the belief persists that when a woman "takes" a man it is assumed that there is magic involved, not unlike the way it is believed that Othello employed sorcery to win over Desdemona, a blonde beauty who could never truly fall for a Moor without the employment of some magic, black or otherwise.

In *Body of Evidence,* a truly terrible Madonna movie, the plot is predicated on the notion that a young, conniving woman can carefully choose older lovers with weak hearts—in the physical, not the emotional, sense—and engage them in sex so tiring and grueling that she finally fucks them into death by way of coital heart attack. Of course, only weeks before the death dance, her men always rewrite their wills to make her sole beneficiary. At one point in the movie, Joe Montegna, pressed into service as a hapless prosecutor, says of Madonna, "She may look like a beautiful woman, but she is a weapon no different from a gun or knife." She kills with her pussy: this terrible movie is the most fully realized version of the *vagina dentata.*

And in the trailers to promote the TNT miniseries of *Samson and Delilah,* the voice-over—narrating a montage of footage of Elizabeth Hurley lying beneath Samson in various orgasmic positions—simply says, "Where just a touch of a woman could crush the strength of a man." Of course, David smote Goliath (thought by some to be a descendant of Samson, the theory being that while in prison the Israelite strongman was put out to stud) with just a slingshot and God on his side—but it never seems to have occurred to anyone that Delilah too had God on her side. In fact, the rabbinical reading of Samson's story vindicates Delilah more than any other interpretation does, because it believes that all activities are God-ordained, we are all pawns in His plan.

This view assumes that everything that happened was part of some overall strategy, a plan for Samson to wage his private, one-man guerrilla war on the Philistines. He married a Philistine woman as a camouflage, so the rulers would never suspect he was actually fighting on behalf of his people—he made it all look like personal vendettas. Samson was far from being hotheaded and a slave to lust; all of his actions were by design, according to the rabbis. This makes Delilah look as if *she* was manipulated by *him* as a way to make the Philistines mad. In a way this is no better: far from being a clever, crafty woman, she is passive and simple like all the other Bible babes. This does not improve matters much at all.

And this interpretation of Delilah is not one that has held much sway. She is almost always seen as a woman working in the service of Satan. Her weapon is her beauty—or if we choose to assume that Delilah did not have the gift of pulchritude in the purest sense, that, as with Cleopatra, her charisma came from a deeper well within, then her weapon is her allure, which we might as well call beauty. But beauty is not innocent, whereas a child's toy, some marbles and a string, a slingshot, is. Beauty is only innocent if it's chaste—and yet, the first thing any man wants to do to a beautiful woman is fuck her silly, thus rendering her used, sullied, discardable and therefore possibly angry and furthermore most likely dangerous. Man in his suspicion creates woman in her danger. For some reason, in the Delilah myth a celebration of her charms is always subordinated to a rank fear of them. "The woman who makes free use of her attractiveness— adventuress, vamp, *femme fatale*—remains a disquieting type," writes Simone de Beauvoir in *The Second Sex*. "The image of Circe survives in the bad woman of the Hollywood films. Women have been burnt as witches simply because they were beautiful. And in the prudish umbrage of provincial virtue before women of dissolute life, an ancient fear is kept alive."

But it seems unfair, once again, that men want women to be beautiful, but when they actually are they are suspicious of it—unless *all* they are is beautiful, which makes it less threatening. But actually, in nature the most beautiful creatures tend to be the least predatory— cats, dogs, birds—while it is the ugly, slimy, gray and grimy—rats, reptiles—who tend to be the most likely to do us harm (this does not take into account the gorgeous lions and tigers who would be happy to devour us if given the opportunity, but somehow, for whatever reason, they don't tend to live among us). One undeniable exception is the beautiful coral-striped snake that bites with lethal poison. And of course it was a snake who was in cahoots with Eve. But it is strange that all the qualities that are supposed to make a woman desirable also make her a target of disquiet and distrust.

*   *   *

Though Delilah may be a minor player in the text of the Samson story, her myth has writ large over time, making her seem significant, which would seem to suggest an anxiety about such a woman and her power. And the cultural artifacts of this desert romance are considerable: Rembrandt painted several depictions of Samson's life, including *Samson's Wedding Feast* and *Manoah's Offering*, both of which hang in Dresden, and *Angel Announcing the Birth of Samson to Manoah*, which is on display in Stockholm. Erté gave a sexy, swervy Art Deco look to his design of *Samson and Delilah*. In his *Duino Elegies* Rainer Maria Rilke imagines Samson pushing against the pillars—his final act of life—as childbirth. Cecil B. DeMille made the love into a sort-of silly Hollywood epic, and Nicholas Roeg made an even sillier—all the more so because of its aspirations of authenticity—TNT miniseries with Elizabeth Hurley as a heavy-breathing Delilah in Estée Lauder's heaviest eye shadow, and unknown actor playing Samson-as-Eddie Vedder. Dennis Hopper makes an appearance as Ms. Hurley's malevolent mentor at court, and the pair are compelled to engage in stilted dialogue that tries for sensual and suggestive banter with a conspiratorial edge, and simply fails. (Hopper: "You are a loose woman, Delilah." Hurley: "And if I were not a loose woman, I should be very insulted.")

I much prefer references to this ancient couple like the allusion made on a *Seinfeld* episode where a ponytailed salesman whom Elaine is dating falls asleep on her couch and has his hair cut off because a Nicole Miller dress he promised to bring home from the store he works at fails to materialize. While it's uncertain if he loses his strength, he certainly does lose his job. But sex and seduction accompany the myth far more than virile vigor—although the former's ability to wipe out the latter is the whole story. The A&E *Biography* show that traced the true story of Samson and Delilah was promoted with thirty-second spots that sketched out their scandalous love, followed by the dramatically intoned question: "Is it *Melrose Place?* No, the Bible!"

Of course, there are Samson myths in many cultures: the Babylonian sun hero Gilgamesh (brought down by the goddess Ishtar, who also, in a sense, brought womanizer Warren Beatty down for a bit), the Greek Herakles, the Phoenician Melkarth, the two Babylonian sun deities Marduk and Nergal, the Assyrian solar gods Sarapu and Ramman, the Sumerians' Tammuz, the Indians' Vishnu, the Celtic Cuchulainn, the Macedonian Alexander the Great, the founder of Buddhism, Gautama, not to mention the more modern cult of the long-haired manly man, be it Gregg Allman, the Calvin Klein model of a few years back whose name was, improbably, Attila, and the many biker dudes idealized in Diane Wakoski's *Motorcycle Betrayal Poems.* Never mind the show/movie *Hair.* Or all rock stars, with all their songs about how they have a right mind to shoot that woman down. Even the cult movie classic *Billy Jack* is a recast of the Samson saga, to the point where toward the end one of the girls asks the title character, a former Green Beret turned protector of Native American kids, about the medicine bag he is carrying. To explain why he always carries the little pouch, Billy tells her, "Without it, I am cut off from the forces of life." She responds, "Kind of like Samson and his hair?" And considering that Samson was conceived, apparently immaculately, to a barren woman following an annunciation via one of God's angels, the story of Jesus Christ can be said to be a variation on the Samson myth, the difference of course being that instead of getting dragged down by a whore, Jesus lifts Mary Magdalene up. By virtue of this, the story of Jesus can be seen as a correction of the Samson saga. In their etymological roots, both Delilah and Lilith are the same name, joining our heroine with the first wife of Adam, the original Eve, the woman who said no and who was recently transformed by Jewish feminists into a historic refusenik, so much a symbol of womanly assertion that a magazine was named for her. Delilah also weaves like Penelope, a woman holding all her suitors at bay while she waits for Odysseus—a symbol of feminine virtue, not malice. Of course, Calypso, the lover on the lam, was a weaver as well. All this may just tell us that way back when, women spent a lot of time at the loom.

Since so few people actually read the text of the Bible itself, few realize that many of our cultural myths that evolve into firm ideas in the collective unconscious are based on notions attached to the characters postscript. It's like a game of Telephone. The Bible is so spare, which is why it lends itself to archetypes and caricatures that reflect readers' beliefs over time.

So for me Samson has come to represent some late-stage version Kurt Cobain. When Kurt first died, what with Courtney strung out and ranting on a dais at his memorial service, it was easy to say that the witch killed him. She broke his heart, she drove him crazy, she annoyed him—whatever. It seemed perfectly plausible that her contribution to married life might well have been the death of him. I myself thought, at the very least, that all the people around him—friends, lawyers, managers, family, band—could only have been feeling homicidal when they left him alone in a house full of guns. And I'm right: that was irresponsible behavior, whether you're going to call it tough love or not. But I have a feeling that a person as miserable, depressed, addicted and reeling as Kurt must have been by the end of his life was a real pain in the ass to deal with. Suicidal souls are exhausting and emotionally draining to all who get near them. And I think, at a certain point, even those who love them completely just say, in deeds if not in words: So fine, blow your brains out.

They don't expect it to really happen.

And Samson was surely one of those people who could make you think enough is enough. Delilah, Courtney, the Philistines, the record industry: blame anyone you want. While the lesson most people take from this story is that if you fall too hard for some broad she will betray you, the truth is just the opposite: Delilah betrayed Samson for not loving her enough, not falling for real. In Eric Linklater's novel *Husband of Delilah*, Samson is portrayed as abusive, battering, snide and sneering, always ordering Delilah around. Delilah is constantly afraid of losing him, and uses her relationship with Philistine authorities and her money to keep him. The Philistines are depicted as reasonable creatures, not barbarians, though there is no mention of any interest in the arts or culture, to be fair to the lore attached to them. Linklater also expresses some notion that Delilah must betray Samson in order to be authentic, in order to become a fleshy, fallible human to this man and not just some sex goddess and comfort creature who he idolizes, but can never quite genuinely love. She is sick of his being obsessed with her, addicted to her—she wants to be loved for herself, to be real. She is tired of being a bit of what he fancies, a distraction from the difficult uses of his strength. She is trying to get the whole situation down to size. The point is that one's motives in betrayal are often complicated—it's not as simple as she did it for the money, she did it because she's a femme fatale and that's what women like that do. They had a complicated dynamic and a full-bodied relationship that the text does not make us privy to. But most women, like most men, are reasonable creatures, and as Jean Renoir said: "The problem is, everybody has their reasons." The line comes from *Rules of the Game,* the masterpiece that in the sexual and other confusion of its plot subtly sketches a cinematic blueprint for the course of relations between the sexes in an age of uncertainty brought upon Europe by the two world wars fought on its land (the film predates the second of the two, but anticipates it as anyone following world affairs at that time would have to). One of the few benefits of being a child of divorce, particularly a contentious one, is that you learn early to construct complex narratives to explain your parents' behavior: while each of them can afford to demonize the other, as a kid who loves both Mommy and Daddy you must ratify a whole new set of laws in your own mind, must learn to assemble a view of the situation where neither is wrong, both in their way are right.

Perhaps Delilah only wanted to know, just for a little while, what it felt like to hold the weight of the world and the strength of the universe in her arms, at her mercy. Maybe Delilah could not reconcile herself with the belief that her love alone could control and consume Samson, or tell herself that her sexual tyranny could compete with, say, the divine rights of Canaanite kings. The delusion-fatigued Delilah, while certainly still a desirable beauty, was worldly enough to trust no one—not even herself: she could not quite accept on faith that her soft, silken charms were enough to hold Samson's attention and hold him beside her, especially with his solo *intifaddeh* for competition. She felt him slipping away, felt it the way lights drain from the sky as the days get shorter after the Summer Solstice, or the way there's that much more darkness in life: she felt it with a terrible, subtle sorrow, the kind that's metastasized deep inside your bones long before it's made it to your conscious mind. And what woman does not know some version of this feeling? Who, born female, has not felt a twinge of insecurity when her man has looked away just for a few moments—and then for a few minutes, then hours, then incalculable time, until love is gone not because it is renounced but because it is forgotten? The lucky few, I imagine, don't fall prey to these insecurities, the ones with confidence and fortitude. But in a world that defines women by the marriages they make—in millennial America, it is *still* like that to some extent—even an independent woman like Delilah can go into paroxysms of panic at the thought of losing her man. Even Delilah, this *shiksa* goddess in the big city who seductively cast a spell on Samson—sorceress of the Sorek—wondered when her boy would tire of her, return to his people: come to his senses. What woman, once again, has not felt that a man's infatuation with her is a delusional state from which he will recover? Somehow, society convinces us that we are nothing without a man, and simultaneously feeds us subliminal messages that make us feel that no man in his right mind would really want us. And this is fucked up enough today; imagine how it was for Delilah in the late–Old Testament era. And I bet she wished that Samson could know her anxiety, her fear of abandonment, if only for a little while. For once, Delilah wanted to have all the power while Samson was helpless, useless, blinded and shorn.

How easy it must have been to turn him over to the Philistines. How empowering. And for Samson too, it must have been some sort of relief from the relentless pursuit that was his life, it must have been some kind of liberation to be finally freed from the quest. At a certain point in life—your late twenties, perhaps—it's got to be nice to know once and for all that you're never again going to spend the night with a whore and carry away the city gate in the morning; it's nice to know your salad days are over. In the novel *Hopscotch*, by Argentine writer Julio Cortázar, narrator Horacio Oliveira spends the whole book questing through a life of philosophical peripatetica centered in Paris' Latin Quarter. It is a book of ideas, a collage of thoughts about blindness and insight, with Klee, Fritz Lang, Saint Augustine, Claude Lévi-Strauss, Anaïs Nin, Louis Armstrong (referred to with the familiar "Satchmo") and post-Structuralist aesthetic theory all thrown in for atmosphere. Oliveira is, to say the least, an avid pedestrian, a street seeker of nothing in particular. "It was about that time I realized that searching was my symbol, the emblem of those who go out at night with nothing in mind, the motives of a destroyer of compasses," Oliveira announces early in the book, not so much to explain as to simply introduce—acquaint us with—his wanderings.

Often he'd wander in the direction of his girlfriend Lucia, always known as La Maga (perhaps another woman possessed of magical powers). In the hyperintellectual, pseudointellectual scene that Horacio and La Maga occupy, she comes to represent the deceptively simple. "She was one of those people who could make a bridge collapse simply by walking on it," Cortázar writes, leaving us to wonder if La Maga is, as her name suggests, that mythically powerful—or simply so clumsy and colossal. The only thing that is certain is that in all La Maga's presumed stupidity, her whole way of being poses huge challenges to Oliveira's sense of self. "[H]e is looking for the black light, the key, and he's beginning to realize that you don't find those things in libraries," a mutual friend tells La Maga. "You're the one who really taught him that, and if he [leaves] it's because he's never going to forgive you for it." Indeed, that is exactly what happens.

"I know you're tired of me and don't love me anymore," La Maga says as their relationship is falling apart. "You never did love me, it was something else, some kind of dream you had." It happens that Delilah says more or less the same thing to Samson: as she attempts to extract the secret of his strength, she says to Samson, "You don't love me, you only hate me." And she's somewhat right. He is obsessed with her, which is not the same as love, and she is finally at a point where she is desperate for him to see her as flesh and blood and need—she is tired of being worshipped like a movie star, a screen goddess, a sexual icon. Both these women are frustrated by men who fail to see them the right way—or fail to see them at all. Delilah, at the end of the day and by the end of this episode, is a woman who wants to be loved for herself, she wants to settle down and be serious. She is made furious by the way Samson has allowed a failure of insight and eyesight to infiltrate their relationship.

It is in this context that Delilah, whose name means "of the night," gives Samson, whose name means "of sunshine," the gift of darkness and blindness. For without his eyes, Samson can finally see God clearly and have a relationship of greater spirituality than he has ever achieved before, even in all those moments of galvanized strength. Samson was distracted by his eyes, made irascible and irrational by all that he saw—and when he came across a pretty girl, he seems to have become silly as a teenager no matter how old he was. Delilah freed him from his visual compulsions; his spiritual self was reborn. And in *Hopscotch*, Oliveira recognizes at first that the intuitive, anti-intellectual La Maga might in fact see with greater clarity than he does, lost as he is in a muddle in the middle of his cerebral cortex. One bit of dialogue:

"Do you think I'm so blind?"

"On the contrary, I think it might do you some good to be a little blind."

"Ah, yes. Touch replaces definitions, instinct goes beyond intelligence. The magic route, the dark night of the soul."

At first Oliveira finds her way of seeing, her choice to valorize emotion over logic, completely silly. He breaks up with her, and naturally finds that he misses her desperately, that he has lost the use of her eyes, that he is bereft of her vision, that he is walking around at least half blinded. "But La Maga was right, as always she was the only one who was right," Oliveira thinks longingly of a time when she was the only one who despaired of getting to hear a Brahms sonata while the rest of the group focused its attention uselessly on some domestic squabble across the alleyway. "La Maga had no idea at all that she was my witness, and on the contrary, was convinced that I was eminently the master of my own fate," he confesses in the reverie of another day of missing her. "But no, what really exasperated me was knowing that I would never again be so close to my freedom as in those days in which I felt myself hemmed in by the Maga world, and that my anxiety to escape was an admission of defeat." The intellectual gymnastics that define his social set start to seem stupid.

"I can make a dialectical operation even out of soup," he thinks with self-loathing as he contemplates his loss. He scours the Paris newspapers for any description of a crime victim that fits La Maga; he searches every pharmacy he can in Buenos Aires since she'd once worked at such a place; he traipsed through the bad neighborhoods of

Montevideo. Finally, despairing of ever finding La Maga again, know-ing that she may well have returned to Uruguay, a place where people disappear and occasionally turn up as corpses in a football stadium, Oliveira is overwhelmed with regret, wondering: "perhaps I should have spent a little more time in Montevideo and done a better job of searching."

In desperation, Oliveira just admits, without restraint, how desper-ately he feels the loss of La Maga—an absence that he brought on all by himself—and how right she always was. "There are metaphysical rivers, she swims in them like that swallow swimming in the air, spin-ning madly around a belfry, letting herself drop so that she can rise up all the better with the swoop. I look for them, find them, observe them from the bridge, but she swims in them. But she doesn't know it, any more than the swallow. It's not necessary to know things as I do, one can live in disorder without being held back by any sense of order." Of course, glorifying her naïveté, as if she were the unwashed exotic in Truffaut's *Wild Child*, he once again tries to classify her, find the phylum for her nature. Finally, knowing he is stuck in his linear, Car-tesian, enlightened thinking, Oliveira begs her revenant for deliver-ance. "Oh let me come in, let me see some day the way your eyes see," he cries out.

The only way Oliveira could possibly see the vistas of La Maga is without her; and the only way that Samson could see the world as Delilah did was dismantled, effectively eviscerated by the Philistines. She knew that. All his life Samson had been this hulking beast that none could vanquish—in his bullying and belligerence, Samson was all-powerful. Delilah, despite her sexual sorcery, would always be es-sentially powerless in a man's world, was still required to respond to the higher-ups among the Philistines, she was still compelled to hand over her man at will—anyone who doubts that she was *forced* to forfeit Samson will recall that the Philistine soldiers and officials waited outside her door as she questioned her husband about the well-spring of his strength, which would seem to suggest to me that this woman was hounded by law enforcement officials; her tent was no less under siege than David Koresh's compound in Waco as it was invaded by ATF troops. So Delilah is first at the mercy of the instabil-ity of her lover, who between her and his private jihad is serving at least two masters; and then she's at the mercy of the demands of her own state, with orders coming from the highest echelons: stretched, divided, cracked, confused, she is, above all, drained. By turning Samson into a helpless blind man, Delilah is forcing him to see the world as she sees it, to feel humbled before God and man alike. She wants Samson to know her helplessness, and she wants him to feel what her devotion to him has cost her. She is also finally putting up the Heisman hand and saying *enough;* she is tired of the craziness. "And that's how blind people are the ones who light our paths," writes Cortázar, expressing the idea that those who say they cannot join us in our ventures can sometimes be an excellent barometer of the sanity of our schemes. "That's how someone, without knowing it, comes to show you irrefutably that you are on a path which he for his part would be incapable of following."

Delilah wanted the pain of her worldview to count, to hold currency with Samson, and though he was blinded in the process, in fact it seems he could finally see, finally feel the darkness and depth of life that one misses when he is a man of action, of thrashing out, of riddles and massacres, but not of solitary sane contemplation. "Reverse everything," exhorts Marguerite Duras in an interview in the literary journal *Signs.* "Make women the point of departure in judging, make darkness the point of departure in judging what men call light, make obscurity the point of departure in judging what men call clarity."

I think, finally, for Delilah, disempowering Samson seemed like the best shot she had at keeping him around. In a very humane reading of the situation, Wolf Mankowitz's novel *The Samson Riddle,* shows her to be a woman in a panic, he's coming around to see her less and less, he may have someone else, she's bound to lose him anyway in this jihad, so she takes the bribe money as a nest egg. She has no man other than the loose cannon that is Samson, and has no other security against old age. We see her as a survivor in a man's world. According to Dr. Gregory Mobley of Harvard Divinity School, she isn't "a conniving femme fatale as much as a woman trying to carve out her own place in a world that was against her." Dr. Carol Fontaine of Andover Newton Theological School adds, "I think Delilah was someone caught in the middle. I think she is trying to save her own life. I don't know how a woman alone—we have no indication that she has brothers or a father—could have said no to the Philistine lords with that kind of force and for that much money."

In a discussion of all the wiles a wife must use to keep a straying husband around, the energy she must expend to reduce all rivals, whether other women or worldly causes and concerns, Simone de Beauvoir writes: "If nothing succeeds, she will resort to bursts of weeping, nervous outbreaks, attempts at suicide, and the like; but too many scenes and recriminations will drive her husband out of the house. The wife thus runs the risk of making herself unbearable at the moment when she most needs to be seductive; if she wants to win the game she will contrive a skillful mixture of affecting tears and brave smiles, of blackmail and coquetry." Or she might cut his hair, subdue and tame him, like Delilah.

But Beauvoir is making the point that the patriarchal, traditional marriage has set woman up to be necessarily wily, and yet it complains when she does only what she must. "This is indeed a melancholy science—to dissimulate, to use trickery, to hate and fear in silence, to play on the vanity and the weaknesses of a man, to learn to thwart him, to deceive him, to 'manage' him. But woman's good excuse for it all is that she has been required to involve herself wholly in her marriage. She has no gainful occupation, no legal capacities, no personal relations, even her name is hers no longer; she is nothing but her husband's 'half.' "

Of course, the women's movement was supposed to change all this, but has it really? We may no longer be "managing" marriages but we are managing relationships, reading books like *The Rules* and *Men Are from Mars, Women Are from Venus* and trying to work things out that we ought to abandon. We are trying to save and cling to what we have, like the wife in Scott Turow's novel *Presumed Innocent,* the woman who is willing to kill a foxy mistress to save our marriage. Delilah just got in over her head and into Samson's hair. I'm sure her motives to begin with were happiness on the home front. We all gladly buy into the notion that marriage is woman's way of taming the wild beast that is man. We accept this, but what we don't like is if she then takes this domesticated tiger, this declawed and defanged feline, and turns him over to the zookeepers because—well, because she can. Which is exactly what Delilah did. The Philistines captured Samson and entertained themselves by observing him in all his weakness and helplessness in the center of the city.

But even if you accept every justification for Delilah's betrayal, I'd still maintain that she did not ever mean to give him over to his enemies. Every commentator points out that she made her intentions plain, gave Samson three chances, and since the first three times he lied about the source of his power, Mankowitz suggests that she believed he may have been lying when he said the haircut would work. Samson's surrender to Delilah with such great ease, so little coercion, and despite her complete lack of guile makes it seem as if he wanted, at long last, to give in and give up the fight, to abandon the one-man war. In the end, Samson was like any fugitive who does something stupid just to get caught, like Timothy McVeigh driving a car without license plates from his Oklahoma City bombing mission, creating through oversight the opportunity to get pulled over by the cops.

And as much as Samson in his tragic heroism resembles suicidal Kurt Cobain, in his forcefulness, in his presumptuousness, in his peacock pride, he also reminds me a bit of O. J. Simpson. Perhaps Samson had no desire for surrender at all, he had simply come to believe that the source of his strength was his own will, not God's—he had come to believe that not even a haircut could sap him, much less kill him. He reminds me of a man who believes he could get away with murder. Samson seems like a man who might give away his secrets, believing himself invincible. Who can say that Samson too wasn't beating his wife, that Delilah kept calling on the authorities to restrain him and they couldn't? Perhaps Delilah was more clever and accomplished at the art of survival than Nicole.

*   *   *

There is no escaping that this is a story about fear of women. In the view of contemporary culture, this is a narrative about the *power* of women, but that is only an attempt at fashioning an excuse for men's irrational dread of this phantom female potency—a dread that is actually a direct consequence of the male of the species' God-honest down-deep awareness that since time immemorial he has had a stranglehold on all the power (and since Karl Marx has proved correct in positing that he who has the capital has control, all I have to say is seventy cents on the dollar to prove my point)—which is why he lives with the fear of one who has something to lose. He's so busy protecting his pot of gold that in all his vigilance he's failing to enjoy it—and to translate that into the subject at hand, it seems that male fear of the world's freewheeling, devastating, difficult and complicated women is actually obviating a hell of a good time. Delilah's punishment for assuming freedom as her birthright—beyond just having the roof fall on her head—is going down in history as a very bad woman. The punishment for similar behavior today, thousands of years later, has its own twists.

Consider this: consider that if a female athlete or performer—a respected one, a role model, a *nice* girl, a Chris Evert or Bonnie Raitt—admitted to being HIV-positive and claimed she slept with a thousand men, she would not be accorded the dignity that's been granted Magic Johnson, who served on a presidential commission, bitches and ho's aside. "Delilah is often referred to as a 'loose woman' but no one calls Samson a 'loose man,'" notes J. Cheryl Exum in her essay "Feminist Criticism: Whose Interests Are Being Served?" in *Judges and Method: New Approaches in Biblical Studies*. In Italy a porn star is in parliament. Here, we can't even elect one woman President and a potential Attorney General, Judge Kimba Wood, was removed from consideration with talk of her training to be a Playboy Bunny in London in the sixties tossed about as indications of inappropriateness. Feminism has taken us far, to far, far places, but it still hasn't made it comfortable for women to be sexual subjects, it still has failed to eliminate the threat of female sexuality from the American psyche—a female cannot be whole successfully. In the case, for instance, of Ms. Wood, it's as if the delight we ought to feel knowing that such a smart and capable creature is also a major babe is seen instead as a threat, an uncomfortable, itchy possibility. Could no one have said: All that and big boobs too? Of course. But no one did.

Women's sensuality, the fact that they are sexual beings, seems to be so distracting, so overwhelming in its vertiginous power that no one can stand it. "In this androcentric view female sexuality, unless controlled, leads to evil and destruction," writes historian of Judeo-

Christian and Islamic cultures Gordon Newby in *The Making of the Last Prophet*. It's not that at this late date women are barred outright from positions of power, but in order to assume the role of serious scholar or intimidating manager or levelheaded leader, she must not be attached to anything that resembles sex appeal. Because the sexual lure, if recognized in a woman, is suspicious and scary because it is believed to be unbridled. Or else it is thought that what is really out of control is men's response to her sexual presence: he simply *will not be able* to think straight with sex just spilling all over the conference room like a slippery mess.

Now, it may well be that sexual tension can keep business from getting properly conducted, but, my God, life is still a great deal more fun with the intrusion of this kind of trouble into life now and again. And for what it's worth, the idea that the President of the United States can be trusted to manage Saddam Hussein but cannot keep a handle on his own libido would seem to indicate that a highly sexed nature does not preclude one's capacity to engage in sensitive matters involving security and international nutcases. I know there are plenty of women in serious policy positions on Capitol Hill, and—a silly argument—no doubt many sexy, lovely, alluring young women work in the White House and in other centers of power, and in many cases they command power. But I'd like to see any one of them go all the way, be completely in charge, without having to become serious and less flirtatious. Men do not have to lose their charm to exude power, but women's sexuality is a dangerous distracter. If you don't see what I mean, consider this: As long as the President's cabinet contains only women like Donna Shalala and Janet Reno, then as far as I'm concerned it is still half empty.

This would be the most permanent legacy of the Delilah story: the dis-integration of woman from her sexuality. Always, a woman is seen as using her sex appeal to destroy a man, to get power, to gain the upper hand. Or else it is out of need, she must display her erotic nature in order to sell her body to make a living: she is a whore, she is desperate, she is cheesecake, she is a stupid girl reduced to this. The notion of a woman simply reveling in her own gorgeousness and sensuality because she can, because she enjoys it, because she wants others to appreciate it, seems not to exist in our cultural lexicon. She is always using it. A woman is never allowed to be integrated with her sexual nature in a way that isn't either demeaning or frightening. Here sex has been set up as this great source of power for women, and yet, when any one of us decides she'd like to put it out there in ways that have not been pre-approved by the powers that be, they take it away or deny it or somehow try to make it suspect. For such a source of all the world's ills that women's sexuality is said to be, few women have access to it in any way that is not manipulative. The feeling that men are more susceptible to seduction can be countered by the fact that women get swept up in romance, and, in the end, in love, we are all vulnerable, and women should not be seen as dangerous because we are desirable.

In the bizarre case of Sol Wachtler, the eminent chief judge of the state of New York who stalked and threatened Joy Silverman, the Park Avenue divorcée with whom he was having an affair when she tried to break it off, the media depicted him as in the wrong—which was hard not to do, considering he was sending filthy letters and condoms to Silverman's daughter. Nevertheless, there was a constant sense that such an eminent man could only have been driven to this behavior by a sorceress, a practitioner of some brand of sexual exoticism of unknown origin. While it is easy to think the situation must have been extraordinary, in fact it was all pretty straightforward. Sol from the start seems to have been a bit disappointed in his marriage choice, not because his wife Joan was not a fine woman, but because like many people married in the fifties to the first person they ever kissed, he was wistful and wondering, and like many middle-aged men, Wachtler chose to have an affair with a younger woman who, over time, urged him to leave his wife and marry her. When this was not forthcoming, she decided to see other men. Now, unlike most women left in the lurch at age forty-five by some man (think Anjelica Huston in *Crimes and Misdemeanors*) who wallow in self-pity and never love again, Joy Silverman went out and found herself a new boyfriend—pronto (whose last name, strangely enough, is Samson). Had she not, I'm sure we would feel much more sympathy for her. She is good-looking, rich and Republican—in other words, easy to hate, a big target. It's easy to dismiss her as a much-married JAP who wreaked havoc on a learned, accomplished man who knew what it meant to work for a living. Just the same, the scenario of their affair, this adultery, is totally common, right down to the fact that Sol never left his wife. The only thing unusual in this story is *his* behavior. But still the focus is on what a bitch she was. In fact, the only thing she did wrong was get on with her life when he could not give her what she wanted and needed. To most people, that is what's known as healthy.

And yet, somehow, echoes of Delilah everywhere.

To be fair, Mrs. Silverman supposedly told Wachtler that her new boyfriend was richer and handsomer. Which is crass and uncouth, though not actionable. And I can think of the occasional occasion when such nastiness might be perfectly appropriate—such as if the man is making obscene phone calls, sending sick letters, threatening your daughter, trying to withdraw your trust, etc. But you know what? It doesn't matter how she behaved. The trouble is with how he behaved, which even in the realm of a scorned lover is a real outlier. Late in life the guy fell hard for someone, probably for the first time ever. His failure to act on that—his decision not to leave his wife and pursue this passion—was his own idiocy. That he could not cope was not surprising—his emotional life until then had been very limited. But that's not Joy's problem. He failed her, not the reverse. The focus should be completely on him.

In other words, let's focus on Samson's behavior, not Delilah's.

Trouble is, even if we do look at the men's culpability, by most traditions women still get assigned the greater share of blame for illicit or ill-considered sexual liaisons on two counts, while men can be found guilty on only one. In her essay "Gendering the Ungendered Body: Hermaphrodites in Medieval Islamic Law," Paula Sanders notes that in ancient Islamic societies, "although men and women presumably bore equal responsibility for illicit relations, that responsibility was construed in terms of certain assumptions about the natures of men and women. Men were considered susceptible to seduction and the actors, whereas women were considered to be both seductresses (that is, tempting men to act in certain destructive ways) and the recipients of the men's acts." While this Islamic view may be an advance over Hindu beliefs that all women were temptresses, that any man who went astray was a victim of her tantric sex trickery, in our modern world, is this what we want? For that matter, do we really want Joan Wachtler idiotically standing by Sol, saying I'm prettier than Joy, I'm thinner than Joy—do we really want women acting like the wife in *The Crucible,* begging the husband for forgiveness for somehow driving him to go astray—acting in some sense as an obverse of seduction?

If we have figured out that the world is a sphere, that no one is going to row their boat right off its delicate flatness, why has our view of women's sexuality in some essential way remained medieval, ancient, perhaps even prehistoric?

But let's assume, for argument's sake that Delilah and Joy Silverman were both sexually manipulative. Let's assume they used their sensual arts to drag men down. They were, indeed, duplicitous, and, by extension, all women are duplicitous. Well, so what? What do you expect? In both instances they were using what little power they had to get what they wanted. And in both instances, that was not anything so outrageous: they both wanted committed, respectful relationships. The only reason either lashed out (besides that both were provoked by the secret police, the CIA, etc.) was that what they wanted was not forthcoming. In this world women have very little recourse, and the solace of knowing there will always be another man is not much relief when there have already been more than enough. We only know how to use what we have, and some of us know how to use sex as a weapon. The details of both the Delilah story and the Joy Silverman story make it clear that it is not so simple—both women were being engaged in battle by many decidedly nonsexual forces—but every time I hear a story of a woman leaving a man in a flurry of heartbreak, in jail, at the gallows, desperate, psychotic, on medication, in a straitjacket—every time I hear a Delilah story, I have to smile. Because the problem is not that women bring men down—it is actually that men bring women down, refusing to fulfill our needs, failing to give us what we want, knowing in some sadistic way that we don't have forever to wait the way men seem to. Biologically, and often socially and economically, men have all the power. And if, every so often, a woman comes along and inverts the order of things just a bit—well, who am I to deny my delight?

Society has made women the sex objects—men at best are matinee idols—but it bristles when women take up that role at inappropriate moments. In truth, over and over women learn that sex is their only weapon—the only professions in which women get paid more than men are modeling, stripping and prostitution. As long as that is true—and it will be a while yet—we will all walk around knowing that while women can certainly be valued for their minds, they are extra specially valued for their bodies. This is not an opinion; this is simple economics. Even women who work as corporate attorneys, bond traders, legislators, advertising executives, news anchors and investigative reporters know that it pays to be sexy.

And yet, when anyone flaunts this a tiny bit too much, when any woman is revealed to actually have been sufficiently aware of her physical endowments to have gone to the Playboy Club looking for a job like Kimba Wood, or, as was the case with Diane Sawyer, to have posed a bit too provocatively in *Vanity Fair,* everyone just gets unnerved. Men have made us into sex objects—every last one of us, but the pretty girls, the daddy's little pumpkins, the baby dolls among us especially—and the fact that we have actually managed to learn a few other tricks, which is to say how to make a living with our clothes on and our torsos vertical, ought to be considered nothing less than a tribute to our ingenuity and the indomitable human spirit that wishes to be mind as well as body. But damn it, do you know how dull life will be when the only women allowed to be sex objects are Cindy Crawford and Victoria's Secret models? It's to the point where no one is even protesting, we all accept that all of us—men and women—would rather look at Pamela Anderson in *Playboy* than at just about any of the men in *Playgirl*. We've accepted that the vitality of heavy-breathingness belongs to woman alone. And we also accept that nobody ought to start stripping in a corporate boardroom. But the fact that women have carried on in previous incarnations, or continue to go on after hours, with all the sexy bravado that we allow to men should not be a problem any longer. And to say that, for instance, posing nude is inconsistent with being a serious scholar or a credible manager or a dynamic leader means we're also going to have to start saying that fucking the slave girls makes Thomas Jefferson unworthy of having been President or makes the Declaration of Independence a null and void document, sleeping with a thousand women makes Wilt Chamberlain a lousy basketball player.

Life is strange; to expect people to be all one way or all another way is stupid.

*   *   *

Delilah's most astonishing distinction, one overlooked amid all the attention to hair and muscle and sensual pleasure, is her independent status. Unlike just about every other woman in the Bible, Delilah is introduced as simply Delilah. She is not called "daughter of" or "wife of," she is her own person. It is often assumed that this lack of marital or familial association marks her as a prostitute or, more likely, since she is acquainted with all the higher-ups, a courtesan in Philistine noble circles. But since the Bible is fast to identify women who ply their wares in the sex trade, I'd prefer to think of Delilah as a precursor to all strong, modern, willful women—even independent career women—who are so feared because even at this late date they continue to threaten the social order. I'm not referring to women who work for a living, because nowadays, married or not, that is usually an economic necessity; I'm talking about women who forgo the whole business, don't bother with husbands or children, or wait until they are good and ready to settle down. Women who just do what they want.

Well before Delilah appeared as the agent of her own desire, the wife of Potiphar made a less advanced attempt at claiming a right to self-determination of some sort—even though she never is named as anything but somebody's spouse. But feminist scholars, so busy mainly trying to show how Joseph escapes a fate that no female character could get away from without a scrape, don't bother to notice what an extraordinary and revolutionary character she is. Reported by later interpreters to be named Zuleikha, this horny housewife is married to the viceroy who Joseph serves. One fine day, she makes a pass at the pretty slave boy, he rebuffs her, and in her humiliation she tells her husband that Joseph raped her. Latter-day readers of this tale often find themselves believing that she's telling the truth: he *did* rape her. But that's not the point. It's more interesting to assume that she jumped him. If that's the case, the wife of Potiphar is the first exemplar of the female gaze, the first woman to objectify a man, to look at him and say, *He's hot; I want him.* She is the first woman of desire, with desires, and the daring to express them. An early Mrs. Robinson, but perhaps every powerful woman who has become attracted to the hired help: Lady Chatterley, Madonna, Bess Myerson, Elizabeth Taylor.

And who is really to say that the feeling between them wasn't mutual: she is the wife, hanging around the house all day, stuck at home while Potiphar is off doing battle, and probably finding herself chummy with the hired hands, because the help are the only ones who are there. Perhaps romance between the two was entirely possible. Patty Hearst married her bodyguard; Madonna had a baby with her trainer. Lina Wertmuller's brilliant film *Swept Away* posits the possibility of a boat yeoman and a millionairess falling in love when they are trapped on a desert island. Why not in desert Egypt? Certainly more than one porn flick has involved the acrobatic possibilities of the plumber, the gardener, the carpenter. Not to mention the pool boy, or the boy in the pool, as was the case in the dangerous liaisons between Mrs. Robinson and Ben, and Gloria Swanson and William Holden. Lonely glamorous women with irregular social lives can find that their most continual sources of intimacy are household laborers. But even if we discount the possibility that Joseph and this woman so much as liked each other, there is something commendable about a woman at long last asking for it—even begging for it. And, in fact, it is such an oddity, one that is never again repeated in the Old Testament, that it makes me assume that she was probably telling the truth. He probably did jump her. Horny young kid and all. It is only his luck that the word of a woman was so worthless that all he got was a prison sentence. But actually, it's more interesting to assume she was the seducer who got elbowed. It's exciting.

In conceiving the wife of Potiphar as a pioneer of female desire, it's not an evolutionary overstep to say that there is, outside of all logical explanations for Delilah's behavior, one that is more visceral and pure. One that is about emotional mayhem, about dreams of wildness, about thrill-seeking and troublemaking simply for its own sake. Of wanting to be as big and bad as Samson, and doing the only thing that came close: destroying him for want of the possibility of creating herself. What horror I felt to hear she was a villainess when it seemed to me there was little evidence to support it. It seemed to me it was about wanting to define her, to line-draw her as if she were Jessica Rabbit and not a spirit too free to obey their rules. In fact, whose rules were they? Even Michel de Montaigne, a man himself, had the good sense to point out all the way back in the sixteenth century: "Women are not in the wrong when they decline to accept the rules laid down for them, since men make these rules without consulting them. No wonder intrigue and strife abound."

I've always loved the old folk song "Samson and Delilah," which most people who know it at all know from Grateful Dead concerts. But actually there is a much more rowdy, angry version done by the group called the Washington Squares. If I'm in the right mood, if I'm the right amount angry, that song can sound like the best thing in the world—especially the chorus, the frustrated insistence: "If I had my way / If I had my way in this wicked world / If I had my way I would tear this building down." Now, of course, it's Samson who's supposed to be saying this, he's the one with all the destructive might. But recently when I was listening to this song, I had this riled-up euphoria and I thought about that feeling that I have all the time, that if I had *my* way, *I* would tear this building down, I would tear lots of other things down. I was thinking that I am just so full of unexpressed rage.

So then, it hit me: What if Delilah was *that* angry? What if she wanted to tear things down? What if every time she looked at Samson she just wanted to kill him because his recklessness and fury had an outlet, he had his strength, he could kill a thousand people with a donkey's jawbone, and he could kill a ferocious lion with his bare hands. But what could Delilah possibly do with all her rage and anger? I mean, it's nearly the twenty-first century and I don't know what to do with mine. So what if Delilah just wanted to be able to act out and feel all these things that are so wrong? What if she'd walked around day in, day out, her whole life troubled and bothered, so that what she did to Samson had nothing to do with spying for the Philistines and had nothing to do with betraying Samson—had nothing to do with anything at all except a pain and destructiveness that she'd kind of ignored until Samson came along and reminded her that it was there, and reminded her that she was angry enough to let a whole city come falling down on top of her.

Now, me, I'm not a femme fatale. Like Delilah I think I just care too much, I fall in love and I get stupid as bubble bath. Or perhaps my emotional involvement is just overdetermined: I get obsessed and over-wrought about whatever man comes along because I don't know what to do with myself, with the *excess* of self I drag around like a hundred and twenty pounds of dead weight. Whether the emotion is true or truly wished for, anytime anything resembling love comes my way, it makes a fool of me. It seems that to pull off the part of the dangerous, deadly woman with any kind of conviction, you must possess a strik-ing indifference, you must be a prickly possum—and it helps if you come by your aloofness by honest means: it helps to be a chilly New England thoroughbred like Marietta Tree, a conniving member of the impoverished British gentry like Pamela Harriman or just a careless, bitchy woman like Pam Smart, who seems to have wanted her hus-band dead just because a divorce would be a hassle and a blemish on her Martha Stewart dreams of a tasteful, catalogue-ready life. (One of the reasons the Smart case interested me is that no matter how many times I studied the situation, there seemed no motive for the murder except an image-conscious dread of divorce; the search led to the con-clusion that she was not so much cold or shallow as altogether empty.) You can't fake your femme fatale-ity, because emotion will lead the cleverest woman to get lost in her own game: in fact, in the cinematic versions of the Samson and Delilah story, even when she is portrayed as an all-business espionage operative of the Philistine secret police, she is also shown as full of regret, ultimately a feeling creature who falls for this man she's supposed to simply ensnare. No director dares make her cold-blooded: DeMille rekindles the romance between Sam-son and Delilah while he pushes a mindless millstone in a labor camp, and shows her unable to not stand by his side as he spreads the pillars apart and sends the temple falling on everyone; in Nicolas Roeg's version for TNT, Elizabeth Hurley is less than convincing though try-ing very hard to be, as she says of Samson, "Even though I betrayed him, he still belongs to me." Delilah, in contemporary portraits, falls in love because she can't help herself.

In the 1988 spy-who-loved-me Costa-Gavras film *Betrayed,* Debra Winger plays an FBI agent who's sent to infiltrate a white supremacist group by seducing a recently widowed father played by Tom Berenger. He is a sick man, playing hunting games in which a black man is set loose in the forest just to be chased down and tortured terribly by Berenger and his buddies. But when this is not going on, he's a good family man, his two children are adorable and adoring of Winger, who feels enveloped in the family life that is so much warmer and stronger than anything she experiences as a government agent. It does not help that her superior officer is an ex-lover who will not listen to her pleas that she is getting too emotionally involved and needs an out. At the end, Winger kills Berenger—it becomes kill or be killed—but she quits the FBI and can never again have real contact with the two children she loves. She is a pawn for forces that seem no less ugly than the white supremacists, she is bereaved and bereft, no doubt very much in the position that Delilah was in when she chose to die with Samson rather than live without him, no doubt the position many women are in when they try to merely be sexual weapons. Few of us are sufficiently dispassionate to play the femme fatale. You must be cool and contained as just about nobody is. The triumph of Sharon Stone's performance in *Basic Instinct* was her ability to convey somehow, between scenes of torrid suggestion and the cool sharpness symbolized by the ice pick as murder weapon, that she was actually fragile and delicate and needed someone (Michael Douglas?) to watch over her. That movie would have been arch and simply laughable like *Showgirls* and *Body of Evidence* and *Sliver* all were, if Sharon Stone had not brought real heart to the part.

There have been, though seldom, some brilliant portraits in film of women who truly are all ice: Barbara Stanwyck as Phyllis Nirdlinger in *Double Indemnity* is dead-on deadly, a woman who seems to kill on contact; in *The Last Seduction,* Linda Fiorentino made a real star turn as Bridget Gregory, a woman who writes backward, talks tough and throaty, fucks with an indifference that is too indifferent to qualify as studied and is so ruthless that her own attorney asks if she's checked her pulse for a heartbeat lately. But the only reason these films have become, respectively, a classic and an art-house classic, is the exquisite performances of the lead actresses, the convincing qualities that are so crucial to keep from the caricature and crass cattiness of, say, *Showgirls*. But in *Basic Instinct*—for which Sharon Stone should have been nominated for an Oscar—it is the softness and sweetness of a woman who is supposed to be all harsh blonde angles, all starched slim dresses, all sangfroid, that make the movie more than mere exploitation. The scenes of Ms. Stone sitting with an afghan blanket wrapped around her in a rocking chair on the front porch in the San Francisco rain—the cliché setup of catching the bad girl off guard in a moment of repose—which could seem contrived, instead work as genuine and revealing. The truism that every shrew is just a woman waiting to be tamed does, after all, have some truth to it. Nobody wants to be alone.

So, as I was saying, I am not nor have I ever been a femme fatale, and I am certain I'm probably missing out on something big. Like Delilah, and like most single women above the age of consent, no one ever refers to me as some man's daughter or another man's wife. I pay my own rent, I earn my own living, I have not had to answer to anybody in many years, and the only people who are likely to tug at me in ways that will feel like some kind of surrender in the future are my own children. I am completely free, and as far as my life goes, I have all the power. In fact, I have turned thirty in an era when for the first time in history a woman can feel as unencumbered and unbound as I do. And yet, for all the power I command in not being some man's dependent appendage, I generally walk around through life feeling pretty powerless. I don't think this makes me unusual, nor do I think this feeling is particularly female: men and women alike, with certain exceptions, walk around feeling small, insignificant and helpless compared to the enormity of the world, and I think it has always been so. People weren't always dwarfed by Calvin Klein billboards in Times Square and a Sony screen broadcasting bombs in Iraq right next to it, but I'm sure there was plenty of ignorance and megalomania to keep the majority of Cro-Magnons fairly humbled.

Just the same, powerless as I feel when it comes to everything, but particularly with love, every so often some guy will come along whom I find terribly attractive and he feels the same way about me and anything can happen, anything goes, and the strange thing is that the strongest urge I will get is to make a mess of him. I don't know where this comes from—compared with my own self-destructive problems it seems too healthy to hash out in therapy—and these attractions have tended to be years apart. But when I have a man in front of me, even one I really like, one who is quite literally putty in my hands and wherever else, I feel the incredible urge to use the power he has given me to ruin his life. The only way I can figure this is that—and this is the reason *The Rules* was written for women, not for men—as much of my life that is my own and that I have made in ways that my mother and grandmother could not have imagined, and as much as in matters of the heart I think right now at my age both men and women are nervously, nakedly groping, none of that changes the fact that as I get older, my real power will diminish while my male contemporaries will see theirs grow. Whether it's biology or culture or both that make this so, it does not much matter: feminism can't cure it.

Now I don't intend to let any of this ruin my good time. I'm glad to see that Farrah Fawcett at fifty can dump Ryan O'Neal and run off with someone younger and thinner and basically, what with the *Playboy* body-painting spread, behave like a menopausal man, but the fact that I can even root for her in all her ridiculousness stems from the same sense of disempowerment I usually feel. Because I don't like the idea that I'll be getting older and lesser; I want to keep becoming more and more and more. My sexual energy is so much a part of who I am, and the idea that it might at some point be taken away is all too horrible. And so there are these moments when I feel this power, this power I have been temporarily credentialed with while I see men only getting more and more and more of it, and it makes me so mad and crazed and I want to jump out of my skin with my desire for MORE MORE MORE. And then, I don't know, there could be some perfectly nice guy sitting there in front of me and the urge to use what power I now have in every which way, to love and to hate, to take this window of opportunity that represents either my childbearing years or my sexual desirability and smash my fist right through it and make the most of it. I don't want to spend any time making lists of things I need to do by age thirty-five or no one will marry me, I don't want to be on this fucking clock that no man on earth is at all concerned with. I want more than that. That's the word that keeps echoing in my head as I think of ways to make a mess: MORE.

And that's how it was for Delilah. Samson loved her. It's a big deal for the Bible to say that. I think she loved him too. But she was an independent gal, and the men come and go when that's who you are. Who can tell who among them might just be so good and faithful and true that he's the one person you shouldn't, say, kill with an ice pick. It's hard to know what to do. History brands you betrayer when really it's just that you were thinking: Why should the men get to have all the fun?

PART TWO

Hey Little Girl Is Your Daddy Home?

Sometimes it's like someone took a knife baby edgy and dull
and cut a six inch valley through the middle of my skull

BRUCE SPRINGSTEEN
''I'm On Fire''

There is only one thought that I ever have about Amy Fisher, no matter how many incriminating, nasty, horrid things I read about her: That she is blameless. She should never have been prosecuted for shooting her boyfriend's wife, all blame should have fallen firmly on Joey Buttafuoco's beefy, bulgy shoulders.

Because she was a teenager. Teenagers are hormones with legs attached to them, and not much else. What I would have done for a boy or man I loved when I was fourteen, fifteen, sixteen—things I most certainly would not do now. I also never would have done what Amy did, but who cares? That just means that I got lucky. The fact that most teenagers get through adolescence without lawyers, guns and money should not reflect badly on the ones who do end up turning into juvenile delinquents in the name of love. Those high school years, they are the time when anything goes, when you're just a flimsy piece of walking substrate in search of a catalyst, and when girls, in particular, are just one man or one boy away from doing something really stupid. In a country with the highest teen suicide rate on earth, no self-inflicted fatality really surprises us any longer: we accept the hara-kiri crash as just another war wound—the drag-racing accident, the drunk-driving death, the overload of a Percodan scrip still lingering after Mom's root canal, the wrists getting ready for a very large donation to the Red Cross. Homicide, on the other hand—that rare occasion when an adolescent actually thinks to do harm to someone other than herself—it seems we ought to be a bit more prepared for it. And when adults are involved, adults who may have influence on the behavior, adults who should be staying out of the rarefied, hyperbolic world of teenland to begin with, adults who above all should really know better—they must be held responsible. When Pam Smart, a grown woman who became sexually entangled with a fifteen-year-old boy, convinced her young lover to kill her husband, she was sent to prison for life without parole. Somehow, Joey Buttafuoco, who did eventually serve a six-month sentence for statutory rape—all the while denying that he'd ever slept with *anyone* underage—managed to elude prosecution for his complicity in the shooting of his wife. Even though the minute he began to toy with Amy Fisher's sixteen-year-old mind, such as it was, he became responsible for its thoughts, rather in the way that when a person drives drunk, if there is an accident, it is the driver who is held responsible and not the car.

Look: you don't get angry at a middle finger for doing what a middle finger does. A pointer points, a pinkie picks, a ring finger wears a symbol of holy matrimony and a middle finger says fuck you. And a teenage girl will kill and die for love, for what she *believes* is love. She doesn't read *Smart Women, Foolish Choices* and decide to get a grip. She reads pulp novels and decides to get a gun. If she's still bothering with school, she reads *Romeo and Juliet* and *Wuthering Heights* and lets the melancholy of these classics teach her that true love justifies any consequences; or else she checks out her mother's copies of Judith Krantz and Danielle Steel (a new one every nine months!) and worse, and creates fictions and fantasies involving all-for-love scenarios as if life were a Harlequin Romance.

Did Joey Buttafuoco tell Amy Fisher to kill his wife? Perhaps not in so many words, but this man was nothing if not a signifying monkey.

Amy Fisher should not be in jail. In college, in reform school maybe, but not in jail. That several years later, beyond eligibility for parole, she remains in Albion State Correctional Center while an array of bozos and buffoons involved in this case get on with their lives— and turn a profit and befriend Howard Stern—proves just how scared we are of the inchoate violence of a woman scorned. Even if she is just a girl.

*   *   *

The events of the Amy Fisher story, the 1992 adolescent/adultery/ attempted-murder case, better known by headlines like "Lethal Lolita" or "Long Island Lolita" or "Teen Fatal Attraction," comprised a lowbrow media event, a situation that was so strikingly tacky it never really got out of the tabloids. It was the kind of story that a newspaper like *The New York Times* would cover only in order to note how much coverage it was getting elsewhere, rather like the nine-teenth-century puritanical pretense of painting someone else painting a nude, or rather like reporting what Gennifer Flowers said in *The Star* as if it were news analysis. Or pretending that the presidential race, the evanescent stump speech promises, were more important news than the story of Amy, a small, shaggy high school girl on the South Shore of Long Island who fell for a puffy, married auto mechanic with a smashed-in face and a really funny name, one so improbably unpro-nounceable that for months David Letterman would get onstage and just, pie-eyed, say "Buttafuoco" as if it were joke and punch line all by itself. Anyway, this bit of extramarital and extracurricular intrigue in suburbia did not become news until Amy shot Joey's wife on their front porch while pretending to sell Girl Scout cookies, puncturing a carotid artery and permanently lodging a bullet in the woman's head—though somehow, miraculously, Mary Jo Buttafuoco lived on. No one particularly cared about this story up until then, no matter that Joey gave Amy herpes, got her started as a beeper-service hooker who made house calls and somehow arranged things so that she joined his gym and ended up sleeping with his personal trainer, who hap-pened to have both a hair weave and a wife, so that, via Joey, Amy at sixteen was involved with two married men and turning tricks as an after-school activity.

But this only really, really became news when Joey claimed that he didn't even know Amy—maybe they had pizza together once—she was just an accident-prone customer, totaled one car, kept denting another, he couldn't imagine why she would shoot his wife. It became news because here they had the actual smoking gun, which meant the third act of this morality play had come off without a hitch, the conventions of narrative obeyed precisely; but in a sudden twist of Pirandello, you had one of the players claiming that the first two acts, the only logical explanation for why a shooting took place, did not exist: in other words, a sixteen-year-old girl with no prior police record had shot a Long Island housewife she'd never met before for no reason at all.

This was akin to, several years later, O. J. Simpson looking at pictures of the now-deceased Nicole Brown with a cleft lip and bruised cheeks and a black eye and saying that he never beat her. And he never wore those ugly-ass Bruno Magli shoes that he was wearing in thirty-six different photographs either. This is about men who approach history with a method that can only be described as Soviet.

Amy Fisher became a story because it was about a teenage girl and it involved sex and violence—and automotive mishaps—and all that other titillating stuff, but it was also a story because it was an attempt to detach these acts of sex and violence from their meaning, to deny life its logical flow at a time—adolescence—when so much of what happens already feels illogical. Amy Fisher personified those strange moments at the end of an Arnold Schwarzenegger movie when buildings start to blow up and bridges start to burn for no reason—the enemy has already been done in at another skyscraper or weapons silo—and yet, viewers watch these scenes of cinematic catastrophe, ignoring the conventions of plot, because the special effects seem like enough. The Amy Fisher story is about an attempt to focus on one girl's special effects and pretend that no story line preceded it. And there's a lot of that going around these days.

Meanwhile, as Macbeth said of his misguided crimes, "We have scorched the snake, not killed it." All the while that Amy claimed Joey had asked her to kill his wife, Mary Jo, made more ferocious by her wounds, refused to consider the possibility that her husband had anything to do with her injuries.

Amy was to be charged alone.

In May 1992, Amy Fisher was arrested and held on $2 million bail, the highest ever in Nassau County for a nonhomicide (to put this in perspective, the child molester who kidnapped little Katie Beers and kept her chained in his underground bunker—another famed Long Island case—was held on only $500,000 bail). Forfeiting a trial, Amy plea-bargained and she is now doing five-to-fifteen for first-degree assault.

By late 1992, in an unprecedented move, all three major networks had produced made-for-TV movies about the case. By early 1993, when CBS and ABC chose to air their versions opposite each other on the same night—it was Alyssa Milano vs. Drew Barrymore, teenage mud wrestling at its best, the truly stupid against the falsely trashy—the ratings war on the eve of Bill Clinton's swearing-in threatened to upstage the inauguration itself. Drew had a 19.5 Nielsen take, Alyssa—in a show based on Buttafuoco lore—got a 15.8, and the version that played a week before, starring the unheralded Noelle Parker, pulled in a 19.1.

In the words of Russ Meyer: *Faster Pussycat! Kill! Kill!*

*   *   *

"Irving Thalberg used to tell me," Anita Loos reports of M-G-M's boy wonder in *Kiss Hollywood Goodbye,* " 'When you write a love scene, think of your heroine as a little puppy dog, cuddling up to her master, wagging an imaginary tail, and gazing up at him as if he were God.' "

(So this is what gave Nancy Reagan the idea.)

But as author of the novel *Gentlemen Prefer Blondes* and the screen adaptation of *The Women,* and as a leading architect of the cinematic flapper girl with her freewheeling, footloose and fanciful ways, it is unclear if Loos ever really took to Thalberg's mandate. No matter: the rest of Hollywood has been following it ever since. Which is why nubile girls on the edge of seventeen—in motion pictures, at least—never had it so good. All those incredible child-star debuts and teenage takes in the spotlight: the preternatural, premature grace and elegance of Elizabeth Taylor in *National Velvet,* Claire Bloom in *Limelight* and later on Olivia Hussey in *Romeo and Juliet;* the European goddess girls, from the stark and Teutonic mystery of Nico in *La Dolce Vita* to the all-blonde, all-bleach, all-nude-beach of Brigitte Bardot in . . . *And God Created Woman;* the more American shiksa goddess worship of Candice Bergen in *The Group* and Cybill Shepherd in *The Last Picture Show;* the hot and bothered babes, from the fifties repression of Susan Kohner in *Imitation of Life* and Carroll Baker in *Baby Doll,* to the full-frontal girl trouble of Mackenzie Phillips in *American Graffiti,* Melanie Griffith in *Night Moves,* Carrie Fisher in *Shampoo,* Jennifer Jason Leigh in *Fast Times at Ridgemont High,* Lori Singer in *Footloose* and Laura Dern in *Smooth Talk;* the accidental seduction of Sue Lyon in *Lolita,* Brooke Shields in *Pretty Baby,* Nastassia Kinski in *Tess* and Juliette Lewis in *Cape Fear;* the latter-day takes on hardscrabble, self-sufficient Shirley Temple types in the wise precocity of Susan Strasberg in *Picnic,* Tatum O'Neal in *Paper Moon,* Jodie Foster in *Taxi Driver,* Linda Blair in *The Exorcist,* Quinn Cummings in *The Goodbye Girl,* Drew Barrymore in *E.T.,* Jennifer Beals in *Flashdance* and Natalie Portman in *Beautiful Girls;* the smart, solid, good-girl sturdiness of Judy Garland in *The Wizard of Oz,* Patty Duke in *The Miracle Worker* and Ally Sheedy in *War Games;* the unexpected sweetness and strength of Molly Ringwald in *Sixteen Candles,* Martha Plimpton in *Running on Empty* and Mary Stuart Masterson in *At Close Range;* and then there is the simply, breathtakingly lovely—Natalie Wood in *Rebel Without a Cause,* Tuesday Weld in *Bachelor Flat,* Mariel Hemingway in *Manhattan,* Diane Lane in *A Little Romance,* Ione Skye in *Say Anything.* What has happened to these girls?

In many cases the jury is still out, in a couple of instances the Oscars and Barbara Walters interviews eventually came, the Academy Award for best supporting actress—frequently given, when it isn't already earmarked for some aging British character actress, as some form of Hollywood imprimatur to this year's starlet—was a lock. But most did not live up to their initial promise, most could not possibly excite the shock of the new ever again, and even if they did, they became drug addicts, they made lousy choices in love, they made claims that Michael Jackson was the most normal person they knew, they made guest appearances on *The Love Boat,* they became beards for Rock Hudson or Malcolm Forbes or both, they became spokespeople for Poly-Grip, they did testimonials for the Psychic Friends' Network, they died mysterious deaths. They faded away, published bad poetry like Ally Sheedy, became full-time manic-depressives like Patty Duke, were found out to be bad actresses like Candice Bergen, chose bad roles repeatedly like Juliette Lewis, lived with Rick Springfield at fifteen and Rick James at twenty like Linda Blair, became fat, old and profligate like Tuesday Weld and found themselves married to a classical violinist and living on Long Island, became ridiculous like Tatum O'Neal. Or worst of all, like Olivia Hussey, so beautiful in Franco Zeffirelli's classic, so archly alabaster and gorgeous as the screen's most memorable Juliet, they simply disappeared, left the time zone, left the continent, went to a faraway place where the extraordinariness of their youthful beauty, the experience of having it photographed and captured and commodified at such a young age, could be lived out in peace.

They—or the best part of them—died young: *Or I swear / I'll die young / like those favored before me, hand-picked each one / for her joyful heart.* So wrote poet Olga Broumas in "Cinderella," the lament of a woman rewarded for nothing more than fitting a glass slipper, raised from plebeian status and her washerwoman's post because of her shoe size, not so much different from little girls loved for a sexuality they are not in control of, a sensuality they might not be aware of, a way of being they are enslaved to though it is not a skill they can develop, it is not like playing tennis or solving quadratic equations. They are revered for a passive trait, an immanence in the eye of the fickle beholder—at a very young age they are endowed with a power certain to abandon them almost as soon as they figure out how to really use it. Adolescent sexuality, which employs ignorance as aphrodisiac, can become a girl's deepest experience of Marxian alienation from the fruits of her labor: as soon as a girl understands what she is doing, she is no longer fit to do it. After all, the most exciting thing about Lolita is that she does not mean to be exciting.

"I defy any pretty girl who is rocketed to world stardom at fifteen in a sex-nymphet role to stay on a level path," Sue Lyon, star of Stanley Kubrick's *Lolita,* told the *London Sunday Times.*

It's not that Willie Aames or Ricky Schroder or Leif Garrett or Troy Donahue have fared so much better—but they were just heart-throbs, teen idols, *Tiger Beat* fodder, not unlike Tiffany, Debbie Gibson, or Marie Osmond, bubblegum girls whose balloons were meant to burst. (Of course, had they the good sense to become country singers like Tanya Tucker, they'd still be at it, because the patron-plutarchs of Nashville—still as entrenched as the old studio system in Hollywood once was—do take care of their own: a girl can get hooked on barbiturates and become a casting-couch casualty when she tries to break into movies, but when she comes home to Opryland, she'll be greeted like a prodigal daughter and given back her old slot on the charts.) Like the Hispanic pop group Menudo, which replaced its members as each hit puberty, they must have understood that their success was glandular, hormonal—they were temporarily privileged by youth. But the women I mentioned were actresses—of the type that would insist, today, on being called *actors*. Somehow, their like-minded male counterparts made the transition into adulthood with a lot less grease and grime. We all know that Warren Beatty lived to achieve superstar status—as an actor, producer and director—long after his youthful debut in *Splendor in the Grass,* that the Hollywood experience made him feel competent and capable, a moviemaker and a womanizer whose appetites and activities were all part of a will to power. Likewise, Dennis Hopper managed to survive playing Elizabeth Taylor and Rock Hudson's eldest son in *Giant* to go on in his twisted way and somehow manage to make something of his life. (I believe that role, as child of two of the fruitiest people ever, with an unhinged James Dean at the other end of the set, in a movie that must have taken a long time to make, is adequate explanation for all of Hopper's oddities.)

But when it comes to young actresses, Jodie Foster is the exception that proves the rule. Of the rest—the remains—mostly, they lost a little something, they shed petals, they stiffened or they drooped, they became thespian models of defloration—a rape by voyeurism—as if something really wonderful and meaningful had been taken away from them. They demonstrated the Heisenberg principle in action, proof that the results of an experiment are altered simply by being watched. They started to look spent. They started to *be* spent: Tuesday Weld's troubled trajectory became the paradigm for Hollywood's jailbait set (Drew Barrymore followed it almost precisely), with her first nervous breakdown at nine, her first bout with drunkenness at ten, her first love affair at eleven, her first suicide attempt at twelve—

all of which meant that by fourteen she had nothing better to do than begin fucking her favorite drinking buddy, the forty-four-year-old pre-Mia Frank Sinatra. A 1996 biography of Ms. Weld was appropriately titled *Pretty Poison*. But even without the private dysfunction, the public dissolution of talent is bad enough. Can anyone detect any continuity between the freshness of Juliette Lewis in *Cape Fear* and the wretched, rowdy ugliness she displays in *Kalifornia*—an unpleasant quality which keeps following her through *Natural Born Killers* and beyond? Can the pure, direct loveliness of Mariel Hemingway in *Manhattan* actually belong to the same actress who seems false, flat and not even particularly pretty in just about everything she has done thereafter? By the end of the century this adolescent deterioration process had been so completely hastened that after completely winning us over in 1995 as nice, spoiled Jewish girl Cher Horowitz in *Clueless*—a Beverly Hills update of *Emma* whose adorableness transcends forteenyboppers-only status—by 1997 Alicia Silverstone could be declared completely over: as Batgirl in *Batman* she was trashed for being fat, and in *The New York Times,* Janet Maslin wrote of her performance in *Excess Baggage* (which Ms. Silverstone, somehow, also produced): "The petulant curl in her lips has deepened into a sculptured cleft . . . she is a surreal, zaftig everyteen who seems eerily larger than life." And while sitcoms have saved a few great beauties found to be wanting on the dramatic front—Lucille Ball was actually the first gorgeous woman to be such a goofball on television that after a while no one noticed her looks at all—the subtle, precocious performances as well as a certain rare elegance that Cybill Shepherd, Brooke Shields and Candice Bergen once commanded seemed to promise so much more. That magic, that teenage bloom, it never can be captured again.

Consider the case of Melissa Gilbert, who appears to have had so much plastic surgery that her face barely resembles that of the girl she once was on *Little House on the Prairie*. Without the fleshiness in her nose and with the red rinse that's been cast on her hair, Gilbert—in a similarly unconvincing quest to shed the farm-girl-fresh face of early fame that drove eldest *Waltons* daughter Mary Ellen to do a spread in *Playboy* and an ad for Scientology—has become a spokesmodel for Belle color hair dye. But she is like a child playing with Mommy's makeup whose proud attempt at glamour fools no adult: a finger-painted face, with smeared fuchsia lipstick and smudged blue eye shadow, it is the overdone job of the underage playing grown-up. Gilbert seems desperate to be an adult, and in doing do she has lost not just the quality that made her Laura Ingalls but also whatever it was that made her Melissa—whoever that was—to become a hologram, a TV-movie version of Julia Roberts, a hollow Stepford Wife replacement for herself. Now, somehow Ron Howard still looks like Richie Cunningham—in fact, he still looks like Opie. Somehow the boy from *Happy Days* has not been transformed into an extra on *Melrose Place*. Somehow his face—and his life—have retained their integrity.

But for women to grow up in public, they must create discontinuities with their old selves, they must disappear, change masks, go off to Yale or go under in Dr. Kamer's office, they cannot just make a graceful, fluid transition. Their teenage quality and exuberance is just too much for the world to take, the mischief and frenzy must go into hiding, and allow us our ritual mourning for the lost adorableness: we ooh and aah over cute little Judy Garland before it all went wrong, we coo over the lushness of Liz Taylor on horseback and eight husbands ago, and we sigh over the way Tuesday Weld was such a dream girl, so obviously the perfect girlfriend that even in 1991 Matthew Sweet used an old movie still of her on the cover of his album *Girlfriend*. We grieve for the loss even though we sanction it—it is our choice to take away the girl's glorious freedom before she mistakes the privilege for a right. But we do it so reflexively that we don't even notice, it seems as normal to us as virgin sacrifices once seemed in pagan cultures. And these former girls come back, thinner and paler, like tubercular patients coming down from the magic mountain, or returnees from the "rest cure," a postlobotomy Frances Farmer, reemerging at peace with the world, blanker and blander, rather like a soap opera character who is sent to live with her grandmother in Florida for a few years while still in grade school before a forced return brings her back as a whole new grown-up thing.

It's the magazine makeover, it's the acolyte who runs away to the desert for several years—Moses, David, Buddha—and comes back a holy man, it's the promise of muscles and manliness from Charles

Atlas, it's queen for a day, it's Grimm's fairy tales, it's a metamorphosis myth that ignores the plodding, slow sameness of reality.

Girlchild stars who grow up in public seem as transformed as someone who has gone into the witness protection program.

*   *   *

"I've never hidden the fact that I love young girls," Roman Polanski yelled at the nagging press corps that pursued him all around the 1977 Cannes Film Festival as he ambled about the Croisette with a fifteen-year-old Nastassia Kinski on his arm. "Once and for all, I love very young girls."

Considering the accelerated aging process that wastes away and wears out Hollywood's sweet young things with a fast-forward so fast it's as if they were living in dog years (bitch years?), it almost seems reasonable that Polanski should be a sucker for raw meat, for milk-fed tank-bred veal. In this context, our culture's fascination with the virginal victim—who is, if nothing else, a break from the tired woman—is understandable. In these oversexed times—when Tracy Lords *retired* from her pornography career by the time she was eighteen—it is only the girl who knows nothing about sex, perhaps doesn't even know where babies come from, who can guarantee that a man will feel his dominance, and will experience himself as breaking and entering. After residing in this erotic gray zone of date-rape confusion, with seduction and sexual harassment and who made the first move all constant questions, there is something so nice and safe about surefire violation, about fucking a child, or a comatose hospital patient, or a mentally retarded woman—all of them offer the relief of certainty, since they are not even in a position to express, experience or exercise volition. "You ain't never had no pussy like that," the pimp played by Harvey Keitel in the 1976 movie *Taxi Driver* says of his underage hooker Iris, portrayed by Jodie Foster in her first Oscar-nominated role. "You can do anything you want with her."

But Iris' appeal is that she is quite knowing, a stray cat made smart by living on street scraps—that she is twelve but not really. It is the untouched and unmolested that fuels our latest array of fantasies. The fascination with the murder of JonBenet Ramsey would seem, at first, like a good example of the public's prurient interest in a tender, taboo sex object, except that there is nothing sexy about a child so done up she looks like she belongs in Madame Tussaud's Wax Museum. Our interest in this dead six-year-old is indeed perverse—but perverse in a social, not a sexual, sense. This little girl is just so peculiar: doomed at birth by being christened with a name that's a cross-pollination of Jonathan with the title of a frequently administered IQ test, a name that, whatever its origins, could only belong to a Bourbon Street stripper, a name that is about as French as french fries, French kisses, French vanilla, French roast, French braids and French-cut jeans, a name with hoity-toity aspirations that are meant to obscure the very trashiness they spotlight. This little girl had glamour photos that paid homage to Francesco Scavullo's *Cosmo* covers, and played dress-up in clothes that actually fit her, with no blue eye shadow misplaced on her cheeks and no coral lipstick smeared sloppily on her chin. This little girl wore "outfits," matched purses and shoes, coordinated bonnets and gloves, symbols of leisured gentility last seen at Sweet Briar College in 1957. Anyone concerned that baby beauty pageants sexually exploit girls so young that even Larry Flynt would blush are missing the point: which is, of course, that it is all just so cheesy. It's embarrassing. It's the kind of thing that allows the French to make fun of America even as they watch their Mickey Rourke movies and Jerry Lewis telethons. It's silly and infantilizing. I'm sure the participants in these pretty-baby contests are thoroughly damaged by the experience, but in ways far stranger than anything having to do with sex. The fuss and focus on this tacky subculture provided a momentary freak distraction from a dominant culture in which the lust for sweet young things—a few years older than JonBenet Ramsey, and more likely to be wearing flannel and blue jeans than broad-rimmed hats and twinsets—has become perfectly normal, and there's nothing anyone can do to stop it.

In the little-seen art-house film *The Babysitter,* Alicia Silverstone has no idea what kinds of perverse and extreme fantasies her charges, the father of the kids, and various teenage boys are having about her as she wanders around, blissfully unaware, attending to the children, giving them baths and getting her shirt all wet, basically lying in wait for whatever may happen because her alarm system is not yet in-stalled. Uma Thurman in *Dangerous Liaisons* is similarly there for the taking as John Malkovich does just that. In the movie *Kids*, the HIV-positive philosopher of the delights of defloration—who is supposed to be sixteen but looks no more than eleven, and actually looks a lot like a walking penis—goes on about how he loves to fuck virgins, loves that there's no "loosey-goose pussy."

And let us not forget the way Bill Wyman, the seemingly most unrolling of the Stones, reminded us never to underestimate still water when at age forty-seven he took up with, then eventually married and later divorced, the thirteen-year-old Bardot-in-a-kilt Catholic school girl named Mandy Smith (for good measure, at some point, *her* mother hooked up with *his* son). It reminds us of some of this cen-tury's great romances: Elvis and Priscilla, Jerry Lee Lewis and Myra, Frank and Mia, Woody and Soon-Yi, Seinfeld and Shoshana, Roman Polanski and whoever, Hugh Hefner and whatever. Harold and Maude, sort of. Charlie Chaplin and his succession of teenage brides, definitely. (Chaplin's second wife, whom he wed when she was fifteen and knocked up, was actually named Lilita, a fact not unknown to Nabokov, whose literary legacy was just a vowel away; by the time Chaplin married his last wife, Oona O'Neill, he was fifty-four and the bride was his oldest yet—at seventeen.) I would add to that list Charles and Diana, but he doesn't count because position compelled him to marry a virgin, and because, frankly, he just doesn't count.

And of course, so many movie jokes would never exist without the May-December possibilities. Woody Allen's now much-bitten line in *Manhattan*—"I can't believe I'm dating a girl who does homework"—became much funnier, or much sadder, when its real-life implications were realized. In *When Harry Met Sally . . .* , Billy Crystal mocks his unserious serial monogamy by saying of his new girlfriend, "I men-tioned something about the Kennedy assassination and she said, '*What?* Was Ted Kennedy *shot?*'" And in real life—more like sort-of real life—Amy Fisher offers the tidbit that when she and Joey met for love in the afternoon at a local motel, he would turn the clock radio to the classic rock station and quiz her to make sure she knew it was the Doors who did "Light My Fire" or the Eagles performing "Peaceful Easy Feeling." And Boston cabby Jimmy McBride, the MTV alter ego of actor Donal Logue, made fun of Alanis Morissette's misuse of the title "Ironic" when he inserted this couplet: "It's like meeting the girl of your dreams / And finding out she's five years old."

Meanwhile, the archetypal virgin—meaning Lolita, not Mary—has apparently been thoroughly misunderstood by posterity. In an interview in *Vogue,* Jeremy Irons, who plays Humbert Humbert in Adrian Lyne's almost unreleased film adaptation of *Lolita,* points out that despite the notion of teenage temptress that has been attached to the moniker Lolita, in Vladimir Nabokov's novel she is actually rather vile, obnoxious, not in the least bit seductive. She chews on gum with bovine vigor and blows enormous pink bubbles that pop into sticky puddles across her face. She prefers her sleeve to napkins and tissues. Her nail polish is always chipped. She may be the subject of blue movies, but Nabokov's Lolita is green, still picking at earwax in public, an unwashed phenomenon. "In the popular imagination, Lolita is this stupendous little kitten," Irons says. "And in the film we certainly paint her so. But in the book she's absolutely ghastly—cheap, not pretty, bad teeth, bad skin, smelly—that's the drama, that he's besotted by this *awful* girl." In the same *Vogue* article, mistress of vampires Anne Rice is quoted as noting that Lolita "was a very ordinary girl who didn't herself have profound sexual feelings and never really enjoyed the illicit relationship." It seems that in the void created by Nabokov's beautiful and complicated text (lack of reading—not misreading—is the culprit here), a cultural version of the game Telephone—with Freudian phantasies and wish fulfillments guiding it along—has turned a girl who is the object of perverse desire into the subject of a rapacious sexual appetite. But the literary Lolita's appeal is not in the way one can partake of her supple, youthful flesh in that moment of ripeness and unspoiled beauty that explains why teenage fashion models are lust objects, girls in their luscious prime. To be a man and be hot for Bridget Hall is perfectly normal; to be Humbert Humbert and hung up on twelve-year-old pudge is to be a pervert, a pedophile—to wag one's tongue after youth with vampiric intent, to pursue it only to destroy it, to be the agent of the girl's downfall, turn her into the wretch that any man preying upon such a childish subject must believe all women are. "Humbert Humbert," British novelist

Martin Amis has said, "is without question an honest-to-god, open-and-shut sexual deviant."

And Jeremy Irons is right: the uncouthness of Lolita is precisely the point. She reminds us that men who take up with teenyboppers and believe that they are getting a woman that has not, in the language of used-car salesmen, been "pre-owned" are not much different from Humbert Humbert. For they are actually hooking up with the same pimply baby that Lolita was in print if not in practice, but fooling themselves with the high gloss of femininity in bloom.

They think that statutory rape laws were written for other men. That Amy Fisher isn't really a teenager and Joey Buttafuoco isn't really a pervert.

Meanwhile, a romanticized notion of what is really a violated little girl allows for the counterimage, the celebration of innocence as front, of ignorance as sexuality. It allows for the lovely, unadorned black-and-white photographs of Christy Turlington in ads for Calvin Klein underwear, a woman in her twenties looking slightly fleshy and all pouty, curves suggesting baby fat, not even showing much cleavage in basic briefs and no-push-up bras that create a sexiness that is the opposite of what one would get with anything that might be called "lingerie." (Interestingly, Victoria's Secret, catalogue of décolletage and dishabille, has mimicked Klein's success by putting Claudia Schiffer and Stephanie Seymour in television and print ads selling its "underware" line of practical, ribbed cottons.) It allows for a magazine—known in jargon as a "stroke book"—called *Barely Legal*. It allows for baby-doll dresses and kinderwhore fashions, for chunky high-heeled Mary Janes from Prada and solid-silver pacifier pendants from jewelry designer Helen Bransford.

It allows for the entire career of Liv Tyler, who in *Heavy, Stealing Beauty, that thing you do!* and probably in as many more roles as can possibly tolerate this act, plays the virginal sweetheart, the very very very nice girl with coltish gracelessness and unscathed beauty, whose mere presence irradiates everyone around her, whose luminescence wakes up the long-dead urges and makes people want, in each of those respective films, to go to cooking school, to face death with dignity or to take up improvisational jazz drumming. It allows for Carroll Baker in Elia Kazan's film of Tennessee Williams's *Baby Doll,* the child bride who lounged in a crib, sucked on her thumb and whom a much older Karl Malden spends much of the movie just trying to keep under *his* thumb. It allows for the ongoing fascination with Edie Sedgwick, the most celebrated of the Warhol superstars, subject of an oral history called *Edie* that portrays her as the Forrest Gump of the demimonde, a dead girl whose memory outlives her life as the Pop Art pop tart, the girl on fire with silver streaks in her hair, an ectomorphic little frame, bone-white skin stretched on her skeleton like a lampshade. But Edie's longevity in the afterlife, which would seem to be because of her youthquaker cool, is actually a product of the belief that all that was just a facade: we're in fact infatuated with the photographs that show her when she wasn't in costume, pictures that reveal such innocence, snapshots of little girl blue with long black hair fresh from a spot of shock at Silver Hill, pictures that focus on her big huge eyes that shine like flying saucers, liquid sky, pure as a really pure batch of Burmese heroin, pure as Ivory soap. This photomontage of a reconstituted Lolita—frail, fragile, dead by her own hand, a girl whose good looks make you imagine potential that was never there, a girl who makes you sigh and say, So beautiful, so sad—allows us to be in love with the Edie we believe was worth saving.

And then finally our sordid romance with the malleable, labile Lolita allows a situation in which, far from not having a clue about her power to drive men mad, this former naïf becomes a knowing menace, a shadowy figure of danger and deceit. It allows for a situation where Pulitzer Prize-winning playwright Edward Albee—who is not, I don't think, a stupid man—amid much frustration while trying to stage *Lolita* for Broadway in 1981 (starring Blanche Baker, daughter of Carroll), actually responded to protests from Women Against Pornography and social worker types by saying, "It is Lolita who seduces Humbert. It is the exploitation of the adult by the child." It allows for a movie like *Poison Ivy,* which brought Drew Barrymore back from the dead, allowing her to play an irresistibly naughty teenage tramp who befriends a lonely, unlovely Sara Gilbert, and manages to move into her house, share her bed (director Katt Shea never makes it really clear what we are to make of that), then seduce her handsome father (Tom Skerritt, a Guess jeans ad veteran at a time when the same modeling assignment was still in Drew's future), "inadvertently" kill her bedridden emphysematic mother (Cheryl Ladd, also brought back from the dead), and basically get the run of the place. It allows for the dangerous curves of *The Crush,* which has a fourteen-year-old Alicia Silverstone report to her twenty-eight-year-old object of pursuit, "Guess what? I got my period!" It allows for girls on an after-school murder spree in the movie *Fun,* and for the girls on a lesbian murder spree in *Heavenly Creatures.*

It allows for avant-garde filmmaker Jennifer Montgomery to re-create her prep school affair with photography instructor Jock Sturges in the grainy, black-and-white starkness of *Art for Teachers of Children*—and it allows for Sturges himself, all his pretty pictures of all the pretty blonde girls with no clothes on. It allows for the Calvin Klein jeans ads of 1995—part of the designer's time-honored tradition of controversial campaigns—that were taken off the air and pulled from billboards because the awkward unkempt models, posed in faux pine-paneled rec rooms reminiscent of the *Brady Bunch* basement, gave some people the impression they were auditioning for kiddy-porn parts. It allows for the disturbing discovery of Lewis Carroll's infatuated photographs of the real-life Alice. It allows for the lingering strangeness of the nude pictures of model-turned-photographer Lee Miller, taken by her father in the 1920s when she was just a teenager. It allows for a situation in which everyone, ad hominem, permanently primed for scandal, gets all nuts about Sally Mann's photoessays of her own children—often unclothed—even though the actual images tend to be rather innocuous, the idea more racy than the implications, a lot of bark for very little bite. And it allows for a situation in which, in a 1977 *New York* magazine profile of Brooke Shields, her mother Teri can be caught looking at stills from the film *Pretty Baby* and saying, "Look at you with your little titties sticking out. You would know she hit puberty the day filming began. When Louis Malle signed her up, she was as flat as a board, but when we got to New Orleans she had her first period and he could see these two little knobs popping up." On the magazine's cover, the mother and daughter are pictured beside a tag line that reads, "Brooke is twelve. She poses nude. Teri is her mother. She thinks it's swell."

But in truth, to differentiate between these types of intriguing teenage personalities, to view one as deliberately seductive, another as helpless and blameless like Thomas Hardy's Tess Durbeyfield or Samuel Richardson's Clarissa, is to miss the point. Because *any* of these behaviors can be thought to be a come-on—some of them may even be—if the excitement of youth itself is turn-on enough. In the end, Humbert Humbert as connoisseur of the nymphet implies a level of refinement that will not be found in the average john purchasing the services of an underage call girl. In fact, unless he is a serial killer whose prey are always prostitutes and who has a very specific physical and psychological specimen in mind, the client in this exchange is probably motivated by a simple salacious admiration for a young, supple body; the subtleties of personality pale against the pursuit of crude, cheap sex. And a teenage girl thrown into a Lolita situation is left unsure of what she did to get there. Endowed with some unearned power to drive men wild, she will wonder what she must to do to stay in this vaunted position—how long she can keep this up, how long she will be able to rely on this very unreliable asset. There's the looming specter of the coach that turns into a pumpkin come midnight. And after a while the girls who are in crisis, who have no career goals or education to fall back on and no future that they can foresee, find themselves willing to give up all of themselves, body parts gone, everything else gone, the girl is an amputee, a human manqué: the weapon of sexuality boomerangs, backfires. As Amy Fisher (with the help of Sheila Weller) put it in her autobiography *Amy Fisher: My Story*: "People call you 'seductive,' as if you have power. But *you* feel you have *no* power. No power at all. You're just going blindly along on tools you picked up. But, if you'd ever been given a choice, those might not have been the tools you'd have chosen."

*   *   *

In recent years, theorists of female development seem to have declared détente in the fight with Freud over penis envy, and redirected those efforts toward extending his models—the Oedipal struggle, phallocentric but still useful—to encompass the very different maturing phases in girls' lives. Their main conclusion is that (surprise!) adolescence is a period when girls go underground, when their personalities are muted, when they lose sense of what they want and who they are, when they begin to scurry desperately to maintain relationships, often at the expense of their own integrity, of being a self. The glow and edge of youth fades away, a process depicted in the disintegration of many of the aforementioned actresses' performances. They lose their natural charm because they lose their fighting spirit: the glory of their early work is in seeing that last gasp, a losing army that won't surrender, the holdouts on top of Masada, or Samson pushing the pillars in a final frenzy of strength before he dies. The beauty of adolescent girls is that all that is beautiful about them will soon be snatched away: they are creatures about to disappear—fireflies, thorn birds, june bugs.

This discontinuity is the subject explored by Carol Gilligan and Lyn Mikel Brown, both research psychologists and professors of human development, in their 1992 book *Meeting at the Crossroads: Women's Psychology and Girls' Development*. The authors and several researchers spent time interviewing and just hanging out with girls between the ages of seven and eighteen, hoping to track the phenomenon of diminished resilience, lost vitality and a faded fighting spirit that they call "losing voice." Perhaps Gilligan and Brown's most astute revelation—although, if you think about it, this is actually rather obvious—is that boys have their cursed bad phase in preschool, but girls experience it several years later. "The pressure on boys to dissociate themselves from women early in childhood is analogous to the pressure girls feel to take themselves out of relationship with themselves and with women as they reach adolescence," they write. "On a theoretical level, the evidence we gathered led us to consider early adolescence as a comparable time in women's development to early childhood in men's: a time when a relational impasse forced what psychoanalysts have called 'a compromise formation'—some compromise between voice and relationships . . . [This adjustment] leaves a psychological wound or scar, a break manifest in the heightened susceptibility to psychological illness that boys suffer in early childhood and that girls suffer in adolescence." In other words, boys have to make a break with Mom and assert their masculinity at a very young age, which is why come kindergarten there are suddenly all those hyperactive boys with their Ritalin prescriptions while their parents are trying to find a cure for ADD. But girls don't assume their sullen, troubled mien until sometime in junior high school when the bloom and blood of burgeoning sexuality forces them to break with Mom, puts their bodies on view in the free-market bazaar that is the world, and they experience firsthand nature's processes as she turns them into baby makers, bodies to bear more bodies.

The conclusion Gilligan and Brown come to is that girls react to the changes by entering a trancelike dissociative state they call "going underground":

> [S]eparating themselves or their psyches from their bodies so as not to know what they were feeling, dissociating their voice from their feelings and thoughts so that others would not know what they were experiencing, taking themselves out of relationship [with themselves] so that they could better approximate what others want and desire, or look more like some ideal image of what a woman or what a person should be. Open conflict and free speaking that were part of girls' daily living thus gave way to more covert forms of responding to hurt feelings or disagreements within relationships, so that some girls came to ignore or not know signs of emotional or physical abuse. And relationships correspondingly suffered.

Everything that is so hard about being a woman, the inherently torn and conflicted nature of choices between career and family, between romance and respectability, between recklessness and restraint, between virgin and whore, between pushing and pulling—problems which were supposed to be resolved by now, but probably won't ever be put to rest—are all rooted in what happens in our teenage years. After all, what Gilligan and Brown are really describing is the process of self-destruction—the wearing down and winnowing away of the integrity of the self—that is better known as becoming a woman. Books like *The Rules,* which essentially instruct women to control their impulses in an attempt to act like they have self-esteem—even though anyone who actually *had* self-esteem would just do whatever the hell she wants—only reaffirm the lessons girls learn early on about self-silence. "Girls, we thought, were undergoing a kind of psychological foot-binding, so that they were kept from feeling or using their relational strengths," write Gilligan and Brown. "Instead, these strengths, which explain girls' remarkable psychological resilience throughout the childhood years, were turning into a political liability. People, as many girls were told, did not want to hear what girls know."

Using the work of Gilligan and Brown it is easy to understand Amy Fisher as well as the many other good girls gone bad—the recent roster of drunk and disorderly athletes like Oksana Baiul, Tonya Harding and Jennifer Capriati, along with the more anonymous middle-class prostitutes and shoplifters and scofflaws—and to see them as the usual array of victims who become defendants. In objective terms, of course, they are not victims at all, but psychologically they must have experienced themselves as suffocated, strangled, stymied and just desperate for air, intoxicated from not breathing, unable to judge, to see, to feel, to imagine what was right. These are the young women who felt the world closing in on them and fought back—and they did it in terrifically unfortunate ways. (The nice thing about these particular examples is that no one can say to them, Why don't you take up a sport?)

Amy's weapon of choice seems to have been sex. Of course, it's not a choice so much as a fallback position: just as some girls figure out that their ticket will be a talent for biochemistry or composing villanelles while others sew beautiful curtains and bake delicious devil's food cake, sex is the thing that any woman who lies down and spreads her legs can do. That some girls try to elevate it to an art form—fooled, I think, by the way we celebrate sex objects like Cindy Crawford and Pamela Anderson, and not quite realizing that the neighborhood tramp is still just a slut—doesn't account for the way that the role attaches itself to them. Girls who try to turn sex into a weapon (I'm tempted to say that this would be like Iraq deciding to welcome SCUD missiles) are only making a virtue of necessity. Hot and bothered is not a cultivated state—it's more like climbing ivy or a weed run rampant or dandelions everywhere, more like something meant to be evoked by the title *The Girl Can't Help It*. Later on, a woman can learn the rules of the game, but a twelve-year-old engaged in wildly seductive behavior is just needy and complaisant.

And still, it happens: Some girls are more attuned to how the world is responding to them—usually in the absence of fathers or big brothers—and have been manipulating and putting the make on any potential protectors almost forever; while others—blessed with uncommon comeliness and a superannuated sense of their own sex appeal—cannot help noticing that men notice, that catcalls and cars follow them wherever they walk, that men mistake them for nineteen or twenty even though they are just thirteen, that friends' older brothers offer to drive them home, offer to pick them up, offer to do anything at all. They discover pussy power. Knowing she can get her way with her wiles—that, for instance, the mechanic down the block will repair the dents in her new convertible for free and Dad will never have to know that half the time she drives like she's asleep at the wheel—she will use flirtatiousness, her feigned naïve helplessness and whatever other effects she has learned from the movies, to get what she wants. Nothing wrong with this. Nothing at all. If you can get through life batting your lashes, it beats the hell out of carrying your own bags.

But then there is the part of this Faustian bargain that is not so savory, and it seems to me it is Amy's story. You see, Amy is not, I don't think, one of those girls who would have inevitably become a sex object, a wild thing. She was apparently shy—all the news accounts seem to agree on these few facts—and she was not one to play with alcohol or drugs. But more to the point—and I feel like somebody needs to say this—she is no great beauty. In the reports that followed Amy's arrest, the media played up her purported pulchritude, perhaps in an unconscious effort to burden her with blame: as Columbia journalism professor Helen Benedict points out in her book *Virgin or Vamp,* "when a sex crime victim is considered attractive, she receives *less* sympathy." But Amy is not like Brooke Shields or Drew Barrymore, two such comely, contained children that people would project adult notions of sexuality onto them no matter what they did. Amy looks pretty enough in pictures, but more than anything she is just cute—cute and boppy, a girl who in an alternate scenario would have made the cheerleading squad, but would never have been voted homecoming queen.

But the sexual strategy imposed itself on Amy because of something that happened when she was thirteen years old, which, by Brown and Gilligan's reckoning is the most vulnerable point in a girl's life, the moment when she first begins to lose track of herself and instead starts to fall into society's sleepwalk, to consent to the brainwash of whatever is around. At this time, Amy and her family moved from homey Wantagh to the more upscale Merrick, and she was quite apprehensive about the change. One day while she was home alone, sleeping in on a Saturday morning in the new house, several men were doing renovations downstairs, laying down the kitchen floor, mixing cement. One of them raped Amy. She says that she never told her parents because she was afraid she would be punished. According to one of her friends, who sold this anecdote during the media feeding frenzy that descended all over Merrick after the shooting, Amy later told her, "I fucked the tile man." Amy claims that she never said any such thing, that she always described this event as a rape. But I am inclined to believe the friend. Because that is something a child would do: take a traumatic experience, one where she lost control, where she was frightened—in fact, I would guess, very frightened—and claim that it was a choice, it was seduction, it was humping the help. (For whatever reason, many gay men I know were raped by uncles or family friends as children, and now say that they don't remember the experience as a violation, that they only recall the various ways that it felt nice—and point to their current sexual preference as proof, never considering the possibility that their psyches may be accommodating an uncomfortable trauma by turning it into a triumph.) Who has not practiced this form of alchemy, converting painful experiences into interesting stories, entertaining anecdotes, cocktail party banter? Sooner or later it all comes out in the wash, or it all shows up on *Jerry Springer*, everything accumulates in packaged, processed words to become a pat, pathetic imitation of life. We all know that memory is basically a construct, that we revise and rewrite history all the time, and most of the time we don't even notice we are doing it. It must have been a reasonable coping mechanism for Amy, at age thirteen, to take on sex, make it her weapon, decide to use her body to take men before they took her.

The trouble is, sex is not a weapon. It's a reproductive act that God in his infinite generosity has made quite pleasurable. So much more has been attached to it, both by puritanical zealots and overzealous pornographers, not to mention by Jewish mothers, Catholic fathers, diseases we didn't ask for, dangers we want to defy, and of course, finally, by our own unavoidable knowledge that it is the life force, that our sexuality is so essentially bound up with what we are, what we are made of, it is our mettle, it is the finest and most delicate and most damaged thing about us.

And still, sex itself, in a workaday sort of way, is just sex. And if you try to use it as a weapon, the only person you will wound is yourself.

You don't have to be Amy Fisher to find this out the hard way. Adolescence for girls in almost any circumstance is a nightmare unmitigated. As William Inge tried to show with the Kim Novak role in *Picnic,* it is a horror even for the homecoming queen—or Miss Neewollah (Halloween backwards), the title of honor with which Novak is crowned at a Labor Day picnic in a small town in Kansas, all the while she tries to explain her desire to run away with a dissipated drifter played by William Holden, because she is just so sick of always being just pretty. And, of course, another homecoming queen from Orange County named Nicole Brown ran off with O. J. Simpson when she was just seventeen, seemingly hoping to escape from herself.

Of course, teenage years are a tough time for guys too, but it is not because they are pushed and pulled every which way: it is in fact because the trajectory for boys is so much more direct. You want to be a man, you want to be stronger, you want to be richer, you want to lay as many babes as possible. The propulsion for the male of the species is utterly forward—more women, more muscles, more money, more power, more scores. There is pressure involved in all this demand for acquisition and accumulation, but at least the rules are straightforward and obvious—if you're going farther, faster, harder and higher, then unless you wind up in a car wreck, you are doing the right thing. Which is why when an adult woman seduces an underage boy—as was the case in the recent episode that found Mary Kay LeTourneau, a married second-grade teacher in a Seattle suburb, already the mother of four, giving birth to a child by a thirteen-year-old former student—it is not the same, not even comparable, to any instance of a grown man messing with a teenage girl. Those who thought this teacher-molestress was let off easy with a minimal sentence and some counseling—those who believed that this Sophocles-worthy sexual tragedy (travesty?) should be treated like any Humbert-Lolita statutory rape case—failed to recognize that girls and boys develop differently, and it's moronic to pretend otherwise. (For what it's worth, we barely ever prosecute *any* episodes of "consensual" rape regardless of gender permutations—witness Michael Kennedy's clean getaway from his teenage babysitter, which allowed him to walk free and finally ski to his death.) But more to the point, this makes the idiotic presumption that boys and girls are the same, that sex means the same things to both, that they are socialized with the same expectations. Regardless of what the law says, most thirteen-year-old boys would consider any female willing to have sex with them a gift from above; that attitude may not be good or healthy, but there it is. The male body must consent to sex in a way his partner's does not quite have to; the simple fact that the woman ended up pregnant means that he achieved the only tangible measure of sexual enjoyment that we know of at least once. Yes, there is the new expectation of sensitivity and caring, but that's just a footnote, a brief break in the forward march—and it does nothing to change the notion that there is no such thing as a loose man, but the world is full of loose women. Consider the foolhardy futility of attempting to attach the moniker "slut" to a man when what we really mean is "stud."

Informed by this realpolitik, a girl's development into the feminine personality is complicated, her desire is bound up in questions of morality and propriety, with physical arousal not much more than a sideshow to the central emotional issues about what sex really *means* (and not, as would be the case with boys, how it really *feels*). The rules, despite the valiant efforts of *Ms.* and *Cosmopolitan* combined, never really change: boys like girls who are sexy, but not slutty—so a little restraint is called for at the same time as one puts out a bit. While the boys can focus solely on their pleasure, getting to first base, then to second, then to third, and maybe even a home run—girls must still temper their desires. If they get lost in abandon, then they will not remember to keep doing the twisted tango, the one step up and two steps back that is a requirement of any girl who wants to have her fun but still maintain her femininity by playing keeper of the gate. In her short story "Lust," a catalogue of the terrible sadness of teenage sexuality, Susan Minot illustrates the inequity: "The more girls a boy has, the better. He has a bright look, having reaped fruits, blooming. He stalks around, sure-shouldered, and you have the feeling he's got more in him, a fatter heart, more stories to tell. For a girl, with each boy it's as though a petal gets plucked each time."

This oddly contradictory approach to the socialization of girls is the reason that date rape has become such a vexed issue. Sometimes I think that one of the problems that both sides—or perhaps I should say all sides—to this issue forget is that many women—and to a greater extent, college girls—don't know how to say no because they don't know how to say yes. They cannot for the life of them register what their desire level is against what they think they should or shouldn't do. How many girls are taught that if it feels nice, don't think twice? How many are told by anyone other than Nike to just do it? How many are lovingly instructed, as Anne Sexton wrote in a poem addressed to her preteen daughter, that "there is nothing in your body that lies"? How many believe in their bodies? Men want or don't want. Women think they maybe want to, but only if he feels the way she hopes he feels, and blah blah blah. Even though I am approaching thirty—and I'm afraid that I am quite typical in this sense—I still never know what I want or why I am doing whatever it is that I'm doing with men. I still, with anachronistic dismay, don't have sex early in a relationship even though that's when I really feel like it because of all the usual reasons that you're not supposed to; but later on, I'll find myself having sex whether I want to or not because it just seems like the thing to do, or something like that. I wish I could get a grip on something as simple as desire, but it is so shrouded in other motives, in what I'm trying to prove, in whether or not I'm trying to accelerate emotional intimacy through sexual contact, in messages playing on an open-loop tape—by now in the extended dance remix version—that won't stop reverberating through the back of my brain. Sometimes I do things that I don't want to because I want to be bold—I want to see what it's like to fuck someone on a barstool or on a therapist's couch, or on my desk in my office at *The New Yorker*—and sometimes I say no when I want to because I don't want to be easy.

I realize my assessment of women's sexual situation as we approach the millennium might seem dated or old-fashioned—just as I also realize that there are women with such equanimity, women who were raised by unneurotic mothers and adoring, dependable fathers, women who know their own self-worth, who know what sex is worth, and can take it all at face value. And it is my hope that the next generation of girls is reared with the freedom to register desire and pursue pleasure and not be afraid to want, to need, to demand, to delight. But in the meantime, rare women like Camille Paglia and Katie Roiphe, blessed with such a sense of certainty in the sexual arena, need to be made more sensitive to the confusion girls feel about their right to erotic abandon and the concomitant right to forgo it. They need to understand that when girls misuse or abuse the term "date rape" it is only because the taxonomy of women's sexual experience has not yet classified all the different perfectly legal and easily avoidable ways that these women-in-training feel themselves being violated—they have no language to express how they had no idea what they wanted until they got what they didn't want. And, I might add, all these confused girls would do themselves a favor by avoiding doing things like taking all their clothes off and then realizing they just want to flee (which I have done many times, so I know the impulse well) until they get clear about what they want and expect from sex. Because the current morass—well, one Antioch College is enough.

In the case of Amy Fisher, you have a girl who figured out that men like sex, and they like it with her, but did not absorb the lesson about displaying her sense of self by putting the brakes on things once in a while. Her pursuit of pleasure was not pure—she always wanted something else, like attention or love. She didn't seem to understand that the men she slept with were in fact in it for the enjoyment and that's all. They had no ulterior motives, they were not looking for Daddy or searching for salvation. During a postpartum and pre-*Evita* interview on *Oprah,* Madonna said that she planned to teach her daughter Lourdes to have self-respect. An audience member then asked what she would teach the little girl about men. Madonna snapped back: "If I teach her to have self-respect, then I won't need to teach her about men." She got that right. Amy Fisher was bereft of any dignity, and because she was completely unschooled in the seesaw of sexual gamesmanship a girl must play—thinking she could just thrust forward like the men—she lost out big time.

It's not that a woman cannot be a sexual adventuress, cannot have escapades and dalliances: of course she can. But if you live by the sword, you must die by the sword, which is to say you cannot expect anything from sex but sex. Even the vamps of film noir, the women who sleep with men to get them to kill their husbands or to help them in some such scheme or to serve home and country by extracting state secrets—even these women wanted something for the carnal acts they committed. But did you ever hear of a man sleeping with a woman to get something out of her? It just seems the way of things that women bargain with their bodies and men don't. The lessons in how all this works are rarely imparted to teenage girls beyond the occasional adage about not buying the cow when you can get the milk for free. But when you're seventeen, you don't want to get married anyway. Teenage years for girls tend to be marked by much regrettable sexual activity, and it often mars their dealings with men in adulthood. The whole situation seems baffling: boys want to have sex with them, will do anything, say anything, to get inside their pants, and then they don't want them anymore. It makes no sense: give them what they want and you get punished.

Susan Minot captures this confusion very eloquently in "Lust": "Then comes after. After when they don't look at you. They scratch their balls, stare at the ceiling. Or if they do turn, their gaze is altogether changed. They are surprised. They turn casually to look at you, distracted, and get a mild distracted surprise. You're gone. Their blank look tells you that the girl they were fucking is not there anymore. You seem to have disappeared." In the August 1996 issue of *Harper's,* this same sentiment was echoed by Kathy Dobie in "The Only Girl in the Car," a beautifully rendered memoir of the horror of being a promiscuous girl in seventies suburbia, a chronicle of the way she was punished, ostracized—and ultimately gang-raped—for daring to be so bold as to want the same thing all the boys wanted: to get laid whenever she felt like it. "Almost all of my early sexual experiences were with boys who wanted me and hated me for it, boys who thought their desires were dirty and were quick to put that dirtiness on me," Dobie writes. "That peculiar mix of lust and loathing, the light in their eyes, the brusqueness of their hands, the begging and then sneering, the whimpering and then boasting—that was sex as I knew it."

And while singer-songwriter Liz Phair is thought of as one of those dirty girls with a rough mouth, one who can be plain and unpretty about sex, people should not fail to notice the exhaustion in her songs, the sounds of disappointment that link her directly to the girl fading away in Minot's story, or to the girl standing by impassive and sullied in Dobie's recollection. Phair's detachment, which is thrilling enough to be mistaken for heat, is absolutely about all things tepid and empty. Sung against the monotony of the piano-practice tune "Chopsticks," Phair's lyrics are deflated, resigned: "He said he liked to do it backwards / I said that's just fine with me / That way we can fuck and watch TV." And on "Fuck and Run," Phair struck a particular note with many women for singing about the frustrations of waking up in bed with someone you barely know, knowing full well that you aren't going to get to know him any better. "I can feel it in my bones / I'm going to spend another year alone," she says in the refrain, and on the final repetition she changes it to the slightly more ominous "I can feel it in my bones / I'm gonna spend my whole life alone / It's fuck and run / Fuck and run / Ever since I was seventeen / Ever since I was twelve." You see, the cross-purposes of sexuality begin at seventeen, at twelve.

*   *   *

Whatever unique troubles adolescence poses, we all know that obsessive love and its murderous tendencies exist just as strongly in human adults as in any teenager, which is why Carolyn Warmus and Betty Broderick and Jean Harris did the deeds that forced them to do hard time. Very often, even with adults, the object of this crazed adoration is of so little consequence—so mild or so icky or so not worth it—that the woman, in extremes and in fragments, starts to look like loose particles in a centrifuge spinning wildly around a dead, still, unmoved center. Obsession is basically an emotional fallacy, a mistaken belief one is thinking about someone else when she is really thinking about herself. That's why obsessive love is often greeted by such intolerance, such lack of sympathy: it is the most selfish emotion of all, disguised as self-negation. It is perverse.

And messy: the desperate, demeaning letters full of begs and pleas, the repeated telephone hang-ups and the evidence that you are the perpetrator via caller ID or *69, the strange looks from security guards as you loiter in the lobby of the love object's office building. All this acting out is just so humiliating, the kind of yucky embarrassment that seems so female, so pathetic—like shoplifting or binge eating or forced vomiting—that the world can't even find a way to make it seem "cool," because the symptoms are so terribly raw, such a florid, uncomfortable eruption of the loneliness and desperation that scare the hell out of us. This is awful stuff, the kind of brute emotional torture that no one is fit to handle, least of all teenagers. Romantic disaster is their natural habitat only because they still haven't learned.

But adults are supposed to know better, they are assumed to be able to control their impulses—that is, I suppose, what makes them fit to be called *adults*. And if an adult woman—i.e., Jean Harris—becomes sufficiently insane over a diet doctor in Scarsdale that she goes to his house with a loaded gun and succumbs to the inevitable, it does at the very least seem like she must answer for the consequences. But to be a seventeen-year-old and adequately infatuated with an older man to have committed an act of violence on his behalf—this by a girl with no police record—seems a crime that *he* must answer for. Whatever troubles Amy had before Joey—and they were considerable: besides the rape at age thirteen, Amy was also traumatized by a schoolyard fistfight she got into with one of the tenth grade's tough mamas that left her with a broken nose and a dislocated jaw that required surgical reconstruction, and resulted in a $1.2 million lawsuit against the school district—none of them imply her complicity in her own undoing. Look, I am as sickened and annoyed as the next person when someone in trouble starts attributing all their bad behavior to falling off the teeter-totter at three or to a recovered memory of sexual abuse at four, but somehow I don't cringe at the thought of seeing Amy Fisher as a girl "at risk." Once she is twenty-five years old, I'll feel that the statute of limitations on pointing a finger at her pubescent perils has expired, but Amy was *still* a teenager, still very much in the thick of some very difficult years, when she met Joey. Like the newly aligned bone structure of her face, Amy was just barely holding it together, as vulnerable as Austro-Hungary on the eve of World War I, a weak and unassertive territory with boundaries and ideologies up for grabs. If any of her activities were immoral, none were illegal. But somehow, sometime after she got involved with Joey, Amy became a call girl, apparently at his behest, at least in part to fulfill some Travis Bickle fantasy he had about turning Amy into a hooker so that he could then rescue her from the life.

Because Joey denies anything more than just barely knowing Amy, there is only circumstantial evidence to corroborate her claim that he hooked her into hooking. In fact there isn't any way to prove much of Amy's story, but somehow we seem to believe the crux of it, if not every detail: the *New York Post,* which in the spirit of tabloid journalism often trashed Amy, asked readers who was to blame for Mary Jo's shooting, and found Joey the winner (in the sense that there was a winner in Shirley Jackson's short story "The Lottery") with 1,416 votes, while Amy received just 324; had this poll been done later, when Joey was convicted of statutory rape after Amy's convincing testimony, the margins might have been wider.

A large part of the reason we believe Amy's story—besides the fact that the big lug she calls her lover is nothing to boast about—is that we see the wreckage, we see Joey's fingerprints all over this mess. If you went into London after the Blitz and saw burnt-out buildings, crumbling edifices, detonated shells, dead bodies and other assorted memorabilia of an air attack, you would not assume that this was just some perverse British gesture at postmodernism, an attempt to give the city that certain bombed-out look at the behest of some new architectural movement that is managing somehow to thrive in the midst of this huge war; you wouldn't assume anything other than that London had been bombed. Similarly, we don't need to work too hard to trace a trail between a girl who was troubled but not criminal to a sudden onset of antisocial symptoms—as well as a case of herpes—that arrived in her life at the same time as Joey did.

In this country we believe that children need special protection before the law, and when kids misbehave, even if there is no older person aiding and abetting, the law understands that they are not supposed to be as morally developed as adults—which is why our system of justice invented juvenile court. And while teenage boys are given to insane infatuations—see Scott Spencer's *Endless Love* for details—in most cases, they don't have an older woman goading them on the way Amy Fisher had Joey Buttafuoco. There's no need to explain this—teenagers in general are gross and obnoxious, rarely managing to fare the ch-ch-ch-changes without aggravated acne or bad posture or strange ideas of what to do with their hair—but more often than not the ones who manage to be cute are girls. Because of advances in health care and nutrition, the average girl now experiences menses at twelve, three years sooner than she could have expected her first period half a century ago. Benzoyl peroxide and Retin-A have further contributed to making adolescence less vile. The faddish, girlish clothes that they still tend to wear—well, if you like 'em young, you like 'em like that. But yummy though they may be, these girls are poison, mostly to themselves. They act like little grown-ups and that makes it easy to forget that they don't know shit. As writer Tad Friend puts it: "The reason sex with minors is immoral is that while they may look and move like nascent Sharon Stones, they don't have any idea what it all means." Or worse, they know exactly what it means, they have an instinct for seductive poses and caricaturish flirtation—or they learn them from old Madonna videos and memorized *Melrose Place* episodes—but they don't understand where their chain of command begins and ends. If the implications of sexiness are clear, the implications of sex itself may not be.

And yet, the multiple portrayals of Amy as a public menace—depictions created both on national television and in the local courtroom—indicate that we have stopped regarding youth as innocent. It is old news that the viciousness of many recent juvenile crimes has resulted in an increased number of minors who are tried as adults. But in Amy's case, because of the seeming sexual bravado of a teenage call girl with a married lover—which was interpreted by the district attorney's office, as well as by the judge who set Amy's $2 million bail, as a sign of strength, not weakness—Amy was treated as an adult by the legal system not because of the wretchedness of her crime but because of the perceived uncontainable nature of her promiscuity. Amy Fisher might as well have been radioactive, the heat of this hot little number made these men—lawyers, judges, police, private investigators, so many men—so damn nervous. In fact, the judge actually called her a "wild animal" and "a stick of dynamite with a lit fuse." It was as if they all feared that Amy, if not carefully regulated, might disintegrate into sawdust, and her dirty particles might infiltrate every nook and cranny with sex and fever and frenzy and lust.

"One might describe this defendant as a seventeen-year-old girl who lives at home with her parents and goes to high school. That would be about as accurate, Your Honor, as describing John Gotti as a businessman from New York City," deputy district attorney Fred Klein said at the arraignment, in an attempt to convince the judge to deny bail. "This defendant is totally uncontrollable, manipulative, violent and extremely dangerous." In an odd instance of the legal system defending the honor of the *il*legal system—as always, politics makes strange bedfellows—Klein pointed out that Amy had "cheated" her escort service out of profits by turning some of their referrals into private customers. Bail was set, but at a prohibitively high sum.

At a later appeal by Fisher's attorney for bail reduction, Klein argued that Amy was a bad risk outside of jail because she could so easily "slide into that sleazy world [of prostitution], and she'll be able to support herself very well, and no one would ever find her." Klein said this as if he'd failed to notice that television cameras had become permanent fixtures outside the courthouse, outside the county jail and outside the Fisher home—Amy could not possibly hide in plain sight. But more disturbingly, Klein treated and talked of Amy as if she were a force of nature, as if her ability to turn tricks was a source of power—and not a simple function of her ability to lie supine, spread-eagle. As Sheila Weller, co-author of *My Story,* points out in a section of her third-person analysis: "The notion that teenage prostitution can as easily bespeak a girl's enormous emotional problems and self-brutalization as the wiliness and resourcefulness Klein alluded to, was unaddressed." (In fact, I think Weller fails to make herself clear here: I mean, when on earth has prostitution *ever* bespoken *anyone*'s "wiliness and resourcefulness"? When has it ever been anything other than a last resort or a form of mental illness? And I defy anyone to find me one prostitute without "enormous emotional problems"—because I think it's hard enough to find one *person* without enormous emotional problems.) Amy's bail held steady at $2 million, and could only be paid with the combined resources of a production company purchasing the rights to Ms. Fisher's story and a kindhearted bail bondsman in New Jersey. In the eyes of the law, Amy Fisher was the Pandora's Box of Nassau County, the Typhoid Mary, the Red Scare, the Black Death, the untamable wild bikini, the female body as agent of demise, the *vagina dentata* contained in a five-foot frame. And in my eyes,

Fred Klein had well earned the Senator Joe McCarthy Award for preposterous hysteria at no cause.

Meanwhile, as Amy rotted in jail, every man she'd ever met seemed to be selling her out. Peter DeRosa, a john she'd serviced in his home in Levittown—the place synonymous with subdivision hell—had videotaped their encounters with a hidden camera, a move that proved to be fortuitous when the prostitute turned out to be front-page news. He sold the tape to *A Current Affair* for $8,000, turning a profit, which meant that rather than paying for sex, DeRosa ended up getting paid for it (a privilege that, from the looks of him, I don't think he will be enjoying ever again). Carnal acts aside, this videotape contained a moment of Amy saying, "I'm wild. I don't care. I like sex." This syllogism was frequently sound-bitten into some sort of slut manifesto. After that, other men came forward, selling stories of sexual favors in return for procuring a murder weapon. With cameras staking out Long Island to a parodic effect that can only be likened to the Albert Brooks movie *Real Life*, men whom Amy barely knew were claiming that she slept with them, while the men she had actually slept with were denying it.

Following Joey's lead, Paul Makely, Amy's boyfriend and the proprietor of the Future Physique gym (more French where it doesn't belong), had always gainsaid any suggestions that he'd had an affair with Amy. Paul had a child with his common-law wife and a domestic life he was determined to maintain. But unlike Joey (who'd sicced Amy onto him in the first place), Paul seemed more available to Amy—he was even going to be her date for the senior prom—and she thought of him as a salubrious influence, even called him "my lawyer-approved boyfriend." Then one day while Amy was out on bail, Paul allowed *Hard Copy* to plant cameras in his gym and intrude on a rendezvous that the couple had planned after her plea-bargain hearing. An undisclosed sum, estimated to be as high as $50,000, was to be tendered to Paul for his trouble and treachery. The result was footage of Amy flippantly (and after the broadcast, famously) asking Paul to marry her so that they could have conjugal visits while she was in prison, and saying things like "If I had to go through all this pain and suffering, I am getting a Ferrari." Paul, of course, was supposed to be the good guy, the antidote, the anti-Joey. (It seems that whenever people deal with the world in binary oppositions, choosing one thing only because it negates another, they are inevitably startled by the discovery that the quest for something completely different has only given them more of the same. That's why Oedipus killed his father and slept with his mother while doing everything to avoid that fate.) On the night the *Hard Copy* segment aired—after falling on the floor, crying and screaming, "Not Paul! Not Paul!"—Amy took an overdose of Xanax and lorazepam, and was committed to Huntington Hospital for a month of psychiatric treatment.

It is strange to me that this *Hard Copy* episode served only to demonize Amy further. The obvious pain and trouble of this girl was turning a profit for others, but no one publicly expressed any urge to protect her, no one seemed to notice that she was a teenager kidding around with her boyfriend when she said whatever things she said: no one gave her a break. It was all face value, all Ferrari = materialism = frivolousness = failure to recognize the seriousness of her crimes: BAD BAD GIRL. Marvyn Kornberg, the lawyer for Joey Buttafuoco, responded to the Makely tapes with the dismissive, "It's just Amy doing what she does best: lying and prostituting herself"—even though, in fact, she hadn't sold herself so much as she had been sold.

And that's how girls get into trouble. Does anyone have a v-chip that they can use to correct that? Because the intrusions of violence, of fear, of all that is bad in the world, are usually out of our control— and all the inhibitors to the negative influences of the media and the arts that people want to build as some glossy gesture at protecting their children's innocence are just false, the silly symbolic acts of people stuck in a closed system, like those warning labels attached to a mattress saying that you can't cut off the warning labels. No gated community, no television rating system, no parental advisory stickers on albums would have helped Amy Fisher at all—bad people and bad parenting are what made Amy bad; not rock music or the Internet. The real test of our character and concern for children is not in the shibboleths we invent to safeguard the ones who are already perfectly safe, but rather in what we do when the system fails and goes wrong. Amy Fisher is a real girl in real trouble, in real need of all those things we supposedly do to protect the innocent—she is the reason there are statutory rape laws and juvenile delinquency procedures that we seem to have forgotten about. And in a pinch, that protection wasn't there. The television exploitation of this minor—are there not some FCC guidelines about what is permissible in such situations?—prompted prosecutor Fred Klein to say that she was even more "revolting" than he'd previously thought, but it made no one angry at the privacy invasions brought on by Paul Makely, a man she trusted, or *Hard Copy,* a nightly tabloid that no one should have trusted. It seemed that if we could be amused and entertained by Amy Fisher, all anyone really cared about was that she's not my daughter.

Meantime, much as Amy is made to look like a girl who needs more than just a good spanking, for the longest time there was a baffling reluctance to prosecute Joey for statutory rape—not to mention contributing to the delinquency of a minor—even though everybody *knows* that he really did sleep with Amy. At first police and prosecutors decided not to press charges because Amy was not a credible witness; later they said that they wanted to spare the Buttafuoco family any further grief. He was finally tried and convicted in 1993. But it's hard to see this hemming and hawing as anything but some form of judicial disapproval of Amy, of a girl who definitely wanted it, and who should have been saved from what she wanted, as Barbara Kruger implores on one of her art posters. Certainly in the aftermath, Joey deserved to be punished. It's not as if we have failed in the past to take a hard line on statutory rape: Roman Polanski—a Holocaust survivor who gave us *Repulsion, Chinatown, Rosemary's Baby, Tess,* and lost a wife and an unborn child to a kind of insanity that seemed peculiarly American until the Tokyo subway bombing cult emerged—was exiled for sleeping with a thirteen-year-old in 1977. How has an auto mechanic been so judicially privileged?

*   *   *

Gloria Steinem believes that women get more radical with age because they become less valuable—their merits as sex objects are diminished, their function as breeders is depleted—as time goes on. She may have a point—Bridget Hall is surely making more money at fifteen, with modeling contracts for Maybelline and Ralph Lauren, than she will ever make as a uneducated fifty-year-old who learned everything she knows during her sixth stay at Hazelden (not that all models are brainless boozers, but by most accounts Hall is). But I can't imagine Amy Fisher will ever feel more worthless than she did at seventeen.

And traditionally, daughters of all kinds have always been infinitely expendable—just ask the Chinese, who in recent years, under the one-child-per-family policy, have sent so many daughters to state orphanages (and often into the hands of childless American couples) that a generation of boys has grown up to find they have no one to date, no brides to marry. It is the wisdom of Confucius that a woman who cannot read, write or work is a blessing, and ritual foot-binding once assured her delicacy: her trifling, decorative, homebound life as a breeder, her impeded and hobbled access to the world. Even today, the literature of Chinese-American women is rich with unfortunate feelings about being born female. Amy Tan's *The Joy Luck Club,* a model of the novel as self-help book, should have been called *Low Self-Esteem Is Worse Than Mao!* Subsequent writers have been both more subtle and blunt: "We were a family of three girls. By Chinese standards that wasn't lucky," Fae Myenne Ng writes in the first lines of her novel *Bone.* "In Chinatown, everyone knew our story. Outsiders jerked their chins, looked at us, shook their heads. We heard things. 'A failed family . . . Nothing but daughters.' "

And the trouble of getting a nubile daughter into a practical nuptial arrangement is just so much literature. One of the reasons there is no point in reading more than any one Jane Austen novel (*Pride and Prejudice* would be my pick) is that they all involve the same dilemma: a good, henpecked man is cursed with daughters, and no son, and British entail laws do not allow any of his distaff offspring to inherit the family house. There is a distant male cousin out there somewhere, often brooding and inscrutable at first, and in the absence of a male heir in the immediate family, he will gain title to the home. In the meantime the girls all need suitable mates. In movie versions of Austen, the elaborate cast of extras and wide crinolines create a claustrophobia that makes it feel like daughters here, daughters there, daughters everywhere—girls more suffocating than a plague of locusts—and *all of them in want of a husband.* Always one daughter is silly, another priggish, another materialistic, and one is good and solid and righteous and noble. The last one, of course, by the end of the book and after a few bouts with hesitation blues, will be betrothed to the cousin who will inherit the house—nearly lost to the family by entail, now saved by incest. The other sisters will also prevail—after a few balls and some afternoon teas and at least one sudden onset of illness that requires convalescence at the future intended's family home—to make proper matches as well, and as the pages stop or the credits roll, Mr. Bennet—patriarch of *Pride and Prejudice*—will heave a great sigh of relief, the gaggle of girls at long last out of his hair and lair.

But if daughters are expendable in an eighteenth-century comedy of manners, they are altogether abusable in earlier settings. The Bible, particularly the more narrative and less prescriptive stories of the Old Testament, offers several crude depictions of daughter destruction. Early in the book of Genesis and late in the decline of Sodom—where bestiality began and prison pastimes were invented—a minor character called Lot found his house under siege by all the men of the city, all demanding that he hand over the two guests who were dining with him (apparently the townsmen intended to, as the etymology suggests, sodomize the visitors). Lot tries to negotiate with the terrorists by making this offer: "Behold, I have two virgin daughters who have not known man; let me bring them out to you, and do to them as you please; only do nothing to these men, for they have come under the shelter of my roof." In this situation, things work out all right because the two sojourners turn out to be angels who blind the madding crowd, and thus a *deus ex machina* prevents us from seeing a man give over his daughters to gang rape to protect a couple of people he's only just met. But that's cold comfort to those of us who realize how unlikely it was for Lot to have a pair of angels at his table; in the absence of miracles, the father opted to ruin his daughters. Later on, after Lot's wife has turned into a pillar of salt while looking back at Sodom and Gomorrah as they burned down, Lot's daughters seduce him while he is in a drunken stupor, each of them ending up pregnant. Apparently, the two girls' intentions were noble: fearing that the twin cities' destruction meant that the whole world had been demolished, they believed they were the last people on earth, and they wanted to ensure the species' survival. Obviously this family was uniquely afflicted.

But then in Judges 11, the prophet Jephthah, a Jew in good standing, promises God that he will sacrifice the first thing that walks out the door of his house if he returns from battle against the Ammonites victorious. In a blatant attempt to blame the victim, when Jephthah sees his daughter approach he yells, "You have brought me very low, and you have become the cause of great trouble for me!" Two months later, Jephthah slays his daughter and burns her on an altar, a virgin sacrifice, as promised, never receiving the eleventh-hour reprieve that Abraham gets before slaughtering Isaac. As biblical scholar Ann Tapp points out in "Virgin Daughter Sacrifice," a study of several episodes of this kind, the moral rectitude of these acts is never questioned or commented on at all in the text. "Nearly as atrocious as the ideological presentation of women in these fabulae is the fact that each fabula is so inconspicuously in a larger narrative that the hideousness of their events reads as a passing detail," she writes. "The cursory, noncritical allusions to virgin daughter sacrifices in these narratives serve to legitimate the atrocity." In fact, Tapp cites a mention of Lot's deeds in the *International Critical Commentary,* published in 1930, which singles him out for praise: "Lot's readiness to sacrifice the honor of his daughters . . . shows him as a courageous champion of the obligations of hospitality in a situation of extreme embarrassment."

Emily Post, take note.

Still, both Jephthah and Lot are only bit players in the biblical epic, and their impact is limited. But two much-studied celluloid heroes— Jacob and King David—were equally remiss. Jacob, one of three patriarchs, progenitor of twelve sons who eventually named the Twelve Tribes of Israel, counted Dinah as his only daughter. As we have seen, it was Dinah who one day went for a walk "to see among the daughters of the land," and instead ended up getting raped by Shechem. After the deed was done, after he "took her and lay with her and tortured her," he fell in love with her, the way Luke fell for Laura after he raped her on *General Hospital.* Shechem then went to ask Jacob for Dinah's hand in marriage, but Jacob stayed silent, stony, refusing to get involved. (By Deuteronomic decree, Shechem is actually doing the honorable thing, since the law commands that a raped virgin belongs to her violator—"she will be his because he tortured her"—which at first seems illogical, since a girl ought to be protected from, not entrusted to, those who hurt her, but obviously the tradition of a woman being branded in blood, or being claimed by way of injury, has very respectable origins. Certainly it is demonstrable in modern life that when violence becomes an open wound which the woman is constantly worrying and the man is forever regretting—i.e., the dynamic between a battered wife and her husband—it can become a form of emotional Krazy Glue far stronger than the usual acts of kindness and tenderness that most couples try to bond with.) After Dinah's brothers massacre Shechem and his people, in a nasty and brutal revenge involving a lot of grown men's foreskins, as well as plenty of rape and looting—behavior that makes it clear that it is family honor and not Dinah's feelings that are at stake here—Jacob finally speaks up, but only to say that this pogrom has brought ill repute upon his home and will invite retaliation. Jacob never expresses concern for his only daughter.

In the case of King David, the crime is within the palace walls, and rape intermingles with sibling rivalry. The trouble begins when Amnon, David's firstborn and heir apparent, becomes infatuated to the point of affliction with his half sister Tamar. Lovesick to distraction, the prince takes to his bed, and convinces his father that Tamar must come to his chambers and tend to him and feed him with her own hands. It is on David's orders that Tamar visits Amnon, so it is under her father's auspices that she is raped. After this defilement, Amnon finds himself repulsed by his pathetic victim, "hating Tamar more than he loved her before," and when he tosses the newly deflowered maiden out of his room, insult overwhelms injury. David, who is consumed by the work of nations and already in over his head with Bathsheba and the scandal involved in getting her husband killed so that he could marry her, can't be concerned with Tamar. Instead, her full brother Absalom takes matters into his own hands and kills Amnon. After that Absalom flees the kingdom in fear of his father's vengeance, David becomes the poet of Psalms and the seeker of Ecclesiastes, and Tamar is never mentioned again, a ruined girl becomes a fallen woman—a woman fallen out of the pages of history, as good as dead in the public record.

In all these Old Testament instances, basically decent men—and Jacob and David surpassed mere decency to become regarded as *tzaddikim,* righteous disciples of God—treat their teenage daughters with neglect, abuse or both. These moral lapses on the part of men who were supposed to have walked in God's footsteps prove that adolescent girls have always been without safety or sanctuary, they are between men, no longer Daddy's little pumpkin and not yet somebody's baby, some big man's little woman. Stuck in the middle—as they were in the age when women did not have careers (when men probably did not even have careers—callings, or sheep to tend, but not careers)—girls of a certain age could ripen and fester as a full-time job. They become a problematic presence around the house, dead weight in the domestic realm because they are just kind of hanging around, expectantly, waiting for something to happen, waiting for life to begin—waiting to get married, basically. In the meantime, their misdirected and undirected and randomly directed sexual energy threatens all the other women in the household—this is assuming a time when harems were a standard feature—because anything that is latent is potentially explosive.

Both the Dinah and Tamar incidents—if we assume their cost to the households they affected and not the emotional toll taken on the girls themselves—caused a lot of trouble and bother for everybody around them, with internecine warfare and fratricide being the worst of the consequences. These girls, silent in the text, but acting as the "McGuffin"—screenplay jargon for a trivial item that the audience will forget about, though it motivates all the action—become the model for every gun moll who causes a rumble when two rival leaders of the pack fight for her honor (though she never asked them to), and the prototype for Helen of Troy, the face that launched a thousand ships and then disappeared from view. And you always get the feeling that all this *Sturm und Drang* could easily have been avoided if their naïve, nubile bodies had not been there, loose, unclaimed, unprotected—basically, just asking to be raped. In biblical times, a teenage girl's betrothal could create kinship among clans or bring peace between nations—her value as a matrimonial object was real, a bride-price could be attached, she was a commodity for her father to trade. But until she could be appraised on the open market, she was just a body housing hormones in flux, her intrinsic worth not yet assessed. "Virgin daughters are, as understood by men, in a transitory state," Ann Tapp writes. "Though capable of child-bearing (a necessity in maintaining male lineage), they remain possessed by their fathers and desired by other males, thus placing them in a dangerous position between two male forces vying for ownership." Back then, it was accepted at the outset that people were functions, a woman was only as valuable as the babies she made, a child was only as good as the crops he tended to or the cows he milked—the notion of unconditional love, Immanuel Kant's vision of a "kingdom of ends" where everyone is a subject, beloved for his human spirit, did not yet exist. In the Bible almost all purely emotional love—Samson and Delilah, David and Bathsheba—is an agent of downfall, while practical unions thrive. A teenage girl, on the verge of becoming the producer of another man's heirs, a sexual being who is forbidden to all the men in her home, cannot be of much use to her father, who may be aroused, disgusted or frightened by her fomenting femininity. He may want to protect her, but he also might prefer to just get rid of her. He might just not know what to do.

It is in this vacuum, the slender ravine between male protectorates, that the Joey Buttafuocos of the world slip in. No father, no husband—open season. There is no story of a teenage girl in trouble where the father is a vigilant, loving presence. Though the Fishers did not divorce until sometime after Amy went to prison, her father looms throughout her memories as distant and terrifying—he was thirty-eight when she was born, her mother was only twenty-one, and in Amy's recall her dad was old, often sickly, with switchback moods and a trigger-finger temper, the kind of father who would punish Amy for getting raped by the tile man, the kind of father who did not protect her when she was sexually molested by a family friend between the ages of three and six. Elliot Fisher was a true failure in the role of father as John Wayne, the patriarch-protector avenging his wronged daughter's honor—but he can rest easy knowing he shares this limitation with Jacob and King David. And he can comfort himself further with the fact that at least he was there, even if he was not *there*.

It's quite normal, at this point, to grow up without a dad. Fathers often feel like a family absence, like heroes of Bolshevism airbrushed out of photographs under Stalin's rule—they are missing figures that nag and tease us with the sense that they must be there somewhere, like an amputated limb. The fact that the institution of fatherhood is in complete crisis in this country is not something that anyone of functional sanity can possibly deny any longer. The Million Man March, the Promise Keepers' rallies—these happenings could never have been elevated to media events unless a return to responsible paternity was on their agendas. According to a Washington, D.C.-based organization called the National Fatherhood Initiative, 60 percent of rapists, 72 percent of adolescent murderers and 70 percent of teenagers in state reform institutions are products of single-parent households; in 1993, 84 percent of the children of divorce were in their mothers' custody, and according to a study published in the *Journal of Marriage and Family,* 35 percent of children who live without their fathers never see them, and 24 percent see them less than once a month. It has gotten to the point where there are now public-service advertisements on television that show a lion teaching one of his cubs how to roar properly, which is apparently basic to the survival of the brood and the species, presenting a parable for the importance of fathers to human beings also. The overdetermined images like the Kodak commercial that shows a hunky, shirtless man holding a baby or the overextended dads of popular movies like *Mr. Mom* and *Mrs. Doubtfire* both belie the absentee fatherhood that is a fact of growing up American, and also pay homage to the struggle that many younger men are in fact undertaking to make their paternal presence known, to be involved parents, nothing like their own distant dads. Though the future of fatherhood is probably a brighter one, all the troubled teenage girls who have made headlines are the products of a lifetime of wondering, Where's Poppa?

Lolita is fatherless, her widowed mother's marriage to Humbert Humbert the intermediary that allows the pedophile to enter her prepubescent life. Most of the child-star sex kittens are fatherless, and many were in some sense *replacing* their missing fathers: Tuesday Weld, Sue Lyon, Carol Lynley, Linda Blair, Jodie Foster and Drew Barrymore all acted as sole breadwinners, supporting single mothers, siblings, stepfathers, whoever. In the Tamar and Dinah stories, both David and Jacob have ceded all paternal duties to the brothers. Nicole Brown's father did not hesitate to hand his eighteen-year-old daughter over to O.J., and continued over the years to mortgage Nicole's life to his son-in-law's generosity, becoming the recipient of a Hertz dealership in Orange County, allowing O.J. to pay for his various daughters' intermittent schooling. It seems clear that girls gone wrong are always either bargaining chips between fathers and husbands—currency, wampum, barter—made into sex objects by the men who should be protecting them and allowing them to cling to their girlhood just a little bit longer; or they are simply without fathers at all.

It is, in fact, a telling detail in this saga that when Mr. Fisher first brought Amy to Complete Auto Body to have her sideswiped mirror repaired after her first car accident, he overheard Joey say, "I'd like to fuck that," in reference to his daughter. "Somehow that remark hadn't bothered my father," Amy says. "He dismissed it as a compliment."

Hey little girl is your daddy home?

Everyone, it seems, protects the boys when they are bad, but no one protects the girls when they are victims. It's true that the Fishers provided Amy with excellent legal counsel, and risked all that they owned as collateral for her $2 million bail, but their support for her always came across as anemic, ashamed—as if they too could understand the objections to a teenage hooker with a married lover, as if they could never summon the strength that Mary Jo Buttafuoco had to just insist that her husband was perfect and that was that. Just as abortion rights activists for so long fought on behalf of womankind with the apologetic "Abortion is a terrible thing, but . . ."—minced words that paled beside the righteous indignation of those championing the cause of the unborn—we seem only to defend our girls gone wrong with "She is a monster, but . . ." We never quite give them the insane and often inexplicable support that boys seem to get no matter what. In his 1997 book *Our Guys,* journalist Bernard Lefkowitz chronicles the overweening kid gloves' treatment that thirteen teenage boys—all local heroes and varsity letter types—were accorded in affluent all-American Glen Ridge, New Jersey, when, in the spring of 1989, they sexually abused a seventeen-year-old mentally retarded girl (she had an IQ of 64), luring her into a basement and treating her to an afternoon of oral sodomy followed by rape with a baseball bat and a broom handle. The next day, the boys tried to entice an encore performance out of their victim. Despite the grisly nature of this crime—and the coldblooded cruelty that could cause these boys to ask for more on the morrow—only three were finally convicted, and not until 1993; they were not sentenced until 1997—to jail terms that could be paroled in as little as ten months' time—and in the intervening eight years, these rapists roamed free. According to Lefkowitz, one of the convicted offenders simply explained, by way of excusing himself, "I used poor judgment."

By comparison, Autumn Jackson, an obviously very troubled teenage girl who was raised by an obviously unstable mother to believe that Bill Cosby was her father (the DNA flies!), was convicted of extortion in Federal Court for feebly and unsuccessfully blackmailing her putative paternal unit into giving her money to prevent her from selling the story of her secret sire to the tabloid weekly *The Globe*. Ms. Jackson may well get twelve years in prison for a crime that ultimately harmed no one and that can, in some ways, be seen as no more than just a pathetic and pathological response to being fatherless, or of disputed paternity, and a product of misdirected parenting. Meanwhile, Melissa Drexler, the nineteen-year-old better known as the "prom mom"—she gave birth in a stall of the ladies' room during her senior soirée and either killed or left the baby for dead—has been indicted for first-degree murder in Monmouth County, an offense that carries a thirty-year minimum sentence—even though it's obvious that what the girl really needs is some serious therapy, probably a stay in a locked ward, and a junior high level course in sex education. In the same vein, in a courtroom in Wilmington, Delaware, prosecutors made much fuss about the fact that they would *not* seek the death penalty against Amy Grossberg—another adolescent in denial about her pregnancy until her baby burst forth in a motel room one day and was found dead in a Dumpster the next—as if it were a sign of their reason or mercy or compassion, or *whatever*.

I can only interpret the severity with which punishment and the attendant moralizing are meted out—or, at any rate, spoken of—when it comes to these very young, very harmless and completely clueless girls as a particular strain of extreme misogyny that can only be directed at women whose sexuality is still just beginning—just barely—to bloom. It seems like some societal attempt to stamp and stomp this burgeoning sexual energy into a vapid, stolid anemia before it has even an opportunity to be enjoyed by its rightful owner, by the girl on trial. Perhaps the cheer that I could not help feeling when nineteen-year-old English au pair Louise Woodward was set free in Middlesex

County after being given a sentence of time served for the accidental death of the infant in her charge was simply in that for once a teenage girl—a thoroughly homely one, it seems worth noting, and one who projected only the dankest, dingiest bit of sexual verve—was given the state's unswerving, unconditional support in her own pursuit of happiness (even if that meant, in Ms. Woodward's case, going to see the touring company of the Broadway show *Rent* twenty times during its Boston engagement). Here, in Judge Hiller B. Zobel's court in Cambridge, Massachusetts, a justice of the Commonwealth was siding with the girl, backing up her version of events as no one had ever offered to do for Amy.

In Amy's case, not even her own parents or attorneys seemed to be with her all the way. The decision for Amy to plea-bargain, which was wise considering there was a grandstanding prosecutor and such a fervid, rabid victim (it is hard to remember that Mary Jo, not Amy, is technically the victim) to contend with, still in some way showed a lack of faith in Amy's essential innocence. Remember, almost all of the Kennedy clan came out to support William Kennedy Smith when he was charged with rape in Palm Beach in 1991. And Alex Kelly, an accused rapist when he was still a high school senior in Darien, Connecticut, was secreted out of the country by his parents before the state had a chance to try him; by the time he returned to face the law in 1996, after several years on a European sojourn, he was completely at ease, his girlfriend and family flanking him supportively on his way into court, their faith in him unshaken. And, of course, there were the Simpson women—two sisters, an octogenarian and wheelchair-bound mother, not to mention his daughter Arnelle and even his ex-wife Marguerite—who stood by O.J. so resolutely, creating a barricade of tough, no-nonsense guardian angels, bolstering their man like a scaffold holding up a crumbling edifice.

In not one of these three cases was the accused convicted. (Alex Kelly's trial ended in a hung jury, and it was considered a miracle—as well as a much-needed opportunity for the state of Connecticut's legal forces to learn from its mistakes, just as the attorneys in Simpson's civil trial learned from the loopholes in the criminal prosecution—that the second time around, after some well-publicized drunk-driving episodes, Kelly was finally convicted. Even then, after the verdict, he was released on bail to await sentencing—an oddity when, by comparison, Mary Kay LeTourneau in Seattle was *in jail* awaiting trial for a lesser crime.)

No one, it seemed, was willing to jump without reservation to Amy Fisher's defense. When I think of the strange spectacle of folksinger Buffy Sainte-Marie speaking out on behalf of Richard Secord during the Iran-Contra hearings, insisting that he was the "Universal Soldier" of her one hit song, a footman in other people's larger designs, it seems incongruous that no one championed Amy's cause until she was safely locked away in prison. An unlikely crusader—Tammy Wynette, say, or Phyllis Schlafly—surely should have shown up. Finally Madonna, on *Saturday Night Live* in January 1993, ripped up a picture of Joey and said, "Fight the real enemy." This made her the only prominent feminist to speak out in any way on Amy's behalf. While Gloria Steinem and company were getting all huffy about Anita Hill, who was mostly just being irritated by her former boss, no one was coming forward for Amy. Anna Quindlen, where are you? Earth to Katha Pollitt—hello? The world needed your wit and reason (I say that about Pollitt, not Quindlen, who has had neither for quite some time). Only Amy Pagnozzi, writing in the definitely down-market *New York Post*, came out on Amy's side—and even befriended Amy a bit, finding common ground with the teenager because she was married to Clive Barnes, the newspaper's theater critic and a much older man.

But the feminist movement's mum response to Ms. Fisher did nothing so much as reveal its own vulnerabilities and defenses—into which, by the mid-nineties, several younger women like Katie Roiphe, Rene Denfeld and even Naomi Wolf would eagerly puncture big holes, as part of a sex-positive wave that came to be known as "do me" feminism. Amy Fisher made us see that the desexed persona of the proper feminist—which made it impossible for feminism to take up her cause—meant that a number of women who wanted to walk on the wild side that was supposed to be part of the promise of liberation had nowhere to turn.

Anita Hill—she was easy to defend, the poor sharecropper's daughter made good, the Yale Law grad who, with so many of her siblings beside her as she spoke at her Senate hearing, was the modern incarnation of the house nigger, the person that every bigot means when he says some of my best friends are black, the one you point to in contrast to inner-city mayhem to prove that stupidity and moral bankruptcy—not racism and poverty—are the reason that *those people* are stuck in Harlem, in East St. Louis, in Compton, in prison, in hell. She was the virtue meltdown. She's the one who—unlike the recalcitrant Jane Roe or the unpleasant and unbecoming Paula Jones—makes the moral fault lines so easy to define.

But what can the women's movement offer Amy, who really needs them? The challenge that someone like Ms. Fisher poses to feminism is the obverse of the trouble that men like Bob Packwood and Arlen Specter—two senators whose private behavior and icky personalities are reprehensible but who have always been good supporters of women's rights and issues when it really counts—cause us: nothing Amy does or says is particularly good for the cause, but she is a grim and healthy reminder of what the women's movement must do for her, how it needs to make the world safe for Amy Fisher and for so many girls who have gotten the worst of the promises of liberation—promiscuity, pornography, prostitution in the suburbs—without the knowledge of how to use sex as a weapon before the Joey Buttafuocos of the world turn their rapiers against them.

*   *   *

It is amazing how many women's memoirs of teenage disaster in the still of suburbia have appeared in recent years—Beverly Donofrio's *Riding in Cars with Boys,* Betsy Israel's *Grown Up Fast,* Susan Gordon Lydon's tale of twenty years of heroin addiction titled *Take the Long Way Home,* the now-classic anonymous diary of a juvenile junkie called *Go Ask Alice,* among others. The fictional renditions of the same source material—Joyce Carol Oates' *Foxfire,* Alice McDermott's *That Night,* Susan Taylor Chehak's *Smithereens,* Joyce Maynard's ambitious novelization of the Pam Smart case, *To Die For*—are never-ending. While most of these books don't become best-sellers, they are literary staples, constants. City-girl stories are never quite so gothic, the pregnancy scares and peyote incidents never quite so brutal, the botched abortions and crime scenes never quite so bloody—possibly because the dreary, dull suburban landscape is fallow ground for a teenage wasteland. Which reminds us why it is the fifties, when everyone migrated out to their subdivisions, and not the sixties, when everyone went nuts *because* of those same subdivisions, that mark the decline of American life.

All these narratives of suburban girlhood seem to revolve around a simple set of plot points: a boredom, almost from birth, that would appear to be depression but is soon mistaken for mischief; a desire, at an early age, to be seductive; a belief, at a later age, that acting on this desire can be fun; and finally watching as it all comes back in haunting horror; followed by a realization that the ghastly consequences—unwanted pregnancy, disease, crime, prison—will be paid for by the girls alone, and the guys are not even going to be supportive. In fact, many of them won't even be *around* to be supportive. And the boys who have not fled in horror will often turn on them: they'll sell stories to *Inside Edition,* they'll pretend they don't know her, they'll be the first in school to spray-paint "SLUT" in scarlet letters across her locker. Parents are always far too far away to notice what is going on until a pregnancy starts to show or a syringe punctures a hole in a trash bag—and even then they try not to notice. Loneliness is the leitmotif, and it hardly seems surprising that sex or drugs become the frenzy in which all this isolation gets lost. But in a strange turn of exuberance, the loneliness that these remedies ultimately only serve to magnify seems an acceptable price to pay for the brief freedom they allow. "There was the daytime world, the public world, in which we all had families, went to school, took directions from adults, and lied all the time without even thinking about it," Kathy Dobie writes in her *Harper's* essay. "Sex blew this world open . . ."

One of the truest, most upsetting and oddly literary portraits of suburbia as hidden hell is actually a movie. *Smooth Talk* is a creepy, unsettling adaptation of the Joyce Carol Oates short story "Do You Know Where You're Going? Do You Know Where You've Been?" Put on film by Joyce Chopra, one of the rare female directors at that time (whose reputation was later destroyed when she was one in a series of people at the helm of *Bright Lights, Big City,* a mistake of a movie for reasons beyond mere misdirection), the 1985 release is mostly about Laura Dern's obnoxious, awkward sexual awakening in small-town California at age fifteen. There is so much in the movie that is so accurate, painfully so—Dern's gawkiness, her poor posture and, above all, her obvious discomfort in her own body that gives a sense of a girl who was not a real cutie pie through childhood, but is now blonde and leggy and not quite able to handle the attention she gets from boys at the mall, boys at the soda-pop joint, boys everywhere. She is mystified by her sudden power at the same time that it makes her feel superior to her plain, homely family (Mary Kay Place plays the mom, if that gives you some idea); it makes her feel that she's got a secret that is too significant to be interrupted by her mother's concern with painting the house or her sister's interest in her dolls.

And, of course, that's the nature of the cleft that occurs at adolescence: the family can't see what the world has started to notice—or, more likely, they willfully ignore it, pretend that sex has not invaded their space with the suddenness of a bad odor—so there's no way for a girl to be a comfortable, integrated person at home. The constant jones to get out of the house is all about going to a place where it's possible for authenticity—or, failing that, the mall, the drive-in and worse—but that too is disappointing because the boys you neck with or the ones who buy you milk shakes cannot recognize you for the sweet little girl you are, they can't see that only an hour before you were washing the dinner dishes or refurnishing your dollhouse. A terrible, sinking personality split becomes inevitable, as Carol Gilligan and Lyn Mikel Brown document so well in *Meeting at the Crossroads,* and the result, as portrayed in *Smooth Talk,* is a lack of conviction that makes Dern's character easy to hate. The loneliness Dern feels when she's trying to talk to her mom, paired with the antsiness she feels out on a date, should inspire sympathy, but instead just meets with our disgust. The audience starts to hope that this girl gets what's coming.

And in this, too, *Smooth Talk* is unusually accurate. Teenage girls, who more than at any other time in a woman's life perhaps, really just need someone to talk to, often sabotage themselves by giving off so many mixed messages that no one around them knows what to do, and everyone is just so sick of the sulleness and snideness. They are like starving stray cats, and all you want to do is bring them some leftover marrow bones and rub them behind the ears because they are so pretty and fuzzy—but all they want to do is scratch your hand and give you rabies because you might be the same person who threw stones at them earlier. The discomfort of watching Dern's act is almost too much, and yet it's one of the few truthful adolescent portraits I have seen at the movies, one of the few where the girl is not a vapid sex kitten or a mother murderer, where she is not sexy and seventeen or acne-scarred and dangerous; Dern comes across as just plain old confused. It is a spectacular performance.

The red-hot center of *Smooth Talk* involves an older greaser, played by Treat Williams, talking his way into the girl's house while the family is away for the afternoon—Dern, cranky and cross as usual, can't be bothered to join them. After about an hour of obnoxious cajoling through the screen door, when Williams finally gets the girl into his car and onto her back for the classic American sexual initiation in the wheat fields, it's hard to know if it's rape or seduction or what. There's a lot of symbolism bound up in the doorway, which gets locked and unlocked and fidgeted with as Williams' harangue goes on and on. It's the movie's one heavy-handed, graceless moment: the house, which is the universal symbol of family, is safe; once Dern walks out the door, she's basically consenting to whatever. And yet, the tribulations of adolescence are honestly stated: Laura Dern played with halters and short shorts and cutoffs and fire and other raw, rough attempts at sexy because she thought boys were fun; the real consequences of sexy—the men who may not be so fun—no one warned her about, because a conspiracy of silence surrounds the grimy thought of what happens to any girl who goes out looking for it, looking for anything. This girl was definitely out there looking for trouble, but no one bothered to tell her that trouble shows up the way it wants to, that it doesn't stop when you say stop, that men read sexual innuendo any which way they like, that as jailbait you can go fishing but you can't know if you'll catch a fluke or a shark, that you've got to expect to be eaten alive. Brooke Shields may not have known what she meant about nothing coming between her and her Calvins, but zillions of men knew just what she didn't know she meant—the pubescent virgin of those ads sums up nicely what post-structuralists mean when they say that the signifier and signified do not have to have a meeting of minds—and this is why parents wish they could just keep their teenage daughters locked up in the house. Meanwhile, Treat Williams is able to achieve his own version of breaking and entering just by smooth talking the girl into going for a ride with him because she doesn't know what else to do.

Hey little girl is your daddy home? Did he go away and leave you all alone? Mm-hmm I got a bad desire

Without particularly meaning to, *Smooth Talk* explains why date rape is so troublesome: she didn't say no, she didn't say yes, she could have refused, she didn't refuse—and yet it seems certain that a real violation has occurred. But the movie doesn't deal with that. That's not really the point. This isn't a movie about the law or personal politics—it's about a girl learning her lot in life as a woman, learning the lesson of Dinah and Tamar, learning that no one really cares how she feels. It ends with Dern, her sister and her mother dancing in the living room while James Taylor sings "Handyman." It's stark and awful, the two sisters doing a box step like an awkward couple during "Beth" or "Endless Love" at the senior prom, both of them seem lonely for company and comfort, and the mother seems relieved, for the moment, to have her little girls back. The father is nowhere to be found—he's out fixing the car or getting the barbecue going, doing some guy thing.

I fix broken hearts / Baby I'm your handyman

It's hard not to be flooded with images of the perfect high school crush, of James Taylor the way he was in *Two-Lane Blacktop,* the sweet preppy boy of unhappy Mnemsha, a blue-eyed beauty with long dark hair, a junkie, a McLean's refugee, a man who would never do what the guy in *Smooth Talk* did, he is the perfect image of the boy Laura Dern went out looking for, someone romantic and off-kilter and tongue-tied with a pretty, pretty voice and an acoustic guitar that he bought from a guy who said it once belonged to Jaco Pastorius. Or something like that. James Taylor, such as he was in the early seventies, is the boy every girl should have lost her virginity to.

But it's never like that.

The lingering image is that women have to fend for themselves, that the father is just a shadow in the house and that this sweet moment, this family dance, is all the more precious because it's nostalgic—far from being a return to innocence it is only a brief reprieve from confusion that is only going to get worse with the years, it is as awful as the final sentence of *The Good Earth* when the sons promise the father that they'll never sell the land, "but behind his back they smiled." These are smiles that imply everything that will go wrong in China for the next century. And the foreboding left at the end of *Smooth Talk* is so thick, thick as anything Pearl Buck could have imagined, because it predicts damage done to daughters for generations.

*   *   *

And yet, for all that Amy Fisher reminds us of teens in trouble, she also stands for all that is riveting and funny and fascinating and riotous about teenage life, of the reason why all subversive art and rock music—much of which is made by people in their thirties and forties—gets grouped under the rubric of "youth culture," as if all that is alive and kicking can only be of and by the young. Ms. Fisher's autobiography, *My Story,* reads like an instruction manual for teenage disaster disguised as a cautionary tale. Its style is picaresque, but also grand, an Italian opera in a shopping mall, with all the stock characters and props that we're all too familiar with from all those recent-immigrant-made-good movies: the plucky, scrappy elders who are street-smart but barely speak English; the simple working stiffs who make enough money to own a boat and a Benz even though all they know is cement or plumbing; distant fathers; doting mothers; churches that all seem to be called Our Lady of Perpetual Sorrow; last names with too many vowels or too few; and children who change Debbie to Debi, Cindy to Cyndi and Amy to Aimee. In the cinematic imagination, the place is always the Bronx or Brooklyn, but in real life, we all know that it is Long Island, the most densely populated Italian-American region in the whole country.

My Story could be the story line for a Russ Meyer movie, or in its darker moments, the treatment for one of those late-sixties biker flicks that star a young pre-acid casualty Bruce Dern, or a not yet respected director John Cassavetes, or a fictional Maria Wyeth as B movie biker mama in Joan Didion's *Play It As It Lays* (the movie version of which starred—*touché!*—Tuesday Weld). But instead of Didion's flat tones on the blacktop, imagine the wreck everywhere, the wreck on the highway, the wreck all over the place, the motif of Andy Warhol's

Accident series, the pictures that showed multiple exposures of the casualties of—to put it in epic terms—America, stock photos transformed into art in that dry, denatured Warhol way that makes their violence and destruction seem somehow only worse. That early work—the electric chairs and car crashes—is so upsetting, so detached at a time when detachment was not mere mannerism, that it explains just what Warhol was retreating from in all that Campbell's Soup, all those consumer goods, those images of Liz and Liza and Jackie and Marilyn, in his invention of a detachment that *was* mere mannerism. The flat, one-dimensional beauty of his silk screens, and the way the women whose images he used were flattened and contained by photographs—ironically, as icons they were larger than life but as people they seemed so much smaller—always struck me as a way to manage the world, to make it nothing at all like Amy Fisher, who as a teenager practically luxuriated in hysteria and melodrama. This girl, an absolute adolescent, is a control freak's nightmare, an accident waiting to happen, a land mine no one knew about until one day someone took the wrong step and woke up the whole neighborhood. She was planning to go to Nassau County Community College to study God knows what, she was worrying that Paul might not want to go to the prom with her, and then she got a gun and shot someone in the head.

If I were the mother of a teenage daughter, I would find reading Amy's autobiography simply too upsetting, the implications too terrifying, because it is hard not to notice, amid so much in it that is so crazy, there is so much more that is all too typical. All the hours spent at the Sunrise Mall, the boyfriends in and boyfriends out, the pathetic attempts at self-dramatization summed up with lines like "I *am* a female James Dean" or the Blanche DuBois-ish "It doesn't take long for a girl to destroy her own life." Even Amy's outsize feelings for Joey, a man who, it seems to me, only a mother—or a teenager—could love, are just business as usual for the besotted babe in the woods. The fact is that teenage girls, suffering heartbreak or a failed crush or even a yet-unrealized rejection, often feel as if the world is coming to an end. Everything seems THAT BIG at that age. In her short story "Lust," Susan Minot's unnamed narrator captures the delirium that teenage girls experience with each new crush: "I could do some things well. Some things I was good at, like math or painting or even sports, but the second a boy put his arm around me, I forgot about wanting to do anything else, which felt like a relief at first until it became like sinking into a muck." The beauty of the Amy Fisher story is that finally a teenage girl gets her heart broken and contrives events such that no one can blame her for feeling like it's the end of the world. She really has sunk into a hell of a muck! The worst thing a nice Jewish-Italian girl from Long Island can experience, barring actual apocalypse, has got to be prison time (contrary to common belief, it is not having your Bloomingdale's charge cards canceled). By going to jail, a girl that's known as jailbait can finally have problems on the magnitude of her emotional life.

Writer Betsy Israel, who chronicled her own Nassau County teenage pregnancy and eventual reformation in a memoir called *Grown Up Fast,* described in a *New York Times Magazine* article her identification and repulsion with Amy Fisher. "As someone who grew up two canals over from—and left high school two years after—the Buttafuocos, I have long had a strangely personal interest in the case and a fascination with the purply haired protagonist, the girl described, as was I in about 1976, as 'totally uncontrollable,' " Israel writes. "Once 'uncontrollable' meant carving words into your skin with a dull-edged razor and devouring the contents of your parents' medicine chest. I could not imagine factoring into that emotional free fall actual guns, or rather I could imagine it, and the idea, decades later, had the power to terrorize me . . ." But the ability to feel both distanced from and strangely sympathetic with our *Hard Copy* heroines is rather usual these days. The tabloid events involving men—Son of Sam, Ted Bundy, Mark David Chapman—tend to lure us with their luridness because we simply *cannot* imagine being them, cannot identify the killer in me; but women's tabloid histrionics—Lorena Bobbitt, Jean Harris and, I would even argue, Aileen Wuornos—draw us in because we all feel that we are one step away from the same thing, a slight shift in circumstance, a move of our emotional trajectories by just a degree or two, a few IQ points more or less, a missed estrogen dose, and we might do the same. Or worse, we might *not* do the same, but wish we could.

These women, somehow, always seem oddly justified, the motive always a bit more, well, grounded than I was reading too much J. D.

Salinger or the prophet Ezekiel came to me in a dream and told me to wipe out all women with red hair, or whatever. The women tend to be motivated by heartbreak, and they tend to attack the victimizer or the perceived rival rather than some abstract stand-in. We understand this, and of course we would never do it ourselves—thus giving us permission for righteous indignation—but we get it. (I often think that if O. J. Simpson could admit guilt, he might be in jail, but he might also earn some amount of public sympathy because we all can understand a crime of passion.) As Amy herself points out, the prison she is in seems like a purgatory for women in trouble because of their dependencies on men. Let's face it, if men's prisons are full of guys who are in because they killed their wives as self-defense against getting beaten or who sold their bodies on the street because their girlfriends forced them to, no one is telling. It is no surprise that Jesus spoke the words "He who is without sin may cast the first stone" to prevent a mob from killing a woman: her sins—in that case, adultery—would never be those that no one else could identify with.

Now, of course, there are people who will, for whatever reason, admire Mary Jo, the woman who stood by her man, got breast implants while he served a statutory rape sentence and has the good fortune to have a half-paralyzed face, so that no one will ever know what she's really thinking. Camille Paglia does this. "Mary Jo even sang praises about their 'better than ever' sex life on Howard Stern's radio show," Paglia wrote in the *San Francisco Examiner*. "It was an astonishing display of female triumph of the will. A betrayed wife had won back her man and defeated her young rival." But Mary Jo partisans are the people who identify with the strong, with the fighting Irish girl who defied even the most optimistic medical prognosis by living after she was shot and left with a bullet permanently lodged in her head—and who, by living, put her husband in a position of permanent guilt, permanently beholden to the woman who took a bullet for him (which, by the way, did not keep him from getting arrested for soliciting a prostitute a couple of years later). These people, these strong people, they don't need our identification, oblivious as Nero fiddling about, marching along like nothing is wrong when everything obviously is, they will always be fine. Their plight is not only uninteresting, it is also one of bare-knuckled survival, and in that way it is rather troglodytical, not unlike Joey Buttafuoco himself. All that stuff that Thoreau once said about most men living lives of quiet desperation—well, if you turn up the volume on that paradigm, and give it a South Shore (of Long Island) accent and a tendency to wear loud, acrylic print outfits, you're left with Mary Jo Buttafuoco.

I guess the point is that Amy Fisher has emerged as a heroine—and even a martyr—in this story, at least as far as I am concerned, because it seems far preferable to be Amy Fisher in prison than Mary Jo anywhere on earth—even before she was shot. It seems better to have Amy serve as our surrogate for the mistakes we will never make than to identify with Mary Jo about the ones that there is a good chance we will make. Amy represents that certain thing that separates us from animals: she has a conscience. It is misdirected, of course, and it may even be a bad conscience. But somewhere in her overwrought, libidinal brain, she sensed that something was wrong with her behavior, with Joey's behavior, with what was going on around her, and she decided to do something about it: she got herself a gun. It was most certainly the wrong thing to do, but this protest against the treatment she got, and that she willingly accepted from Joey and other men, was not as she herself believes the sign that she had lost all self-respect: to the contrary, it was the beginning of her refusal to take it any longer.

Meanwhile, Mary Jo, living in the same house with Joey, with her face sagging on one side and two plastic Baggies of silicone lifting, separating and dividing down below, is refusing consciousness. It is the denial that Mary Jo lives in that keeps the world from falling apart—for if any more people acted out against what goes on around them, all stability would cease, the 50 percent divorce rate would skyrocket, the likelihood that most members of most families would still be able to get together on Thanksgiving and Passover would plummet, we would become an army of emotional desperadoes doing just what Amy Fisher did. And still, we need the occasional Amy Fisher, just as Thomas Jefferson posited that democracy required the occasional rebellion, to remind us how much we deny.

But who cares if Mary Jo Buttafuoco lives or dies. As far as anyone can tell, her consciousness is not much more than that of an alligator who has been flushed down the toilet bowl and must only fight its way out of the sewer. Only she is not fighting. And that is why I am sorry she isn't dead. Look, if she and Joey came to whatever agreement they have that shit happened but their marriage, their kids, the years gone by are more important, that's their problem. But Mary Jo's constant public refusal to admit that her husband might have actually had an affair (unless, of course, her presumption is on the basis of who would want him?) makes it everyone's problem. Because her continued insistence not that she has forgiven him, but rather that *he never did anything wrong*, makes idiots of us all. When the couple appeared on *Donahue* shortly after Amy went to prison, Mary Jo's demeanor of denial was such that, had there been a sandbox anywhere nearby, I'm sure she would have stuck her head in it and remained in this ostrich stance for the rest of her life before she'd concede the possibility that Joey did anything wrong; finally, one woman in the studio audience, frustrated with what seemed like the obvious obtuseness of this wife, pointed to Joey and yelled, "If it looks like a snake and acts like a snake, it must be a snake!" When police detectives showed Mary Jo at least thirteen receipts for four-hour stays at the Freeport Motor Inn & Boatel, signed by Joey and documenting that he was there either with Amy or with *someone*, Mary Jo just stonewalled the evidence, saying that "if they or anyone said they had a dozen motel receipts, then a dozen times *I'll* just say that *I* was in that motel with him."

Here's how it looks: there's one woman in jail and another woman with permanent physical damage, but in all this Joey Buttafuoco appears to have been punished not at all. In fact, he's gone Hollywood, and is making appearances on *Geraldo* to talk about his new career, with roles in upcoming films as a bouncer, a Mafia heavy, a villain in a horror movie—playing to type, you might say, though his agent was quoted in *Esquire* as insisting, "We just want to prove that Joey has an incredible amount of talent." And Mary Jo comforts herself with the knowledge that the enemy is in jail. But that's where she is wrong. Amy is not the enemy. Mary Jo is sleeping with the enemy.

But Mary Jo and the rest of the family's reaction to this case pretty much proves that men will band together and defend each other even when it's wrong (an atavistic tendency from a more militant time when "my country right or wrong" led us into Vietnam and all that), but women not only rarely bother to band together with each other—even worse, they tend to band together with the men. So that not only do you have Mary Jo with the IQ of a fence post defending her husband—you've also got her mother calling John Gambling's morning radio show on WOR in New York just to say that her son-in-law is a son to her, she's known him since he was sixteen, and in her mind he's just perfect, Jesus of Massapequa. "I told you before, John, and I will say it again," Mary Connery said with insistence, "I will lay down my life for my son-in-law. And they'll have to go through me to get to him."

Long Island: where the men are men, the women are men, and the pets are scared.

To read accounts of the Amy Fisher story, one is extremely struck by this strange collective denial on the part of all who were close to Joey, that same playing pretend that we mostly associate with Mafia movies—and with Jonestown. Or Waco. Amy herself, the dope, was said by police to have protected Joey even after they told her in interrogation that he turned her in. Attorney Eric Naiburg claims that when he took on Amy's case, he "spent the first two weeks convincing her that Joey was not going to come to the rescue."

* * *

But even though neither Betty Friedan nor the justice system nor her own father did much for Amy Fisher, a funny thing seems to have happened: the world of the teenage girl suddenly opened up at the same time that incarceration shut Amy down. The adolescent age group is a huge market—with a population of 25 million (which will be more like 31 million in 2006), it is worth $89 billion a year to industries—and teenage girls are renowned for spending like crazy. Even Humbert Humbert, with characteristic glee and disgust, noted little Lolita's status in the marketplace: "She it was to whom ads were dedicated: the ideal consumer, the subject and object of every foul poster." So it's not like the teenybopper world, at least from the consumer perspective, was not a full one, not like there wasn't enough Maybelline and Clairol's Herbal Essence and Benetton to go around.

But the glaring absence in mass-market goods for girls was, for lack of a better word, darkness: shopping malls were filled with glum, sullen, alienated girls being sold cheery, pretty things. The world of the girl was still believed to be big pastel ribbons and acrylic appliqués for blue jeans and Claddagh rings exchanged between friends and *The Baby-Sitters Club* and prom dresses by Gunny Sax. My God—even Amy Fisher had a roomful of teddy bears and stuffed animals! The brutal truths—that girls drank whole bottles of Robitussin to get high, that they cut up their legs with razor blades for fun or psychic relief or whatever, that they were into scarification, that they gave themselves homemade tattoos with India ink and sewing needles, that they hated their parents, that they lived at the food court of the mall—all this ugliness was not reflected in the popular culture aimed at them. *Seventeen* was for twelve-year-olds; New Kids on the Block was for ten-year-olds; John Hughes had abandoned Molly Ringwald for Macaulay Culkin; and exactly *who* were all those people buying all those Tiffany albums? Now and again there were movies like *Heathers* or *Mystic Pizza* or *Sid and Nancy,* and if you lived in a big city or college town there might be a radio station that played Minor Threat or Green River or something other than pedophile Michael Jackson, but "alternative" did not yet exist as a noncategory catchall, much less as an entire culture. Archie comics were starting to seem more realistic than most of what was coming at the typical teen.

So sometime in the early nineties, the girls all by themselves, with no assistance from any international conglomerates, invented the Riot Girl movement, starting punk-rock bands and fanzines in suburban garages and rec rooms just like boys used to do, linking up with other girls in disparate cities like Washington, D.C., and Vancouver and Olympia and Toronto through Internet chat rooms and newsletters. And they forged a manifesto, a two-page document that declares, "We seek to create revolution in our own lives every day by envisioning and creating alternatives to the bullshit christian capitalist way of doing things." Indeed the drafters of this manifesto had read Carol Gilligan and Lyn Mikel Brown's book and urged their constituents to "resist psychic death," to "cry in public" and to plan for the day when "girls rule all towns," when "all girls [are] in bands." And in zines like *Chainsaw* and *Girl Germs* they wrote about why they loved Kristy McNichol and why they hated *Twin Peaks* and how even though they were just teenagers, they knew enough to tell that Gloria Steinem's *Revolution from Within* was completely dopey and had nothing to say to them. And they made their own tapes and put together their own tours, started their own labels like K Records with bands like Bratmobile and Huggy Bear and Bikini Kill, which were great even if they couldn't play for shit. And they called what they were doing "revolution grrrl style." And they sang about how just because you want to get laid doesn't mean you want to get raped, and they were fun and feminist at the same time.

And eventually, this little movement became part of a big huge deal, as Debbie Gibson was replaced by Tori Amos and the Breeders and Hole and Veruca Salt and Liz Phair. And even the boy bands weren't presumed woman haters anymore, especially when the leader of the biggest boy band of all, Kurt Cobain, married Courtney Love—and not a more traditional rocker wife like Angie Everhart or Naomi Campbell—and even carried the couple's baby around in a Snugli, and was known to wear the occasional dress. (Kurt even admitted he got the name for Nirvana's biggest hit after Tobi Vail, his then girlfriend and Bikini Kill drummer, spray-painted a bathroom wall at Evergreen State College with the words "Kurt Cobain smells like Teen Spirit.") Clearly, Axl Rose was not the only kind of rock star out there anymore. *Sassy,* which for a while was the cool alternative to *Seventeen,* had a column called "Cute Band Alert," and now those slouchy gorgeous boys like Evan Dando from the Lemonheads and Steve Malkmus from Pavement became sex symbols of substance. And instead of *The Facts of Life* there was *My So-Called Life,* which got canceled but even still, and *Clueless* was sweet without being stupid, and *The Craft* was sweet even if it was about teenage witches, and *Welcome to the Dollhouse* was definitely not sweet but it had a strong enough impact to get beyond the art house and into the occasional multiplex. And in short order, Jennifer Capriati and Tonya Harding went nuts or went psycho and Lorena Bobbitt wasn't convicted and Sharon Stone and Shannen Doherty became role models. And Alanis Morissette made it seem like a good idea to root for the Glenn Close character in *Fatal Attraction* after all, and a world that had been so resistant to all that Amy Fisher was, now that she was in jail, was starting to look like one she could have lived in.

Meanwhile, in the Albion State Correctional Center, Amy has received more than twenty disciplinary citations, and has even been found guilty of sexually harassing a guard. Which, I'm sure the Riot Girls would agree, means she must be doing something right.

*   *   *

On 10 December 1996, after serving four years in prison for first-degree assault with a .25 caliber handgun, Amy Fisher was denied parole by the state board in Albany, New York, on the grounds that "there is a reasonable probability that [Ms. Fisher] would not live and remain at liberty without violating the law, and her release at this time is incompatible with the welfare and safety of the community." The board also criticized Amy's decision to leave the crime scene without calling for help for Mary Jo, opting instead to return home to wash off the blood. "Your pattern of intention and the severity of your criminal act coupled with your lack of insight into your criminality do make your discretionary release not appropriate at this time," the parole report said, addressing Amy.

Nowhere in these written conclusions, however, was Amy Fisher ever referred to as a "wild animal."

According to the Justice Department, the United States prison population consisted of 1,182,000 inmates by the end of 1996, more than double what it was in 1985. This increase was attributed to the conviction and incarceration of more black drug offenders and more white violent criminals. While the length of sentences has not increased, the likelihood of paroling prisoners has decreased—though I doubt this reflects a sudden new trend among assailants to flee a crime scene without calling an ambulance first. The habit of running to scrub the blood from your hands is, I believe, time-honored.

Federal prisons now operate at a 25 percent rate of overcrowding; state prisons, like the one Amy Fisher is in, have a population excess of only 16–24 percent. Our penal system is one of the only government-sponsored growth industries left; states like Missouri that lack the capacity to hold all its convicts have been known to contract them out to private, for-profit jailers in states like Texas, where patrolmen fired by local sheriffs and police departments for excessively violent behavior and the like can find employment and have been known—as was captured on videotape proudly recorded for training purposes—to beat their charges with stun guns and fire hoses, have them slither across the floor naked while guard dogs bite them and spray them with pepper when it's all over.

Amy Fisher will next become eligible for parole in June 1999.

The Buttafuocos now live in California.

* * *

Here's the real Amy Fisher story, the way it should have been:

This is about a girl who is shaggy and small, hair in her eyes—you just kind of know, you can imagine, that her mother is always pushing it behind her ears or trying to get her to put it up. And that's probably Amy in a nutshell: solidly defiant, but up until Joey, it was probably pretty innocuous, hair on her face, clouds in her eyes.

When Amy met Joey she thought he was cool. If she had followed the college-bound course she was meant to—85 percent of the graduates of John F. Kennedy High School attend four-year institutions (and I don't mean jail)—then in ten years, she'd have thought he was gross, a terrifically recherché relic of days gone by, she'd have looked at him the way Stephanie in *Saturday Night Fever* looks at Tony Manero— with a twinge, with a sigh, and finally with a sense of relief that she got out, that 2001 on the weekend is not what she lives for, that the back seat of a car is a place for passengers and not for sex, that she became a grown-up.

This ought to have been a story of the road not taken, of the crush Amy had on the guy who fixed her cars, the white 1989 Dodge Daytona which was later replaced—in one of those moments when life offers symbolic justice that is almost literary—with a black 1991 Chrysler LeBaron once it was totaled, in one of those many accident situations that seemed as much a part of Amy's dazy dopey adolescent days as, say, the four major food groups or a toothbrush are to other people. This could have been a distracted driver in disarray, the kind who would still have to bring her car in on college vacations for a tune-up here, a dent there, who would always make Joey Buttafuoco smile when she turned up in December or May, the unspoken frisson always there, never spoken, never certain.

This is the story of a girl and her car because that is what it would be had Amy taken the road she did not take. Because really I don't think she wanted Joey or Paul or Rob or any of the boys she turns to like they're salvation, like they are mighty as Michelangelo's *David*. I think she wanted out. I think she wanted to drive as far and as fast as a Bruce Springsteen song, to run like hell from herself and her life, to let's get lost. I think she wanted speed, absolutely elsewhere, to escape the depression that she describes as hanging with her from the time she was a little girl: "Dread is what I feel upon awakening," she recalls early in *My Story*. "Sadness has me inside of it. It's like a big tub of water I'll never get out of. It's not fair to wake up, six years old, and feel like that." This is the story of a girl who wants so badly to be free that she finally ends up in jail, doing five-to-fifteen, dreaming not of boys, not of lovers, but of Ferraris.

This is the story of a girl who pretty much just wants what boys are guaranteed as their birthright—to go out there and hunt and make claims and take lovers and take chances and take in and take off and take out and say gimme gimme gimme and never once be told that a lady must wait and all that stuff.

See, if Amy had really listened to her own desires, had really tried to know what she knows, all her energy would have been focused with the precision of an electron microscope on that great big open vista, that forward trajectory, the place anywhere on earth that even an American-made car will take you to, and the place beyond that, the place where Emily Dickinson, who never left Amherst, could be transported to in the comfort of her own mind, the place she described with the line "There is no Frigate like a Book."

You can drive forever and never find that cool calm, but the chances are certainly a lot better than if you're fucking a thirty-seven-year-old married man with herpes and a funny name, in a little apartment above the garage, the kind of place where men keep their etchings, the kind of claustrophobic setup that is so enclosed that you don't even notice that you're always having sex during the gray of afternoon—the adulterous hour—never in the black of night or the sunny bright of first thing in the morning, never when people who are not in illicit liaisons manage to do it.

Look, a girl can get in trouble anywhere. But a car, even on Dead Man's Curve, even on a very dangerous road, will take you a lot further than a man. And when the time is right, if it comes to that, you can drive that car into a garage, turn on the engine, feel the air fill with carbon monoxide, feel the onset of asphyxia, feel your breathing slow, feel your body stop feeling, feel the only real freedom you will ever know.

PART THREE

There She Goes Again

I want to be the girl with the most cake
I love him so much it just turns to hate
I fake it so real I am beyond fake
Someday you will ache like I ache

COURTNEY LOVE
"Doll Parts"

The calm before the storm: most of us understand this reference to the peaceful, dark gray of the sky in the moments preceding thunder crack and lightning bolt and a cloudburst of torrents of rain as meteorology's metaphor for the way that when things seem the most stable and contained, it is often just a decoy for disaster, a respite nature grants as a cruel joke before a big huge mess, before the hangman shows up, before the bomb drops, before really bad things start to happen.

This simple and commonplace expression, the kind busy people use to describe a rare period of downtime, the kind of saying that seems so obvious, that reminds us to trust the silences no more than we trust the noise, that makes note of the way the signals we receive are often counterintuitive, that tells us not to get too comfortable with our assumptions—this stupid expression about the weather whose meaning and implications I never gave any thought to at all—suddenly struck me as rich and resonant when I realized it is completely wasted on friends and relatives of suicides.

It seems like every suicide was healthy, happy, sane and sanguine—

a few problems, nothing serious—at least as far as the mourners are concerned.

Consider the case of Margaux Hemingway, a former model and failed actress, who, at the age of forty-one, on 28 June 1996, died in her studio apartment in Santa Monica, her body bloated beyond recognition, her hands folded over her nightgown as she lay tidily on her bed, her position that of a corpse in a coffin. The news of Hemingway's passing was mentioned on television bulletins or in wire-service stories in the newspaper almost as an afterthought, more a confirmation than an announcement. It was as if to say that if you wondered what had happened to that Idaho-fresh pretty girl with big bones and baby blues and bushy brows and that whole seventies outdoorsy glamour thing, the one who appeared in a movie called *Lipstick* and seemed to be recovering from the humiliation ever since—if you wondered what happened to her and occasionally thought that she might be dead, then it turns out that you were right.

None of these early reports mentioned the cause of death, which was not to be determined by the Los Angeles County coroner—chastened to caution by the public relations fiasco of the O.J. trial—for seven more weeks. But even without the benefit of the autopsy report, it seemed obvious that this was a suicide: relying on only the meager details about Hemingway obtained through media osmosis, through a fame that had become as indelible and unnoticeable as invisible ink, I knew that nothing about Margaux's situation—nothing about being a woman in your forties living alone in one room without a view—sounded especially happy.

I remembered Margaux Hemingway as a thing of beauty, the model graced with a million-dollar contract—unheard of in 1975—to be the face of a fragrance called Babe, created by a company called Fabergé, in what seemed like an effort at forging a female counterpart to Joe Namath's success as spokesman for an aftershave called Brut. I could envision the famous photograph taken of Margaux at Studio 54, appearing—either by design or by default—as the quintessential Quaalude casualty, a picture-perfect depiction of disco decadence with the spaghetti strap of her camisole insouciantly and sloppily slipped over her shoulder, her left nipple bared, her spaciness outspaced only by the blank stare of her kid sister Mariel in the background. (It is this

picture of these two granddaughters of a Nobel Prize–winning author—along with the alleged careers of Sofia Coppola, Julian Lennon,
Ashley Hamilton, Zoe Cassavetes, Charlie Sheen, the Phillips sisters
Mackenzie, Chynna and Bijou, and the Wilson girls Carnie and
Wendy—that makes me wonder why famous people continue to
breed.) I could recall images of Margaux on the cover of *Time* and
Vogue and *Harper's Bazaar* as the model of modern American beauty,
the inside pages of her fashion spreads and face shots that frame her as
the first supermodel: I'd seen them all in the dentist's waiting room
during my prepubescent cavity-prone years, and they came back to me
after her death as recovered memories that were not false so much as
vague. But the images were vivid enough to remind me that for Margaux to have been in that glossy, glittery place—sheltered by the
sweet, slippery safety that success at a young age secures for you when
you are too busy to want it, and snatches away from you when you
are finally desperate enough to need it—and now have her life, at
forty-one, enclosed into one small room, was a sure sign of suicide.

I didn't, when I heard those first news reports, know the gory details, the twenty-eight-day detox at Betty Ford, the subsequent stay at
a private clinic in Twin Falls, Idaho, or the fact that her death was a
day shy of the thirty-fifth anniversary of her grandfather Ernest's suicide via Abercrombie & Fitch shotgun. I didn't know about the failed
marriages, the declared bankruptcy in 1991 with debts of $815,900
and assets totaling $6,795. I didn't know about the posing in *Playboy*,
the infomercials, the Psychic Friends' Network endorsements, the public claim that her grandfather molested her and the resultant estrange-
ment from her family. I didn't know that she had changed the spelling
of her name, née Margot, to the more exotic x-variation, chosen for
the wine her parents drank the night she was conceived, and I did not
yet know that she had been named for Margot Macomber, a character
of Papa Hemingway's invention blessed with a face "so perfect that
you expected her to be stupid." I didn't know that she dropped out of
high school, that the only real job she'd ever held involved doing
publicity for Evel Knievel, or that her first husband picked her up in
the Palm Court at the Plaza Hotel on her first day in New York when
she was just nineteen. I didn't know that she had to lose forty pounds
to be a model, that she did a half-hour television show for the BBC in

which all she did was talk to Lynn Redgrave about her struggle with bulimia, that she was traumatized by a skiing accident that caused her to gain seventy-five pounds from immobility. I didn't know all the New Age nonsense, that she consulted with a Cheyenne medicine man, that she learned the art of shamanism from the Northwest Coast Indians, that she studied the philosophy of the Hawaiian kahunas, that she hoped a chiropractor might cure her epilepsy, or that she ended up in jail in India for reasons that are unclear while on a trip to visit holy sites. I did not know that at her funeral, held at something called the Agape Church of Religious Science, an ex-boyfriend said, "I feel her, you feel her, she's in the wind." I did not know that she'd moved into the apartment that she chose to die in less than a month before, that the boxes were still unpacked. I did not know all the other pieces that make this seem like a life worth interrupting.

I did not yet know that Margaux felt like nothing, and she was nothing. Nothing but a great beauty, and one who had, by most accounts, through the ravages of alcohol and time, completely lost her looks. But never mind that, because at one time she *had* been a great beauty, and even then that was not worth much. Beauty is not, after all, worth anything more than beauty: it did not mean she could act, dance or sing, and in spite of her literary heritage, it did not mean she could write, think critically or even think at all. "She thought they were going to have a creative marriage, like Jean-Paul Goude and Grace Jones," a friend said of Margaux's second attempt at matrimony—to a man from Venezuela who lived in France—which pretty much proves my point: only an idiot would see Goude and Jones as a paradigm of creativity or anything else.

But we valorize beauty so highly, we believe in it, we revere it, we have given supermodels more space in the public pantheon than we afford to just about anyone else who does just about anything else for a living. What was once a rough trade of underpaid girls in overpriced *schmattes* has gleaned a professional sheen enticing enough that Elite Model Management—in a reversal of the usual flow of talent—now has a division for actresses who want to model (it represents, among others, Drew Barrymore, Ashley Judd, Ivanka Trump and Nastassia Kinski). Beauty is so powerful to us that we forget that it is only what it is, it is its own closed system, open it up and it contains nothing, it signifies nothing and it implies nothing other than the premium of pleasure that beauty itself provides: it does not bestow goodness or braininess or anything more, and yet the omnipotence of beauty by itself is enough to make it perhaps the most desirable asset in God's creation. Other heritable attributes, like intelligence or talent, can be a passport for a simple soul into an exceptional life, into premature fame or fortune for which, by definition, no one can ever be adequately prepared. But smarts and chops are more than skin deep, they are an inner resource, they demand motion and motivation, while modeling asks for stillness and static. Of all the assets that can take a girl away from her hometown, beauty is the most dangerous, the desire it inspires seems to entitle people to abuse it, the luckiness we attribute to the beautiful people makes us feel just fine about anything we might do to them—they *must* be immune to heartbreak, they *must* be impervious to pain. (So entrenched is the collective sense that those gifted with good looks lead carefree lives of no consequence that even as I defend the feelings of a supermodel, I have trouble believing that what I am saying is true.) "Don't hate me because I'm beautiful," Kelly LeBrock coos in Pantene commercials, which I'm sure makes many people want to ask, *Why the fuck not?!* If beauty can excite love, then it can also incite hate. (In LeBrock's case, it ought to elicit our pity: until recently, she was married to Steven Seagal.) "Only God, my dear, / Could love you for yourself alone / And not your yellow hair," W. B. Yeats wrote in "For Anne Gregory," a poem that omits its implied inverse, that neither God nor any man could love her *without* her buttercup-bright tresses. (The corn-silk mane as an ideal of beauty has become such a resonant metonymy for all that is oppressive in our culture that when Whoopi Goldberg did her one-woman show on Broadway many years ago, her today-I'm-gonna-be-a-white-girl routine entailed little more than draping a towel over her head and asking the audience to admire her "beautiful blonde locks.")

In the movie *Wolf,* Jack Nicholson plays a polite editor forced into one frustrating situation after another with a chilly, unpleasant Michelle Pfeiffer, cast as a spoiled heiress who cops a streetwise attitude that Nicholson finds simply insufferable. "I think I understand what you're like now," he says, exasperated after one affront too many. "You're very beautiful and you think men are only interested in you because you're beautiful. But you want them to be interested in you because you're *you*. The problem is, aside from all that beauty, you're not very interesting: you're rude, you're hostile, you're sullen, you're withdrawn. I know: you want someone to look past all that, at the real person underneath. But the only reason anyone would bother to look past all that is because you're beautiful. It's ironic, isn't it? In an odd way, you're your own problem."

Margaux Hemingway seems to have spent the last twenty years thinking that she should have been able to do something with herself because she was beautiful, when in truth, on the evidence, she was capable of absolutely nothing. Here was a simple girl, who should have led the simple Idaho fishergirl's life and found some version of the happiness to which we entitle most Americans, and which most seem to accept. Beauty carried her away from her Idaho home, and by the time the good looks had taken their leave, Margaux could not find her way back. "She was just a gentle soul who got lost in fame and fortune," her friend, chiropractor Caren Elin, said.

So she retreated to that refuge for the dull-witted, the world of New Age therapy, a brain-dead insult to the very Native American culture it is supposed to revere, and she found herself saying things like, as she told *People* in 1994, "I needed to go inside and clear the blockages, because nothing was coming to me, no jobs, no work."

She thought the problem was "blockages."

In August 1996, nearly two months after Margaux Hemingway's life-drained, lifeless body had been discovered, the Los Angeles County coroner reported that she had died from a deliberate overdose of phenobarbital, a sedative and occasional epilepsy treatment that also happens to be one of the few orally imbibed drugs that—when taken in excess—can be relied upon to induce death, and not just coma or vomiting or a cry for help. In fact, phenobarbital is so dependable that it was also used in the mass suicide of the Heaven's Gate cult less than a year later with a 100 percent rate of effectiveness. Nevertheless, when Margaux's friends and family were faced with such irrefutable evidence of her desire to die, they seemed to think there must have been some clerical or bureaucratic error. They, too, seemed to think the problem was "blockages."

"If she were going to commit suicide, everyone would have

known," her sister, occasional actress Mariel Hemingway, told *Vogue,* rejecting the autopsy report. "She would have made a big flipping deal about it. I don't even mean that as a bad thing, but she let people know. She was not suicidal at all. She was never in a better place in her life. She was physically in great shape and getting herself together mentally. She was only going forward."

"At any other time in her life, it wouldn't have been so shocking," Mariel's husband, Steve Crisman, concurred in *People,* pointing out that Margaux had been very involved with yoga and meditation. "This was the best I'd seen her in years. She had gotten herself back together."

"No matter what the coroner finds, it's a mystery," said Stuart Sundlun, an ex-boyfriend, in *Vogue,* denying the possibility of suicide because Margaux had made doctor's appointments for the coming weeks, and besides, "She would have left a note."

"Her career was coming into fruition, she looked amazing," added her friend Gigi Gaston, though the only evidence she gave of Margaux' booming career was Gaston's own desire to write a script with her.

As for whatever sense of peaceful well-being Margaux might have projected at the end of her life, while living in a single monastic room with unpacked boxes—cartons conveniently ready to go, a courteous act typical of suicides—I can only say: *the calm before the storm.*

Caren Elin, the chiropractor, might have been the only one to sense a serious problem, and that was only because it had literally been spelled out for her when, on the day of her death, Margaux Hemingway left Elin a message that was transcribed onto her pager. It was just two words: *help me.*

* * *

With the possible exception of Kurt Cobain—who was surrounded by too many people who were too fucked up to stick to any kind of party line and who was just too florid and exultant in the pursuit of his own demise for any pretense of life-love to be presented—it's hard for me to think of any recent famous suicide who was not, for the record, completely happy, healthy and sane at the time of his death.

It was an accident; she just slipped; he lost control; these sound like excuses for domestic violence used on a triage nurse at the ER. Everyone falls; no one jumps. In fact, Gloria Vanderbilt maintains that her son Carter Cooper toppled off a roof because the medication he was taking made him dizzy. Had he been a government official, by now a theory would be making its way through the Internet about how he didn't jump or fall—he was *pushed,* with evidence of an FBI cover-up of a CIA fuck-up vis-à-vis campaign contributions from Maoist Chinese factions and a paper shredder full of documents to follow. Or something like that. The White House, particularly Hillary Clinton, did such a good job of convincing people that Vince Foster was delirious with delight in his Washington post—save for some nastiness from those John Birchers at *The Wall Street Journal*—that his decision to go to Fort Marcy Park and shoot himself in the head was instantly fraught with suspicion and intrigue and doubt. "Of a thousand people, of those who *might* commit suicide, I would never pick Vince," the First Lady was said to have declared, according to *The New York Times* columnist Frank Rich. Even after Whitewater special prosecutor Kenneth Starr declared Foster's death an unequivocal suicide, the conservative lunatic fringe continued to play on-line sleuth. Christopher Ruddy, a journalist fired by the *New York Post* for refusing to abandon his Foster conspiracy theories, has since found employment at the ultraconservative *Pittsburgh Tribune-Review,* and has managed to turn his inquiry into the lonesome last moments of a depressed and despondent attorney into a book-length account called *The Strange Death of Vincent Foster* (which, amazingly, was published by the Free Press—definitely a haven for right-wingers, but probably not the kind of place that would publish *The Turner Diaries* or, I'd have thought, one man's obsessive fantasy of government cabals).

Even Sylvia Plath, whose suicide had a certain poetic inevitability, has been portrayed as one hoping to be saved: British writer and literary critic A. Alvarez posited in *The Savage God,* his 1971 study of suicide, that Plath expected her course of death to be disrupted by the arrival of an au pair girl, a rescue that did not come off when the gas from the oven that killed Plath also drugged her neighbor downstairs, so that no one was conscious enough to get the door.

But beyond the world of bitter fame, in every encounter I've ever

had with a person who was close to a suicide—particularly when the
method was ambiguous, a drug overdose that could be construed as
accidental—that person always insists, police report or coroner's conclusion to the contrary, that the death was definitely a mistake, the girl
obviously botched up her tranquilizer dosage, she was doing so well,
she had finally made a turnaround, the new medication seemed to
really be working, she had just bought a ticket to Venice for the Bien-
niale, she was coming to lunch on Saturday, she had paid off her
American Express bill, we were going to get our nails done on Sunday:
she was doing fine.

The main thing those close to suicides want to make clear is that she
was doing just fine.

I don't think that this is just a way to get themselves off the hook, to
claim that they did not come running because there was nothing
wrong. Frankly, if they offered these upbeat reports on the end of days
because they wanted to shirk responsibility and stave off blame and
make themselves feel less guilty, it might be an improvement over the
emotional fallacy that they are in fact committing: these claims of the
happy, healthy suicide show a lack of insight into the human condition, an inability to see that when you decide you are going to end it
all, the relief brings a reprieve to your suffering for the remainder of
your days, and you will be cheerful—gladdened, as no one else is, by
the thought that the light at the end of the tunnel *is* the oncoming
train. Knowing that you have finally found a solution to your suffer-
ings—knowing that after the uselessness of est, of psychoanalysis, of
behavior modification, of Anthony Robbins, of chakras, of crystals, of
herbs, of Prozac, of Ritalin, of Valium, of Librium, of lithium, of
drinking Blue Nun for breakfast, of recreational heroin use, of addictive heroin use, of AA, of NA, of Zen Buddhism, of graduate school,
of meditation, of primal screams, of Dr. Laura, of Deepak Chopra, of
plain old psychodynamic therapy—knowing that this fatiguing and
futile search has finally yielded the resignation of failure, you will most
likely at long last be in good spirits. The big sleep is a big reward.

That is why the most difficult, histrionic hysterics in life can become
models of efficiency in death, assuming an air of clear-eyed order of
the variety that makes people say, If only they had tended to their lives
with such care, they could have been happy—completely obscuring

the fact that, obviously, they *just couldn't.* It's like thinking a disastrously failed marriage can be saved just because the couple got along well for a weekend in St. Barts. For successful suicides, the death wish and its execution allows a refuge of reason that is not applicable to any other areas of endeavor. "Dying / Is an art, like everything else / I do it exceptionally well," Sylvia Plath wrote in "Lady Lazarus," a poem concerned with resurrection. "I guess you can say I've a call." Despite the claim to dying "exceptionally well," Plath did not have the foresight to put her papers in order (more evidence for partisans of the rescue theory) before her suicide in 1963, which is why her sister-in-law Olwyn Hughes, whom she didn't much care for, ended up in charge of her posthumous career. This lesson was not lost on Anne Sexton, who attempted to kill herself nine times before getting it right, and complained to her psychiatrist that Plath's suicide "took something that was mine—*that* death was mine!" In anticipation of her 1974 self-asphyxiation, Sexton made up a will, appointed her daughter Linda literary executor, prepared a folder with detailed funeral instructions, and settled her affairs. The tidiness of a planned death has even found its way into fiction, with Edith Wharton's talent for the telling detail on display at the end of *The House of Mirth,* in the aftermath of tragic beauty Lily Bart's fatal overdose of a soporific called "chloral": when Lily's thwarted lover, Lawrence Selden, goes to her rooming-house digs to sort through her things, steeling himself for a disarray of debts, "[t]o his surprise he found that all the bills were receipted; there was not an unpaid account among them."

Unlike those who use suicide attempts as cries for help, those who are serious will do all that they can to conceal their intentions from anyone who might get in the way. They will buy plane tickets they never plan to use, make leg-waxing appointments set for dates long after rigor mortis will have set in, and enroll in courses on flower arranging that have nothing to do with pushing up the daisies. They will not, as Mariel Hemingway believes, "make a big flipping deal about it."

For the first time in their lives, they will be discreet, subdued—they will be fine.

In some ways, the nonsuicidal cannot be blamed, and may even deserve commendation, for not understanding the mind-set of one who has abandoned all hope, of one who has made a commitment to death. None of us intent on living knows what it's like on the other side of the proverbial little-tugboat-that-could that pushes us all along, that creates an expanse of optimism, a hope against hope, and provides a buffer against self-destruction that is so sturdy that even the most depressed and most cynical people are usually cushioned against any final gestures of ending it all. Almost everybody is holding out, often idiotically, for that 0.001 percent chance that things will get better, a belief so pervasive it must be genetically coded, or else many more people waiting for Prozac to work or waiting for the delirium tremens to subside would be found with a finger on the trigger and a gun to the temple. Most of us, embarrassingly enough, actually *want* to live, have a rage to live, and we don't know the pandect of the would-be dead, can't understand the counterlogic of their behavior.

"Suicides have a special language," Anne Sexton wrote in "Wanting to Die." "Like carpenters they want to know *which tools.* / They never ask *why build.*" If suicide is governed by its own laws and logic, the response to suicide has also been codified, the Talmudic twists of human behavior after such a death made practically predictable by sheer repetition, the contentious response of family members, the disputed cause of death, the stupid and crass things people say because they don't know better: all of these reactions follow a pattern as certain, and as indecipherable, as the flight formations of birds.

My guess is that Margaux Hemingway's passing will be recorded as the death at a young age of an aging beauty, it will be entered into whatever cultural logbook it is that lists similar casualties of too much too soon or too little too late, that lists the self-destructed geniuses of jazz and philosophy and jive and poetry, that lists the mad scientists and dissipated drunkards and vein-dead junkies and survivors of Auschwitz who could stand the world no longer and fashion models who didn't know enough of the world to begin with. In the shorthand of this suicide sign-in sheet there might be mention that the cause of death is "disputed" or "denied," but there is no room for the mythologies that accompany the premature, premeditated death of any famous person, long the province of book-length studies and doctoral dissertations.

And such detailed biographical analyses are themselves likely to be disputed or denied once the author's worldview falls from favor. The lives of the dead are retroactively subject to change as the ideology of the times changes, so that a "difficult woman" can be reconstructed as a "misunderstood perfectionist," and a "dumb blonde with big boobs and small talent" can be transformed into a "victim of the patriarchy," and a "sensitive artist" can suddenly be downgraded into a "psychotic nutcase." Every suicide, even in private life, gets this speculative treatment, note or no note, since nothing can possibly satisfy the search for meaning in a gesture stemmed in frustration. Suicide, like death itself, is of necessity not a coherent construct to anyone still living.

But a beautiful woman, especially one who fashions intrigue in such a way that she mixes mystery and access just so and becomes an icon in her lifetime, a living screen on which people project their fantasies about womanhood, femininity, art, insanity—a Rorschach test so convincing everyone believes that he alone sees the inkblot the right way—can become a monument to such a variety of meanings—to meaning itself—in the afterlife. Since suicide is often the act of a person who feels dehumanized and objectified, it seems a cruel irony that this self-inflicted death is likely to increase our tendency to view the buried woman as a symbol of whatever ills of society helped to construct the hothouse in which her personal woes flourished. As film critic Molly Haskell points out in her feminist exegesis *From Reverence to Rape,* a movie star's suicide "casts a retrospective light on her life. Her 'ending' gives her a beginning and a middle, turns her into a work of art with a message and a meaning." Death seems like an inflated price to pay for respect and integrity, but remember that until she killed herself, Marilyn Monroe was laughable—a luscious, lusty Hollywood parfait, her body parts viewed as much greater than her whole. The posthumous "discovery" of Marilyn's untapped, unappreciated talent—her revision as feminist icon, as victim of a misogynistic, male-dominated system—which would seem to be a sign of progress is really just craven, cheap and self-serving—compensation for exploitation with more exploitation. It's easy to mourn the dead, but it's hard to help the living.

Even Margaux Hemingway, in her blank beauty and in her failure to have a life that meant much of anything, will eventually have those fragments subjected to a coherent narrative: someone will find a message in her death, and, absurdly, a purpose to her life, unconcerned by the fact that if Hemingway could not feel and believe in it with enough conviction to stay alive, it would do her more honor to just accept this assessment and let it be. It is a little-known detail of Margaux's life that her failed performance in *Lipstick,* one of the big-budget, big-gobble true turkeys that the motion-picture industry occasionally likes to grace us with—Anne Bancroft in this movie is even more shameful than Laurence Olivier in *The Betsy*—has been redeemed by some with time. Her character's assumption of vigilante justice—when the law won't punish a rapist because he was not a stranger to his victims, Margaux gets him with her very own gun—has been belatedly recognized by feminists as the first example of the avenging female heroine: Margaux as a girl with good aim in *Lipstick* could be the prototype for roles that would crystallize in more critically and commercially successful films like *Thelma & Louise, Terminator 2* and *The Long Kiss Goodnight.*

It is also a barely recalled footnote to Margaux's life—a detail that would merit a complete chapter in anyone else's—that legislation in the state of California that was passed to make it easier to convict those accused of "acquaintance" or "date" rape was named for Ms. Hemingway. This previously unacknowledged crime—which was used in *Lipstick* strictly for titillation purposes; like most Dino De Laurentiis movies this one was not an attempt at consciousness raising—accidentally and ultimately made its star a martyr. And perhaps, one could argue, it was *Lipstick,* not Women's Studies 101, that served as the most potent weapon for imposing certain parts of the feminist agenda on a mostly apolitical public.

In time, Margaux's friends and family could take this shred of a thread and try to find in it some real moral fiber. They might try to make it seem as if Margaux had planned it this way all along. They could point to a California law that bears her name and insist that she was a feminist force. They could pretend not to notice that most of her life was whatever she stumbled upon—she was conscripted into her modeling career, it was not some Cindy Crawford-style scheme—which is how it is when you spend most of your life loaded. They could let the waste of it all speak for itself: they could see that the true life story is almost always more poignant than the ordained narrative. Or they could try to find reason in her life, pretend Jean-Paul Sartre had never invented Existentialism, had never explained the nauseating emptiness inside every being, this big hollow that all of us fight so hard against, wrestling with a phantom because it is all we can do to make this big nothing bearable. But suicides are the people who have given up the battle: they deny reason. They are tired and they want to go to sleep.

And no one else can leave it at that. Suicide has a cult following: the fan club of self-destruction resulted in the 1981 *Rolling Stone* cover of Jim Morrison in one of his famous lizard-king, enlightened-savage poses with a caption that read, "He's Hot. He's Sexy. And He's Dead." Whatever strange and fanatical response the men who died too young inspire, the books on Jim, Jimi, James and Kurt combined don't come close to the amount of literature that is devoted to reinventing, reassessing, and redeeming Marilyn. Add Sylvia, Anne and Janis to the list and the library almost doubles. As interesting as these women— gifted with the force and talent and beauty to turn their emotional disasters and chronic hysteria into performance art—were in their short lives, there is no way they could have anticipated the sweet hereafter. These women, rich with interpretive possibility, become mental-health pornography once dead.

*   *   *

Madness has always had great visuals, its ugly affliction often creating a freakish beauty when it preys upon and plays upon the young and lovely and charmed and blessed, inflicting the bipolar image of the female grotesque: the luminosity of beauty is matched only by the stupefaction of insanity, the opaque eyesore of sadness and despondency, a mixture of prettiness and pollution so striking and inexplicable that it is as hypnotic and paralyzing as a skyscraper burning down, so strange that mystification becomes inevitable.

Logic would seem to dictate that there could be nothing comely or charismatic about a woman in extremis, mid-breakdown, caught in an emotional car wreck, but the illogic of fact has made the history of beautiful women coextensive with the history of miserable, depressed women. Certainly, most men will insist that nothing is less alluring than a woman in a straitjacket—even a very beautiful woman is just a lunatic at that point, insanity acting as the great leveler—and the seizures, vomiting, drooling, tics and assorted side effects of Haldol and other medications are a putrid sight on a pretty face, an anaphrodisiac. The first mention of a woman beset by sorrow concerns the matriarch Leah, in the book of Genesis, and a presumption of beauty deficiency has become her unfortunate legacy. The text refers to Leah as "tender-eyed," which is interpreted as an idiom for lachrymose, since the Bible never concerns itself with ophthalmology unless it is to point out that someone is completely blind. Because of her sorry disposition, Leah is thought to be unattractive; because Jacob was in love with her younger sister Rachel, but was forced to marry Leah—by a ruse pulled by the girls' father to ensure that his elder daughter was wed first—Leah is thought to be pitiful. But in spite of this particular indignity—not merely a mercy fuck but a mercy marriage, one so steeped into Jewish traditional memory that in Orthodox weddings the bride always wears a veil across her face, which she pulls back before the end of the ceremony to prove that she is "Rachel" and not, heaven forfend, the undesirable "Leah"—nowhere in the text does it describe Leah as ugly or even homely or plain. And yet lack of looks seems to be the aspersion cast upon this older sister over time, as if the only explanation for her depression or downbound spirits was a failure to attract suitors—as if unhappiness were an affliction of the unbeautiful. Yet despite the popular axiom that beauty = happiness, ugliness = misery, both the cinematic treatment and the cultural mythology of the madwoman and the sad woman have almost invariably turned her into a sex object, a dead and voluptuous artifact of some misunderstood other time, a creature whose tragedy is not that she was in pain, not that she was gifted, not that she was mistreated, but rather that she was an exquisite bauble that the world destroyed.

I have always found the gargantuan dichotomy between what we find sexually arousing in the abstract and who we actually want to sleep with to be, frankly, frightening—and I assume this gap will only grow as time and technology make all sorts of fantasy lives possible and accessible. I find this particularly disturbing when the persona of the depressed woman is involved, because in real life, while plenty of men have a Jesus complex and want desperately to rescue the sad-eyed lady of the lowlands immortalized in song, for the most part most guys who are emotionally stable enough to actually be purposefully involved with a woman breaking down have the good sense just to keep away. Most guys do not want to get involved with a girl on fire—the ones who do seem only to want to add fuel to the flames, but very few seem interested in finding a bucket of water. Relationships as therapy are rare, and yet the romantic possibilities are such that they are constantly dangled before us in popular culture as a rather wistful, visible temptation—love as refuge from a world gone mad in *Hiroshima, Mon Amour;* love as refuge from a world so false in *sex, lies, & videotape;* love as refuge *for* madness itself in *Sid and Nancy.*

In the Jean-Jacques Beineix film *Betty Blue,* the sexy and seductive fleshpot of the title—played with French exoticism and zaftig ease by Béatrice Dalle—makes her way through a hysterical crack-up, a natural disaster of the mind that blows through her with the amorality of a dust bowl, brutal and fatal without even meaning it. The breakdown is manifested by inexplicable, almost whimsical episodes of violence and self-destruction—the kind that make people around her say, *But a minute ago she seemed just fine*—that escalate in severity, until, finally, Betty picks up a scissors and pokes out her right eye. By the end of the movie, she is buckled down, bandaged up and shrouded in white sheets in an insane asylum, her beauty useless, her condition repellent.

But this ultimate ugliness does not nullify the film's overall effect, its illustration of the reigning attraction of the madwoman. Up until the lockup, and until her final destruction, Betty is a force who keeps her lover Zorg—a hapless nice guy, a housepainter she tries to turn into an author, a man who has no idea what to make of Betty—and everyone in the movie, and everyone in the movie theater watching, in her complete thrall. The film has such a relentless and overwhelming feel, Betty's personality seems to demolish and dominate everything in her wake, that it starts to seem perfectly possible that the whole world is being held hostage to this woman's moods and turns—even if it is just a movie. I know plenty of people who walked out of *Betty Blue,* or just plain hated it, resenting its reverent, adoring, painstaking attention to a woman they saw as an immature, indulged nutcase. But people who like it love it, and watch, fascinated, as Betty lives on impulse—trapped by her own insanity, she appears to be completely free: she defenestrates one household appliance after another from a beachside bungalow, adds lighter fluid and a match, creating a bonfire of ironing boards and crock pots, *à la plage;* then she tosses a kerosene lamp into the emptied cottage, and sets it ablaze as well; she dumps paint on Zorg's boss' car in protest of some undetectable slight to Zorg's undetectable genius; she stabs a woman who is rude to her in the breast with a fork.

But the most riveting of Betty's tantrums is in her bestial, raw sexuality, the way it runs rampant through her relationship with Zorg, the way its purity and strength threatens to destroy the woman who contains it and everything that comes near her. *Betty Blue* opens with one of those blunt, unforgiving European sex scenes—no music, no flattering lights, Betty's saddlebags jiggle a little, Zorg's male frontal nudity is completely uncloaked—the kind of scene you'd never see in an American movie, the kind that really does make you want to go home and fuck the first person you see. And so from the start, the film promises to flesh out the fantasy of the madwoman as an animal in the sack, the notion that it is her unhinged erotic drive that is making her so crazy, with Dalle's bad-mood beauty the plot's best accessory, her astonished blue eyes, lush black hair, carefree fleshiness, and high cheekbones on a sucked-in face making her impossible to resist.

Betty Blue, by design or not, is actually an updated variation on the 1964 film *Lilith,* with Jean Seberg as the mental patient in the title role and Warren Beatty as a directionless war veteran who finds some purpose in the employ of a luxurious, liberally run insane asylum whose director believes the patients are delicate geniuses damaged by a coarse, cold world. (This enlightened atmosphere seems to have been modeled on R. D. Laing's theories of curing the mentally ill by allowing them the freedom to act out.) Beatty falls for the blonde caprices of the promiscuous, seductively distraught Lilith—wild-eyed Seberg wears flowery sleeveless dresses and swallows broken glass on a dare—who is both too clever and too much of a draw for Beatty, and the whole mess ends with her suicide and his ruin. Other cinematic portraits of a woman breaking down have been similarly sexy or, at any rate—perhaps because few actresses are *not* physically blessed—the afflicted heroine is always beautiful: Think of Natalie Wood in *Splendor in the Grass,* Catherine Deneuve in *Repulsion,* Carrie Snodgress in *Diary of a Mad Housewife,* Ann-Margret in *Carnal Knowledge,* Tuesday Weld in *Play It As It Lays,* Gena Rowlands in *A Woman Under the Influence,* Diana Ross in *Lady Sings the Blues,* Ronee Blakley in *Nashville,* Demi Moore in *St. Elmo's Fire.*

In 1965, Julie Christie won an Oscar for her performance in John Schlesinger's *Darling,* a portrait of a troubled model who is fashionably mod against a backdrop of swinging London, when Mary Quant and David Bailey and the Rolling Stones defined the times, when even Americans flocked to see *Blowup* and *Alfie* and *Look Back in Anger,* when England still dreamed. (Christie's role actually inaugurated the era of the British blonde—Anita Pallenberg, Marianne Faithfull, Vanessa Redgrave, Jean Shrimpton—with her beautiful hair, bad choices in men, and attendant addictions.) The movie is eager and excited, Christie an avatar of London in its butterfly burst: the dowdy, dingy, corrosive crust of war scraped away at last, the fustian pretense of the infallibility of all things British blown away by the smarmy sex and cheap tricks of the Profumo Affair. This is London with libido rising, every angry young man master of his blooming, blushing English rose: British heterosexuality has not shown such buoyant good health since Pamela Harriman decamped for Paris back in 1948.

The booming, heady cultural atmosphere of *Darling* is important to keep in mind because its presence is practically a character in the movie, it all feels so fun and rich and fabulous and micro-minied and motorcycled that it could easily distract us from the empty, sinking sorrow that is the real story of the leading lass's life. Which is, of course, precisely the point: if the delights of decadence can distract an audience that is only inhaling its secondary smoke, imagine what hedonism can do for the pretty girl in the picture who is getting a direct hit. With so much to live for and so much of so much, *Darling's* heroine soon goes wrong in all the usual ways, and we are meant to understand that her wrecked romances and unhappy relationships and sense of alienation are the result of her beauty and the opportunities it gave her, the places that it took her. (Maybe Margaux Hemingway should have seen this movie, whose premise is confirmed by the book

Model, Michael Gross's best-selling exposé of the mannequin trade—
and its many young and beautiful casualties.)

Whatever preposterous notions were played out in *Betty Blue,* and
however much the movies prettify depression, *Darling'*s thesis seems
to be borne out by real life, and by a world that exposes the pretty
young things to so much more, invites the beautiful woman to venture
forth so much more readily, takes her to a place that her mother told
her she shouldn't go, and makes her believe that she is safe, that she is
so gorgeous and people adore her so much that nothing could *possibly*
go wrong. Good looks in moderation and within the dictates of convention are always a good thing: a girl who is cheerleader-pretty will
be popular and blessed with boyfriends, having the time of her life in
high school, when no one else is. It is a girl who is exquisite, or
preternaturally sexy, or possessed of a talent that makes her beautiful—it is a girl who is special, radiant, a sensitive artist, a delicate
flower; it is a girl whose loss to the world would be viewed as the
greatest tragedy; it is the prized China doll who has the most reasons
to be careful—she is precisely the one who is most likely to mistake
her own delicacy for invincibility.

The roster of renowned women who had bouts with depression,
who were treated for mental illness, who had chemical dependencies,
who tried suicide, who died by their own hand, or who lived out their
lives between mood swings and crying jags, between bad spells and
psychotic episodes, a sinking feeling always chasing them down—and
whose charisma, charm, beauty, style, sex appeal and talent almost
never gave out—is legendary: screen dream Greta Garbo, screen gem
Natalie Wood, screen goddess Rita Hayworth, sex goddess Marilyn
Monroe, sexpot Dyan Cannon, tragic beauty Vivien Leigh, noir star
Gene Tierney, Godard gamine Jean Seberg, dance innovator Isadora
Duncan, ballerina Gelsey Kirkland, it-girl Edie Sedgwick, debutante
designer Tiger Morse, stifled southern belle Zelda Fitzgerald, French
songbird Edith Piaf, singer/junkie Marianne Faithfull, jazz vocalist Billie Holiday, rock chanteuse Nico, schlock chanteuse Karen Carpenter,
Nordic-boned and American-bred model/photographer Lee Miller,
great grande diva Maria Callas, Mexican painter Frida Kahlo,
lobotomized actress Frances Farmer, newscaster Jessica Savitch, royal

immortal Princess Diana, country star Tanya Tucker, dead model Gia Carangi, battered model Esmé Marshall, cokehead model Janice Dickinson, English writer Jean Rhys, Algonquin wit Dorothy Parker, several women who were married to Jackson Browne, Robert Lowell or Ted Hughes—and these are just the ones that are most obvious or emblematic.

To me the most intriguing example of an unraveling glamorous life—perhaps because it keeps going on, an extended near-miss experience—involves excess and insanity and eccentric behavior, along with a lot of physical illness, more than it does depression. Still, it's a mess. If beauty were the cause of ruin, and degree of beauty defined just how bad things could get, Elizabeth Taylor's crazy life would be granted the grace of inevitability. It's hard to remember back to the gorgeous girl on horseback in *National Velvet,* to the romantic beauty caught in a kiss with Montgomery Clift in *A Place in the Sun,* to sex-starved Maggie in a slip and in a bad way in *Cat on a Hot Tin Roof,* to the classy call girl driven to doom in *Butterfield 8,* to the generous Yankee lass who marries into the Texas ranch life in *Giant,* but rest assured, God gave Elizabeth Taylor one of the all-time awe-inspiring faces, blessed her with the kind of beauty that seems like it ought to have meaning, a surface so perfect that it must have risen from something very deep. With luscious, lustrous mahogany hair, skin that was the last word on alabaster and inexplicable eyes—no one had ever seen orbs so purple, so blue, so violet—Taylor seemed to be otherworldly, and had she never become an actress, never played such strong, difficult parts, she probably would have become one of those forbidding girls, a delicate piece of crystal too fragile to touch.

But at this point in her life, which has been punctuated by brushes with death and accidents with chicken bones and wedding ceremonies and divorce proceedings and rehab stays, with visits to Michael Jackson's Neverland and attendance at Luke and Laura's *General Hospital* wedding, all that elegance is gone. "My life seems very supercilious to people who only look at it on a superficial level," Taylor told Barbara Walters in 1977, sliding into the casual, glossed-over malapropisms that seem to be the lingua franca of celebrity—a symptom of stardom and its infantilizing privilege that could easily make one believe that, if there is a hired hand to polish every toenail, then there must be some script girl in Mr. Goldwyn's office assigned to speaking proper English. Elizabeth Taylor is such a star that it seems perfectly reasonable that she ought to be able to delegate sleeping, breathing, eating, drinking and speaking to some assistant: her existence seems hugely exhausting. She is one of the few people who were not imprisoned in a concentration camp who could call themselves survivors without making me want to puke. I'm not sure what she has survived—fame, I guess—but it seems like *something*.

But if Elizabeth Taylor is the purest distillation of everything, good, bad and crazy, that can be extracted from a life spent on the sound stage and the movie set—if the unquestionable, paradigmatic nature of her stardom makes it her birthright—it goes a long way toward explaining her resilience. Elizabeth Taylor is not a stranger in her own life. Few other women, particularly those biologically predisposed to mental instability, will ever feel so at home in the world. Anne Sexton, the strikingly strong-boned poet who won a Pulitzer Prize in 1966, had the wherewithal to advise her daughter in a poem to "let your body in, / let it tie you in, / in comfort," but was never able to feel comfortable enough living in her own skin to keep herself from committing suicide in 1974. The impending emergency of everyday existence seems to have been the only guiding principle in Sexton's life, with the simplest acts—she was petrified, for instance, of going grocery shopping—fraught with potential for crisis, so much so that the hugeness of her need resulted in the enormity of her appeal: somehow, she managed to cultivate a magnetism so electric that she was able to draw lovers and friends and fellow poets and distant relatives into her quotidian melodrama with the force of a high-powered vacuum. She needed attention, and she got attention. It may have driven Sexton's mother-in-law crazy that Anne was a "flamboyant, pretty child who wore too much lipstick and slept all morning while the housework lay undone," as daughter Linda Gray Sexton recalls in *Searching for Mercy Street,* but just the same, Anne *did* sleep and her husband's mother *did* do the cleaning—a pretty impressive swindle, if you ask me.

And this feat of enlisting help through helplessness can only be understood in the context of the kind of personality that refuses to suffer in silence—and by making noise may well inspire pity or invite resentment, but no matter what *always gets her way.* "I don't recall ever having been with Anne Sexton when she did not require someone to take care of her," poet and editor Peter Davison writes as the first line of a chapter on Sexton in *The Fading Smile,* his memoir of the Boston poetry explosion that occurred at mid-century. Davison goes on to recall a scene that illustrates all the inventions of din and drama that indicate the desperation, idiocy, neediness, largeness, loudness, selfishness, not to mention the compelling, demanding and dictatorial nature of the depressive personality. "I can remember an evening at dinner at Arthur Freeman's house when Sexton, who smoked continuously, struck a match and seared her hand with a fragment of phosphorus," Davison writes. "For the next two hours her pain was a presence in the room larger than that of any of the guests: ice was brought, her hand was immersed in a plastic bag full of ice water, her ululations rose and fell, her husband comforted her again and again. The guests tried to speak of other things, but it proved impossible: it was the pain that governed."

As irritating as it must have been to be at that dinner party, as an anecdote this mostly makes me want to congratulate Anne for taking over, for holding prisoners, for making her pain everyone else's problem. What a triumph of the will, what a spirited assertion of self from a person in pieces, like the twisted but logically sound behavior of the man who only kills himself after he's killed everyone he knows: *If I don't get to live, you don't either.* Anne refused to let anyone else feel complacent in her discomfort: *Someday you will ache like I ache.* This uppity unrest was what ultimately destroyed Sexton, but it was also what kept her alive for as long as it did. Davison notes that she required somebody to take care of her, and somehow she never went without: if Sexton's loved ones were sick of the noise by the end of her life, they ministered to it for a long time. And I am certain that, more often than not, they did so happily; I believe that her beautiful, lively, functioning and fruitful hours must have been shimmery and brilliant enough to make everything about her seem like a precious, delicate gift from God. In the last year of her life, several of Sexton's women friends worked out a schedule of shifts so each could be assigned a time to keep track of the increasingly suicidal and sloshed poet. As degrading as it must seem to be the object of this kind of pity and to be so thoroughly in need that you are bound to cause resentment and exhaustion among the ranks, Sexton surely must have been gratified to know that her life was so dear. "Anne was very seductive. Enormously so," her close friend Pulitzer Prize-winning poet Maxine Kumin said in an interview. "She probably had more personal charisma than anybody I've known since."

Whatever the purpose of this charisma in private life, it was a boon for her public persona as confessional poet and woman of letters with a smutty mouth and a vulnerable soul. Audiences were drawn into her overcrowded readings by the promise of her Boston Brahmin good looks, and the shock of such a lovely, elegant creature admitting desperation for love in "The Ballad of the Lonely Masturbator" and desperation straight up in "Wanting to Die." Though Sexton's features were a bit askew—an oddity of slant that is shared, to greater advantage and stronger effect, by actress Mimi Rogers—her eyes flashed aquamarine, and the white skin and dark hair that topped off a slender body with charm-school posture gave her the appearance of poet as fashion model (in fact, earlier on, as a bored housewife, Sexton had given life as a mannequin a brief try). With these physical endowments as a starting point, Sexton could easily work her hunger for attention, her voluptuous bearing and her dramatic use of small gestures into a strong stage presence: she read with a husky, throaty voice, and unlike the bespectacled poets of her day, Sexton wore bright red lipstick, high-heeled shoes, slim slit skirts and halter tops. "In addition to the strong feelings Anne's work aroused, there was the undeniable fact of her physical beauty," Maxine Kumin writes in her introduction to *The Complete Poems*. "Her presence on the platform dazzled with its staginess, its props of water glass, cigarettes and ashtray."

Toward the end of her life, Sexton saw herself as almost a movie star—of the public television variety, no doubt—with prima donna airs, the tendency to send back meals in restaurants without cause, a flair for every dare that caused her to set a hundred-dollar bill on fire at the dinner table, a flamboyance that meant she wore orange chiffon negligees and cut a wide swath with spilled pills all over the breakfast table, an inability to sign books without just the right Waterman pen and an interest in her image that meant she had a special reading wardrobe. Most notably, there was a long, clingy red dress with big, bright gold buttons that was meant to convey strong, dangerous female energy, intended to announce *the girl with the most cake;* this was the dress that she wore for her last reading, it was the dress she wore when she danced on the banks of the Charles River in front of her daughter's Harvard dormitory as she gulped down equine-quality tranquilizers with milk from a thermos in her final failed suicide attempt, it was the dress she wore for her cremation after she finally got it right.

Another of her reading outfits is on display in a famous photo by Gwendolyn Stewart that was on the cover of Diane Wood Middlebrook's controversial 1991 biography of Sexton, which was a *New York Times* front-page cause célèbre when the author was given access to the dead poet's psychiatric records and taped therapy sessions by daughter Linda, who also revealed that her mother molested her repeatedly. Just the same, the image on the front is so glorious and alive, it reveals a lust for life that makes it perfectly understandable why the book's terrible revelations of character deficiencies—Sexton's infidelity to the husband who cooked dinner and tended to her daughters so she didn't have to, her constant drunkenness and relentless promiscuity after her divorce, the usual poet's problems—are delivered in a tone that is sad and loving and forgiving, that is mostly just full of dismay that the gifted beauty and the ugly monster are both chained to the same weak and faulty life-support system, that neither will loosen its grip, like Siamese twins who will surely die if separated—but won't live long if they are not. The photo is all charisma and charm, the poet is shown twisted into place, her legs tightly crossed, her feet in white shoes with a crisscross buckle, her sleek black-and-white dress aswirl in Matisse-style geometry, bangles spangled down her arms, her hands lively and expressive, as if arguing a point or responding with glee to some juicy gossip, a Salem menthol draped between her fingers. This same image became a poster to advertise a reading Sexton was to give at Harvard, enhanced with white letters delivering date and time, but all that really matters, all the eye can see, alongside Sexton's twisted-up body and her wide-open gaze, is the insistent line, "Hurry up please it's time." It does not much matter what this is referring to, if it came from a poem (T. S. Eliot's "The Wasteland," as it happens), if it's tossing some levity at Anne's inevitable lateness, whatever. Because in retrospect it can only speak to the urgency of life, a brilliant excess that is the mark of the madwoman, the reason she is fascinating, fun to watch, that these positive features live with her in the collective memory a lot longer than the tyranny of her personality disorders, the obnoxiousness that was the result of her sickness, the sickness that made her horrible, even though the struggle to overcome it made her great.

Depression in all its dreariness is an unlikely focus for literary or any other kind of intrigue, and yet it has structured the plots of lives and stories as juicy and jumbled as the freshest Hollywood gossip. Its sufferers have been cast into the roles of icons and idols, the brilliance of what some of the afflicted did in what little bit of life they lived was truly heroic and beatific, in the Christian sense of the word: even while they were still alive, often they did not live much, often they were engaged in a slow rowing toward death, absorbed by blackness as if it were not a color but an atmosphere as thick and suffocating as the inside of a steam room. And yet, with what little brightness seeped though the slats and bled through the shades, they did *so much*. Sylvia Plath, who has by now been dead longer than she was alive, wrote *The Bell Jar,* composed her Pulitzer Prize-winning poetry, put together a collection of short stories, had a Fulbright Scholarship at Cambridge, graduated *summa cum laude* from Smith, taught a couple of semesters at her alma mater, had a couple of stays in a mental hospital, managed to have many love affairs that ended badly and one marriage that was on its way to ending badly, gave birth to two babies—and still she was able to die at age thirty, a suicide on schedule preceded by a life that ran at a breakneck pace. I point out this prodigious output because I think depression ought to be understood as much more than a monolithic force—in fact, it ought to be understood as something so mighty and complicated that it drives its sufferers in a multitude of directions, and occasionally gives the impression that if behind every great man there is a woman, then behind every great woman there is a madness. If the male driving force is the need to make a living, the female ambition is fueled by suffering.

But I also point to Plath's numerous and voluminous achievements because I want to make clear that her depression was a useful motivator only insofar as she fought against it with these accomplishments. People romanticize insanity because they believe it is the thing behind the art; in fact, it is the thing *in front of* the art, the roadblock and police barrier and phantom tollbooth that you are pushing against. Plath happens to have fought a valorous, mighty battle, and in that sense she is fit to represent all the other women who were "difficult" or "bitchy" and were probably behaving badly—resulting occasionally in great art and, more often than not, only in frayed tempers—because they too had demons to fend off. Suicide and depression are words that often punctuate the life of Sylvia Plath; they mark the atmosphere that she travels in, but they do not describe the whole of her life, they do not define a body of work more complicated and nasty and funny than all that; as *New Yorker* writer Janet Malcolm points out, if all Ms. Plath had to offer was the extravagant effulgence of her misery, "we wouldn't be reading the poems; they would simply be the inarticulate cries of an anguished woman." Or, as Oscar Wilde put it: "All bad poetry is sincere."

And in contrast to her heart of darkness, Plath seems to have taken great pains to present herself as a fifties fixture of sweetness and light, a Seven Sisters version of Doris Day, a girl who always traveled in a neat little suit with reliable Samsonite luggage in tow. In a *New Yorker* article that filled an entire issue of the magazine one week—it was later bound into a book called *The Silent Woman* in 1994—Janet Malcolm quotes a teacher Plath had at Cambridge who was greatly impressed by the way the young poet was "always neat and fresh, wearing charming, girlish clothes, the kind of clothes that made you look at the girl, not the garments; hair down to the shoulders still, but ever so neatly brushed and combed . . . This charming American neatness and freshness is what I chiefly recall about her physical person." Alfred Kazin, who taught Plath while she was still at Smith, wrote of the prim undergraduate: "When we met at home, she was the first to clear the dishes after coffee. She was certainly a 'regular' girl, full of smiles." All of Plath's attention to grooming and styling and decorum—a trait mentioned in every account by every acquaintance—is notable because it indicates a person who wants to be normal and well adjusted. Granted, this pre-hippie and pre-grunge era did not avail itself of eyebrow rings and nose studs and purple hair, but there were beatniks, and there were Vassar girls in black turtlenecks who did not wash their hair. More likely than not, these deliberately filthy girls were posers and Plaths manqué who mistook despair for depth: one of the surest signs of a person who is deeply depressed is in all the things they do to not be depressed, how willingly they will cop to a huge desire to just be normal and happy, to find stability and start a family. By the end of her life, Plath had abandoned all pretense to vanity—Alvarez recalls a visit he paid her a couple of months before her death, remembering that "her hair gave off a strong smell, sharp as an animal's"—which was a sure sign she'd surrendered all hope.

What I am trying to get across here was that this was a woman who put up a huge fight for her own life and happiness—but the fight was not against sadness so much as it was against *largeness*, against the outsize and oversize emotions she felt about so many things, too many things—a way of thinking and being that is intolerable to the world under any circumstances, but certainly had no place in the quietude of the fifties. It is not hard to love the poetry this emotional life produces, to appreciate it as a stand-in and catharsis for the petty problems we have that are a dollhouse version of her overwrought Taj Mahal, but that does not mean we love the poet or the person. And it is not hard to love the struggle that the poetry represents: with the perfectionist's precision of language that is a literary analogue of Seurat dot-by-dot paintings, Plath's extraordinary care—which you would think would be stifling—is the exhilarating expression of a soul dying to be free.

No one should make the mistake of thinking Plath and Sexton—the alpha and the omega of the poetry girl-gone-wrong on the page—offer the world no more than their dreary surrender. They fight and struggle against their demons the way anyone else created in God's image, with a lust for life, is driven to do. They fight in the brilliance of their poetry, images so sharp and neat, they fight by falling in love, they fight by giving birth, they fight by wearing high heels to do housework, they fight by wearing bright red lipstick just to run to the market, they fight by refusing to get out of bed ever again, they fight by giving readings with great elegance and eloquence, and sometimes they even fight by making Sunday brunch for their mothers-in-law. They also fight by being fucking impossible: they are late or they are very late; then they pretend they thought they were supposed to be there then. You want to help them, but they don't answer the phone, and when you come over to their house to find them, they get mad. You lend them money for rent, they go for a facial. The notion of the damsel in distress that accompanies the posthumous vigil-type atmospheres that occur when a famous depressive does herself in, the loved ones saying we tried, she was so sad, nothing helped, must be discounted as agitprop. Any truthful rendition of a woman falling apart will make it clear that what is happening to her is terrible and what it is turning her into is also terrible. "Angie is a deeply sympathetic character," film historian Jeanine Basinger writes in *A Woman's View*, referring to the drunk and disorderly and career gal-cum-neglected homemaker Susan Hayward played in the 1947 film *Smash-up, the Story of a Woman*. "Although it is understood that one sympathizes with her situation, not with what it makes her do."

To make this point about Plath is to make it doubly so about Sexton, who lived a lot longer and wrought far greater damage. Here's what I want you to know: Neither one of them died of sorrow, because if sadness had been the whole story, then the whole world would have delivered them hankies on a silver platter and eventually the sympathy would have made sense and seeped in and they would have gotten better. They died because they were complicated, because they were large, because they contained multitudes that Walt Whitman could not have begun to imagine. They died because, indeed, they were frequently quite sad, and they did not like it one bit, and they did not want to stay home and feel sorry for themselves, so they left the house and it only made them sadder: they refused to accept the limits of their mental conditions, and instead were confronted by the limits of the world's ability to tolerate them. They died because they were difficult and incredible, and because no matter how many people want so badly to have wunderkind children that they send their little three-year-olds to preschool enrichment programs or get their high school juniors tutored for the SATs, not one of these poor benighted parents has any idea how undesirable a truly talented child actually is, none of them can see that everything about brilliance and beauty and excellence and genius leaves us absolutely awestruck until we realize that the personality disorders and maladjustments and mental diseases that tend to accompany these gifts are not optional features. "I have known no man of genius who had not to pay, in some affliction or defect either physical or spiritual, for what the gods had given him," writes Sir Max Beerbohm, offering an appraisal of the modern human condition. "For with much wisdom comes much sorrow; the more knowledge, the more grief," opined King Solomon in Ecclesiastes, weighing in on the ways of the ancient world. In the Old Testament, God extracted huge tolls and brutal trials from his most favored mortals, and not a damn thing has changed since then.

And it's worse for women.

Plath is a far more gifted, refined and elegant poet than Sexton, pushed as she was into painstaking and exacting use of language at the hands of the British literati who surrounded her when she moved to England with husband Ted Hughes. Sexton is more confessional and Plath is more conventional, but it seems inevitable that the two would be paired within the pantheon, as if in a high-concept sitcom noir, the New England poetry babes, girls who would go for a drink at the Ritz Hotel after a workshop at Boston University with Robert Lowell (can you *imagine?*), the women who seem stuck in the wrong era, lost in America with no magic carpet to ride. And like Marilyn Monroe, they invite speculation about feminism as salvation: dark and down during the postwar boom when the world was bright with I Like Ike, Sexton and Plath are to the fifties what acid casualties are to the sixties— victims of the times who were also given their best material *by* the times. Sexton, uneducated, often sloshed and slutty, is the bad girl, while Plath, the A student with all the prizes and awards and degrees who is quiet and sweet, the good girl: Sexton's overbearing crazy woman is balanced by Plath's submissive, sympathetic depressive.

Now, as far as I know, there is no such creature as a "submissive, sympathetic depressive." Of course, there are people who suffer with the ailment who are quiet and polite and gentle—often enough, that's how they got depressed in the first place—but this is not a disease that plays itself out quite so pleasantly as that. And it's a disease that sucks you so deep into your own needs that rudeness becomes inevitable, as is the case in people's recollections of feeling put upon by Plath in her indifference to good manners. Dido Merwin, erstwhile wife of the poet W.S., wrote in a brief memoir, quoted as an appendix in Anne Stevenson's Plath biography *Bitter Fame,* that on a visit the Hugheses paid to the Merwins' farmhouse, Sylvia "used up all the hot water, repeatedly helped herself from the fridge (breakfasting on what one had planned to serve for lunch, etc.)," and worst of all, devoured a *foie gras* "for all the world as though it were 'Aunt Dot's meat loaf.' " Now, there are certainly worse sins than an insatiable appetite—and there are harsher crimes than being an American accustomed to long, steamy showers and large plentiful meals without persnickety, nitpicky hostesses keeping track. On the other hand, it is very annoying to have a guest lick pâté off her fingers as she digitally digs it out of the serving platter; among other things, it's gross to watch. This behavior is both self-centered and unselfconscious, and despite the petty nature of the ire it arouses, the end result is a less than sympathetic Sylvia—not sad and sweet, but depressed and demanding. Perhaps because, as Woody Allen pointed out in *Annie Hall,* Sylvia Plath is an "[i]nteresting poetess whose tragic suicide was misinterpreted as romantic, by the college-girl mentality"; perhaps because these same starry-eyed English majors have mistaken all depression for something intense and sweet and feeling and Byronic—and not something violent and obnoxious and bitchy and trying and exasperating; or perhaps because *The Bell Jar*'s cover art, since the day it was published in the United States by Harper & Row in 1971 (it had been released in Great Britain in 1963 under the pseudonym Victoria Lucas, to protect the guilty, as it were), has had this faded rose painted in dots by some aspiring Monet with that certain look that paint-by-numbers done in art therapy has, which would seem to suggest that sorrow and suicide are like a red, red rose drooping in its vase, and blah blah blah—perhaps it is for all these reasons that people don't realize that Sylvia Plath was a maniac and depression is simply not a pretty thing.

This mistaken assumption not only reveals a failure to grasp the cult of the madwoman; it also betrays an ignorance about the process of the cult of personality as a whole. Where women are concerned, nobody gets noticed just because of early death or quiet desperation or haughty mystique (Jacqueline Kennedy is the exception, a marvel of the power of playing hard to get). The women who inspire wonder with a longevity that is greater than their own life span, the women who become subject to and of many biographies that take sides in arguments and situations that are only nominally about the woman herself, the women who become a *pretense*—a woman like Sylvia

Plath—did not get into this predicament by being sweet and sad while still alive. Unfortunately, Plath is more likely to be remembered for her emotional hell and her shock treatments than for her precision as a poet in *Ariel* or for the remarkable achievement of *The Bell Jar,* which is very funny, smartly detached and often nasty in a voice too honest to be unsympathetic. And though interest in the work itself has kept it all solidly in print, with HarperCollins publishing a twenty-fifth anniversary hardcover edition of *The Bell Jar* in 1996, interest in Plath herself and her jam-packed, truncated life is such that it gave Janet Malcolm a pretext for studying the nature of biography—hagiographers and pathographers, critics and propagandists, Plath has all aplenty—in her cover-to-cover *New Yorker* piece. Even after death, Sylvia holds sway.

This frenzy of biography is fueled both by the posthumous rescue possibilities invited by the ambiguous circumstances of Plath's death and by fascination with her and Hughes as the last really glamorous literary couple, the last attempt to mate genius before all the brilliant poets figured out it was all too much trouble, best to just settle in with an accountant or practical nurse or carpenter. It is this coupling that overhauled Plath's appearance as a nice American gal with Samsonite luggage in a camel-hair coat, arriving in England to study poetry, prim and proper as any girl enrolling in her mum's shorthand class, the very thing that became a metonymy for all Sylvia snubbed and disparaged Stateside. It is through Hughes that she says goodbye to all that, it is with him that the Sylvia Plath persona was invented at the same time her person was destroyed. The hot-blooded madwoman with red hair and bloody red lipstick emerges on the night Sylvia met Ted, at a party in Cambridge, when, drunk out of her mind, she recited two of Hughes' poems to his face from memory, and after much groping around, bit his cheek with vampiric intent, drawing blood. As she recorded in her journal: "the door was shut and he was sloshing brandy into a glass and I was sloshing it at the place where my mouth was when I last knew about it . . . And I was stamping and he was stamping on the floor, and then he kissed me bang smash on the mouth . . . And when he kissed my neck I bit him long and hard on the cheek, and when we came out of the room blood was running down his face. And I screamed in myself, thinking: oh, to give myself, grasping, fighting, to you." Of course, it is easy to see that it was at this party in 1956 that the intriguing, alluring Sylvia Plath came into existence, but it is the fact of this literary merger, as well as the separation at the end of Plath's life, that invites endless and unanswerable speculation: Would this suicide have happened if they hadn't broken up? Would they have gotten back together had she lived? In light of the Hugheses' marital collapse, should the future fate of Plath's work—by dint of a legal technicality that made Ted next of kin at the time of Sylvia's death—be controlled by a man who betrayed her?

Sylvia Plath provokes such disproportionate speculation on the lost possibilities because, in fact, they are so numerous. There may have been other husbands, more children, better poetry, bigger novels, academic appointments: if Courtney Love, once thought to be just a Nirvana groupie whose best songs were really written by her husband (remember?), has managed to construct a life that places Kurt Cobain as a mere footnote, imagine what Sylvia Plath could have done (especially when you consider that Hughes, in spite of his ascension to Poet Laureate of Great Britain, is still, in some sense, a footnote in his dead wife's life). In contrast, Anne Sexton, while certainly a fascinating woman, has not been claimed and clawed at quite so hungrily in her corpse form, because we know the dreary development of her life only too well, we know the story—it is a whole story and it is a common story—and it reads as one miserable version of what Plath's life might have become: by the time of her death, Sexton had quite thoroughly exhausted all possibilities, had been married for a long time and found that wanting, had a multitude of men and women for lovers and was never satisfied, had years of therapy, was on many drugs, and lithium seemed possibly promising, but evidently not promising enough. "The woman is perfected. / Her dead / Body wears the smile of accomplishment," wrote Sylvia Plath in "Edge," which seems a prescient epitaph for Anne Sexton. "Her bare / Feet seem to be saying: / We have come so far, it is over."

Plath died young, died without, died a world still waiting to be born.

*   *   *

Of course, dying young with possible Prozac beckoning at some van-ishing point off in the future, the blunt chemical corrective to the dark side of genius, may romanticize the futility of suicide. But to be a beautiful body living among the ruins of a ravished, zapped-out mind is almost as compelling. In other words, even someone who *forgets* to commit suicide—who in all the hysteria of being so miserable some-how never manages to fit her own death into the schedule—can end up in the cult of the crazy woman. Frances Farmer, who made her home in Seattle before it was suicide central, did not have a particularly memorable film career. Not because Farmer wasn't talented or mar-quee-famous in her day, but—like Linda Darnell and Jeanette Mac-Donald and Jean Arthur and Joanne Dru and so many other movie stars whose names mean nothing to noncinéastes today—Farmer somehow failed to be legendary, to be a Garbo or a Bacall, a Marilyn or a Rita. But in spite of Farmer's career obsolescence, her life's ex-tended resonance made it the subject of the movie *Frances* in 1982. Starring Jessica Lange and her beau, playwright Sam Shepard, this film is a variation on losing one's mind, Hollywood style. Starting with the tedious stereotype of the miserable and misunderstood actress who just wants to be taken seriously and talks about longing to return to the true grit of the theater and blah blah blah, *Frances* quickly twists into something inexplicably hellish and harrowing. It is a loony-bin trip in which the inmates at the asylum are so knocked out and ne-glected that Nurse Ratched would be a welcome presence, and one wonders why the doctors don't just let them kill themselves, let them be dead instead of just deadened. (The offscreen antics on this film set were a drama all their own, with Lange already the mother of Mikhail Baryshnikov's child and now seducing Shepard away from his own house and home; she ultimately saw a prodigious professional payoff amid all this personal upheaval when she was nominated for two Os-cars in one year—for a supporting role in *Tootsie* and a lead role in *Frances*—taking home the trophy for the former, and Shepard from the latter.)

But before things descend into this institutional squalor, Farmer is portrayed as a precocious beauty, her movie-star future is shellacked with the high gloss of destiny, it's all so lovely and hopeful and inevi-table that nobody bothers to notice that the poor girl is too naïvely and pathologically honest—just too *damn sensitive*—to play the Hollywood shuffle. She becomes one of those "difficult" women whom the studio system tolerates with about as much enthusiasm as Winston Smith facing the rats of Room 13 in *1984*. Their resistance fuels Farmer's obstinacy. She goes to a party where her presence is expected, but then sneaks upstairs into the master bathroom, fills the tub with hot water and fluffy bubbles and spends the evening taking a bath; when Clifford Odets turns out to be a cad who just happens to play the liberal party line—and just happens to be Hollywood's screenwriter darling for the moment—she calls him a hypocrite to his face. She can't fake it, she can't even try to fake it—the problem after a while is not that she has too much integrity, but that the self-destructive nature of her integrity is such that she will only know that she's succeeded in respecting it when it has ruined her. So it does. Psychiatric wards, shock, medicated somnambulance: this is the price.

But as Frances falls apart, the movie *Frances* has her defiance and sorrow serve only to make her prettier, her madness acting as a beauty elixir. Of course, after the frontal lobotomy things are not so lustrous—after all, it takes some ability to focus to comb your hair—but the indelible impression of what she once was seems to be a constant. At the end of the movie, we watch Jessica Lange shuffle listlessly along, a wiped-out waif reduced to work as a celebrity guest on game shows. But we also see Sam Shepard in the part of Harry, Farmer's long-suffering sweetheart, a fantastically romantic character, the man who found her when she was still in high school, fell in love with her idealistic moroseness and rescued her from stupid dates with stupider boys. All these years later, Harry still loves Frances, pays her puppyish attention and follows her around adoringly, as if, even with a chunk of her brain excised, she's still the same girl. And it starts to look like maybe a lobotomy is better than suicide. At any rate, Frances Farmer has lived on, not as an actress, but as a symbol of the systematic destruction of the difficult woman. She has been particularly cultic since the whole grunge thing turned the Pacific Northwest into an American dystopia, even lending her name to the Nirvana song "Frances Farmer Will Have Her Revenge upon Seattle," and to Kurt Cobain and Courtney Love's daughter, Frances Bean.

Zelda Fitzgerald, too, has had her internationally acclaimed schizo-

phrenic tendencies outlive almost all other facets of her thwarted, distorted—but still somehow thrilling and riveting—southern belle
turned literary babe's existence. So much so that in the movie *Manhattan,* when Woody Allen is trying to describe the maddeningly frustrating and fickle Diane Keaton character, he refers to her as "the winner
of the Zelda Fitzgerald Emotional Maturity Award." And for a
woman who functioned strictly as a figure and fixture of a certain
smart set—a party presence, a fabulous flapper—Zelda has achieved
great renown, almost all of it predicated on her problematic mental
health, and almost all of it infusing her with more intrigue and inquiry
in the afterlife than has been enjoyed by her drunken, brilliant, middle
western (as they'd have said back then) mess of a husband, the writer
F. Scott.

The particular twist that Zelda's legend offers up for those looking
for an ideology to attach their curiosity to is her function as a Jazz Age
artist manqué, a writer of great natural gifts, a woman who thought in
the peach-pulpishly rich metaphors of the southern mind—as becomes
clear to the reader of her short stories or her 1932 novel *Save Me the
Waltz*—whose literary ambitions were alternately dismissed, discouraged and, some say, plagiarized by her possessive, protective but, most
importantly, insecure husband. When Zelda sent the manuscript of
her novel, completed during one of her many institutional interludes,
to her husband's own Scribner's editor, Maxwell Perkins, Scott was
apoplectic, resentful that for four years he had been "unable to proceed [with his own book] *because* of the necessity of keeping Zelda in
sanitariums . . . her novel is an imitation of it, of its rhythms, materials . . ." One can't completely blame Scott for feeling the fatigue of
having a mentally ill wife—but surely he must recognize how his own
alcoholism was an equally likely culprit for his four-year lag. Just the
same, Scott's books—particularly *The Great Gatsby*—are taught, almost uniformly, in English classes all over America, while Zelda's
novel, only intermittently in print at all, is the kind of thing that you
might read in a women's studies course as a female work of literature
worthy of resuscitation, but one read more as a document than as a
novel. In fact, I would guess that few people even realize that Zelda
wrote a novel, or even *wanted* to write a novel, or that she was an
artist whose paintings were exhibited and collected—that she even

took temporary leave from a psychiatric hospital upstate to come down to her opening at a gallery in New York City. Her fame is both frivolous and gruesome, based not on her accomplishments but on an intrinsic beauty and an intractable sorrow.

Denied the writerly right, Zelda was reduced to being a combustible showpiece, with her husband very much a part of her mythology, acting as her alcoholic accomplice, an aider and abettor just barely balancing on the edge himself. Together, Scott and Zelda were self-destruction's power couple. Shuttling their unstable household and unhinged personalities around from St. Paul, Minnesota, to Montgomery, Alabama, to Paris, France, to Rome, Italy—with odd moments in Africa and Delaware and Hollywood thrown in between—the Fitzgeralds only managed to remain in any given place long enough for people to remark on their charismatic charm. "There have been dozens of memoirs written, wherein one catches glimpses of Scott and Zelda sleeping in each other's arms at a party," writes Nancy Milford in *Zelda,* her definitive 1970 biography. "Everyone wanted to meet them, to have them for dinner guests, to attend their parties, and to invite them to their openings. The youthful handsomeness of the Fitzgeralds, their incandescent vitality were qualities they possessed jointly and effortlessly." Milford goes on to quote personages no less esteemed than Dorothy Parker, H. L. Mencken, Ernest Hemingway, Edmund Wilson, John Peale Bishop and so many others, all paying homage to the Fitzgeralds' striking gorgeousness, which was enhanced by their talent for mise-en-scène.

But when it came to public displays of affection, Scott was more the motionless maypole while Zelda created the brilliant hues of long rope and ribbon spinning all around him: she was known to dance on tables at the Etoile in Paris (upstaging Isadora Duncan); was remembered for taking a thirty-foot dive, during low tide, late at night on the Riviera; was credited with jumping into the fountain in New York City's Union Square while completely sober; and the couple together were said to have celebrated a move from one hotel to another by spinning in the revolving doors of the lobby for half an hour. As seems to be the pattern with emotionally disturbed women, the frightening lightning flash of Zelda's madness was coupled with a delightful, infectious sparkle at other times, something that Scott understood, as he wrote in *The Crack-Up:* "I was in love with a whirlwind and I must spin a net big enough to catch it." But captivating as they were, many of Zelda's displays were more troubling than entertaining, several predating her life with Scott: once, while still a teenager in Montgomery, she got mad at a date and kicked in the storefront window of a photography studio (the boy had been staring at a picture and not paying enough attention to her); at a fraternity party not long thereafter, she got drunk and broke Victrola records over her date's head; and later on, she was caught taking a bath in her hostess' private chambers while a large gala was going on in the ballroom below. (This echo of the film *Frances* would seem to suggest that perhaps a major symptom of emotional instability is a desire to bathe at inappropriate times.)

But with the Fitzgeralds moving around so much, many people were only able to catch a glimpse of the grace notes, flying by as quickly and effervescently as a comet, leaving an impression of glamour and godspell. While many peripatetic souls travel a great deal because they are blessed with a feeling that the whole world is their home, Scott and Zelda were more likely motivated by a sense that *nowhere* in the world was their home—there is no restful haven for an unquiet mind. In any event, mental institutions in locations as various as Geneva, Switzerland, and Asheville, North Carolina, were the few places that Zelda was ever settled in for long stretches of time—in one case, for over four years. She died alone in a fire in a psychiatric hospital, charred by smoke and bloated from insulin treatments. Not terribly glamorous.

But if Zelda deserves to be remembered as much more than the premier beauty of between-the-wars Bedlam, Edie Sedgwick really and truly owes all her fame to having body and bones orchestrated in such a way that she made depression look fascinating, she made mania look fascinating, she made drug addiction look fascinating, she made nodding off look fascinating, she made wired look fascinating, she made speed freakouts look fascinating, she made bad trips look fascinating, she made burning down your hotel room while too sedated to care and almost dying of smoke inhalation look fascinating: Edie is such a convincing representation of the benefits of life gone wrong that were she still around today she would probably have to be a lobbyist for the tobacco industry. The scion of an old and large New England clan,

Edie was a Warhol superstar celebrated in the August 1965 issue of *Vogue* as a "youthquaker," a shining, shocking symbol of the dark, complicatedly arty counterpart to the hippy-dippy sixties scene that would be associated with San Francisco and Woodstock and college kids with shaggy hair and backpacks who had not yet arrived at the sophisticated, studied indifference that Edie and her lot were pioneering. Still, the only thing of consequence that Edie ever did with her life—and even in this case, not deliberately—was to end it early, at age twenty-eight, in 1971, by way of a barbiturate overdose.

But Edie was exquisitely beautiful, all big baby browns with indelibly dilated pupils that made her eyes look like black spots Dalmatianed against eggshell-pale skin—a contrast so absolute that it evoked both the astonished openness and sweet opaqueness of a deer caught in headlights. It is this ineluctable projection of innocence that makes all of Edie's bad habits look so good: the delicacy is never hardened, but the cool visual effect of self-destruction still shows against Edie's pristine, pure backdrop, as fine and gentle as organza. You want to save her; you want to join her; either way, it's all about *her*. "To see her in sunlight was to see Marxism die," Harold Brodkey wrote of the leading lady in his short story "Innocence," a line reminiscent of references to a face that launched a thousand ships and other evocations of a potency beyond ideology—of falling for someone so hard that the whole world, or, at least, left-wing political doctrine, seems to topple down with you. Edie, addled and addicted, seems to have had this effect on people, functioning as an often inanimate objet d'art even when she was still alive, and seeming to only further potentiate her power as a muse postmortem. Edie was said to be the subject of Bob Dylan's "Just Like a Woman"—"with her fog, her amphetamine, and her pearls"—and the platinum streaks in her hair against the pallor of her complexion were thought to be the images evoked by the album title *Blonde on Blonde*. There is no such ambiguity in the Edie Brickell song called "Little Miss S."—"Living the scene out of her limousine / Little Miss S. in a mini dress"—inspired by a shared first name that otherwise seemed to be attached to absolutely no one under fifty. Ms. Sedgwick was also the subject of an eponymously titled elegiac poem by proto-punk Patti Smith, beginning infectiously with the plaint "she was white on white / so blonde on blonde." She is also the centrifugal force that unifies disparate factions and themes and scenes and settings of a best-selling oral history jigsawed together by Jean Stein and George Plimpton under the heading, at once simple and grandiose, *Edie: An American Biography*.

The book is an awesome accomplishment—reminiscences cobbled together with such precision that it smooths into sensibility the serrated edges and irreconcilable absurdities of Edie's life, of old money and boarding schools and Groton and Harvard leading into Warhol's Factory and the Velvet Underground and Viva and Billy Name and silicone breast implants. When it was published in 1982, *Edie* became a best-seller in spite of its putative subject's lack of a legacy of any apparent import, and it started a craze for oral histories—even fiction modeled on that form (*Boy Wonder* in 1988 and *Boone* in 1990)—none of which equaled *Edie*. Between the book and an art-house re-release of the feature-length Edie extravaganza *Ciao! Manhattan* in 1983—a film as busy, jumbled, noisy and ridiculous as its star—the long-dead Edie Sedgwick became a role model of sorts for teenage girls of a self-destructive bent. Clumpy, chunky platinum streaks in dark hair and a refusal to wear any form of hosiery other than black tights to re-create Edie's signature anorexia aesthetic were the essential elements, but more ambitious acolytes could accentuate the basics with acid-green matte jersey, the curtain-ring earrings, the white mink coat, leotards, hiphuggers, Kenneth Jay Lane jewelry, anything by Rudi Gernreich, anything by Pucci.

I think Edie's appeal as a fashion icon and as a depression idol—over a decade after her death—may be because of, not in spite of, her seeming worthlessness, and the frivolity of her existence that meant her only meaningful pursuit was that of losing her own mind. Edie so thoroughly and singularly stood for going crazy—and yet this negative, often irritating and certainly destructive trait was enough to make her life memorable to others, enough to work up a fuss about the very nothingness that defined her. As a result, Edie is an ideal role model of what to do with yourself if depression is all you are, all you've got, all of everything. Even people who are not clinically depressed spend a good deal of time feeling bad—and at a certain point one thinks, If I have to feel bad, I might as well be stylish and glamorous while I'm at it. Edie did it. Most misery is just plain miserable, and no amount of purple mascara and gold lamé and dark sunglasses can change that. But Edie managed to make it something more, a fashion statement, a desirable mien. She is a beacon of hope to the hopelessly unhappy in her hypnotic intoxication.

Edie, who was never gainfully employed in her entire brief life, is further significant because she set the tone for the vocational crazy woman, for the person who unravels not so much as performance art, but as a life endeavor. It is true that depression, if it is chronic and systemic, can be more a personality type than a limited-run disease. But for many public figures, mental health has become the whole story. Patty Duke is better known as a manic-depressive than as an actress (even though she won an Oscar for *The Miracle Worker*). And with Superman replaced by Batman as the movie superhero of choice (I'll refrain from making a joke about Christopher Reeve), Margot Kidder is definitely better known for being a nut than anything else she's ever done. Marianne Faithfull, despite a cult following for her throaty, drug-damaged voice, is best known for the drugs and the damage and for being perhaps the most famous subscriber to England's heroin-maintenance program before cleaning up at Hazelden. And does anyone really know what Dorothy Parker did for a living? While every memorable quip and biting insult in the American idiom seems to be attributed to her—and there is some vague sense of theater reviews and screenplays—like everyone else involved in the Algonquin Round Table scene, Mrs. Parker is most likely to go down in history as a colossal, suicidal drunk. On the other end of the spectrum, Nico would seem to illustrate that the less said the better; the silence of the lamb is always heard as deep and meaningful, rarely presumed a symptom of stupidity, vapidity or shrugged shoulders of the mind. The inscrutable Nico never really did much of anything—though spooked with a voice as comatose and indifferent as she herself seemed to be, and this kind of fashionable, club-scene approach to her dirgelike songs that made her seem like the hipster Warhol world's answer to the German cabaret's smoky singers. Despite her distraught elegance, in the end Nilo was just Elke Sommer as junkie, or Joey Heatherton with dirty hair, a blonde lounge singer that the Rat Pack had somehow neglected to notice. And yet, it was still possible in 1995 to devote a two-hour documentary called *Nico Icon* to her deceased zeitgeist, to a life whose prevalent activity was doing heroin. But the blank résumé is the very thing that, as Hilton Als noted in *The New Yorker,* "allowed film directors and, in the end, rock audiences to project their dreams across her face, which she kept more often than not immobile as a screen, unmoved by their projections."

But there are others whose talent is recognized and renowned— whose work has not lost its luster as history marches on, whose legacy has actually appreciated in value over time—but who still seem defined by death, whose choice to die has become more memorable than the way they lived. It goes without saying that most people have not read a single poem of either Anne Sexton or Sylvia Plath, but many are aware of them as martyrs to suicide. And were it not for the fact that every child in America (on earth, for all I know) sees *The Wizard of Oz,* often with repetitious delight, most people who are even a few years younger than I am will know of Judy Garland only because of her bouts with the blues and pills, because of her drag-queen symbolism as an oppressed spirit. Billie Holiday and Janis Joplin will be nothing but junkies tossed in a heap of show-business roadkill not too far off in the future; Columbia and Decca will reissue old albums and assemble boxed sets, and still very few people will know what either of them sound like. People will know nothing about these two great singers except that they reached early and self-destructive ends. Many will never hear Billie Holiday sing "Good Morning Heartache" or "Strangefruit," they will never know that soul music is nothing new, and many may even avoid the huge hungry voice of Janis Joplin, will hear cover bands do "Piece of My Heart" and think that's how it's supposed to sound. But as sacrificial songbirds, they may have a legend of quantum longevity. I don't mind that Patty Duke or Margot Kidder has come to this, but women of real talent who are only identified by their pathologies are kind of like trees that are only good for timber, as if their gracious green leaves that provided shade and shelter and aroma, as if all the fruits and flower blossoms they bore in life don't matter nearly as much as the way they will be pulped.

In a way, none of these women has to do anything more than be remembered as crazy to maintain a fame that may even be eternal: certainly, Sylvia Plath is much more famous now than she was at the time of her death. But the allure of the madwoman seems to work both ways, with insanity giving the appearance of intrigue or intelligence to someone like Edie Sedgwick, but with it likewise detracting from the talent of many other well-known nutcases because it becomes all that matters. Evidently, as a personality trait, madness is a thick air—were it an odor, it would be strong as skunk, undiminished by any deodorizing forces. I think this goes far in explaining why many of these women ended their lives in suicide: they were consumed by a personality disorder of mammoth strength, from which, eventually, not even the brilliantly intense opiates could shelter them unless they took in so much that it ended up killing them along with the ache—the usual baby and bathwater scenario. But it is also because of the large nature of the mental illness that the people close to them were as likely to feel resentful, exhausted, used, abused and angry by the end—and too far away and alienated to come running to the rescue that one last time. "I wished for my mother to die," Linda Gray Sexton writes in her memoir *Searching for Mercy Street*. "As much as I dreaded her suicide, I also craved it. I longed for freedom from the tyranny of her many neuroses that seemed, in the last year, to have overtaken her personality."

* * *

These days, so many images in fashion and culture thought to be beautiful and—yes—marketable are actually quite depressing, or even suggestive of mental illness, with expressions of distress and despair so reflexive in the current aesthetic that they have assumed the reverse fixity of the Cheshire cat's unfading smile. The "college girl" romanticization of suicide and despair has been put to mod and manipulative purpose by clever art directors and commercial photographers, many of whom no longer seem worried at all that their ad campaigns may come across as negative, may make their perfume or blue jeans or bustier seem like a sullen, luckless albatross of a product that will bring a pox upon the purchaser's home. In fact, it often seems that anything that *doesn't* come across as morose will also fail to be seen as desirable and beautiful, as worth the price of a designer label or fit to be called haute couture: hence, a frail Amber Valletta lounging in a damp, dank rowboat with smudgy, kohled eyes illuminated only by a gray, sickly light is in an ad that is meant to make us want to wear Prada; for the same Fall '97 season, a whited-out Stella Tennant, with hair sticking every which way—in what appears to be an attempt to do to her head what Richard Dreyfus found himself compulsively doing to mashed potatoes in *Close Encounters of the Third Kind*—looks thoroughly mad in an ad that is supposed to make us want to buy Giorgio Armani. In the May 1997 *Allure*, Niki Taylor, the fresh-faced Floridian whose healthy glow has been a persistent counternarrative to glum glamour, is posed in a layer of spray-can sweat, smeary blue eye shadow, her stringy hair combined with ripped-bodice slips to achieve a tacky streetwalker stance. In the same *Allure* issue, a black-and-white photograph of Academy Award winner Mira Sorvino puts her at the center of a chaotic tableau, with the actress kicking and screaming, carried off by police officers, a nurse in attendance, with a caption—amid mentions of a suit by Todd Oldham, shoes by Sonia Rykiel—offering the offhand language of fashion copy: "Going mental: An ode to actress Frances Farmer, who was committed to an insane asylum in 1944 and later lobotomized." On the next page, in full color, Sorvino is in a gold lamé gown—by Jacques Fath, we are told—a bandage on her forehead, a nurse carrying both a hatbox and a jar filled with would-be formaldehyde and Farmer's frontal lobe, an image that is meant to be beautiful.

But even before the instrumental break in "Smells Like Teen Spirit" was played over highlights of the bobsled and luge races during the '92 Winter Olympics—thus confirming my suspicion that no one even knew how to identify what was depressing (Nirvana) and what wasn't (snow sports) any longer—the salable nature of that which is both beautiful and upsetting was understood. For years now, music videos and television spots and print ads and all manner of popular culture have routinely appropriated erotically unnerving and seductively sick images from sixties cinema like *Belle de Jour* and *Persona* and *La Dolce Vita*—film stills so commonplace that they have lost their context, pictures so pretty and fashionable when removed from the unpleasantness of plot that Anita Ekberg's busty blondeness or Liv Ullmann's remarkable gaze or Catherine Deneuve's sunglasses are all that there is. These images are all bright colors and dull despair, used by creative executives who don't even necessarily know who Buñuel and

Bergman and Fellini are or what the French New Wave was all about or what continent Sweden is on or what makes certain situations Felliniesque—or what made the characters the films depicted so arresting to begin with.

Alongside these visually compelling movie reels, many stock photographic images have themselves formed the template that art directors draw on when they want to depict despair, insanity, madness and the like: the "shock therapy" effect of Man Ray's Surrealist solarization technique; the Depression era poverty and dignity in the work of Dorothea Lange and Walker Evans; the grotesques, freaks and lost souls depicted by Diane Arbus; Bob Richardson's mid-sixties photographs of models in desperate straits, of Nena von Schlebrugge (Uma Thurman's mother) lying on a couch crying to her psychiatrist on the phone, or of Donna Mitchell in various states of sexual rapture, always looking, as Richardson puts it, "drugged and beaten"; the glamorous violence of Chris Von Wangenheim's 1977 campaign for Christian Dior jewelry, in which the diamond-bedizened Lisa Taylor sits impassive, nonplussed, unfazed—and, to all appearances, sedated into submission—while a red-eyed Doberman pinscher clamps its bare teeth on her braceleted wrist; the sadomasochism made beautiful by Robert Mapplethorpe, and the many very beautiful women made stark and sometimes ugly by Richard Avedon; Nan Goldin's 1986 photoessay *The Ballad of Sexual Dependency*, a collection of Polaroid-blurry snapshots of strung-out people in seedy settings, some trapped and violated by love, others putridly at the mercy of their addictions; the chilly sexual cruelty of Helmut Newton, well into his seventies and still the reigning risqué fashion photographer, a native of Germany whose work has always given me the feeling that his parents read to him from Sacher-Masoch's *Venus in Furs* instead of *Emil and the Detectives* or some other Berlin bedtime classic—so primal is Newton's decadence that it seems almost pre-Oedipal. (For instance: Now that whips and chains and handcuffs have been done to death, Newton has decided that disability—paralysis, limping, deformity—is his new frontier, or at least that's the only conclusion I can draw from the layout he did of his compatriot Nadja Auermann in crutches, splints, braces, wheelchairs, as well as other corrective bodily gear, as part of a fashion spread for *The New Yorker* in 1996.)

The impulse that draws us to these depressing visual images is pretty much the same one that allows essentially sane and well-adjusted sorts to enjoy the dark art of a band like Hole or Marilyn Manson or a poet like Plath or a novel like *She's Come Undone* or a movie like *Shine,* which was considered a surprise success even though it had the obvious appeal of allowing any parent who saw it to congratulate himself because *he* wouldn't beat his child and *he* wouldn't drive him crazy with Rachmaninoff—without that same parent having to concede that David Helfgott is one of those needy, annoying people he couldn't possibly abide if this were real life and not a movie. While the conventional wisdom would insist that a happy ending is required to make something a "feel-good" movie, in fact plenty of films that allow us to smugly applaud ourselves for never falling that low—but for still having the sensitivity to appreciate and care about those who *have* fallen that low just enough to spend two hours watching *Frances* or *Betty Blue*—seem the very definition of "feel-good," from a certain liberal humanist perspective. Let's face it: they don't have movie theaters or bookstores or music emporia in mental wards. The audience for crazy art is mostly not crazy people. And no matter how many functioning dysthymics there are walking the streets on Prozac, they are not a large enough special-interest group to constitute the entire audience for Metallica albums or even for Kieslowski films: there is, apparently, a whole world of perfectly normal people who dig other people's pain.

And glum photography put to commercial use capitalizes on our need for sullen art, our culture's attempt to invent a medicine man, the shaman who suffers so we don't have to: he provides the 1 percent homeopathy to the public—the catharsis experience, the leading edge without the deep fatal wound—while he himself is infected with 100 percent of the disease. And just as inoculations are a bodily blockade against microscopic predators, the unhappy visual images that flood into popular culture screen out the ugliness of depression and insanity and make it all so beautiful—through an artist's rendering, or through a camera's lens, with the help of a light meter and proper play between a bright flash and frightened, frozen eyes, a scared and sad woman, a body caging vulnerability—can be converted by art into a breathtaking image. Charles Peterson's unruly, uncontained black-and-white photographs of Soundgarden, Nirvana, Green River and other Seattle bands in motion—using a slow shutter speed and flaming-flash technique that's become his trademark—create quite a commotion, lots of toppling over and falling into drum sets, lots of drunk and disorderly incoherence, so much disturbed energy that so captures the exuberance of grunge's downward spiral it is easy to forget that many of the people in Peterson's pictures have since died. But if Peterson's lens tended to focus on men, music videos stalked distraught, unstrung women. While MTV was still in its infancy, Paulina Porizkova was already the windblown damsel in distress for the Cars' "Drive"; Sofia Coppola plays the drugged-out roughed-up babe of the Chateau Marmont variety in the clip for the Black Crowes' "She Talks to Angels"; in the video for "Silent All These Years," Tori Amos is boxed into fetal position, in a striking concoction of photographs hued in blue and orange and purple, artfully Xeroxed onto stark white paper so that the singer looks as delicate as a watercolor painting, even as the song affirms her strength; in "If It Makes You Happy," Sheryl Crow casts herself as a caged animal on display in an indoor zoo, paving the way for the black-and-white follow-up video for "Every Day Is a Winding Road," a chronicle of coming to terms that's full of Clearasil close-ups and introspective wanderings.

In fashion photography, heroin chic has become an idiom of choice, beginning in 1990 with pictures Corinne Day took of a newly discovered Kate Moss, making her the face of the British magazine *The Face*—in a layout whose cranky, incandescent lights and bathroom-tile setting posed Moss' waifishness as dope-sickness, hunger. People dug it. Suddenly fragile, delicate, troubled looks were a trend, and waif models like Emma Balfour, Beri Smithers and Amber Valletta became the antidote to the bigness that was Cindy, Claudia, Naomi and Linda. British photographer Andrew Macpherson described these somber babies as "elegantly wasted," two words that were also the name of an INXS album whose title track was accompanied by a fashionably brooding video. (For what it's worth, the band's lead singer, Michael Hutchence, committed suicide by hanging himself in his room at the Ritz-Carlton in Sydney in late 1997.) Since the early nineties, Kate Moss has herself filled out a bit, she has joined the ranks of the first-name-only supermodels and her looks have proved unexpectedly versatile. But the bored slouch of the world-weary continues to style ads for Calvin Klein's cKOne and cKbe, the sex-neutral fragrances that are sold with campaigns picturing both men and women, standing around looking unwashed and unhappy, for a total effect that makes them appear to be playing a game of charades and doing their damnedest to pantomime "existential angst." These commercials have been around so long that they actually parody themselves, but in case anyone is not in on the joke, Boston Market now has a television spot that shows models blabbing inanities at no one in particular and talking about hunger as if it were an intellectual concept, until some nice, ordinary-looking guy steps onto the set and tells these skinny people dressed in black that the pain they're feeling inside is just what most people call an appetite and they just really need to eat.

Pasty, starved, disheveled, dirty: the heroin chic look begs the question of whether it is dictated by fashion or if fashion is dictated by the drug itself. After the war in Afghanistan ended, the country's 800,000 poppy growers who had fled to Pakistan for refuge returned to their homeland and resumed their tradition-bound agrarian trade; at the same time, with bumper crops of opium in Myanmar, Southeast Asian heroin traffickers were able to flood New York and its environs with a cheap street brand called China White, a strain of smack so potent that snorting it is a realistic, nonprohibitive alternative to shooting up. Becoming a junkie in New York City has never been so easy. As teenage girls all alone in Manhattan, models are natural candidates for substance abuse, making it a lucky coincidence that, as Stephen Fried writes in *Thing of Beauty,* "some girls [are] even more attractive to photographers when they [are] high than when they [are] straight: certain drugs produce certain faraway looks or stoke certain inner fires that work for certain pictures." Fried's 1994 book, a biography of Gia Carangi—the dark, brooding lesbian junkie who made it to the cover of *Cosmopolitan* and *Vogue* before succumbing to an AIDS-related death in 1987, at age twenty-six—may actually be contributing to junk contagion by creating a cult around Gia. A group of young models, calling themselves "Gia's Girls," have apparently taken up heroin in homage, heartened by the knowledge that the large, bloody abscess on Gia's hand that eventually rendered the cover girl unemployable will never be a problem for them, since they don't use needles. "There aren't a lot of signs, aside from the way it makes you itch and keep scratching," Zoe Fleischauer, a twenty-one-year-old model and recovering heroin addict told *Allure,* in a profile the magazine did of her habit. "People aren't likely to notice. Models don't have tracks on their arms; it's more common to snort it rather than shoot up." If enough young models are using, perhaps heroin chic is fashion's elastic attempt to accommodate what it can't contain, to give dull eyes and empty stares and limp limbs a forum for expression, to make languor and helplessness seem glamorous. "The nineties," Amy Spindler wrote in *The New York Times* in May 1996, following fashion shows full of red-eyed models with stringy, slimy hair, "may well be remembered as the decade when fashion served as a pusher—a pusher of what appear to be the best-dressed heroin addicts in history."

It would be easy enough to just say that's fashion, hemlines up, hemlines down, ho-hum, who cares? But drug addiction and mental illness are serious things, they claim lives. And while many suffering souls have beautified and embellished themselves in various ways to gain sympathy for their cause, the effect is often like a charity ball with too much glitter and champagne and conspicuous consumption—all that luxury makes us wonder why the cause needs our help. For some strange reason, a woman crying out in pain is less sympathetic than one suffering in silence—and pictures of fashion models are always silent. In *Carnal Knowledge,* Ann-Margret delivers the best performance of her career as Jack Nicholson's frustrated, depressed girlfriend, buxom in black lace nighties that she never takes off because all she does is sleep—a firecracker when she first met him, she has been reduced by his neglect and her boredom into a nagging shrew, a pill-popper of the classic sixties demented homemaker variety, without the benefit of even being married. But when she takes an overdose, calculated to catch Nicholson's attention, the movie maneuvers us into siding with him, all calm and charm, stuck with this manipulative nightmare. In this surprisingly realistic portrait of a typically annoyed response to a suicide attempt, even a hot tomato like Ann-Margret seems shrill and vile: while there is no way to draw attention to her desperation other than to make a lot of noise, it is that very shriek that drives people away. In real life, the beauty is dwarfed by the overwhelming nature of the mental disease, which is something that still lifes captured through a camera's lens cannot show.

But even worse, sometimes it *is* the pain itself that is so beautiful—instead of masking the beauty, the madness only enhances it. One of the most striking photographs of Edie Sedgwick was taken in 1967 after the second time her Chelsea Hotel room had gone up in flames as a result of her drugged indifference. She sits on a couch, dangling earrings contrasting her pixie-girl haircut, her burns wrapped in bandages, her hand close to her face, her eyes gently closed, heavy with mascara and glitter and fake lashes—she is all eyes even when her lids are so weighed down. It's as if she wouldn't leave her room without putting her face on, fire be damned—a vanity that is sick in its stupidity and touching in its tenacity. The picture I am describing is of someone who has just had her wounds dressed after surviving a fire, it is a horrible thing, but the beauty is in the plainness of the pain, the glamour of fire, the bohemia of it all. We look at this photo and get sucked into its brute loveliness, rubbernecking through a lens across several years, knowing that its subject is a woman who could have been killed, a woman who did indeed die by her own means shortly thereafter. It is a picture of somebody who should be dead, and is dead. It is madness in repose, and the allure is so blatant that it's hard to remember what a miserable person Edie Sedgwick was.

And the photography and artwork that portray and celebrate depression not only fail to enlighten us about the emotional illness of the ravishing subject—if anything, they make us appreciate it *too* much, enjoying the aesthetics rather than aiding with an antidote—but also fail to increase our generosity toward the majority of mentally ill people whose pain is not so pretty. Anyone who has ever taken a tour of a loony bin can tell you that there aren't terribly many Zeldas or Edies in the schizophrenic ward, and even the ones who are there look terrible—slack-jawed, slouchy, spacy, sallow from institutional lighting, puffy from institutional cooking or just plain ugly from indifference to appearance or exhaustion or any of the many other side effects that the lockup can result in.

But forget mental institutions—already the rarefied hospital air could have a salubrious effect on the inmates. Instead take a look at the sick among us. Anyone who walks around the streets of a major metropolitan area will notice that the gutters and sidewalks are littered with the insane and infirm bodies of homeless people, most of whom fell into their destitute, deracinated poverty because of mental illness. These street people, the ones talking to angels or just plain talking to themselves, the ones panhandling on the subway or standing with placards on the median of the highway—these people are smelly, filthy, lousy, shameless, plainly unappealing. And yet, their schizophrenia or manic-depression or alcoholism is no less worthy of sympathy than that of a gorgeous heiress. Mental illness is incredibly ugly, and it is these devastated casualties of deinstitutionalization that walk our urban streets who give the truest illustration of just how ugly the experience of emotional breakdown is. They *look* the way Anne Sexton *feels*. They don't allow us to deny how bad things are.

While Mary Ellen Mark and other Arbus acolytes would seem to provide a countervailing force to heroin chic by photographing the *real* homeless and the *truly* dispossessed, this work only comes across as some politically correct gesture at—at what? It's a tired theme, these pictures of what is ugly and sad, so overdone that it doesn't make us feel anything except occasionally grossed out, and the photographer-as-do-gooder starts to seem just plain exploitative—I mean, at least Kate Moss is getting paid. Worst of all, these portraits of poverty do nothing to connect the emotional life of, say, Frances Farmer with that of a greasy, grimy homeless woman—they do nothing to show that the mental state may be the same, but one was born beautiful and talented and the other was not. (It is worth noting, for instance, that supermodel Niki Taylor, who is twenty-two and the single mother of twin boys, with no skills or education, would probably be regarded as just another burdensome welfare recipient living off our tax dollars if she weren't so beautiful.) In all these pictures of society's marginalia, the subjects remain wholly Other, their humanity restored not at all. The Edie cult, the Gia cult, the Zelda cult: everybody gets trivialized as a result of these icons of insanity—the pretty babies because they are too beautiful to be seriously suffering, and the ugly deranged because no one wants to pay attention to them because they aren't attractive enough.

We blame the repressive times for the madness of Marilyn, we blame the excessive times for the schizophrenia of Zelda, and the cries of Sylvia Plath and Anne Sexton—along with novels like *The Golden Notebook* by Doris Lessing and *Surfacing* by Margaret Atwood—played some part in the spark of the women's movement in the early seventies. But finally, now, with Prozac and all these new drugs and more humane treatments of mental illness of all sorts—and better understanding of depression and its biological nature—it is easy to pin the troubles of all of these women in the past on bad chemistry. It's easy to say—and not wrong at all—that their ailments would have been greatly ameliorated by serotonin reuptake inhibitors. So whether we turn the madwoman into great art or portray her as a victim of bad science, we still end up with the same result: we still end up failing to acknowledge that maybe, just maybe, she had a point, maybe her anger and sorrow and sadness were as justified and valid as Cassandra's prophecies. Maybe their craziness spoke the truth. There are lessons in these lives, but we are no longer obligated to learn them.

*   *   *

Since the publication of *The Bell Jar* in the United States in 1971, nothing has succeeded its significance as a cultural document, no work of fiction has assumed its literary role as *the* narrative of an adolescent girl's rebellion against the forces that will straitjacket her into a frightful, flightless femininity—and the way this willful fight is so thwarted that it just turns around, the loaded gun that should be pointing Out There is instead a weapon of self-destruction. It's the story of the moment when girlishness and womanhood meet at a desperate crossroads, and confront the pushes and pulls and demands and choices that are as daunting as the fright that bluesman Robert Johnson felt at the fork in the road of "Crossroads Blues" when he "got down on my knees and prayed." Plath's novel is still the template, the book to read for a girl going through a depression or breakdown.

It's not that many novels chronicling a girl falling apart have not appeared since 1971—this plot probably constitutes the subject matter of at least half the bildungsromans published each year—but most of them have revolved around, to pilfer a term from legal circles, the abuse excuse. Most are about incest, molestation, rape or battery victims who go crazy as a result of the cruelty and torment that was visited upon them; many employ an *up from slavery / I saw God in myself and I loved her* type of conversion narrative that delivers recovery and redemption by the end, as is the case in popular novels like Wally Lamb's *She's Come Undone* or Pat Conroy's *The Prince of Tides.*

The Bell Jar—while absolutely implicating a prefeminist society in which a brilliant young woman writing a thesis on the motif of twins in *Finnegans Wake* is encouraged by her mother to learn shorthand to increase her secretarial prospects—is about a world that is fine, fine enough for most people to function in at any rate: no beatings, no bruises, no blood on the kitchen floor to be hid under the rug. But Esther Greenwood is just too sensitive. She can't handle it. She gets depressed, she breaks down, she takes a large overdose of pills, she lies comatose in a crawl space in the cellar of her house, she is resuscitated, she gets shock, she gets therapy, months in a mental hospital: in summary, Esther has a taxing and extensive bout with emotional illness, for no particular reason, for causes that shuffle around, appearing and disappearing as if they were part of a shell game, a street con—as soon as one thing starts to make sense, another is revealed. The death of her father? Her rather dim mother? *What* can it *be?*

At no point in *The Bell Jar* is a model of cause and effect, an Exhibit A, an item that can be committed to evidence, offered for Esther's self-destruction. There are a zillion good reasons, but ultimately no real smoking gun, no father who raped or maimed her, no mother, like the one in *Sybil,* who systematically sexually tortured her. There is just stenography and scholarship worries and a simultaneous translator and sexual curiosity and an annoying consumptive Yale medical student for a boyfriend and a hot summer in New York City with a lucky magazine job—there is just a lot of lucky everything, more than enough reward to compensate for a father who died while she was still young and a mother who taught shorthand to make ends meet. *The Bell Jar* rather daringly exposed suicidal depression as the rage of the privileged class, as a killer without cause and a disease without the precise DNA tests or brain-scan results that would hold up in a court case against its existence: its symptoms are purely circumstantial, in an evidentiary sense, and rely on the account the sufferer, who is unstable enough to be thought an unreliable narrator even though it is that very instability that she is testifying about.

Sylvia Plath was a brave soul—and perhaps it helped to live in Britain while writing her novel at a time when in America "important" books like Michael Harrington's condemnation of poverty, *The Other America,* and Rachel Carson's environmental Cassandra cry, *The Silent Spring,* were the real publishing news. Civil rights and the Bay of Pigs and covert operations in Southeast Asia and Kennedy's assassination were the real political news. To imply, even in fictional form, that the plight of a Smith-girl basket case was worthy of anyone's attention in this charged, "serious" climate was quite a statement. Even Ken Kesey and, thereafter, Milos Forman had to make *One Flew Over the Cuckoo's Nest* something of an exposé of mental institution mismanagement—and his characters were seriously sick, not just depressed college girls (or should I say "college girls"?): Kesey wrote about men—ailing men, macho men, deranged men, delusional men—and not sensitive sappy little poetess types who suffer from nothing that couldn't be cured by a husband. Failing that, they could be calmed and balmed with Valium or Librium or Miltown, a housewife pandemic of pills that became a rock music commonplace when the phenomenon was documented in the Rolling Stones' song "Mother's Little Helper."

While *The Bell Jar* is beautifully, carefully and agilely written, full of tart edge and detached bewilderment at Esther's ineluctable disarray—"I wondered what terrible thing it was that I had done"—it can be diminished as not quite the achievement we would expect to receive from a more mature, more developed (and presumably undead) Sylvia Plath. *The Bell Jar* as a novel can be reduced within the Plath *oeuvre* to the status of precursor: what *The Colossus* was to *Ariel,* so *The Bell Jar* would have been to her later lengthy fictional offerings, the ones obviated by her early death. In Ted Hughes' 1970 correspondence with Sylvia's mother, Aurelia Plath, initiated in hope of enlisting her support for a United States publication of *The Bell Jar* (he needed the proceeds in order to purchase a house in Devon), he denigrated the novel as a mere "curiosity for students."

But to view *The Bell Jar* as simply part of a progression, as consequential only in context, is to be an idiot: it is a failure to see that to render a nervous breakdown honestly and truly as it happened, to write in accessible language that richly renders the pathetic minutiae of a mind come undone—"The reason I hadn't washed my clothes or my hair was because it seemed so silly . . . It seemed silly to wash one day when I would only have to wash again the next"—is a worthy and proud accomplishment. Its message about the limits women feel is daring and rebellious, perhaps even now: when Courtney Love sings, "I want to be the girl with the most cake," the demand she is making for, frankly, her just desserts is not so different from the lust for life that Plath was wishing would be permissible for the narrator of *The Bell Jar;* Love's desire to gobble up the most of the most is close to the sense of entitlement Plath wanted for herself. As Mrs. Greenwood urges her daughter to learn shorthand and speaks of what an in-demand secretary she will be if she can take dictation with dexterity and ease and "transcribe letter after thrilling letter," the poor girl just feels horror at the stymied smallness her role in the world seems fated to be. "The trouble was, I hated the idea of serving men in any way," Esther explains. "I wanted to dictate my own thrilling letters."

At the time, Plath could not even contemplate wanting *all* or even *most* of the cake—she was having a hard enough time getting a piece of her own. And the image that she creates to vivify the famine of her future does not have the richness of anything yummy at all—it is instead a fig tree, the Edenic bearer of fruit that the still-graced Adam and Eve ate from and inadvertently prompted their fall (it was not, contrary to common belief, an apple that tempted the first couple; the expression "fig leaf" is derived from what it was that Adam first grabbed at to cover his newly discovered nakedness): "From the tip of every branch, a wonderful future beckoned and winked. One fig was a husband and a happy home and future, and another fig was a famous poet and another fig was a brilliant professor, and another fig was Ee Gee, the amazing editor, and another fig was Europe and Africa and South America, and another fig was Constantin and Socrates and a pack of other lovers with queer names and offbeat professions, and another fig was an Olympic lady crew champion, and beyond and above these figs were many more figs I couldn't quite make out," Plath writes, imagining Esther's future possibilities and impossibilities. "I saw myself sitting in the crotch of this fig tree, starving to death just because I couldn't make up my mind which of the figs I would choose. I wanted each and every one of them, but choosing one meant losing all the rest, and, as I sat there, unable to decide, the figs began to wrinkle and go black, and one by one they plopped into the ground at my feet."

Sylvia Plath suffered from wanting so much in a world that did not allow women to want anything at all—anything, that is, outside of their allotted roles as unmarried women in the steno pool and married homemakers in the neighborhood coffee klatch. In *The Bell Jar* and in a good bit of her poetry, Plath is the voice of one who wants to be *allowed* to want—she wants the luxury of not just one desire, but many. And in Esther Greenwood's fig tree future, the girl who wants so many things that no Santa Claus could ever deliver—the kinds of life-choice combinations that women today struggle to juggle, though we take for granted our right to try and often enough, to succeed— becomes a woman who ends up *needing* so much more. Denied the delicious nourishment of all that is happy and hopeful in what she desires, she is drained and empty, an emotional wreck. The need is a burdensome absence whose weight is so much greater than her brilliant presence: in the end, it is psychic starvation that kills her.

Courtney Love is a controversial figure for a vast assortment of reasons that touch on all aspects of sex, drugs and rock and roll, and still, I think that ultimately the scariest thing about her is that *she wants*. She wants and she's not afraid to say *that* she wants and *what* she wants. She is not afraid of her own desire, and that desire is huge: she wants everything, the most cake and the most of the most. She wants the freedom to be who she wants to be whenever without reprimands and reproaches from those who are not so bold. She wants to attend all the fashion shows in Paris and New York and Milan, she wants to wear ladies-who-lunch respectability in the form of a Chanel suit and a Garren bob, but she wants artistic integrity, the true grit of a girl rocker who is angry and achy and has the hedgehog hair and torn-up tatters of sweaty threads to prove it. She wants to be accepted in the White House and the whorehouse. "Rock is all about writing your own script," Love told *Vanity Fair* when the magazine put her on the June 1995 cover in full seraph gear, feathered wings caped out of her shoulder blades. "It's all about *pioneering*."

When Freud asked, "What do women want?" he felt safe knowing that none would dare to say. "What would happen if one woman told the truth about her life?" asked Muriel Rukeyser in the poem "Käthe Kollwitz," published, as was the American edition of *The Bell Jar,* amid the women's movement's 1971 heyday. "The world would split open." But in truth, it would more likely derogate such "truth" by reducing it to no more than a silly girl's excessive emotionalism before it could even create the kind of threat that actually would cause the earth's faultlines to crack. Sylvia Plath herself dismissed *The Bell Jar* as a "potboiler," and when the British edition was published by Heinemann in 1963, she chose to use a pseudonym. Though *The Bell Jar* received fine reviews upon release in England, the novel by unknown "Victoria Lucas" was rejected out of hand by Knopf—the American company that published Plath's poetry was baffled that they'd even received such an objectionable submission by a complete unknown talent from Heinemann—and editor William Koshland wrote that he was "knocked galley west" to discover that the true author was Plath. Koshland explained that he and his colleagues at Knopf felt it was just a typical first novel that the poet had to "get out of her system," and that it read "as if it were autobiographical, flagrantly so"; Harper & Row, which would ultimately publish *The Bell Jar* in 1971, rejected it at first because "the story ceases to be a novel and becomes a case history."

Speculating on the novel's presumed unpublishability in John Kennedy's America, Paul Alexander, author of the Plath biography *Rough Magic,* posits that *"The Bell Jar* seems to be a victim of its time. Society allowed a man to write about going mad—Salinger and Ken Kesey did, to name two—but when a woman approached the subject, she was disparaged." But to see it as a case of a failure to be fashionable fiction is not quite fair. Certainly, things are a lot better thirty-five years after Plath's book was shunned by the very publisher that would eventually see it spend six months on *The New York Times* best-seller list when it was finally loosed onto an American audience. But I'm not sure we ought to be too optimistic: it's not as if women today who try to be blood-and-gory-guts honest and unabashed with their emotions are greeted with great reverence by arbiters of culture. Excessive displays of emotion are always reduced to merely "manipulative" or "artless." Though the screams of Nirvana and the Sex Pistols could be easily dismissed as no less infantile than the cries of a baby in his crib desperate to get his mum's attention—which is not, by the way, how I feel at all; I *love* both bands—each of these groups has a permanent residence in credibility heaven. Meanwhile, Sinéad O'Connor's public displays of aggression have practically destroyed her career, Alanis Morissette's raging debut American album is undermined by repeated reminders and gibes at her earlier teen pop star status in Canada, and Courtney Love's temper tantrums and crying bouts both at her husband's funeral and onstage are just annoying, just inappropriate: *there she goes again.*

Of course, Courtney Love has certainly become a force and a figure in pop culture, and she has surely got record sales and movie roles to reckon with. But her prodigal and prodigious talent is often ignored in favor of lumping her in with the likes of image geniuses like Madonna, a woman not to be trifled with—just as the gift for perpetual persona reinvention should not be denied in a culture where were it accessible to all, everyone from Deborah Harry to Sheena Easton to Pat Benatar would continue to have viable careers—but a woman with none of Courtney's audacious artistic abilities. Love, despite her great gifts, is more renowned for being a "potboiler": when *Rolling Stone* finally put the whole Hole on the cover—and not just its overfocalzied front woman—the tag line read: "Hole is a band (Courtney Love is a soap opera)." But the sad side of watching such a talent as Love's eclipsed by bad behavior—calculated or otherwise—is that it is just not fair: Kurt Cobain, her deceased husband, was every bit as much the it-boy of grunge with his changing hair hues, his dress-donning for videos, and even his willingness to be half of a very public pair of junkies heading for the junkyard; but in the collective consciousness, his talent takes precedent over his image.

Meanwhile, Love's train wreck approach to her public life has incurred professional penalties with regard to recognition for the work itself: it is simply *unthinkable* that Love was not nominated for an Oscar for her role in *The People vs. Larry Flynt*—and the fact that she was in the running in the category of supporting actress when she so commanded that film is almost worse. I might add that, after being dissed by the Academy, her need to conform to some imaginary standard of respectability—all the plastic surgery she has plainly had, the exchange of a silk charmeuse thrift shop nightgown and *Carrie*-inspired prom queen tiara as an Oscar outfit in 1995 for unironic Versace elegance in 1997—is baffling: when Cher was overlooked by the Oscars in 1986 after a blustery performance in *Mask*, at least she countered the oversight by showing up in Bob Mackie's idea of an Indian chief outfit—complete with gold lamé detailing and sequined feathers for a headdress—and preceded her presentation of an award by saying, "This is my serious actress look." (Cher did receive not just a nomination but the Oscar itself for her part in *Moonstruck*, just two years later; obviously, chutzpah is no object.) But when Love acted as a presenter, she read straight and without expression from the Teleprompter, and she did not seize upon the opportunity to deliver a silly and disrespectful (as if an institution that gives *Forrest Gump* as best picture award really deserves respect!) counter-dis. Her model of decorum in the face of such undeserved unrecognition spoke Twelve Step volumes: *Hi, my name is Courtney, and I am ready to play your game.*

It's not that Courtney Love should not be encouraged to grow up and outgrow a junkie existence of wardrobe by Salvation Army, but both Jack Nicholson and Marlon Brando have won Oscars and commanded artistic respectability while behaving in ways that are completely outside the system. To court Hollywood, Courtney seems to have recast herself; this may well be simply what she genuinely wants to do, but the impulse is such an about-face from her previous projected persona that it seems one or the other must be false. I mean, Dennis Hopper is no longer the nutcase who could only be marginally employed playing marginal characters in *Easy Rider* and *Apocalypse Now*, but he is still patently eccentric, he's still weird and proud.

It was cool, it was gutsy—it was even *ballsy*—when Courtney could boast to *Vanity Fair* back in September 1992 that she was starting her own Hole fanzine called *And She's Not Even Pretty* because "a lot of the anti-Courtney factions say, 'And she's not even pretty.' Here's this new rock star—Kurt—and he's supposed to be married to a model and he's married to me." It was great that she took pride in her unconventional beauty—or the lack thereof—and strutted the seductive sex appeal of her dangerous mind. But now—no more. I am happy to see such a talent as she on the cover of the crucial, telephone-book-thick

September 1997 issue of *Harper's Bazaar* as one of "America's Most Stylish Women," but I'd have liked it a lot better if she'd done it on her own terms, in her own kinderwhore dresses, or even in Vivienne Westwood or Anna Sui—but not, dear God, in Ralph Lauren!

But as much as I am sickened by what appears to be a hard survivalist calculation that has turned a woman who made music that—at least for me—expressed a rage that was frightening, honest, upsetting, sickening and ultimately rather beautiful into someone who just wants to incorporate all that into a marketable act, doing lunch with Demi, playing the Hollywood shuffle and generally fleeing from the kinds of intense and honest emotional experiences that made her talent thrive, I finally have to shrug and ask: What choice has she got? She simply could not have gotten anywhere at all without reigning that stuff in. "It's preposterous to say, 'We *love* your personality. We *love* what you are doing and who you are in front of the camera—but when you step off the stage, you have to be *one of us!*' It doesn't work that way," Milos Forman, director of *Larry Flynt*, perspicaciously observed of his female lead in a *Premiere* cover story on Courtney. "You want brilliance? Don't expect you'll have it for free." But Hollywood does not want brilliance—it wants box office, and Forman notwithstanding, the only thing the powers that be in the movie world are likely to indulge are the special Scientology holiday schedules of its biggest stars. Courtney Love wants what she wants and she will behave properly to get it. She has become, in this way, a model for the New Post-Depressive Woman: saving her tears and hangovers for her private life, in public she is harsh and hard, like Roseanne, Carrie Fisher and other rehab refugees and loony-bin-trip survivors making a Hollywood living, she is witty, overweeningly wise and wise-cracking, smug and smart—but not *that* smart. Courtney Love believes a career will set her free, and she is not dumb about doing what it takes.

And when we get away from show business and get back to Plath's world, the world of letters, it seems worth noting that while at long last women have been given credit and granted success by writing memoirs of breakdowns—both Susanna Kaysen's *Girl, Interrupted* and Kay Redfield Jameson's *An Unquiet Mind* were big best-sellers—the plentiful array of novels women have churned out about losing their minds are largely ignored. In fact, the only fiction I can think of that deals very directly with depression that has had any cultural impact—*The Prince of Tides* and *She's Come Undone*—has been written by men, as if the right to artfully redraw madness into a creation and not just a personal history that can be granted the forgiveness for mistakes in metaphor or purple prose has been left only in the hands of men. That both Conroy's and Lamb's novels are dishonest accounts—the vulnerability of the characters they create is well within the boundaries of what readers can handle, the ugliness of emotional illness is drawn in such a way that the audience believes it is receiving revelation when in fact it is just a canned version of what the distasteful state is really like (the tone is that of one of a racist who apologetically says, "I have nothing against black people but . . .")—is, I think, what makes them accessible in a way that women's work is not. With such a dearth of novels that re-create that state of misery, it is no wonder that Sylvia Plath has not lost her relevance or reason for readers today.

The thing to know is that people tend to think of Sylvia Plath and Anne Sexton as victims of that fifties prefeminist *Feminine Mystique* culture that wanted Smithies and Cliffies to take shorthand and change diapers, and not read Proust and compose sonnets. People think of Zelda Fitzgerald as a frustrated artist of the freer flapper era, a victim of her husband's literary success, his second fiddle with a few strings missing. We're meant to believe that feminism was what these women needed, not lithium. And it may be so: things are a lot better now that women no longer must marry and have children lest they be old maids at twenty-three. Depression is more prevalent than ever, but the voices like Plath's have been silenced. We now have loud women, difficult women, forthright women, impossible women, shocking women—but we do not have sad women in the public view. Feminism seems to have erased that possibility. Courtney Love has chosen noise over nausea of the Sartre variety; she has opted to be a "character," a "personality," instead of a tragedy. Feminism occasionally seems to have silenced the silence of depression: it's not that it by any means denies the existence of this obvious malady, but by politicizing it, it has destroyed the personal possibilities—and the political *is not* always personal. Which is why the prospect for artistic expression drawn from despair for its own sad sake—which was the task of confessional poetry—no longer seems useful in women's creativity if defiance and anger do not accompany it; and, as is well known, once defiance and anger are part of the picture, depression abates and subsides. The whining is over—let the fighting begin! No more Joni Mitchell or Janis Ian or Joan Baez—bring on Hole and Veruca Salt and Alanis Morissette!

I, for one, like both parts of the equation—I like the sorrow and the fury, but only Liz Phair seems able to balance them. Meanwhile the latter drowns out the former, and it isolates us all a little more. Ultimately, that alienation always leads right back to Sylvia Plath, to the last days of the art of confession. A zillion clinical reports in the *Journal of the American Medical Association* that translate into articles in the "Science Times" section of the Tuesday *New York Times* and features in women's magazines talking about epidemic rates of depression have nothing on the evocations of this catastrophic mental state that Plath created so clearly.

To be fair, Sylvia Plath's narrator in *The Bell Jar* is tart and detached, always aware that compared to the execution of the Rosenbergs—a death sentence with which she is obsessed—her problems are all about tempests in teapots. But she doesn't care: the book itself is testament to her belief that this is a story worth telling, a malady worth understanding. *The Bell Jar* is still one of the few titles that speaks to depressives who cannot blame their mental state on any life event dramatic or traumatic or concrete enough to qualify as a topic for Sally Jessy Raphael to explore. Her prose and poetry tell of untethered unraveling and purposeless pain. That Plath later wrote poems invoking Dachau and Auschwitz in the framework of her emotional life proves she truly did not fear the censure of the *Casablanca*-ists, the ones who think personal problems don't amount to a hill of beans, et al.

And Plath was able to compose such a book in the way that someone else might have caught the last train out of Berlin before the Nazis took over: after that period of time, mental health could only be politicized if it was to be heard of at all—in Betty Friedan's *The Feminine Mystique*, in Phyllis Chesler's *Women and Madness*, in Juliet Mitchell's *Feminism and Psychoanalysis*. Her story would have been polemical, rhetorical—not nearly so good as the novel it was. It would have been read as a "text": as the precise case history the American publishers had initially reduced it to. But the result of the diminished acceptance of the concerns of the self—except in the broadest, Me Decade movement sort of way, or in the vilest *Leeza–Jenny Jones–Ricki Lake–Jerry Springer* sort of way—is that serious and accessible literature has tended not to deal with nervous breakdown without incest or some other suburban catastrophe being implicated, or without taking a harsh, ironic, been-there, done-that tone. *The Bell Jar*—in the same sense that Bob Dylan is the last American folksinger and Allen Ginsberg is our last popular, populist poet—was the last novel that exhibited the confessional poetry impulse of the fifties, an impulse driven by the fight against the era's repression, and later drowned out by the far louder voices of protest in the sixties.

Ever since then, depression has mostly been agenda-ized out of literature's aegis—although once in a while a surprising work of truth and depth will sneak into the marketplace. *Smilla's Sense of Snow,* author Peter Høeg's beautiful thriller embedded within a melancholy interior monologue, was a huge critical success and best-seller here in the United States in 1994, a rarity for any book in translation, but as an import from Denmark it is probably the first success in these parts since Hans Christian Andersen. The novel is ostensibly about a Danish Inuit woman's attempt to solve a murder, but it is actually a meditation on sorrow and longing and exile, it is about deep-down defining depression, it is about luxuriating in loneliness, it is about lusting for the darkness of Greenland, it is about finding truth and all the world's secrets in the coldness of snow—it is in fact a novel about a woman in love with snow. Though it was written by a man, Høeg understands the truth of this woman's mind the way D. H. Lawrence felt for the drives of Lady Chatterley and Gustave Flaubert understood intimately the ennui of Emma Bovary. I have to assume that this study of a woman who takes a strange pride in her sorrow only managed to register on our cultural charts because the murder mystery aspect obscured its emotional content. Or maybe, as is the case with the many successful memoirs that have come along to fill a void where intense and exploratory literature once resided, there is a hunger for Høeg's lucid rendering of an alienation that is preferable to a compromised life integrating with an indifferent, cynical world—*Smilla's Sense of*

Snow gave readers a bottled SOS from another coast, assuring the most deserted and isolated person that she is not alone.

More to the point, since the death of Plath in 1963 and her fellow confessional poet Sexton in 1974, no American poet—and, to my thinking, artist or writer—has replaced these two as icons of insanity. For the life of me, I could not tell you what the typical poem published in *The New Yorker* or whatever other journals still contain poetry is actually about—trees, stalagmite and stalactite, and what the fall does to the landscape is all I can grasp—but I am sure that none have the dread immediacy or ache or honesty of "Elm" or "The Tulips" or "Wanting to Die." For a refreshing moment, confessional poetry reigned supreme and then when all the practitioners made good on the promises that their work offered up—which is to say, one by one they died by their own hands—poetry went back to being a gentleman's art, an intellectual parlor game, and all that crazy manic energy instead got packed up and sent off into rock and roll. Certainly, plenty of depressing stuff has appeared, but no one has achieved icon status for sorrow—perhaps because death is a prerequisite, but Diane West Middlebrook chronicles how even when she was alive, Anne Sexton's followers would come see her read in order to see her go crazy. Even as rates of female depression accelerate, with men's speeding up as well, somehow this culture cannot find a place for art that is intellectual, accessible, glamorous and depressive all at once. Finally it reemerged in grunge rock, and pop music in the early nineties achieved the elusive "relevance" it had been masturbating over ever since the death of Jim, Jimi and Janis, ever since the Beatles broke up. But, alas, Kurt Cobain died before it could take hold, before the momentum that qualifies anything as a movement could be felt.

*   *   *

When the movie *Quiz Show* came out, dramatizing the young congressional attorney Richard Goodwin's prosecution of the television game show riggings, I was mostly struck by a dark little corner of the movie—barely even a subplot—a small personal speck within a film that was otherwise notable mostly for its sweepingness, its big themes. I was struck by the character of Sandra Leverant, Goodwin's Vassar girl and graduate student wife, played by Mira Sorvino, in what I thought was quite a star turn. In fact I thought that Mira, who had been a classmate of mine at Harvard, ought to have won an Oscar for her portrayal, and I rightly predicted, when she wasn't even nominated, that it was only a matter of time before she did receive that honor (only a couple of years later, as Linda in Woody Allen's *Mighty Aphrodite*).

Anyway, Sandra as movie character was only vaguely sketched, but she wore berets and accused her husband of being the "Uncle Tom of the Jews" when he seemed reluctant to press charges against Charles Van Doren, the handsome blond blue-blood who was deemed too elegant to drag into this muck, too heroic. Of course, Sandra is right, she is probably always right, and she becomes the moral center of a movie which is mostly about Goodwin's frustration at his paper-pushing job and his attempt to kick up some dust and make a name for himself that is better suited to being number one in his class at Harvard Law. Meanwhile, he comes home to Sandra and finds her doing the crossword puzzle when she should be writing her dissertation, finds her using her obviously considerable intelligence—more considerable than his, it seems clear—mostly to set him straight, to question and criticize the probity of his crusade.

I mean, they are, after all, only game shows.

Well, anyway, I really liked her. I loved the way she would be doing crossword puzzles when she should have been doing serious intellectual work because, frankly, I am an obsessive doer of the daily puzzle, get the *Times* only for the crossword and spend a lot of time when I should be working just filling in those little boxes. And I liked the niche she had carved for herself in her marriage because I always believed it was what I, as a wife, would be best at: as someone who hides at home, writing what is on my mind and disengaged from the politics of business, of life or of politics themselves, I always thought I'd be good to come home to, a person to put things in perspective, to point out the stupidity of the pissing contests most men seem to find so engaging. For instance, I could say, if I married a studio executive, *How stupid you are to give Jim Carrey $20 million for just one movie*, and I could point out why these Faustian bargains never are worth it. Or if I were married to a Democratic pollster who was fretting over

Clinton's approval ratings I could tell him that they don't matter because Bush had a 90 percent favorable read and was thought unbeatable a year before the '92 elections, and things change so quickly. I could, I guess I'm saying, do what I do on the page but in real life: I could point out over and over again how very little any of this matters, how huge these things seem and how quickly they then subside.

As someone who has mostly functioned at a strange remove from life, I am often the first one who is able to say that this or that is not worth it, that the whole point is being missed. And while this occasionally looks like prescience or good judgment, it is really disinterest, it is numbness and detachment.

But Sandra Goodwin, protesting the stupidity of this and that, gave me an idea of how it could make one a good wife, a helpmate—yes, I suppose, the woman behind the man.

So I loved her part in the movie, saw it more than once and told the guy I was dating at the time that it really reminded me of our relationship, and he even agreed. When I read Richard Goodwin's memoir, *Looking Back on America,* the book from which *Quiz Show* was derived, I was annoyed to find only two passing references to his wife—in fact, I think it's fair to say I found her absence suspiciously egregious, the telltale heart of darkness that kept pumping through the plywood of the floors, pounding to be heard.

About a year after the film came out, I met someone who had been involved in the *Quiz Show* production and went on and on about Mira's fine performance, about how her few lines and appearances suggested so much, how much I liked and related to the Sandra character.

And this man said to me: "You know, a few years after the end of the events of that movie, sometime in the sixties, she killed herself."

And I thought to myself: *Shit.* Of course I related to her, she was a complete depressive who slept and did the puzzle instead of working on her thesis, who looked at the world and mocked it from the sidelines, never quite managing the immersion that is happiness, that is the hallmark of her husband, a man who was quite compromised, who did things for the wrong reasons—or who did them because they were part of playing the game, because after all it is only a dance.

It is a lot easier to pay Jim Carrey $20 million and to sit behind a desk at a studio, allowing it to produce bad movies if you understand that it is only a dance.

But what if you believe that life is the real thing, that it is serious, that it is huge? As Sylvia Plath wrote in a letter to a boyfriend in 1955, "Perhaps when we find ourselves wanting everything it is because we are dangerously near to wanting nothing"—which is not so different from saying that you are given to caring so much because you fear how perilously close you come to not caring at all. Depression, the disease of not feeling, starts to manifest itself as tantrums, hysteria, excess—the disease of feeling too much. And after a while, I defy anyone to define the difference.

Depressed women, alternately distant and overwrought, are the most difficult women of all. And behavior that is mistaken for any number of things—lasciviousness, insanity and bitchiness above all— is rarely mistaken for what it actually is, for one of the oft-forgotten sins against society, the illness at the center of so many ills: despair.

PART FOUR

The Blonde in the Bleachers

There are women and there's pussy

SAM PECKINPAH
interview in *Playboy*
August 1972

There is an apocryphal story, which, like most bits of folklore, ought to be true even if it isn't. According to this myth, Bill and Hillary Clinton were driving along one day, when they pulled into a gas station and had their car serviced by a man who turned out to be an old high school beau of Hillary's. So Bill said to her, "If you had married him, you'd be the wife of a gas station attendant."

To which she replied, "No, I wouldn't." Pause for effect. "I'd be married to the President of the United States."

I probably don't need to explain that the assonance of this anecdote is in that it confirms our notion of Hillary Clinton as kingmaker and string-puller, as back-door and back-room woman who's so good at what she does that if Bill Clinton had not existed, she would have invented him.

But then there is another story, one that ought to be true because it is true. This one is recounted by Gloria Steinem in her essay "College Reunion," published in *Ms.* in 1981, on the eve of the twenty-fifth anniversary of her graduation from Smith College. As Steinem recalls, a reporter approached her for an article about why so many women of accomplishment had attended Smith. Steinem asked, "Like who?" Well, the reporter replied—completely glossing over the obvious ones, the Sylvia Plaths and Betty Friedans—like Jean Harris, the school headmistress who killed the Scarsdale Diet doctor. Like Nancy Reagan and Barbara Bush (who dropped out after a year to marry George Bush and become a full-time undergraduate war bride in New Haven). "Don't you think it's remarkable," the reporter asked, referring to the First and Second Ladies, "that the two top women in the country went to the same college?"

"Look," Steinem replied, "do you think a reporter is interviewing Mr. Thatcher's schoolmates to find out how they were trained to marry a chief of state? Is Mr. Thatcher one of the top men in England?"

Some years later, during George Bush's presidency, when Barbara was the "top" woman in the country, she was scheduled to deliver the commencement address at Wellesley College. While Mrs. Bush did ultimately give the graduation speech as planned, there was much protest beforehand from students who could not see why an institution devoted to the advancement of women's education and opportunity should bestow the honor of this platform upon a woman whose primary accomplishment was getting married.

Which is fair enough. (Mrs. Bush, ever the good sport—the woman who gets twenty-five pairs of Keds from her husband as a birthday present, and insists that George would never commit adultery because it would cut into his golf game—gamely remarked to the Wellesley grads: "Who knows? Somewhere out there in this audience may even be someone who will one day follow in my footsteps and preside over the White House as the President's spouse. I wish him well!")

Hillary Clinton, of course, is an alumna of Wellesley, where she herself addressed her graduating class as president of the student government in 1969. She was the first undergraduate ever to speak at Wellesley's commencement exercises, and her remarks fairly exude the typically overexuberant twenty-two-year-old's mix of idealism and idiocy. Sixties cant seems sweetly sincere: "We're not interested in social reconstruction; it's human reconstruction." And psychobabble is as psychobabble does: "We can talk about reality, and I would like to talk about reality sometime, authentic reality, inauthentic reality . . . the potentiality for imaginatively responding to men's needs." But Hillary Rodham was at her Creative Writing 101/Rhetoric 11 best when veering into foxy, frisky, juicy thoughts about "searching for more immediate, ecstatic and penetrating modes of living."

It is no wonder that after this podium delirium, Ms. Rodham was photographed for *Life* magazine as part of a roundup on the rising youth culture leadership. Even looking so serious and dowdy in big, decidedly non-Steinemesque, nonstylish aviator glasses, bottomed off with sensible shoes and horrible stretchy striped trousers—you know the kind, the ones that don't even flatter people who look good in everything, and are inevitably worn only by those who look good in nothing—even in all this frump adornment, the picture suggests the possibility of wildfire.

In fact, in a less frequently published photograph from the same era, Hillary makes her best play for this year's model, captured by the lens in a clingy ensemble of an itty-bitty miniskirt and knit T-shirt with a necklace of bangle links suggesting some style sense, after all; but most of all, Hillary, looking lost in reverie, reveals a huge beatific smile and mischievous mien—the picture is clearly posed but the expression is all candor, all fun. Stuck up as she seems these days, she looks like she might have once had awesome sexy potential—or, shall I say, *potentiality?* She looks like she might have actually *inhaled.* (Could there be any other explanation for that speech?)

But, like Barbara Bush many years before her, Hillary Rodham took all her buoyant rocket fuel and headed to New Haven. She went to Yale Law School, and she believed passionately in things and she learned that justice could be another word for salvation and she wanted to make right all that was wrong in the world and she thought she could fly spaceships to the moon (indeed, quite literally: at age fourteen, astronaut aspirations drove Miss Rodham to write a letter to NASA to find out the requirements for entering its burgeoning space program; of course, they told her there were no girls allowed in their very tall tree house).

Instead she went to Arkansas and became the little woman behind a big man.

Instead she ended up no different from Barbara Bush: Hillary is just her husband's wife. Her decision for—or descent into—complete devotion to the man with the Memphis-thick sideburns and the thwack of black pompadoured hair (his mod styling made the young Bill look like the bass player from a second-tier British invasion band) and a serious, seductive drawl began with her resolve to graduate from Yale Law a year late so that she could be in the same class with her beloved Bill. How he affected her so is anyone's guess, but love and lust have made people weak since time immemorial, so why not Hillary? And, of course, one can only imagine that such an intense and purposeful sort as the young Hillary was said to be must have been particularly susceptible to the rare man who saw her sensual possibilities. The courtship of Hillary Rodham is the horror story of every woman who has lived right, who has balanced her own checkbook, who can change her own flat tire, who lives for files and piles and index cards and in-boxes and out-trays and all the order these things imply, only to find it all wrecked by some man who lives to make bonfires out of other people's to-do lists, who makes her forget to do the laundry until he asks her to do his. Hillary's Wellesley speech reveals a young woman who is clearly about to burst if somebody does not find access to the corruptible, disheveled part of her that has had it with doing homework for the boys she has crushes on, that wishes they'd at least feel her up now and again. As Michael Medved, a Yale Law classmate who is now a conservative/family values film critic, recalled to David Brock in his book *The Seduction of Hillary Rodham,* "[Hillary] was somebody who was not considered date bait, because of her weight and her presentation. She was not a glamorous figure by any stretch of the imagination. She was everybody's best friend."

Even old boyfriends, whose feelings were presumably romantic, are rather bloodless when talking about Hillary. "The thing that I remember most were the conversations," Jeff Shields, Hillary's Harvard boyfriend during her Wellesley years, told Gail Sheehy in *Vanity Fair.* Not that it isn't lovely to have men remember how great it was to talk to you, but he isn't even saying, *We spoke all through the night and then we went skinny-dipping in Walden Pond* or *We had crazy dreams and we told each other everything and we were young and I never felt closer to anyone on earth.* It sounds more like lengthy debates on farm subsidies and the Great Society and should they come clean with Gene or just stick with Bobby. I suppose one has to think of Hillary as Minnie Driver in *Circle of Friends* or Janeane Garofalo in *The Truth About Cats and Dogs* or Emma Thompson silently longing for Hugh Grant and living this muted, muffled emotional existence in *Sense and Sensibility*, all the while reminding us that even plain and practical girls are entitled to their dreams. Even Hillary Clinton once read *Cinderella*.

And if most of the boys saw Hillary as comfort and conversation, Bill Clinton uses words like "dumbstruck" to describe his earliest response to Hillary, claiming he was so awed by her goddess-like presence that he could not speak (I'm sure most of his staffers must think: imagine *that!*). One can only assume that their first encounter was like the scene in *The Big Sleep* where Bogey wanders into a bookstore and the librarian-like schoolmarmish salesclerk takes off her glasses, lets down her hair, shuts the shades, gets some paper cups and pours them a pair of drinks, and suddenly this sweet, severe young woman is not so sweet—and not at all severe—anymore. It's the Bogey magic. Or, at Yale Law in 1970, the Bill magic. And for someone like Hillary, who is wound as tight as coils of copper wire, the feeling must have been like the life force, like electricity.

To be suddenly noticed as a sexual object is supposed to be the downfall of every smart, self-assured young woman who once had goals and plans of her own. Known as "Sister Frigidaire" by her Wellesley sisters, Hillary was bound to melt—but not like the Wicked Witch of the West; no, more like the Siamese cat of a girl in the Rolling Stones' "Under My Thumb" or the hardened hellion down on her knees in the Velvet Underground's "There She Goes Again"—both songs that reflect the misogyny implicit and explicit at a time when women's liberation was just getting underway, both songs suggesting the appeal of surrender, of just giving in, of abandoning the fight. Which is the closest I can come to an explanation for Hillary's decision, after lingering in New Haven an extra year, to follow her heart and follow Bill to Fayetteville, Arkansas.

Somehow, after serving on the precedent-setting prosecution team for the Watergate hearings, which was her first job out of Yale Law, with a promise for more and better, Hillary put aside her goals—not just her career, but the causes that mattered to her, among them some kind of fundamental belief that a woman should be her own person—for Bill, who would not compromise at all on his plan. "If you want to run for public office, you could be elected," Bill told her. "But I've got to go home. That's just who I am."

The wisdom or stupidity in the choices Hillary made so early in her career are for her and history to judge. But the one thing all who are watching are in a position to know is that she truly did choose marriage *über alles*. That she has come to stand for hardheaded, hard-hat feminism is just ridiculous. In fact, when I see that people have that impression of her but deem, for instance, Elizabeth Dole as more traditional and more of a soft touch, I am reminded of the way people used to misread Betty Friedan in opposition to Gloria Steinem. You see, Friedan has always been pro-marriage and pro-family within the context of her feminism—it's just that she also wanted equal rights and opportunity; Steinem has never married or had kids and has always taken a harder line on most feminist issues (she's against pornography, for instance). And yet, years ago, when both of them were out there, actively campaigning for the ERA, people preferred Steinem to Friedan always, thinking of her as less acerbic and less radical because she had her hair streaked at Kenneth's, she had beautiful long legs, she dated and dumped bald-but-otherwise-eligible bachelors like director Mike Nichols (now married to Diane Sawyer)—basically because it was nice to think that a woman who didn't "have" to be a feminist would choose to be one. People liked Steinem because she was pretty and disliked Friedan because she was so damn froglike, which is just fine by me: given the choice between someone aesthetically pleasing and someone else whose appearance is somewhere short of offensive, I will always take the former. But we should not get Steinem and Friedan's positions—which were essentially similar—confused on important matters. In the seventies, the president of one university actually said, when asked his position on feminism, "I don't subscribe to the radical anti-male views of Betty Friedan, but I think I can be comfortable with Gloria Steinem's ideas." If he'd just said, "I like Gloria Steinem, she's got great legs," he would have proved that at least he can see, even though he obviously cannot hear.

And today, Elizabeth Dole has never been seen as anything but an asset to her husband, even though her feminist bona fides are lined up just right: a graduate of Harvard Law School, she has never had children, she gives the impression that everything she knows about mothering she learned from Grimm's fairy tales, she married rather late in life and she has had a very high-profile career of her own. In fact, Hillary's life choices have been the opposite of the ones Liddy Dole made. Liddy never lived in Russell, Kansas. But with her high-end, high-class degrees and all her high-minded notions of a better world, it's hard to see that when viewed as a blueprint, as the human essentials, the vital organs shown in the transparencies of *Gray's Anatomy,* Hillary Clinton is something much more basic: an all-American rugged Midwesterner with wide childbearing hips, muscular stocky legs, and, most likely, a strong back and utilitarian body inherited from the middle-American gene pool that is designed to deliver a baby one day and carry sacks of corn and grain from silo to pickup truck the next. Whatever attaching words like "the sixties" and "Wellesley" and "Yale" and "civil rights" might do to this equation, it is still a picture descended from Grant Wood's *American Gothic,* it is a painting that is a bit creepy and defensive, but the farmer with his pitchfork and his wife with her tight, taut bun are synecdoche for this country, and Hillary too, a native of Illinois, is part of agrarian America, descendant of a long line of indigenous personae: she is a political *wife.*

And Hillary makes no effort to hide this from anybody. "I'm proud of my marriage," Mrs. Clinton writes in *It Takes a Village.* "I have women friends who choose not to marry, or who married and chose not to have children, or who married and then divorced, or who had children on their own. That's okay, that's their choice. This is my choice. This is how I define my personhood—it's Bill and Chelsea."

And yet, so much expectation has been thrown upon Hillary: On the one hand, farthest to the right on the spectrum of insanity, there is the Rush Limbaugh crowd who call Hillary a Feminazi, claim she wants children to disown their parents, parents to disown their children, all this nonsense to be avoided with abortion for all, while her pal Joycelyn Elder advocates masturbation talk in school and buddy Lani Guinier explains that it isn't really about quotas, it's about taking turns, the way children play, so everybody wins. Blah, blah, blah. These are the selfsame people who bumper-sticker their cars with slogans like "IMPEACH THE PRESIDENT—AND HER HUSBAND

TOO." Point is, the various political fiascoes and confirmation screwups, the sudden onset of women with names like Zoë and Kimba (the truly qualified made way for the truly available) being offered and then denied cabinet positions in the first term, were hung on Hillary, which, well—who can say? There are a lot of very loud advisers operating in the White House.

But frankly, the blustery blame from the Limbaugh/*American Spectator* nexus is not nearly so disturbing as the hopes pinned on Hillary by those close to her, those who work in Democratic politics or for Bill Clinton. "I was less interested in Bill's political future than Hillary's," admitted Betsey Wright, Clinton's notoriously loyal, nutty and tenacious gubernatorial chief of staff—and "bimbo eruption" bomb squad—to Clinton biographer David Maraniss. "I was obsessed with how far Hillary might go, with her mixture of brilliance, ambition and self-assuredness. There was an assumption about all the incredible things she could do in the world." The precise content of this "assumption" was fleshed out later, when Wright said to *Vanity Fair,* "She has been absolutely critical to Bill's success, but then I had images in my mind that she could be the first woman President." Dorothy Stuck, another Hillary pal, has not given up hope: "Regardless of what happens to Bill, the nation will be exposed to Hillary Clinton, and Hillary could—and should—be our first woman President." Her mother had intended her to be the first female Supreme Court Justice, but Sandra Day O'Connor put the kibosh on that, and there was talk of her taking the Attorney General position if her husband was elected, though her brother Hugh Rodham seemed to think it was beneath her. "Attorney General is only local lawmaking," he said, with derision, to Gail Sheehy. "There's treaty negotiations she could do. There's labor stuff. There's Secretary of State."

Of course, what is interesting about all this speculation on Hillary's possibilities is that they are precisely the assumptions and ambitions you project onto a gifted youngster, a very bright child, or an adult—no older than twenty-five or thirty—who is thought to be so full of promise. These are not really the kinds of things you say about someone who is full-grown—unless, of course, that person has somehow failed to live up to expectations, or just plain failed and disappointed by any measure. Because all these notions—serving on the Supreme

Court, heading up the State Department, getting an elected office, maybe becoming the first woman to chair the Arms Services Committee in the Senate, or perhaps withdrawing to the academy and achieving tenure at some law school or having a chair endowed in her honor for the study of family law or children's rights—all of these grand ideas are pie-in-the-sky dreams. As far as Hillary is concerned, it ought to be clear to everyone that these dreams are gone—not *deferred;* they are *gone completely.* But it doesn't matter, because she has surrendered it all to wifedom. Looking after Bill Clinton has been her job.

Though Hillary was a partner at the Rose Law Firm—a corporate concern of some genteel southern prestige (and some really icky scandals and skeletons to go with its Confederate roots), she never earned more than $100,000 a year until after 1990, and lived with an income that was only about a third of what the other Rose litigators with equal seniority took in because her outside commitments were so extensive. "Her partners estimated that on average she spent less than three quarters of her time on firm business," writes David Brock in *The Seduction of Hillary Rodham,* explaining that she spent the remainder of her working hours conducting state policy, serving in an unpaid position as chair of a committee on educational standards, which sent her on reconnaissance missions to all seventy-five counties in Arkansas. She also put in a lot of time on corporate boards like Wal-Mart and TCBY, both Arkansas-based companies. Though these board directorships were remunerative positions which could not be filled by the completely brain dead, they were political appointments, the kinds of quasi-community service, quasi-corporate sinecures where having a friend at the statehouse—i.e., marriage to the governor—is always useful.

Meanwhile, charity aside, Hillary brought home $160,000 in combined salary and board directorship fees that she earned in 1990, a sum that bankrolled the Clintons' lifestyle and Bill's political ambitions while he took in his $30,000 a year in state pay. (Thanks to the relatively paltry sum of both spouses' take-home income, the Clintons will be the first couple in recent memory to leave the White House with no family home to retire to.) Many have seen the Clintons as the first two-career couple to occupy the White House, but anyone who examines the record knows that both were working for *his* career, that her breadwinner status in the family is practically akin to a woman working in a steno pool to put her husband through medical school.

Ever since the Labor Party's watershed victory in 1997, people have been comparing the baby-boom Clintons with the age-analogous British Prime Minister Tony Blair and his successful London attorney wife Cherie Booth, since both couples would appear to be the creature quintessence of postwar Anglo-American hopes and dreams. But this was rather demeaning to Ms. Booth, who has run for office (unsuccessfully) on her own, who still uses her maiden name professionally and who still has a profession to use it in, donning the barrister's black robe and white wig as she does each day in court. (Of course, it is easier to pull this off in Britain, where you have the royal family to take care of the ceremonial tasks, and the Prime Minister can stick to the role of governing.) For Hillary Rodham, who was, as she said in her Commencement address, "searching for more immediate, ecstatic and penetrating modes of living," corporate law was the equivalent of a job in the mailroom—menial and meaningless.

And when you compromise yourself that much—you change your hair, your name, your personal style, and you finally invest all your hopes for an idealism that you hold dear into another person—you become thwarted, frustrated and neurotic, like a parent living through his child or, more to the point, like a nagging wife. In fact, feminism got its start precisely because the expansion of the leisure class in postwar America left more and more women with nothing to do except be wives, and the limited stimulation that scrubbing away mildew in the bathroom or wiping runny noses in the car pool provided over time drove a lot of them quite crazy. (This is why, though there was a women's movement in the nineteenth century, it filled less of a void in the predominantly agronomic society where everyone, including wives, had to work in the fields; this does not mean that women were not frustrated by circumscribed roles or a desire for suffrage back then, but it does mean they weren't bored or idle: people who are bone tired rarely foment revolution—except in France, where everything is weird. Which is precisely why many liberal social movements—feminism, communism—tend to remain products of the chattering class, and fail to reach the overworked and underpaid who could benefit from them the most.) The main symptom of "wife sickness"—by which I mean the malaise of just being the supporting player in someone else's star vehicle, only this one doesn't end in two hours—is the way these women become self-involved with someone else's life: this is actually an impossibility, to see yourself so completely in another person's life that you forget about your own, but this is exactly what happens to corporate wives who spend all their time planning dinner parties for their husbands' clients and to political wives who spend all their time on someone else's campaign trail.

The insanity of being nothing but a wife can be maddening enough to move a Westchester homemaker, fed up with the daily struggle to achieve a Mop & Glo kitchen, to write a book called *The Feminine Mystique*. It also happened to be irksome enough to have sent millions of women in 1963 out to buy Betty Friedan's kitchen-table manifesto—in one of the later episodes of *Happy Days,* Marion Cunningham even starts quoting the book to Howard while Joanie eggs her on and Fonzie stands by, sort of looking distressed and sort of savoring the idea that whatever girl trouble is yet to come, it won't affect *him.* But the particular madness of political wives is, well, *special,* perhaps because its necessarily hush-hush nature means that, like most wild things bred in captivity, it develops twisted intractable strains while hiding out, and emerges as particularly sordid and bloated. In other, nonpolitical public walks of life, people may not advertise their plans to check into Payne Whitney, but at this late date it needn't be cause for embarrassment, and it certainly shouldn't ruin anyone's career or future plans.

But in politics, many are afraid to even admit they so much as visited a psychiatrist for fear the stigma will push them out of office. And heaven knows, while coming back from hardship and overcoming adversity is always a favorite stump speech theme, only Marion Barry has ever parlayed drug addiction and jail time into elected office. A crazy wife is potentially damaging to a public servant's rising star, so political wives have become the last bastion of womanhood that has learned to keep a stiff upper lip, not for themselves or for their own career advancement, but for the sake of their husbands—which they probably tell themselves is really for the sake of America or the sake of Tennessee or the sake of Wichita, or the sake of the big cause that this will someday fulfill: *Someday health-care reform will make this all worth it.*

Running on this Ponzi scheme of political and personal promises and compromises, it seems an unusual number of crazy ladies have haunted the governor's mansion or the White House throughout our history. Entire documentaries have been made about Mary Todd Lincoln's mental condition—please note that she is the only First Lady besides Hillary whom we know by three names—but I get the feeling she was not quite right in the head long before she married Abe. Images of Kitty Dukakis drinking rubbing alcohol because the Massachusetts governor's residence had been emptied of all other booze are complemented by images of Betty Ford drinking quite openly in the White House, getting fall-down drunk while her husband presided over an era John Updike calls "America's longest-running one-night stand." One of Watergate's more amusing sideshows was provided by one of its more unstrung minor characters, John Mitchell's now ex-wife Martha, who drove reporters crazy by calling them from her bathtub at all hours of the day and night with promises of inside information that turned out mostly to be her marital troubles. And one can imagine that Pat Nixon spent her share of dark nights of the soul listening to Rachmaninoff while her husband went outside to chat about football and surfing with anti-Vietnam War protesters. Rita Jenrette, former wife of the congressman turned ABSCAM convict John Jenrette, Democrat of South Carolina, was driven crazy by Washington, wrote an article called "Diary of a Mad Congresswife" that was published in the *Washington Post Magazine,* posed nude for *Playboy*, and suggested in the accompanying text that she knew she'd never fit in inside the Beltway when at "the Congressional wives' luncheon for Mrs. Anwar Sadat, I was the only one in a gypsy outfit." Ms. Jenrette then decided to become an entertainer, and has since faded into obscurity.

And the statesman's wife losing her mind, first furtively, then utterly overtly, is, like unfiltered Camels and M-16s and the Church of Scientology, one of those American exports whose growth potential in the worldwide marketplace is too large to estimate. Margaret Trudeau, whose name is barely recognizable today, was fantasy fodder for every gossip rag in the late seventies when she, as wife of Canadian Prime Minister Pierre Trudeau, was caught in all-night unladylike dishabille at Studio 54, the only Canadian in the club's celebrity coterie of Bianca and Andy and Liza and Margaux and Halston and Mick and a revolving assortment of famous fashion victims and cokeheads. Maggie was beautiful and young and bored by her deadly dull husband—she was oomphless in Ottawa. In her autobiography, she confessed, with no regrets, that on the night her husband lost his bid for reelection, she was fucking Mr. Jagger. Unless you count Hamilton Jordan's reportedly cocaine-filled forays into Studio 54, Canada's First Lady was the only associate of an elected official anywhere to hold court in the discotheque. She was a *cause scandale* for a country that had not shown too many signs of life since the War of 1812, and what little talent it exported seemed to migrate to Malibu. Though Maggie eventually divorced, remarried and remained in Ottawa, for a brief shining moment she suggested an alternative approach to the life of the wife-of.

Princess Diana, the first "American" in the British royal family—Dr. David Starkey, a scholar of English common law, has gone so far as to call Di "essentially Californian"—needed to sneak to the BBC and "leak" to author Andrew Morton to let the world know that the Windsors were trying to, as she said to the interviewer on the show *Panorama,* "dismantle [her] personality" by isolating her. In another instance of a foreign ruler's residence imitating an American soap opera, the First Lady of Peru had a fight with her husband and locked him out of their residence in retaliation for perceived slights, which moved him to have the electric power in the house turned off in order to force her out. These examples are not meant to imply that political wives necessarily have it worse than, say, athletes' wives—when you consider what Mrs. Magic Johnson must live with, it's clear that's not the case—but government, particularly elected office, is the last arena where wives play a role as wives per se, where their reflective value to their husbands has not really changed since 1955. But where Bill and Hillary were concerned, she was advertised as more than just a wife—it was "buy one, get one free," in some weird attempt to appeal to the thrifty national character—and she was not going to be a Valium-silenced zombie leading first graders in the Pledge of Allegiance and squeezing the Charmin at supermarket openings in Compton.

"If I get elected President, it will be an unprecedented partnership, far more than Franklin Roosevelt and Eleanor," Bill Clinton said on *Meet the Press* during the 1992 campaign. "They were two great people on different tracks. If I get elected, we'll do things together like we always have." This assurance that Bill Clinton delivered is meant to be Hillary's payoff for having to concern herself with the name Rodham and for the blonde hair—hers and many others'—and for Gennifer with a G and Paula with a shiny complexion and for investing in futures and giving up glasses and apologizing to Tammy Wynette and pretending to bake chocolate chip cookies.

But, of course, it did not work out that way. Instead people have come to dislike Hillary so much for her duplicity: America's disenchantment with Hillary, which has been seen as a referendum on career women, feminism, baby boomers or even power couples, is, if anything, about our distrust of those who don't earn their own keep, who don't prove their own worth. No one minds Elizabeth Dole, extraordinary and accomplished as she is, because what threatens most people is not women who work for a living (which is, after all, what most women must do whether they like it or not), but rather women who linger and connive behind the scenes, the shifty shrews who operate without position, and therefore have no real responsibility and therefore are not accountable, cannot be fired, cannot be trusted. Legendary termagants—Lady Macbeth, Anne Boleyn, Marie Antoinette—were given their due for overexerting their influence as wives; of course, back then women rarely exercised power in any capacity other than wife or courtesan. But Queen Elizabeth I and Mary Queen of Scots were both, for want of a male heir, properly crowned in front of God and everybody, and were therefore never reduced to stealthily sneaking their power like a couple of bulimics secreting away food to binge on, rightly embarrassed by the thought of anyone discovering that they are going to follow the entire box of Mallomars with an entire bag of Doritos. For these British rulers, power was their due and their duty—they had been anointed as queens by the divine right of kings, and their position, far from being a privilege, demanded that they serve more than that they be served. They could proceed with the integrity of knowing that, basically, *they got the job!* Not only was neither beheaded, but both remain among the most well-regarded of the British sovereigns in the eight hundred years of the monarchy's existence—Mary even led her country into war—which would seem to indicate that even in the sixteenth century, the people could occasionally abide a woman in charge. For most of us, who actually fear authority figures more than we fear women, the main concern is: Is she *supposed* to be in charge? (Remember, Alexander Haig's Iago act was not very popular either.)

While it infuriates me to see Hillary Clinton impugned and despised with attitudes reminiscent of prefeminist misogyny, she has probably earned it because, well, *she hasn't got the job!* She's a power sneakbinger, stealing pints of Ben & Jerry's Chunky Monkey from someone else's freezer. Although she came of age in the women's movement and ought to know better, she is living completely through a man, and seems to want the privileges of an independent woman without being willing to go through congressional confirmation or elections or whatever process one goes through when serving the public in a given capacity. It's not just that Hillary's health-care reform proposals were disliked by both liberals and conservatives, it's that the plan's lack of a constituency was a reflection of her own want of a clear base of support, since she was never elected to any office or put through the usual personnel procedures and entered into the government payroll.

"Hillary isn't under attack for being a strong independent woman with ideas," wrote Barbara Ehrenreich in *Mirabella* in September 1996, by which time Whitewater was more than just up shit's creek without a paddle or raft or anyone saying that you're going to be the first female President any longer. "Hillary's career is only a minor update on Barbara Bush's. Yes, she had a job at the Rose Law Firm, but Yale Law School does not take great pride in seeing its graduates run interference for sleazy S & Ls and real-estate dealers. Hillary Rodham, the Wellesley valedictorian, was meant for better things, but chose to follow Bill. Even at Rose, her success depended on her being married to a governor who would reportedly jog over to Jim McDougal's office and beg him to throw business Hillary's way.

"But the political wife plan worked better for Barbara Bush's generation," Ehrenreich continues. "Back then, when a husband philandered, you retired into a discreet depression and then emerged with undyed hair and a determination to write the autobiography of a pet dog. Hillary got mad, but even that didn't lead her to conclude she needed more Bill-free space in her life, like a job where her second last name didn't matter. Instead she dug deeper into his career, made herself indispensable as a strategist, even, at times, a co-candidate."

It is this, precisely this, that people despise.

So what is strange about the story of the gas station attendant who would be king is that it offers a succinct illustration of what it is that makes so many Americans suspicious of Hillary—her controlling nature, her puppeteer position, her fingernail grip—and has resulted in disapproval ratings that have at times surpassed even those of Madame Just-Say-No, Nancy Reagan (who, you may recall, spent taxpayer money replacing perfectly good china *and* flew her hairdresser in from California). What is even more strange about this story is that it's meant to depict Hillary as the strong, strong-arming woman, the bull-dyke nightmare feminist, the woman in charge. It is meant to remind us how scary it is to have a powerful woman living in the White House.

It is meant to make us forget that this woman is not the President, and therefore does not really have any power at all.

It is meant to make us forget that there have been female Presidents and Prime Ministers in countries as varied, as religious, as backwater and as forward-thinking as England, Israel, Pakistan, India, the Philippines, Ireland and Australia. It is meant to make us forget that in the United States, we couldn't even elect an unmarried *man* into office, much less a married woman. It is meant to make us forget that the ceremonial duties of the First Lady are so essential to the executive branch's success that to elect anything less than a man and his wife would be to vote for much less than we believe we need—although, in a survey commissioned by *Vanity Fair* from Yankelovich Clancy Shulman during the 1992 campaign, 84 percent of the respondents said they would condone a First Lady with a second career. Christopher Buckley, however, expressed displeasure in a September/October 1996 issue of *Mirabella*. "Hey, look, this country needs a First Lady. And the last time I checked, it was a full-time job," he wrote. "We need her to be the nation's mother and, to an extent, wife." Of course, Mr. Buckley's own mum is a society grande dame, so perhaps it's hard for him to imagine a woman who wants more than to lunch out on the taxpayers' expense, but he is at least being honest. "What sort of demands will be placed on Georgette [Mosbacher] as the wife of a Cabinet secretary?" asked John Davidson with regard to the famously redheaded cosmetics company CEO in the February 1989 *Vanity Fair*—a grim reminder that "First Lady" duties even extend to a woman who happens to be married to a man whose job is pretty much to do PR for American industry abroad.

And still the notion that being the power behind the throne is akin to being the power itself goes on. During the 1992 presidential race, the high quality and caliber of wife folk was a favorite topic, with Hillary only the biggest chick among a whole pack of Chiclets. The charismatically challenged (though aquatically gifted) Paul Tsongas joked that he ceded charm duty to his attorney wife, Niki. "If you don't have charisma, you marry it," he remarked. Marilyn Quayle, another lawyer—both she and J. Danforth went to Indiana University Law School, though she got in on the merits and he got in, mysteriously, as an affirmative action applicant (don't ask; the school couldn't explain and neither can I)—insisted at the 1992 Republican convention that women would not want to put career before family because that would deny "our essential nature." Just the same, Mrs. Quayle commandeered a six-office suite across the hall from the Vice President's work chambers, and acted as gatekeeper and screener to any of those who might wish to bring their agendas to her husband. Ruth Harkin had once been a prosecutor, but became her husband's full-time adviser for his half-dead campaign. And Hillary Clinton— well, she tended to inspire remarks like: "She's a spectacular candidate in her own right. She's got my vote." "You can't help but think, Why isn't *she* the candidate?" Or, as her own husband said at a dinner roasting the then-governor's wife, "Some say the wrong Clinton is in the statehouse, and I wouldn't disagree with them."

But all those women wielding power—really, what did that mean? Because it wasn't *their* power, it was their husbands' power, which they could occasionally touch by proxy or by persuasion. Clinton's remark about the wrong person being governor is clearly the good-natured condescension of a man who knows that it is his to offer or deny. As Marianne Moore wrote in her poem "Marriage," "men have power / and sometimes one is made to feel it." There is no greater display of power than apparent nonchalance.

Americans' inability to bring themselves to elect a woman to its highest office—and the fact that the Democrats made it appear that they had to beat through all the bushes (double entendre *absolutely* intended) to come up with a fairly obscure, hopelessly unelectable Queens, New York, congresswoman to share the ticket with an even more unelectable Walter Mondale in 1984—has become something of an international joke. Of course, the fact that Italy has had a former porn star who is now the former wife of American artist Jeff Koons in its parliament is also something of an international joke—but it is one that should only serve to highlight that even in the land of the Vatican, they are not nearly so uptight as we are about girls in government. This squeamishness is the sole reason that, if we assume pragmatism before principles, we can justify Hillary's decision to realize her own political ambitions through her husband: in a country where even Ivy League schools and snooty white-shoe law firms and wheeler-dealer Wall Street concerns and other ancient male bastions all have their share of women wielding power as they do nowhere else on earth, we have not even come sort-of kind-of close to sending a woman into the Oval Office. And it's at the point where we just accept it, we think it's normal for it to be that way, we think it's acceptable that the best we can come up with is a First Lady with a fancy law degree and no job, we think it's normal that the Vice President's wife is a grown woman called Tipper—we don't even notice how strange this political impasse is. And maybe Hillary figured it out, and decided she'd rather light than fight.

"The American failure to understand women is most strikingly evident in the case of Hillary Clinton versus Margaret Thatcher," wrote Julie Burchill, a British feminist of observant wit, in an issue of *The New York Times Magazine* devoted to the way the world views the United States. Ms. Burchill is of the opinion that when it comes to sex, Americans are not too swift, strangely uptight, swinging harum-scarum between talkety-talk-talk-talk—with Jerry Springer and Jenny Jones acting as confessional priests to teenage boys who are bedding down their girlfriends' mothers, or promiscuous twelve-year-olds who complain that everyone thinks they are sluts—and then disregarding all this ghoulishness to say that we are afraid that a woman who might be going through menopause while in office is a threat to national security, as if Bill Clinton's dick is not. "Hillary was a woman of great ability and intellect active in a party that was, in theory, sympathetic to the idea of the equality of women," Burchill continues. "Margaret Thatcher was a woman of middling ability and intellect active in a party completely hostile to the idea of the equality of women. Yet it was Mrs. Thatcher who ended up radiantly in power, while Mrs. Clinton ended up pushing her chocolate-chip-cookie recipe, being humiliated on a scale that would have shocked Jackie Kennedy and generally standing by her man to a degree that would suggest that women come not from Venus but rather from Planet Dog. A country at ease with women and sex would not have effectively castrated its First Lady."

That any prerogative that is handed to anyone in a democracy is meaningful only if it is given by direct mandate is shown in the fact that the proud display of Hillary as the unsalaried half of the slogan "buy one, get one free" has recast her as the Wicked Witch of the West Wing, banished by popular demand. And if in 1992 all the candidates were showing off their sassy, brassy, capable and competent better halves, the 1996 campaign was about the silence of the ewe. Liddy Dole spent her sabbatical from the Red Cross on levity duty, insisting that she'd keep her job and keep her hands off policy decisions even if her husband actually *were* elected, and rode a motorcycle with Jay Leno to prove that she's at least as wild as Tipper Gore.

As mutilated and vitiated as the First Lady is by virtue of our protest that we didn't elect her, and as much as she is made to be female eunuch—possibly, in Hillary Clinton's case, even minding the harem—anecdotes like the story of the gas station are meant to make us forget that we seem to want June Cleaver as First Lady.

As much as we need a First Lady, as much as this distaff appendage is necessary for the presidency—even though we need her so badly that we let her have a staff, a secretary, aides, foreign policy advisers and an office that I would guess has lots of big picture windows and a view of the Rose Garden and a rolltop desk with Mont Blanc fountain pens and an unlimited supply of Post-Its—even though we think she is worth this much trouble, we don't give her a salary. Even Lady Bird Johnson, who long learned her place in Lyndon's life after years in the trenches of Texas politics had the wherewithal to gripe, "The First Lady is an unpaid public servant elected by one person—her husband." The current First Lady is in the unique position of having a degree from Yale Law School and earning even less than the undergraduate interns she employs during the summer.

The First Lady earns less than her secretary. (Sylvia Plath's mother was probably right to insist she learn shorthand.)

The First Lady earns less than you do.

And she has thick calves.

The First Lady, be it Hillary Clinton or Mamie Eisenhower, replicates the plight of every woman writ large: not being paid to do tons of work that you could not pay most men to do. Ivana Trump, first bouffanted blonde wife of the Donald, may be silly and surgeried into midlife Barbie-dom, but she still places a premium on the fact that throughout her marriage she was a hardworking woman, helicoptering to casinos in Atlantic City, purchasing chintz to redecorate the Plaza Hotel and generally making herself useful to the Donald's pursuit of gaming and gilding the lily. When asked to reveal Ivana's salary for services rendered, Trump once put it at a dollar a year and all the dresses she could buy. Now, I know she lived well, and marriage makes for strange money arrangements, but Donald is effectively saying that Ivana does not need proper payment for her labors—ironically, she prided herself on the fact that she personally signed every check issued by Trump's Castle—because she can just trust him: *Let Daddy take care of it, little girl.* We all know where that attitude has landed many a good woman, including Ivana, whose new motto is "Don't get mad—get everything!" Receiving money from a man like a girlish gift is not good, nor is extracting it from him in divorce court terrifically attractive behavior. So Ivana did necessary work for exactly what she'd have received if she had only had manicures by the pool in Palm Beach all the livelong day, and without a payroll entry or job description attached to her tasks, she became a unique thing: a volunteer in the service of a capitalist venture.

Ivana tailor-made her dress-indentured servitude, but for First Ladies it is part of the rules of the game—so much so that no one even thinks to question it. In fact, when Hillary Clinton became the chair of the commission on health care, she was not being paid at all to do tons of work that most men would get paid tons to do. And furthermore, she was also accepting the role as fall gal for Bill—if health care had worked, he'd get credit; when it didn't work, she got blame—participating in a psychodynamic where she plays unappealing policy wonk to his persuasive pol part, all in all not much appetizing in it for her in any of this, and she's not even getting paid for it. In fact, all the while she is working on health care she is also doing all the ceremonial afternoon-tea work that is First Lady as usual. As Ginger Rogers once said of her gig with Fred Astaire: she had to do everything he had to do—only she had to do it backwards and in high heels.

Of course we will never have a woman President. What man would accept the role of First Gentleman? What man would take afternoon tea with a bunch of "woman's page" reporters without receiving a paycheck? What man would willingly lead a Christmas-season tour of the White House and show off a gingerbread model of the family home? In fact, I would wager that, should we ever see the day when there is a female Commander-in-Chief, her husband will keep his job back home in Portland or Minneapolis or Waxahachie, and the first couple will have a commuter marriage because *that's how important his career will be to him.* They'd be forced to import one of those swishy-walker types, like Jerry Zipkin or Truman Capote if they weren't dead, anytime there was an occasion involving finger sandwiches or marzipan.

Suddenly it would be impossible not to notice that being forced to deal with the head of protocol or to take advice from Letitia Baldrige or to take a stroll through Gorky Park with Raisa Gorbachev or to restructure the entire health-care system or to work on a regular basis with Ira Magaziner is the kind of job that anyone thinking clearly would not put up with for anything less than the Intel CEO's year-end bonus, and yet going as far back as Martha Washington (who probably had to organize sewing circles to darn the socks of local infantrymen), the American taxpayers have gotten a huge break.

But this is precisely why people are so suspicious of Hillary Clinton. She's kind of like Banquo's ghost lingering in the White House, this nagging presence roaming the corridors of power, trying to be useful when she should really go to her own workstation and play with her own little widgets. Between changing hairdos and hair-don'ts as if she were still in eleventh grade and displacing and misplacing documents as if she were a CIA mole, Hillary has left the American public with this quivering, queasy feeling like: *Doesn't she have anything better to do?* Shouldn't such an ostensibly qualified person have some sort of *job?* With all the government agencies and think tanks based inside the Beltway, wouldn't it be nice to actually bring home a paycheck? I mean, with unemployment so low that Alan Greenspan is about to have a coronary, it seems like Hillary has a patriotic duty to get a job and help keep down inflation.

During the 1992 campaign, Americans assumed and the press tended to confirm that the Clintons saw themselves as the dynamic duo, as co-candidates. But that's not how it works: Clinton and Gore were co-candidates. While Hillary could have run for Vice President, given that she'd never run for any elective office, never held an official position in national politics (of course, in these days of the Ross Perot/ Steve Forbes/Morry Taylor lunatic fringe, perhaps simply being over thirty-five is enough), she'd have been given such a slot only because of her matrimonial status. Elizabeth Dole, married to a man who reminds us all why *The Wizard of Oz* could never have been set anywhere but Kansas, has actually had a career completely independent of her husband's. She could easily succeed where he has failed—and who can say that the sort of Howard Hawkes romantic comedy quality of a Dole-Dole ticket might not have worked better than a former Buffalo Bill and a tendency to misuse the third person singular did. (It has often been noted that Republican women tend to be a more solid lot— Jeane Kirkpatrick, Wendy Gramm, etc.—which is obviously the result of no one in that party much wanting them around until recently, and without affirmative action, only the tough survived.)

At any rate, Hillary was not interested in being VP, seeing it as somehow beneath her: "I'm not interested in attending a lot of funerals around the world," she said at a Hollywood-ladies-who-lunch-but-don't-eat fund-raising luncheon in 1992. Somehow cabinet positions were not considered (the nepotism rule could probably be overturned), but the First Lady still proceeded as if it was her birthright to make policy decisions because she happens to be married to the boss. "No one gives George Bush a hard time when he gets advice from Jim Baker," Hillary complained to Gail Sheehy. Well, *hello*, Mr. Baker could be the biggest dope on earth, but he got himself confirmed by Congress (who may be the mega-biggest dopes on earth), he basically went through what would be known as personnel procedures in any company in this country, so his job is to advise and consent.

For whatever reason, Hillary seems resistant to these standard procedures—she took on the task of health care without getting paid, rather like Ivana's situation—and I believe it is ultimately what has gotten her in over her head with Whitewater and its offshoots. There's no reason for this, it's as if she fears failure if she just agrees to play by the ordinary rules, and the result is an assertive, even aggressive woman who projects a forthright independence that is both incongruous and inappropriate coming from someone who is, after all, just some guy's loudmouthed wife.

Now, let me ask you: Is this not precisely the kind of situation feminism came along to get rid of? People think the nagging discomfort they get about Mrs. Clinton is a consequence of her position as a nontraditional First Lady. But that's wrong: what bothers them is that she is so utterly traditional, but she goes through life with the steely visage of one who is keeping secrets, keeping it all in that this was not what she bargained for—it is, in fact, more like what she gambled on.

The fact is that America is so frightened of a truly independent woman that someone like Hillary—who appears to be just that, even though her entire identity is derived from her marital status—gets demonized as a cautionary, warning shot, lest a woman who keeps her name, her job, her personhood ever dare to enter the White House as anything other than the President's mistress.

* * *

If Gennifer Flowers had not existed, somebody would have invented her, but she is the only character in the drama of Bill Clinton—including the man himself—who is absolutely inevitable. The political groupie who knows nothing of politics, the erupting bimbo on every political campaign trail, the blonde in the bleachers who may even be a brunette—like Judith Exner with John Kennedy and Gloria Swanson with his father Joe—she is the only certainty of any charismatic pol's entourage. Even Jimmy Carter, delivering his famous malaise speech in his cardigan sweater to encourage fuel conservation during the energy crisis, still admitted to *Playboy* that he had "lusted in [his] heart." Richard Nixon—who knows? Even paranoids have enemies, but I don't think that they have mistresses. (Although I have to admit, I fantasize about Nixon having a brief tryst with Karen Carpenter when she and her brother performed for him at the White House, but that's just my creepy little perversion.) This is what politics is all about: just as skinny guys with acne scars pick up guitars and start rock bands in order to get chicks, geeky guys and policy wonks run for office for the big-haired girls.

But these women, it turns out, are often the only people who keep politicians in touch with the real people, they are ordinary as no one else in the pol's life is—they are a retreat from a life that's all pollsters, lobbyists, fund-raisers, all special interest groups with not especially interesting needs. She is his great escape to normal life. The backwater country girl who became Blaze Starr, the ecdysiast for enthusiasts in New Orleans' French Quarter, stripped her way into the aging Earl Long's ailing, populist heart and became his consort and sole source of vigor for his fading days. Somehow, the still-sweet Southerner, sobriqueted "Blaze" because of her auburn mane, became the original church-going stripper—an innocent nude back when there was still such a thing. Miss Starr was an Appalachian escapee with big-city, show-business dreams, and unsuspecting naïf who took her clothes off on her first night on a vaudeville stage—she thought she was supposed to be playing the balalaika and singing a blue Kentucky girl tune— because she just wanted to be pleasing, because it was easier than fending off the itchy, ornery men in the audience—who really were the dearest things once you got to know 'em. If we think of striptease today as a tense, titillating form of seduction, for Blaze Starr it seems to have been more a form of submission; she seems to have performed without guile. And somehow, with his electoral career becoming a past-tense affair, when Earl Long felt displaced in the state of Louisiana—the only place any of the Longs could possibly *not* feel displaced—Blaze Starr made Mr. Long feel right at home, an unpolitical animal once more.

This sexpot-as-girl-next-door quality seems to animate a lot of mighty men's excitement in their mistresses: Donald Trump is not actually a politician—but don't tell him that—and still, Marla Maples, when first revealed as Ivana's rival, attributed her appeal to the real estate mogul as simple earthiness, as lack of socialite polish. "I'm, like, of the soil, of the country, of a solid firm belief in God," Marla said in a *Vanity Fair* profile that was most notable when it ran in November 1990 for including a picture of the pretty peach standing outside the Plaza Hotel in a pink-sequined Bob Mackie gown, gobbling on a New York City street hot dog, in a decidedly suggestive oral gesture. "I would be happier living out on a farm away from everyone and not being in this concrete world." By contrast, Marla said of the then-Mrs. Trump: "The lifestyle she has grown accustomed to is outrageous. It's outrageous spending I can't even conceive of"—which is definitely saying something: at the time of Marla's famous do-you-love-your-husband confrontation with Ivana at Bonnie's, the Aspen bôite at the bottom of the slopes, the mistress was ensconced in a $10,000-a-week penthouse triplex paid for by the Donald. Still, despite such signs of a slight spoiling, Marla's essential claims to ingenuousness seem to stem from sincerity. "There was nothing distinguishing about her except her genuineness," an old beau of the future Mrs. Trump said in the *Vanity Fair* piece. "She was a sweet girl from Georgia, all southern charm, the antithesis of high-society megabucks-type people . . . She invited me to her church." In fact, Marla and Donald often rendez-voused in a pew at the Marble Collegiate Church, adding a touch of the sacred to their sinning.

And if political wives occupy an age-old role of unpaid female labor, the mistresses play the paradoxical part of fantasy *and* reality: he escapes to her, and yet, because he functions in the netherworld of doublespeak and agenda-mongering, where missiles that can blow up the world are called Peacekeepers and where the difference between committing a felony and fund-raising as usual is whether you use a phone in your office or one down the hall in your bedroom (as if telephones are such rare and prized commodities that we measure the legalities by what most of us consider just a matter of convenience)—given this fantasy world he lives in, his mistress' fleshy and full-bodied existence is an escapist reality. Which is how it always is—or at least was before women were in the workforce beside men and with their mates: women were the great escape, the body as leisure. Men escape *to* women, not *with* women—they are land, home, colony, country— all states are female nouns. She is shelter: "Come in, she said, I'll give you shelter from the storm," Bob Dylan sang on a cut from *Blood on the Tracks* that was used in the movie *Jerry Maguire* to remind us how much the tensed-up title character really *needed* the sweetness of his wife to go running to. "You're my castle, you're my cabin and my instant pleasure dome / I need you in my house, because you're my home," sang Billy Joel two or three wives ago. Women are less likely to own property than men—they couldn't legally until pretty recently—and yet their bodies are home.

On the other hand, sometimes politicians are married to women who don't understand what they do, and they hook up with women who do. In 1996, when Secretary of Commerce Ron Brown died in a plane crash on a trip to the former Yugoslavia, he left behind an afterlife of evidence of a long-term, complicated involvement that encompassed both the professional and the personal with a Texas businesswoman named Nolanda Hill. Ms. Hill—who owned three Harley-Davidsons, drove a little red Corvette and flirted wildly—was, right down to the red hair and the three failed marriages, in all ways the characteristic caricature of the Lone Star state's favorite female mascot (think former governor Ann Richards): a loud little lady who cuts a large swath.

"For almost ten years, Hill was Ron Brown's business partner and his closest political adviser, and, for the last seven years of his life, she was his lover," Peter J. Boyer wrote in *The New Yorker,* in a posthumous profile of the relationship. Brown remained married throughout the affair; Hill's third marriage disintegrated toward the end. The adulterous connection seems mostly to have occupied a space separate—and not entirely in conflict with—their respective spousal unions; the pair would apparently talk on the phone for hours in front of their families, who seem to have willfully ignored the passionate pitch of their conversations that most people would sense went beyond business as usual. "The political mistress is a stock Washington character, yet the relationship between Ron Brown and Nolanda Hill was a distinct nineteen-nineties variation of that arrangement by which powerful men acquire and maintain paramours," Boyer explains. "They both were resourceful, charismatic operators who loved to make deals." When Brown's nomination to the Cabinet was threatened by Republican opposition, Hill was called into the war room for strategy sessions, partly because her grasp of his business dealings was stronger than his; as the owner of several television stations, Hill employed Brown's daughter and daughter-in-law; she negotiated the divestment package for certain assets Brown had to relinquish when he became head of Commerce; and, when Hill moved her base of operations to Washington, Brown "often came to her apartment after work, and she'd make him a scrambled-egg sandwich."

Though Boyer sees the "distinct nineteen-nineties variation" on the classic extramarital affair in the Brown–Hill bond, in fact this same setup was anticipated on a smaller scale in the 1979 movie *The Seduction of Joe Tynan*. As the title character (and screenwriter of the film), Alan Alda is a charming senator at just the right age with just the right appeal to make him a serious presidential prospect; he is even tapped for the precursor to all White House ambitions: the keynote address at the Democratic Convention. He is politically obsessed, seized by the vertiginous energy of Washington power plays—he's the kind of guy who likes cutting the deal, maneuvering IOUs around the favor bank so that a vote on a bill comes out just so: He's at that point in his senatorial career when the smoke-filled rooms are still romantic, they still bespeak an atmosphere of macho potentates duking it out until the best and fairest side wins. Senator Tynan has even come to believe that corruption works, that it is a good thing because it automatically eliminates the weakest positions that don't have the wherewithal for a fight; it's not that might makes right—but nothing else does either.

Barbara Harris is the senator's wife, a throaty-voiced beauty who is starting to become what people call handsome, a successful psychologist of great grace and polish who has her own career to attend to and her own life to live, and who is simply sickened and alienated by the power-mad pursuit her husband puts himself through. Naturally, the couple grows apart, and Joe ends up in an affair with Meryl Streep, in one of the actress' early accented roles as a Louisiana lawyer and lobbyist on Tynan's case. The shared obsession of their pursuit of the Senate's vote on a bill is an aphrodisiac: when they have sex, both partners seem like the Faye Dunaway character in *Network,* both seem to heighten their orgasmic responses with every strategic thought that comes up during coitus.

And the situation set up in *The Seduction of Joe Tynan* is the paradigm for any political affair or any office romance, regardless of the specifics: nothing like working closely together to create the heat of achievement, the height of shared excitement.

In late 1997, when *Vanity Fair* and other publications alleged that New York City's hound dog of a leader, Mayor Rudolph Giuliani, had long been having an affair with his high-level, highly trusted and expeditiously promoted aide Crystine Lategano, it had the ring of truth to it that did more to confirm the veracity of this bit of gossip in public opinion than even catching the pair *in flagrante delicto* would have. After all—Giuliani does not seem like much of a sex machine, and a heated affair for him may well be almost the opposite of physical. No doubt what would fuel his City Hall relationship with Lategano would simply be their mutual preoccupation with the politics of the metropolis and their joint desire to conquer the world.

Meanwhile, back at Gracie Mansion—or at a rental unit she may have moved into across the street—Donna Hanover seems a ridiculous mismatch for the bellicose, bloodthirsty, bullheaded mayor. She is so blonde and perky and pug-nosed and peachy keen, dividing her time between socialite luncheons and hanging out with Courtney Love and cooking it up on Food TV. A workaholic like Giuliani seems like a man who must be with a fellow laborer; similarly, Bruce Springsteen traded in Julianne Phillips, his beautiful, seemingly benevolent and certainly generically desirable wife, for the redheaded, rough-edged, plain but still sexy Patti Scialfa, the background singer in the E Street Band who was the only woman who could possibly be right for him: for Bruce, work and life are one and the same, and marriage to a pretty baby who makes movies with Chevy Chase is never going to be engaging and enrapturing enough.

Men like Rudy and Bruce need women they can fuck *and* talk shop with: they have both—assuming the rumors about the mayor are true—basically traded in their secretaries for their wives, the adorable lovelies for the working partners. For what it's worth, even President Clinton met Gennifer Flowers on the job, since the lobby lounge singer was then a reporter at a local TV station covering Clinton's stint as state attorney general. It seems that the intimacy of working together might be the most bonding experience two people can have—which is also perhaps why Hillary Clinton has chosen to make *her* career her husband's career.

And then there are the extramarital affairs that are definitely of an extracurricular nature, definitely with women apart from the political hoopla, women who offer vacation from the obsession rather than a warm, loving body to share it with. These are the groupies, the girls backstage, the babes in bars, the earth mothers and sexy sisters, the comfort girls who make life on the political trail or on the road with the band a bit more bearable. And it may be good that politicians in particular get involved with these more earthy creatures—it allows them to press the flesh of the hoi polloi—but the problem is that when the relationship ends, the women have no recourse, no financial means, very little incentive *not* to go public if the opportunity arises. The have-not women are scandal bait for have-all men, and no one has any business judging Gennifer Flowers for selling her story to *The Star* or Sherry Rowlands, Dick Morris' prostitute of choice, for doing the same. No one should dare to air their disgust when Jessica Hahn moves into the Playboy mansion, when any woman dethroned by a dangerous liaison with a man chooses to defrock and dine out on the notoriety: What else, after all, are they going to do? Who will have them—other than more men who are willing to cash in on, and in turn help the women themselves, in some marginal way, turn a small profit from this astonishing, amazing celebrity? After all, when all is said and done all these women have gained from these relationships—besides, perhaps, a broken heart or a child to raise or an abortion faced all alone—is an anecdote that's worth somebody's money. If the romance remained viable, the roman à clef would remain unwritten.

* * *

Gennifer Flowers, who'd been to the big city enough to know to call herself a "shiksa" in the acknowledgments of her memoir *Passion and Betrayal,* wanted the world to know her side of the story. You can't blame her for using what little public value power she had to the best of her ability. Apart from being a lounge singer, apparently not a very good one, the one bit of power accorded to her and afforded her is that she was, for twelve years, mistress to the Commander-in-Chief. So she sold and told her story, first in *The Star*, then in *Penthouse* (which gave her opportunity to display just what the President quite literally saw in and on her), and finally in her obscurely published book. Some of Flowers' more damning, though entirely predictable, revelations included that she saw the then-governor smoke pot, and he did indeed inhale; that Bill was not very well endowed between the legs, but he made up for it in stamina and eagerness to please; that when Gennifer told Bill she'd heard rumors of Hillary's lesbian liaisons, he shrugged it off by saying, "Honey, she's probably eaten more pussy than I have"; that she aborted a baby by Bill; that she sometimes applied a full face of makeup to Bill; that Bill sometimes liked to be spanked. Still, with all this dirt, perhaps the most damning discovery concerns the President's musical proclivities: "We both loved the Commodores," Flowers admits. " 'I'm Easy' and 'Three Times a Lady' were special favorites."

But the really interesting aspect of Gennifer as mistress is the juxtaposition it offers between herself and Hillary. Proper and educated vs. wild, blonde, sexy: class vs. trash. But Gennifer Flowers was not poor—she comes from a comfortable Little Rock suburb—and she isn't stupid. And Hillary Clinton is much more the girl next door, the traditional wife, than most would think. Camille Paglia describes Flowers as "Hillary without the ice," and in her book Flowers herself recalls being mistaken for the First Lady in a hotel sundries shop. In fact, while a woman with Hillary's credentials ought to have been able to look at Gennifer Flowers as just some tramp, the threat that this mistress posed was probably more palpable. Hillary had a lot to lose: she had tossed everything to come live with Bill in Arkansas; Ms. Flowers, as a local yokel, had never made any substantial sacrifices for her lover. And still, though Gennifer may have had momentary fantasies of having Bill without Hill, the fact is that Flowers didn't—and never would—stand a chance. Because she's a mistress: she's somebody's chippy and nobody's wife. With her big blonde hair—not to mention her stint as a backup vocalist for Roy Clark—Flowers' lock on the extramarital role is a force as ordained as a Calvinist's fate of salvation or damnation.

The bottom line is that some women are always the mistress, other women are always the wife and others are always the groupie. Men are likewise husband material or not, but this difference is more in their control: they can choose outlaw status, they can opt for gray-flannel respectability—they can even switch back and forth between the two quite literally; but women are deemed unmarriable by others. At one time, everybody got married—even sluts settled down—because it's what people did, but now it's not like that, droves of those in middle age have never married or are long divorced, and strangely women seem even more split into camps based on marital status than they were before by feminism.

Gennifer Flowers had nothing to lose and everything to gain by going public by the time Clinton ran. Her behavior in selling out her love life and privacy isn't dignified, but what dignity has she anyway? Women who are cast aside will do what they will and do what they must, and the rest of us are in no position to judge. The main argument against behaving like Gennifer is the dignity. But if you think about it, dignity is really a patriarchal notion—it is about being proud, about keeping a stiff upper lip, about hiding your feelings. In the aftermath of an extramarital affair, the man may want his former mistress to keep her mouth shut, and he may invoke dignity as a reason for doing so, as in: It was so undignified how Gennifer Flowers sold her story to *The Star*. As if the real indignity is not in the extramarital affair that *he* had. Silence is a good mistress.

In a shocking pink bold-lettered endorsement on the back cover of *You'll Never Make Love in This Town Again*, a book in which three Hollywood hookers-to-the-stars—and one woman who's been around—tell all, Gloria Steinem points out, "The powerless always know the powerful better than vice-versa—which is why they're pressured to be silent. In *You'll Never Make Love in This Town Again* four women break that code and tell us what the Emperor is really like—with no clothes on." In fairness, hookers are paid for their silence—unlike mistresses. But in *Esquire*, in an article about shamelessness, John Taylor scolds these call girls for their, if you will, candor—calling them out particularly on claims that they did this book in the hope of helping other young women avoid their fate, which may be so, but it is true that most of us read the book for the dirt, not for the brimstone and hellfire. Still, whatever these überwhores' motivation, everyone should realize that none of these women have broken marriage vows or done anything wrong, their stories are their only currency because of a culture that values youth, so that a prostitute in Hollywood cannot make a living hooking beyond a certain age—but she can tell secrets anytime. The book tells the story of women who are doomed to remain nobody's baby, the ones on the side, the supplementary babes, and it's a grim story. If the men who were tattled on—Don Henley, Warren Beatty, Jack Nicholson, Gary Busey, Dennis Hopper—are so eager to keep these women quiet, they should take up a collection: hush money is a real concept. I bet all these women would shut up for cash.

A few months later, John Taylor wrote a lengthy article about his own adultery and his marital collapse.

Generally speaking, these women who get caught in the midst of political scandal don't ever rise above it, unless it is by self-parody, like becoming a professional Jell-O wrestler or, like Jessica Hahn, moving into the Playboy mansion and getting enough plastic surgery to enter the witness protection program. Donna Rice went Christian, so she is traveling in the opposite direction from Ms. Hahn. Fawn Hall, Ollie North's loyal steno, told Barbara Walters that she wanted to be a television interviewer, was denied backstage passes by Bruce Springsteen, finally went to LA, married Doors' biographer Danny Sugarman, got addicted to heroin and is now writing about her junkie days. But on whole, these are women attracted to power by their own lack of it, the kind of women that in more conventional dating situations would make most men run because they give off vibes of calling sixteen times a day and stalking your ex-girlfriends and stuff like that. But powerful men, for whatever peculiar reasons, luxuriate in this neediness even if they know that should they ever let this woman down, it will be a very bad day for the family pet. One of the reasons the men in trouble (Dick Morris, Sol Wachtler) have their reputations resuscitated so readily is that the trouble that the men get into is the result of their *power*, whereas the trouble the women get into is the result of their *powerlessness*. The only thing these women usually have going is the relationship that is the cause of their sullying and their notoriety. The test case of a powerful woman being an idiot for love has not yet happened.

On the other hand, there are the Pamela Harrimans of the world who show us how a woman can triumph over being just a mistress, or can use it to make herself powerful. But it's hard. How it is that Pamela Harriman, a woman who even by today's wanton standards was a complete slut, managed to become the Ambassador to France and not the Whore of Babylon is anyone's guess. "Basically, I'm a back-room girl," she said in an interview with reporter Michael Gross in 1992, which he made public only after her death. "I've always said this and I've always believed it. I prefer to push and shove other people. I don't really like to be put forward myself." At least two recent biographies have tried to make sense of the situation, and at least one possible explanation for her restored respectability may reside in her skill with a particular word beginning with "f." It's fund-raising, of course, and she was apparently quite good for Bill Clinton's war chest, and who, after all, is he to judge? But of course, as to how she got to be so dexterous on the Democratic Party circuit, well, that probably comes down to class. Never mind that this is supposed to be a class-free society, everywhere on earth the highborn can behave as they wish and maintain their standing—so, sure, she had affairs with married men like Bill Paley, Edward R. Murrow and Jock Whitney—but somehow that air of breeding and blue blood made it impossible to judge her as you'd judge a two-bit slut like Paula Parkinson or Judith Exner. Even at Harvard it was like that. The girls from old Yankee families could sleep around with impunity, while the rest of us got bad reputations.

At the same time, despite my general sympathy for downtrodden women who tell all, I would say that Paula Jones should just shut up. She has probably been given more of our attention than she deserves because she has become an avatar of all our guilt about how we don't take these "trashy" women seriously, feminism fails them. For all the time upper-middle-class women spent in consciousness-raising groups and orgasm-improvement classes in the seventies instead of organizing pink-collar laborers into unions in rural America—and believe me, plenty of feminist leaders *did* do that kind of fieldwork—we are now *all* doing penance with Paula. But, in truth, the only person who dragged Paula Jones through the mud was she herself.

I do find it interesting the way Paula Jones insists that this is not for the money. But if it's not, then what is it for? I know, I know: to recover her dignity. But one has to ask if this is really a good use of our court system. In truth, the courts have the power to bestow punishment, but rarely can they offer vindication: witness the O. J. Simpson case, in which, despite a not-guilty verdict, the majority of Americans still believe he did it. It seems that we tend to assume that a defendant is guilty before the trial even begins, and not for no reason: the district attorneys are not obligated to try any cases (witness the JonBenet Ramsey situation), so they usually don't go forward unless the evidence for prosecution is pretty strong—which is one of the reasons that when Marcia Clark says that she has won nineteen of twenty of her homicide cases, you should not see that as a sign of her courtroom brilliance: despite the impression that high-profile cases with hefty heavies for attorneys may give of the neck-and-neck race to the finish, for the most part the deck is stacked against defendants.

Paula Jones is not filing a criminal complaint against the President, but the point still stands: people are going to think what they will, and either she walks away with some money or she doesn't. Let's face it, many Americans hold the jury system in questionable esteem—wondering how it is that twelve people whom you would not hire to work in your typing pool, much less have deciding matters of life and death, can be rendering a complicated verdict—so the decision of this panel of ordinary people is not likely to change anyone's opinion.

In the meantime, it is Paula Jones herself who is responsible for ruining her reputation, since no one knew who she was until she claimed to be the Paula mentioned in the David Brock article which appeared in *The American Spectator*. In fact, many of the details were botched, which shows how many women were mentioned, how little impact the report had on any one of them, how unrecognizable and random it all was. She outed herself, heaven knows why, but that's her problem, not the court's. If, as Ms. Jones claims, she must clear her name because her family members thought less of her when they heard about the article, I'm not sure how a lawsuit helps: in fact, her sister

Charlotte was still telling *Prime Time Live* that she's in it for the attention, so evidently with them nothing works. As for the rest of us, I think Jones' essential trashiness is going to show through. She will still have too much hair, both on the top of her head and in the high-fluff angora sweaters she favors. (When somebody, probably Republican handler Susan Macmillan, finally convinced Ms. Jones to get a new look, her long and straightened dark hair and toucanish face combined to make her look quite a bit like Pedro Almodóvar's star actress, and model of Mediterranean ugly beauty, Rossy de Palma.) She will still look cheap, and the elongated nose and high-gloss skin that seems desperate to take a powder will still make people say, She's not that good-looking, why would he want her? Jones suffers by being in a situation in which none of the consequences of someone else's abusive actions could render her a working-class heroine, a Melanie Griffith in *Working Girl,* a Roseanne, a Karen Silkwood or a Rosa Parks: Paula Jones' struggles with whatever happened during and as a result of a little bit of time in a hotel room in Little Rock are not great enough to make her mere existence so admirable that she is heroic for just living to tell. Most martyrs are supposed to arrive at their heroism by accident—but like the guy who demanded the reward for inadvertently chancing upon Andrew Cunanan's body, Paula Jones wants to be rewarded for what no one else seems to see as virtuous. So, with very little to complain about and quite a lot to irritate us with, Paula Jones would have been better off never bringing any of this up. This is not *Roe* v. *Wade,* it is not important legislation, and an unsympathetic complainant could hardly do herself any good here.

The one thing she could get out of this is some money. And that seems fine. Evidently enough happened between Ms. Jones and the President to inspire his willingness to make a settlement, and she ought to just take it. She shouldn't give it to charity. She should go to Frederic Fekkai for a haircut and ask him to do something to her hair, so long as it's not what he did to Hillary. She should get a facial at Mario Badescu, and buy herself some custom-mixed face powder at Prescriptives. She should do whatever a girl can do with "mad money." She should do anything she wants, but for God sakes, don't be ashamed of getting some money. This is America, where capitalism is a virtue so long as nobody says so. Every day in everything we do we are all in it for the money or we are truly stupid. It doesn't mean that love of our work isn't a primary concern or that many people earn less than they could because they choose, instead, to do something they like. It just means that this is no time to get sentimental about Marx; under the Clinton administration, we have dismantled welfare as we know it (kind of like God as we understand him) and as we don't know it; anyone who hurries can still catch the last days of Fidel, but let's face it, we like the measure of man and everything he needs and wants to be expressed in numbers, and every time somebody gets handed a large sum of money and says they'd do it for free, I wish they'd prove it. But no one does that—donations to charity don't count, because that is still your choice—because money offers comfortable demarcations of what we are worth and who we are: mere praise or simple blame are not as effective ways to convey an assessment as, say, giving $36 million to Evander Holyfield or extracting $35 million from O. J. Simpson. The reason totalitarianism tends to be part of communist regimes is that in the absence of hierarchy established by degrees of wealth, only complete state control of the populace can impose order. Somehow men tend to be much more comfortable with their capitalist pursuits and desire to make money than women are. They feel more entitled and perhaps they've been made to feel so.

The fabulous illustration that Paula Jones offers of why all women should be forced to do meaningful work outside the home—lest they become the daydream daytime hookers born of bored housewifedom like Catherine Deneuve in Luis Buñuel's *Belle de Jour,* or lest they turn an afternoon's affront into a political football by being Paula and proud—is perhaps worth the price of this whiny public crusade. Because most of her plaint basically comes down to wanting to be unbranded, to lose her reputation as the town whore—and a lack of global perspective has allowed her to mistake this whole country for a gossipy little Peyton Place.

Anyone aware of the rules of the game knows that any political blow is parried with counterattacks and sheepish dismissals. You don't even need to be inside the Beltway to know that: just getting into the sandbox teaches you that if one kid calls you a loser, you must retort by calling him an asshole. But Paula, who started all this by going public, seems outraged that White House spin doctors are not saying that *yeah, the President did pull it out and say kiss it, he likes to treat all his girls to the goods.* She is actually alarmed that no one is eager to embrace her need for emotional justice. While willingly entering the arena by announcing—frankly—her existence to a world that already knows that many, many more of her kind haunt the Clinton presidency, Jones was then dismayed to discover that her sound and fury signified nothing—and only produced a lot of unpleasant noise in response. In her suit, Jones' attorneys complained that, "The outrageous nature of Clinton's branding of Jones a liar is aggravated in that a greater stigma and reputation loss is suffered by Jones by the statements of the President of the United States in whom the general public reposes trust and confidence in the integrity of the holder of that office." Though I defy anyone to diagram that sentence, I think the gist is that if *he* says she's making stuff up, it's *really* damaging.

Now, of course, no one puts much stock in the word of any politician, least of all Bill "Slick Willy" Clinton, who has made being full of shit not just a mere peccadillo, but in fact the greater part of his personality. How can she seriously make this claim? More to the point, how can she fail to see that *she* started this slugfest, and after accusing him of outrageous exposure, aren't all bets pretty much off? Why should he be kind and considerate in response, even if what she claims *is* true. In fact, the horrible thing about Paula Jones' case is that it might even be true, but every aspect of her legal and public presentation make it such that it is hard to take seriously. She has allied herself with conservatives like Pat Robertson and antiabortion activist Randall Terry of Operation Rescue, which necessarily excluded feminist groups from rallying to her side: as NOW president Patricia Ireland said in a 1994 statement, "We find the involvement of right-wing leaders in her case disingenuous . . . They are not known for supporting women's rights but rather for opposing them." Ms. Ireland sees the religious right's interest in Jones' cause as no more than an attempt "to impeach President Clinton and to portray harassment suits as something women file to bring down powerful men." In fact, the feminist agenda is so alien to Jones' backers that it is hard to see her lawsuit as anything other than some sort of conservative dessert tray carting around various right-wing delicacies for her supporters to delectably select from. In general, on the liberal side of things, when legal moves like this are used—and misused—the one thing that can at least be said is that there is a direct relationship between the red herring (a sexual harassment claim) and its true goal (women's rights). In this case, impeaching Clinton and beating the liberals at their own game is the true motive (no point even finding a pretense of alteriority).

With all this freighting down Paula Jones' claim against the President, she still somehow wants him to apologize and to say that she is a "good person." Why? What would it mean if he is doing that under duress of legal action? And who is he, with all his foibles and faults, to declare her good or bad? What is this all about? And does it really belong in court?

I find Jones' goal of admission and apology particularly disturbing on what are perhaps the highest feminist grounds I know of: honesty and self-respect. In this country, the way the courts are set up, you can sue for money—not for goodwill or sweet talk or a half-assed apology from an angry adversary. I believe that the system was established in this way because, as they say in the best legal circles, money talks and bullshit walks. This nation was founded on many principles of liberty, but the most important one is surely free speech, which ensures that you cannot be compelled to say anything you don't want to ever (except in criminal proceedings, when you can be held in contempt of court—but unless it's a high-profile, politically charged case, witnesses can usually take the Fifth). No one can make you tell someone you like them and want to be their friend if you'd sooner cement their feet together and dump them into a slow, noxious death at the bottom of the East River. No one can make you recant an editorial you wrote when you were a sophomore at Dartmouth and infatuated with certain strains of German romanticism that somehow led you to say that other than genocide, Hitler had some pretty good ideas about government. No one can force you to admit you majored in sociology or dated Carl Bernstein. The only thing that the civil courts do when they want to mete out punishment is penalize you where it hurts—in your wallet. These are the rules here in our democracy: in the Soviet Union, they made people renounce creature comforts and pledge allegiance to Stalin's Five-Year Plans; in Red China, intellectuals had to labor in the fields and claim a fealty to Mao's *Little Red Book*. But here, we just make you pay traffic tickets and other more taxing fines. And if women want to engage in the legal system to forward freedoms or just because we're stark, raving, plumb-crazy mad and we're fed up and we want revenge, we've got to learn to collect the cash and laugh all the way to the bank or Barneys or the beach island paradise of our Rousseauvian escapist dreams.

We women need to learn to exact a pound of flesh by good, capitalist means.

It seems clear that Paula Jones has made a mistake in staking out Clinton by wishing to be comforted and liked, even though nothing she's done merits either response from the public or the President himself. This is a little-girl impulse, it is the same needy, wanty sense of worthless begging for approbation and affirmation from those who have no intention of bestowing any such thing upon you that gets women into compromising sexual—and other—positions in the first place. I don't mean to blame the victim—just because it is so damn easy to manipulate many women into sexual servitude does not make it moral or lawful and does not allow us to let men who break our boundaries in bad ways get away with it—but it does mean that we women must behave firmly from the get-go. It means that we know, with no exceptions, that it's a bad idea to go up to the executive hotel suite for a rendezvous of any sort with any man who was previously unknown—and that if you do somehow get cornered by a drawer-dropping higher-up who demands that you pay oral homage to his private parts, you take swift action, you don't wait until conservative interest groups and fringe publications pull you into a brouhaha that is no longer even part of your happily married life and the two kids that you are raising in Long Beach, California. You don't wait until the statute of limitations on filing a sexual harassment suit has expired and you must therefore concoct a claim of civil rights violations to even get the case into a courtroom. And you demand lots of money, refuse to apologize for your really wretched hair, don't demean your integrity with wishes for confirmation, consolation or any words like I'm sorry—and you ask for more money than you want or deserve or would even satisfy Marie Antoinette. And you simply smile with no concern when you are disliked or despised: you do what you have to do because you must, because it is right, and fighting fair—like the many female employees of Mitsubishi, *The New York Times,* Goldman Sachs, AT&T and other companies who sued for sex discrimination and got justice in the form of cash—will be found to have its own compensations, including, occasionally, a respect that can become genuine goodwill. But if you want sympathy, cry to Mommy.

I wonder what it will take for people to learn this lesson: you can't make people like you, and all the efforts to do so (such as filing suit that would appear feminist when it is actually just nihilist) will usually have the opposite effect. Willy Loman wanted to be well liked, and he died with the certainty that his insurance was worth more than his life.

In Jones' case, her attorneys are asking the President to say things we will all know he doesn't mean, although the gesture—along with a sizable payment—will satisfy them. Obviously, the only thing Bill Clinton can possibly be sorry about at this point is that whatever he did to this woman has caused him so much trouble. But he can't truly be sorry for how she might feel: this woman has filed a lawsuit against him, she's consumed his energies, she's spoken of distinguishing characteristics that one can only blush over. If there ever were a point where he felt sorry about hurting her in some way, that's long gone. Now he just wishes she'd disappear. And yet, she wishes he would say patently untrue words.

Look, at the moment we live in mea culpa hell. People are so sorry so often and so quickly—within forty-eight hours of the ear bite, Tyson was apologizing. Of course, he had to do it, the way people always say "Fine" when asked how they are. Very rarely are people honestly sorry—if they were, they would not have done it in the first place. Except for in small chance mishaps, "sorry" is an obnoxious trivial word. There was briefly some talk of President Clinton making a formal apology for slavery, as he had recently apologized for the Tuskegee incident, and this idea was patently idiotic. There were some obvious problems—the events took place too long ago for the current American population of immigrants to feel for slavery as a crime, the hundreds of years that the practice went on made it more a lifestyle than a behavior per se, all of which is to say that the enormity of the crime is beyond the scope of anyone accepting its onus—but the main reason we ought never apologize for such a thing is that it's just too easy. It is so facile, so self-satisfying, so meaningless. With Tuskegee, we can calculate the cost of the error some, we can pay reparations, we can localize the evil and do our best to undo it, but to apologize for slavery would be to say we're sorry for racism, hate, exploitation, the dark side of human nature, that first fall from grace, the day Satan entered Eden as a slivery snake and opened man's eyes and taught him to hate what he could see rather than loving what he could feel. Ever since then it has been a world of men behaving badly, of women sometimes behaving even worse, and everyone just covering their tracks, saying I'm sorry, I'm sorry, I'm sorry. Saying, basically: *I'm sorry I ruined your life.*

But there is real dignity in the occasional moment when some public figure says I'm *not* sorry. I mean, any idiot can say I'm sorry, but it takes a real mensch to say I'm not sorry, or better still, to just shut up. Quiet—or quiet resignation—and a reluctant, pained acceptance of one's responsibility for how he has hurt and harmed and maimed and destroyed others is the only real way to do penitence. After a long and thoughtful time of living with the burden of whatever wrong it might be, then maybe there might be an appropriate moment to ask the wronged party for forgiveness. But remorse is not a rhetorical device.

I found it extremely amusing when both Sol Wachtler and Dick Morris had their respective memoir/public policy books come out at the same time, and both had to do the talk show circuit and discuss the various wrongs they'd committed against their wives and mistresses. Both would sit there and say, "Larry, I did something wrong and it was inexcusable." "Oprah, no one involved in this deserves any blame except for me. I am sick. I am compulsive. I have an addictive personality. I have hurt wonderful people whom I love very much, and I deserve every terrible thing that ever happened or happens to me." My favorite was all the times Morris would talk about wanting his wife back. And I sat there, thinking to myself, these poor, benighted middle-aged men, thrown into the recovery movement fairly late in life, pelted with touchy-feely terminology; forced to "claim responsibility"—a phrase first used to explain how the PLO admitted to having blown up a building—for all sorts of acts that they thought they wouldn't have to answer for before St. Peter at the pearly gates, at which point they could just offer what I call the Portnoy Defense ("I'm a nice Jewish boy! Even when I was bad—the worst—I was still a nice Jewish boy!"), and here they are, unable to continue their professional lives unless they find a way to discuss their behavior that will be palatable to the public. So they think that by saying that it's all their fault, they are—paradoxically—getting themselves off the hook. They are plea-bargaining with the world, offering up their candor—which is not the same as honesty—for a sentence that is no more than humiliation, unemployment and prison time already suffered. They adopt this strategy not just because it's preemptive but because it creates the appearance of penitence. And because it is all they can *do:* here are two men who are accustomed to doing and deciding, faxing this one, phoning that one, forcing, forcing, forcing.

But redemption is about reflecting and lying low, it's about conceding and surrendering. It is not about results-oriented speech, but about slow change, about waiting for that weightless state of grace that is the opposite of demand and want and need. Redemption is big and godly and generous and good. But these men can't sit around all day waiting for the real thing, so instead they try to manipulate and force and cajole it, as if it were a policy decision, an unruly aide, an intractable bloc of senators, something they can announce in a press release. Dick Morris seems to think by telling every interviewer that he is desperate to win his wife back, he will do so, that a grand gesture is a meaningful one. He seems not to understand that he owes none of us any explanation for why he behaved as he did, and if he wants to give his marriage the dignity it deserves—and prove that he really has changed—he'll just shut up.

How about trying no regrets. How about saying that these things, these apparent humiliations, were all part of the process of becoming. No one needs to restore my good name, no one needs to make me into a good girl, to give me lady status after a lifetime of tramp, because I am who I am and what I am and not what others define me as. I don't need someone else to legitimize my claims. Both Paula Jones and Gennifer Flowers made the mistake of seeking absolution in the wrong places. Both want to be understood and accepted and vindicated for their bad experiences, but in truth, their personal pain is between them and their Maker. Court is meant to establish legal claims and award damages—if Clinton did what Paula Jones said, he is pretty scummy.

There is a brute, juvenile crudeness to a man pulling out his dick and saying suck it, even if the woman seems dirty and maybe even is dirty. But she needs to make peace with her misery herself. Gennifer Flowers too. Both women have relationships with other men that are stable, both are okay, and the courts really should be used for real cases of illicit behavior, loss of employment and ruined lives.

Look, it is hard to be a girl, a person, these days. We are single for so long, we are hurt in a million different ways, and we wish we could just have restitution, a little recognition of our heartaches. But we can't. This is just the price of freedom, and I doubt bondage is prefera-ble. People go running to court like they ran to the teacher to tell on the playground bully. Autumn Jackson seems to be taking out her sorrow of not having a family on Bill Cosby. Dorothy Hutelmyer, the North Carolina woman who sued her ex-husband's new wife for adul-tery and was granted one million dollars in damages, and Kelly Fisher Dodi al-Fayed's former fiancée who, prior to his death, was basically suing him for falling for Princess Diana, also seem to be misusing the courts to help assuage their private heartbreak. Nina Sharavan, an emotionally disturbed topless dancer, accused Eric Williams and Mi-chael Irvin of the Dallas Cowboys of raping her to satisfy some need for attention, or to cry out for help (even Irvin and Williams said that they didn't want her punished as much as they wanted her to seek psychological help, because they could see she was traumatized). We are begging for the law to give us not only what is missing in our lives but that which we keep losing over and over again with every new little loss. It is like emotional hemophilia—every time we are cut, the wound threatens to never heal. Early-life damage, instead of making us tough, turns us into delicate creatures seeking repair in ill-advised places. And then we want to drag the law into it—we want the lousy things people do to each other to be illegal, even though more often than not they are not even immoral. They are mostly just business as usual.

*   *   *

The truth is that sexual indiscretions committed by our leaders are our business because they do put them into compromised positions. After all, how much of the Clinton administration has been bogged down and clouded over by scandal which, by its own admission, has obscured many of its accomplishments and often allowed members of Congress to take the President less than seriously? Bad behavior, a checkered past, whatever you want to call it, is a heavy thing, an annoying thing, a distracting thing. Traditionally, spies—CIA officers in particular—were checked over for sterling character, for lack of adultery or personal embarrassment in their background, because a person with secrets is a person who will spill secrets under pressure from the enemy—or rather, a man who cannot be blackmailed is a man who can be trusted. Bill Clinton, on the other hand, lives with the threat of bimbo eruptions exploding beneath every step he takes. And it is rumored that it is only because of J. Edgar Hoover's fear of being exposed as a homosexual with cross-dressing tendencies that the FBI was kept in check during the Kennedy administration. It was a bit of a Secret Service game of brinkmanship, at least as effective as anything George Kennan conjured up to help contain our cold war with the Soviets.

But the mysteries and allure of uncovering the scandal lives of contemporary figures is not nearly as remarkable, fantastical and inexplicable as the modern mythmaking that retroactively attaches devastating powers of attraction to historical characters about whom our knowledge is sketchy, negligible or nonexistent. Surely the most impressive groupie—married or not, political or pop—has to be Sally Hemings, a would-be or could've-been presidential consort. For one thing, with the exception of a small fringe element, no historian seems to believe that there ever was a relationship between Jefferson and his slave girl, a Caucasianly aspected house servant, alleged to have been the daughter of John Wayles, Thomas Jefferson's father-in-law. The only contemporaneous report of President Jefferson's sexual liaison with Ms. Hemings is in the form of an 1802 editorial in the *Richmond Recorder* by one James T. Callender, a frustrated office seeker whose political antipathy for Jefferson, then in his first term as President, discredits his claims. "It is well known that the man, *whom it delighteth the people to honor,* keeps, and for many years has kept, as his concubine, one of his own slaves," Callender begins. "Her name is SALLY. The name of her eldest son is TOM. His features are said to bear a striking though sable resemblance to those of the President himself. The boy is ten or twelve years of age. His mother went to France in the same vessel with Mr. Jefferson and his two daughters. The delicacy of this arrangement must strike every person of common sensibility. What a sublime pattern for an American ambassador to place before the eyes of two young ladies!" Beyond this, the recollections of Jefferson's later-emancipated slaves put many of Sally Hemings' children in a physical gene pool that seems clearly a cognate of that of our redheaded founding father—although historians tend to attribute this likeness to liaisons between Sally and the President's nephews; all of her descendants were, apparently, white enough looking to have "passed" into non-Negro society undetected.

Sally Hemings' alleged relationship with Thomas Jefferson notwithstanding, what is perhaps more notable is the way she has become a figure of legend on the basis of so very little. There is no reason for her *not* to have passed into history unnoticed as most of us are, since only two descriptions of this bondmaid exist at all: in one, a slave called Isaac Jefferson recollects her as "mighty near white . . . very handsome, long straight hair down her back"; in another, Jefferson's grandson Thomas Randolph says she was "light colored and decidedly good looking." These two lines are all the information we have on Sally Hemings, all the hearsay evidence that the record has to work with, and both—in, say, a court of law—can only be regarded as opinion, not fact.

But that has ceased to matter: the myth is everything. From Los Angeles apocalyptic novelist Steve Erickson's imaginings of Sally in *Leap Year* and *Arc d'X* to the Paris-based African-American writer Barbara Chase–Riboud's fictional account *Sally Hemings* and its sequel *The President's Daughter* to rock songs like "Long Tall Sally" to the Merchant–Ivory rewrite of the French Revolution in *Jefferson in Paris,* it is taken as a simple fact that this was a lifelong and loving affair. Sally and Thomas are a presumed-innocent (as in: innocent of prejudicial feelings) and assumed-groovy interracial common-law couple in an era when *Hair* was not yet heading for Broadway. In the November 1992 issue of *The Atlantic Monthly,* Douglas L. Wilson laments that historians now have to prove to their students that this affair did *not* take place, it is so assumed within common culture to have been a certainty. This certainty began in 1974 when Fawn Brodie published *Thomas Jefferson: An Intimate History* and suggested that the truth of the affair had been repressed by scholars who tended to view its existence as a black mark, so to speak, on their hero's record. But by understanding Jefferson's love for Sally from an early seventies perspective—an error of judgment that Wilson calls "presentism"— suddenly, Brodie writes, it is "not a scandalous debauchery with an innocent slave victim," but "a serious passion that brought Jefferson and the slave woman much private happiness over a period lasting thirty-eight years." Suddenly, far from being an injustice for Susan Brownmiller to catalogue, we instead get something like . . . *Guess Who's Coming to Dinner.* Whatever chord Brodie's idea struck with a popular audience, historians have mostly remained unconvinced; in 1997, the University of Virginia published *Thomas Jefferson and Sally Hemings,* attorney and law professor Annette Gordon-Reed's attempt to repore over the evidence, an undertaking that would seem to indi- cate an unremitting need for proof positive.

It is no wonder that people love the idea of this story, that it has inspired mash-note B movie fantasies (as well as some B-movie reali- ties) and has become American history's unholy grail, with Hemings becoming to this country what Mary Magdalene is to Christianity. But while it's completely understandable that New Testament faithfuls, Catholics in particular, should want to believe that Jesus was made weak by at least one woman (from a cinematic perspective, I think most of us prefer post-collagen Barbara Hershey to pre-*Saturday Night Fever* Yvonne Elliman), there is no need for long tall Sally to confirm Jefferson's lust. Whether it is because he has red hair, that he was a Francophile stationed in Revolutionary Paris or simply because it is true, Jefferson was known to be a ladies' man. Sally is hardly necessary for his mystique.

But the Christ comparison is apt because Jefferson was the primary author of the American catechism, he was the Jesus of the religion of liberty. If the possibility of Christ carrying on with Mary Magdalene is meant to remind us of the intrinsic weakness of his loving-kindness and tolerant teachings—i.e., if you take in a whore, you will eventu- ally lie down with a whore—then miscegenation would seem the logi- cal mishap in Jefferson's enlightened worldview. That he was racist on the record does not seem to matter because this fits too well into a well-hewn story structure. And no wonder: it really is a lovely fable, whether false or true, a counternarrative to *Mandingo* and Emmett Till, but also to all the purple pieties that patriotism, patriarchy, all those grandly historic traditions have left us with: one black woman, written into history, can carry the mantle for everyone else who has been left on the margins.

It seems sad, pathetic and telling that President Clinton, whose middle name is Jefferson, should most closely resemble his namesake only in that his sex habits are a public scandal that his political adversaries use to make hay. But if we remove the threat to statesmanship that extramarital affairs can pose (and the closest we've seen of this with Clinton is Susan McDougal, who is not talking), if we look at Gennifer Flowers as a relationship Clinton had as a philandering private citizen, it is easier to put into perspective. Other than that, I have to say that the impressive thing is not that Bill Clinton had a long-term affair with Gennifer Flowers, and received some under-the-desk blow jobs from some other gals along the way, but that he is still married.

The funny thing about whatever extramarital liaisons have been part of the Clintons' union is that it has always struck me as odd that people think of them as indications that their marriage is a sham or a convenient political partnership or worse. According to an array of statistics, affairs are business as usual in American coupledom: in fact, the term "extramarital" seems a real misnomer when speaking of a kind of relationship that seems to be part and parcel of marriage. Dr. Joyce Brothers, therapist for the *Good Housekeeping* set, believes that "situational infidelity"—at a business convention, after a career disappointment—does not necessarily reflect badly on the state of a marriage. Gary Smalley, marriage counselor to Frank and Kathie Lee Gifford, says couples should not split up over an affair, which can be "a medication of sorts." Which is not to say that I think it makes for a happy home or that the violation of trust that an affair brings forth is not hugely painful, often devastating and frequently homewrecking. But the way things look to me—and I have never been married—when I see people who have been together for fifty or sixty years, when I look at my grandparents, my great-aunts and -uncles, when I gaze upon long, strong bonds of love—when I look at people whose particular histories and plot developments I am not aware of, people whom I know only as conclusion, as denouement: when I look at aged love what I see are people who have come to terms with their turbulence.

I don't mean turbulence in a small way: I mean it as the feeling that *I am going to jump out of my own skin,* that *I have had enough of this life,* that *I am sick to death of the choices I made.* This is not just about infidelity, though no doubt there is that too: and I see people who have been tempted and succumbed, people who have hurt and hated and forgiven and made a little bit of shaky, awful, awesome peace with themselves and the person they are married to every day. I see people who frequently can't remember why they took their vows all those years ago in the first place, and who live not just with the vague sense but with the utter certainty that if they had to do it all over again they would be better off with almost anyone else. I see people who have made peace not with their spouses but with themselves, and with the mundane tedium of daily life that is so often so empty that to stay trapped in a marriage that is so hollow, so "unfulfilling," seems like succumbing to the abyss in ways that existence should not demand of anyone. I see people who understand that love is a nightmare, not just once in a while but as a matter of course, because people you love will disappoint you and betray you as a matter of course, they will do it without thinking about it, without knowing about it, without meaning it. I see people who understand, not that love, not that marriage and not that relationships of any sort are a long, long road, but that life itself is trying.

I see people who are happy. Because they have built a life, a real life, something so substantial that not only is it invulnerable to the whims of daily, petty emotion, but it has withstood years of bad moods and ill will and guilt and sorrow and sickness and misfortune and grievances so long-held that no one even remembers where they started. I see people who live in the world, who are anchored and tethered and attached to the world. And they are happy.

The evil of *The Bridges of Madison County,* a hideous book for so many reasons, was in its implication that a three-day love affair is the real thing and a marriage that lasted for years and years and produced good, happy children is a sham. The leading man, the traveling stranger with a camera, never even has another girlfriend thereafter until he dies: the daily importance of life and love is thrown away for some fake notion of *the one big love*. The banality of the ideas presented in the book, passed off as romantic, is more frightening than all the sex and violence in all other aspects of American popular culture that make everyone so hysterical. The problem with Arnold Schwarzenegger movies is that they are dumb and senseless—the violence is all for special effect. On the other hand, Sam Peckinpah's chiaroscuro Westerns are beautiful, full of red red blood in black and white. And they don't pass off a three-day affair as the great love of one's life. What I am trying to get across is that the ruin of this country will not be the bombs and machine guns and blood and guts flying through the air that constitute a large part of what we consider entertaining; what will kill us is the inability to think critically about these images or to raise children who know how to interpret them sanely. And as long as there can be a national craze over the notion that three days in Iowa does a great love make, I think it's safe to say that we're not thinking straight. People who ought to know better bought into the *Bridges* version of romantic love, imagining that all the love inside you—which is enough to last a lifetime—can be meaningfully spent over a long weekend. It's not that movies should only celebrate life-long love stories, but that the *real* romance is the staying together. No one should stay in an oppressive relationship, there should be no Noras, no Nicole Simpsons, but the fact is that a couple staying together only because they are already there is more substantial than people give it credit for, that the rewards of having a partner for life is hugely gratifying in ways that are so surprising and probably understandable only from the other end. The beauty of faith is that it requires faith, it is not a certainty, and the worth of a marriage may not be clear until the couple is eighty years old, but growing old together—just sticking with it—is no small thing.

In this context, women like Gennifer Flowers, the mistresses, these evil interlopers, become much less dangerous, much more a thing that can happen in a long-term relationship. Not that it's okay to cheat, but in the event of such a thing, the most important part is how the couple works it out. Are they in it together for life? Or are they like

Robert James Waller, believing the great love of your life can be three idyllic days? Do they understand that love is cumulative, that quantity is more important than quality because ultimately it *is* quality?

All this is to say that one of the most impressive things to me about the Clintons, either individually or together, is their marriage. The very thing that most people study askance seems to me their greatest accomplishment. Clearly, these are both people who have made peace with their own turbulence. And that is why my judgments about the deals that Hillary Clinton has struck with the devil along the way are not about the choices she made: those choices are her business. My quarrel is with the way she has been perceived, with the way she has been looked upon as a nontraditional First Lady or simply as a willful, independent woman. In fact, this is a woman for whom being a wife clearly comes first.

And heaven knows it took a strong woman to keep the Clinton marriage together—my Aunt Esther always said that the woman makes the marriage, and I think that's probably right—and I am sure Hillary worked long and hard at that. She succeeded where so many others have failed or given up or snapped, and sometimes I think people resent her for that more than her career woman bravado or anything else. She has the smugness of the one he comes home to. She has the arrogance of the one who has won. In fact, it is the fictional account of the Clintons in the novel *Primary Colors,* which finds both Susan and Jack Stanton—as the campaigning couple are called—cheating on each other time and again, and letting each other down in different ways, but still somehow sticking with it, that does the Clintons' marriage more justice than either one of them is able to give it in their own awkward and defensive presentations. In a paraphrased version of the *60 Minutes* interview that the Clintons did following the Flowers free fall, Susan Stanton makes Cokie Roberts understand what it takes to hold a marriage together—and it is her strong speech beside Jack's lame and guilty mumblings that makes it clear that this is a woman of valor. "You are making an assumption," Mrs. Stanton interjects, regarding some assessment of the state of their union. "I mean, Cokie—where have you *been* these past twenty-five years? People have suffered and struggled and been through all sorts of crazy things. So yes, we did have some tough times. But we're still here. And if you want to draw a political lesson from that about Jack Stanton's character, it has nothing to do with inconsistency, or what was the word you used? Untrustworthiness. It's the exact opposite: This man does not give up. He will work through the tough times. He will wake up every morning and bust his *butt* for the American people."

Joe Klein/Anonymous has rendered this speech in close approximation to the real *60 Minutes* vituperation. Both fact and fiction have Hillary as way more competent and confident than her husband, rushing to defend his honor after he has insulted hers. There is something masochistic about this whole approach of hers, but the individual acts, the tough rhetoric, is in itself quite impressive, in fact astonishingly so. She really is very capable. Julie Burchill's estimation of Hillary's abilities as superior to Margaret Thatcher's is likely correct. Somehow the atmosphere she has developed her almost-political career in has not helped her to thrive.

*   *   *

Many political babes and professional girlfriends avoid unseemly display by becoming über-groupies, courtesans in the corridors of power, like Pamela Harriman or Marietta Tree with their harems of husbands and lovers, their series of international affairs that allowed these women to end their lives while serving at high appointments in the world of diplomacy, with no further need for assignations with Averell or Adlai or Agnelli: their social skills in political salons ultimately displaced their slut status in private quarters. Judith Campbell Exner, while never quite becoming America's idea of a classy dame, became a bit more than a simple Kennedy conquest when it was discovered that this babe-a-licious brunette—she had that real early sixties lush femaleness, a womanly heft that made her a voluptuous version of the thin, dainty Jackie—was a sometime moll to mobster Sam Giancana, was some kind of sweetheart to Frank Sinatra and was, by her own admission at the Church hearings, a liaison between the White House and the Mafia, delivering bribe money on behalf of the Kennedy boys in some last-ditch effort to get Fidel Castro assassinated. When Ms. Exner revealed to Liz Smith in an October 1996 article in *Vanity Fair,* as she lay dying of advanced metastatic breast cancer, that she had aborted JFK's baby, she may have increased her mystique a bit more, but probably not: heaven knows, Exner is likely not the only woman who did such a thing, and no doubt there are even a fair number of John F. Kennedy's unidentified offspring floating around the population, an inevitable result of the President's purported rampant promiscuity in an age immediately preceding the Pill and much before legalized abortion. It is perhaps Exner's extraordinary triad of lovers—Sinatra, Giancana, Kennedy—that will ensure her place in history. As Smith, who believes everything Judith Exner says, is still moved to note about her reaction when first hearing of Exner's triple hit: "I remember wondering if she was just bragging. It was like baseball's famous play: Tinker to Evers to Chance."

Mary Pinchot Meyer, another JFK mistress, is little known outside the world of D.C. gossip fetishists, but she might well have been the President's most elegant and exquisite, pedigreed and patrician, altogether unusual paramour. Ms. Meyer was an artist, an abstract painter and partisan of the Washington Color School, a movement led by the better-known Kenneth Noland, who was four years Mary's junior and one of many of her lovers. In her non-Bohemian life, Ms. Meyer was a Vassar graduate, a would-be medical student, a sister of Tony Pinchot Bradlee—first wife of retired *Washington Post* editor Ben Bradlee—as well as a former manuscript reader at *The Atlantic Monthly,* a feature writer for United Press, a great beauty, a mother of three boys and a woman who unorthodoxly divorced her diplomat husband Cord Meyer, a deputy director of the CIA, to pursue her painterly life. Mary was said to enjoy skinny-dipping *ensemble* at her family's Poconos estate, and her irresistible beauty was described to reporter Ron Rosenbaum, in a 1976 article for *New Times* magazine occasioned by the revelation of the Meyer–Kennedy affair in the *National Enquirer,* as that of a woman "who always looked like she had just taken a bath. A man once told me that she reminded him of a cat walking on a roof in the moonlight. She had such tremendous poise."

In every comment included in Rosenbaum's piece, the mention of Mary Meyer's gorgeousness cannot go without an allusion to her large array of lovers kept both pre- and post-divorce, which her forty-odd years did nothing to dwindle. Apparently President Kennedy was among Mary's men, not even necessarily a particularly important person within her selection of suitors. Perhaps Mary Meyer's story would not even merit telling by the few people—like Mr. Bradlee, in his memoir *A Good Life*—who bother to do so had she not been murdered one day in 1964, shortly after Kennedy's assassination, on a towpath beside a canal near the Potomac River in Washington; the crime has never been solved, but James Jesus Angleton, the fanatical CIA counterintelligence man who made a mountain out of a mole hunt, was found stealing Ms. Meyer's diary from her studio shortly after her death. Kennedy conspiracy theorists get good grist from this. Murder mystery aside, as a harbinger of a feminist future, this most independent of JFK's lovers gives a peek at imminent revolution, at a moment in time when it became clear that the women's movement was certain to happen, that female frustration was bound to burst open in a bad way. Reading accounts of Mary Meyer, one is invited into a world of strange bedfellows and crazy liaisons, artistic and sensitive wives married to gruff, bluff CIA husbands—the era of genteel gentleladies stymied and squashed in marriages to strong-jawed men with hardy names like Cord and Jack and Clem and Cap and Fritz and, yes, Oz (short for Osborn Elliot, a *Washington Post* executive). The discrepancy between what these women need and what these men can give is about to go haywire. Mary Meyer's sexual adventures in reaction to that repression actually make her actions in general more interesting than anything that went on with John F. Kennedy in particular.

So it was in the rock world, where uninhibited free love was often equated with liberation. Hence, grande dame groupie Pamela Des Barres has turned her *affaires d'amour* into two books—the first one, *I'm with the Band,* a major best-seller—and has recast her hippie chick days as a consort of choice into a kind of performance art, an act all her own; in fact, Miss Pamela—as she was known around the Whiskey-A-Go-Go and the Fillmore West—and a few fellow supergroupies became a sideshow for Frank Zappa under the guise of GTO (Girls Together Outrageously). The main thing one gets from reading Des Barres' memoir is that being the old lady for a boy rocker—which is now reduced to the pathetically prefeminist terms of servitude and suffering, waiting at home while this modern-day highwayman hits the road—was at one time a rebellious statement of sexual liberation.

Like pornography in the days of *Deep Throat* and *Behind the Green Door*—when the sexual exploitation was purposeful to some plot, when it was not all the money shot on an overlit videotape with a boom mike visibly hanging in the center of the set—to be a groupie involved a sensual, stylish mode of self-expression available in no other way to women. *Rolling Stone* devoted an entire issue in 1969 to groupies, illustrating—in a certain backward way that would occasion most of the radical left's attitude toward its other half, its essential misogyny, its inability to extend its notions of liberation of the human spirit to ones about freeing the *female* spirit from typing pool tedium—the way in which these lady libertines were pioneering a form of women's liberation predicated on a self-determined promiscuity, a choice to *enjoy* men for what they were.

Later on, Bébé Buell emerged on the scene: a blonde, blue-eyed willowy model with a slouchy seventies way about her at a time when the look had not yet been codified and categorized into what's now known as *waifish*. Beull was a Playboy Playmate back when high-fashion models did not cross that particular line and back when the centerfold girls could be nearly flat-chested and barely made up and still exude adequate sexual aroma. Hopelessly uncareerist and lazily unambitious, Bébé gained renown as den mother to rock stars of all kinds, real mother to Liv Tyler, lover of Todd Rundgren, Steve Tyler, Elvis Costello, Stiv Bators and others in the New York punk scene. But somehow she radiated an air of rarity and honor—she was *nobody's* one-night stand unless she chose to be—befitting a groupie who knows that while other girls line up to sleep with boys in bands, those same guys are breaking down doors and windows to get next to *her*. In fact, certain groupies became particularly desirable for band members because they became a rite of passage of sorts: a band going through Arkansas had to get it on with Little Rock Connie, and in Texas there was Dallas Alice (alluded to on Little Feat's live version of "Willin'," on the two-record set *Goodbye Columbus*); to be worthy of the honor of having one's penis molded into a statue for posterity by the Plaster Caster girls was a sign of a rocker's arrival; in *Please Kill Me,* an oral history of the punk scene, Hollywood groupies like Laurie Maddox, Sable Starr and Cyrinda Foxe (who mothered another of Steve Tyler's love daughters) speak excitedly of having David Bowie desperate to bed them down, to join the elite club. "They weren't competitive. They didn't have to be," Bébé Buell says in tribute to her fellow super-groupies. "Every rock star that came to L.A. wanted to meet them, it wasn't the other way around."

In the athletic setting of the movie *Bull Durham,* Susan Sarandon is a fanatical devotee of the North Carolina minor league baseball team attached to her town, and each season she takes on a different player with promise as a lover but also as a student: she tutors over toenail polish, she teaches the rules of the game, the rules of life, the secrets of confidence, the ways of winning; she is a groupie who can affect a player more persuasively and meaningfully than any coach. She ends up with far more power over her chosen charges than they will ever have over her. In the world of show business, it would seem that no groupie worth the goods would give it away for free—and it seems that there are certain prize prostitutes who men have decided are worth a price of thousands of dollars a night. In *You'll Never Make Love in This Town Again,* the highly compensated—if not exactly high-class—hookers who wrote of their "dates" with famous men like Jack Nicholson, Don Henley, Don Simpson and Timothy Hutton, among others, seem rather more proud than sad that a dollar figure—a large one, but none as infinite as the size of love—can be attached to their beautiful, buyable bodies.

Perhaps because of the proliferation of this kind of pricey prostitu-tion—along with a sort of mass-production of groupie girls who lacked the distinctions of their pioneering foresisters—as the seventies and eighties arrived, even in the rock world of anything goes, being a full-fledged wife became uniquely important, in ways disproportionate to the outlaw status this community is supposed to occupy. Women bartering babies for vows became a phenomenon among rock girl-friends as if it were 1958 all over again. Sting had out-of-wedlock kids with inamorata Trudie Styler, but he did ultimately marry her—in a Shakespearean ceremony on his lordly manor with all the pompous pomp you'd expect from a bass player who claims that he once taught both Nabokov *and* differential calculus—after showing footage of her giving birth in a Paris hospital in his concert film *Bring on the Night.* Patti Scialfa had a son with Bruce Springsteen before a backyard wed-ding bash and the arrival of two more little bosses. Jerry Hall, the

Mesquite model who went from boredom with the overly elegant Bryan Ferry to a roller-coaster relationship with Rolling Stone Mick Jagger, finally got him to marry her on the island of Mustique after giving birth to two of his children (a third was delivered down the road); though Ms. Hall has suffered through a marriage made of infidelities and indignities that her husband seems at least as committed to continuing as he is to being with her, she seems gratified to know that while there may be many chicks, only she is Mrs. Jagger. Seventies Staten Island-born model Patti Hansen has stuck it out with Keith Richards through several blood changes, and she even managed to get married *before* she got pregnant.

There are, of course, certain women who seem always to get the guy. Imagine being Jessica Lange, going from Mikhail Baryshnikov to Sam Shepard—two distinct and differently desirable men—and managing to bear children with both. Or Patti Smith, the one woman that gay photographer Robert Mapplethorpe is known to have been in love with, the woman who shacked up with Sam Shepard and settled down with the MC5's Fred Smith. Victoria's Secret model Stephanie Seymour, whose public persona is so strictly photographic that she may well be preverbal, could be Warren Beatty's transitional babe between Madonna and Annette Bening, she could be Axl Rose's heavy metal honey with a tattooed ankle and a *Playboy* nude spread, and she could finally settle in with the horsy set, commuting between estates in Bridgehampton and Greenwich she shares with businessman and *Interview* publisher Peter Brant (whom she married after bearing his baby—and getting her tattoo taken off). Mia Farrow has gone from Frank Sinatra to André Previn to Woody Allen, an impressive array. Claire Bloom has been with Richard Burton, Rod Steiger and Philip Roth, another assortment of types. These women, these always well-manned maidens and matrons, the ones who still seem lucky or at least luxuriously endowed in the matrimonial department even when it all goes wrong—both Farrow and Bloom have recently written memoirs that catalogue much devastation on the home front—always make the rest of us, whether the bare-bottom feeders of dating or just the ordinary women who can't attract men with such seeming ease and can't keep them around with any sort of regularity, wonder what on earth the secrets of these seductive creatures are.

And if we ever do figure it out, the fashion, cosmetic, women's magazine and self-help wing of the publishing industry will find a complete erosion of their customer base, and the whole economy will probably cave in as a result.

* * *

In 1791, Mary Wollstonecraft wrote *A Vindication of the Rights of Woman,* which has come to be known as a feminist classic, and which, like Henrik Ibsen's *A Doll's House* (1879), Charlotte Perkins Gilman's *The Yellow Wallpaper* (1892) and Virginia Woolf's *A Room of One's Own* (1929), still seems fresh and lucid today. Many of the absurdist cant manifestos written under the auspices of consciousness-raising in the early seventies are by now ridiculously dated, male-bashing and silly and as embarrassing as classes in masturbation and other cultural arcana that occasioned these writings and render them mere artifacts, while the clean, well-reasoned works of literature by Wollstonecraft and these others remain frighteningly alive.

Wollstonecraft was a friend of Thomas Paine, whose pamphlet *Common Sense* was said to have galvanized the American Revolution (this was back in this country's infancy, back before the days when the only political action a book could inspire was a book-burning), she was moved by the French Revolution and its ethos of enlightenment, she was as epileptically giddy as the rest of the Western world at the sudden discovery that there was no need for monarchs, that the simple dignity of the individual person invested at birth with the ability to think meant that no person by reason of royal birth (a position that often seemed accompanied by reason of insanity) should be allowed to tell anyone else what to do.

Perhaps, particularly in the United States, which I still believe to be the only nation founded on principles of democracy, it is hard to say what the big deal is in casting off kings, but mankind had simply never done it. Even the Israelites in the Bible, despite a relationship with God so close that they received manna from heaven daily, demanded a royal ruler, could not be satisfied with a "common" prophet or judge as a source of counsel. So the end of the eighteenth century was heady as hell. It took a world defined by the dictum of René Descartes, a place that believed I think and therefore I am, that finally said that the guiding principle of man should be the one quality that separates him from the ranks of animals: that he is not bundles of instincts and impulses, that clear thought allows him access to kindness and fairness and freedom from artificial and often unkind and unfair rule.

It was natural, in this atmosphere, that some woman should insist that gander and goose go together. "Bliss was it in that dawn to be alive," wrote William Wordsworth of that era. "But to be young was very heaven!" (This couplet, in its simple depiction of human events that pervade society like a weather system, is recalled when Bob Dylan's "Tangled Up in Blue" can conjure a whole decade with the lines "There was music in the cafes at night / And revolution in the air.") Mary Wollstonecraft felt that there was no reason that only the men should be allowed to have all the fun. She wanted to live in sin and fuck around with the other utopian philosophers of her day, she wanted to be a mother (in fact, her daughter was Mary Shelley) and still be all these other things, which is why she wrote her book. "A husband is a convenient part of the furniture of the house," she wrote in a letter to her betrothed, the equally open-minded William Godwin. Wollstonecraft is generally credited with spearheading the free-love feminist spirit such as we know it, and her simple point—that a woman is more than just a wife or a would-be wife or a widow; that a woman is not defined by her relationship to a man—has been made quite a lot, and quite often, and it is on these simple truths that contemporary feminism is predicated.

The point of feminism—of any civil rights movement—is every person's right to be who they are.

And that is the American project: it is a human potential movement that is over two hundred years old, it is all about the largeness of the human spirit compared with the petty smallness of everything that would quash it. It is about judging people by the best they can be and not the worst they can do. Feminism, and art that has a feminist agenda, serves to remind us of all the things we could be, all the shackles we can shed from our lives if we wish. It reminds us that we can be anything we want to be this time around. A play as old as *A Doll's House* is still performed regularly—in 1997 it had a controversial and acclaimed run on Broadway—because the image of Torvald calling Nora his "little skylark," his "little squirrel" and his "little featherbrain" still rings true for some people or is a grim reminder of what is no longer true for others. (In fact, Liz Phair's song "Canary," about the oppression of being a good, obedient girl, seems to refer right back to Ibsen.) Every single person still loves the moment when Nora tells Torvald, after a whole play of being treated like a helpless child, that she is leaving him, that this "gives me great pain, for you have always been so kind to me, but I cannot help it. I do not love you any more." People love it the same way they love the moment toward the end of *sex, lies, & videotape* when the Andie MacDowell character tells her husband, whom she discovers has been fucking her sister in her own bed, that she is leaving him, enough is enough. People love it the same way they love the moment in Mary-Chapin Carpenter's hit "He Thinks He'll Keep Her" when the little woman who married at twenty-one and has been good ever since finally decides to be bad: "When she was 36 she met him at the door / She said I'm sorry I don't love you any more." People love it the way they love the video for the country song "Independence Day" that shows all these women whose husbands beat them but who have somehow managed to pack up and leave to the chorus of "Let freedom ring." People love it the way they love ntozake shange's play *for colored girls who have considered suicide/when the rainbow is enuf,* when the four female characters, after describing bleak lives of poverty, abuse, rape, racism and really bad hair days, finally say, "i found god in myself / and i loved her fiercely." They love it the way they love the quasi-inane, quasi-spiritual writing of Maya Angelou, a woman whose mediocre pop poetry comes this close to making me want to say that just because she's black doesn't mean her clichés are art, and yet, somehow, when she writes, "I am phenomenal woman," even I feel something that sounds like *yes!* They love it the way they love a beaten Tina Turner leaving Ike while on tour in Dallas, convincing a hotel to let her stay even though she has no money, no credit cards, no nothing on her.

They love it like they love Diana, Princess of Wales, a true reverse Cinderella story for our time. I have always liked Diana, and thought her insistence on self-determination within the straitening confines of the royal family was particularly admirable in that it did not result in random, obnoxious rebellion, but was instead about wanting to be a good mother, a good humanitarian, a good person—to be lovely and graceful in all the ways that the royals just weren't. She beat them at their own game, all the while insisting on the dignity and generosity of the self, and of all people. When she finally got rid of Charles and got on with her life, particularly in the last couple of months, she seemed to be saying, *I was wood and now I am alive.* Of course I liked her! I *identified* with her in some strange way. But I never would have thought it would feel like a light just suddenly went out in the world when she died. I think maybe what it's about is that someone who had such glamour and style and loveliness but was still able to radiate so much warmth and compassion and caring is rare. A woman who can master beautiful gestures that can make people feel good and loved and recognized can be more important than having a solid economy or a good government or a lot of other things that seem necessary and are necessary—but not any more so than grace and beauty and a person whose mere existence makes it possible for everyone else to dream. People loved Princess Diana, and they were right to: I mean, man cannot live on bread alone. You can train five thousand or ten thousand or a million political theorists and economists and theologians and bureaucrats, but charm and charisma and charity and the desire to put celebrity to good use: hundreds of years of training can't teach that or invent it. Diana had this quality, and it was all of a sudden lost.

Professor Michael Adler, head of the National AIDS Trust, described her as having "the royal touch," by which he meant almost the opposite: by being so tactile, she reminded people that you could show warmth to those afflicted with HIV. But if we put aside Diana's public life, we basically have to see her as a woman who found herself in 1985, at just twenty-four years old, already the mother of two in a bland marriage, who decided to get out there and do something with herself, beginning with an impromptu trip to Belfast, which blossomed into a full schedule of rubbing noses with Maoris, holding the hands of AIDS patients, blowing candles with little girls, lifting children aloft in gestures of affection, freely expressing an empathy that freed her from the royal reserve.

People love these moments of women breaking free—they are our favorite human dramas. We love the breaking-free part, whether it involves convicts cutting loose from Alcatraz or Ron Kovic finally finding his way home from Vietnam or gay men coming out of the closet: the freedom to be oneself and the fight for it is a universally loved story. And we cheer on the woman who slams the door on her husband not because we hate men and not because we despise the institution of marriage and not because we want families to fall apart and not because we are romantic failures and like to see love die. People love it because we love to see human beings born—we love to see a person come alive and say *I am a person,* I am more than what you define and delineate me to be, *I was wood and now I am alive.* People love those episodes because we love life.

Which is why I cannot understand how the dead misery of the Stepford Wife lives on. Every summer, the Brattle Theatre in Cambridge, Massachusetts, would have its "Bored Housewife" film festival, showcasing the movies that showed the martini-and-Valium nightmare of being a woman whose life is in the home: *Who's Afraid of Virginia Woolf?, Montenegro, Diary of a Mad Housewife, The Graduate, Up the Sandbox, The Stepford Wives.* Most of these films date back to the seventies or earlier, but it seems amazing that even today it's still perfectly normal in movies to show at-home wives, though that is not the norm in the world any longer, as much for necessity as anything else. Stepford Wives, Hollywood wives—and, while we're at it, John Grisham wives. Yes indeed, the problem of the little woman behind the man or under him or anything but beside him, acting as an equal partner in an equal marriage, is such that one lawyer turned novelist deserves to be singled out for creating wife characters in book after book (and, more to the point, movie after movie) who do nothing but wear flowered sundresses and offer people lemonade when they come by the house to discuss *big, important* things with her *big, important* husband. (Why is it that dynamic actresses like Jeanne Tripplehorn and Ashley Judd agree to take these sorority sister roles?) The partnership marriage, which should be just typical in this day and age, does not emerge (Bill and Hillary have fucked it up) in popular culture, except with Mary Matalin and James Carville, which is more the rivalry as marriage.

And in movies, the two-career couple—which is, statistically, the living situation most married people find themselves in—is almost never portrayed. Honestly, I could not tell you what possessed Michael Douglas to cheat on lovely, throaty, elegant Anne Archer in *Fatal Attraction,* but it has occurred to me that maybe the woman ought to get a job. Volunteer work doesn't count. Like housework, it is yet another example of the economy exploiting women to do for free what most men wouldn't bother to do for all the money in the world. Colin Powell included. We live in a capitalist country—making a pittance as a legal-aid lawyer or a doctor at a clinic is perfectly honorable, and counts as "real" work, but if you're not being some-how remunerated, you don't count. "Money dignifies what is frivo-lous if unpaid for," wrote Virginia Woolf in *A Room of One's Own* in 1929—and we should have understood this by now. Even going back as far as 1898, Charlotte Perkins Gilman could assert that when women agree to take on the work of running a household for no pay, even though they perform tasks that are absolutely essential—surely society's most important job is to raise children—we show no real respect for them or for what they do. "The labor of women in the house, certainly, enables men to produce more wealth than they other-wise could, and in this women are economic factors in society," Gilman wrote in *Women and Economics*. "But so are horses."

So here's how it is: Being just a wife doesn't work. It works for no one. Lawyers leave their wives for paralegals, doctors leave their wives for nurses. But even if they don't, women get bored and men get bored with them. Life is tedious. There's a reason women reacted so strongly to *The Feminine Mystique* so long ago, and we should not forget those lessons.

We are a nation of splitters and quitters and cheaters whose mar-riages have been shown to have little staying power. That the divorce rate holds steady somewhere around 50 percent is a cause for opti-mism. Other than Joanne Woodward and Paul Newman, it is all but impossible to think of a celebrity marriage that's lasted. *Vanity Fair* published a feature, "Staying Married Is the Best Revenge," which served to point up the rarity of the eternal union. Even those famous couples that seem to mysteriously mesh—Farrah Fawcett and Ryan O'Neal, Tatum O'Neal and John McEnroe—even alliances and alle-giances that radiated the spell of great romance—Elvis Presley and Priscilla, Elizabeth Taylor and Richard Burton, Laurence Olivier and Vivien Leigh—were purely evanescent. Those Hollywood couples that have surprisingly stuck to it—Demi and Bruce, Tom and Nicole—still seem likely to part sooner or later. Often when a friend reveals a crush on a married person, I feel compelled to point out that the odds are that they will be single sooner or later, better to wait than get into the mess.

This is also the society that invented the prenuptial agreement, that wrote the plan for the marriage's demise before it's even started. It is the marital equivalent of our creation of the atom bomb, of our orchestration of our own extinction while every other species fights against it. But just as we also disarm and dismantle on a regular basis, the humorous aspect of these prenups is that it seems that almost none go unchallenged, every item is open to negotiation—perhaps mitigating the damage, but also in their flimsiness mirroring the very delicacy of the marriage contract that is so easily broken.

The point is: it is normal for people to love and unlove, to couple and uncouple—just as it is normal for us to rage against this sorrowful state of affairs. The hypocrisy of it all is a falseness of the best kind—rather like the generation gap, which creates an unfortunate divide between age groups, the demonstrable facts that people born in different eras are different for their different experiences is a sign of the passage of time, a reminder of the elasticity of civilization, and surely proves that all is well in the world.

The point is, we are a nation of individuals more than we are a country of units and families and clans and couples. We are a nation of individuals that wants desperately to be a country of kinfolk, so we marry again and again, we keep at it, we try and try. I think that is to our credit. But it is for this reason that every person should not only want but most certainly needs, requires—must have—her own identity. Being a wife, being a member of any group, can no longer be assumed to be a permanent position.

History has demonstrated again and again that being a full-time wife can drive an intelligent woman nuts. When Jann Wenner, editor and publisher of *Rolling Stone,* left his wife of two decades for a man, many of the couple's friends commented on how they had become estranged because she didn't do anything, she just shopped, she got bored and she began to bore him. I have no idea how accurate these comments or assessments were—it seems to me that to change your sexual preference in your late forties is a bigger deal than just having a wife who lives in Bergdorf Goodman—but there was one smart thing that a friend of Jane Wenner (Jann's ex) said: "A mind needs to be occupied." Those words sum up my point pretty well. People need things to do, men and women, they need to be challenged and given a chance to dazzle. Without this, a smart person will go crazy. And when women are circumscribed into roles of wife and mother, it will always feel as if men are the ones putting them there, even though, at this point, it is really up to us to say, I am larger and smarter and better and grander and greater than the little box you have tried to shut me in.

Every time women agitate it is against an oppressiveness that is euphemized as "patriarchy" but it is really just men. And these are women who love men, who are crazy about men. The women's movement is always about some limitation on what is understood to be the proper female role. But, in truth, women do have choices, feminism has basically worked. Most of the men I know my age really do long for partnership and equality in their relationships. It is better for everybody. And yet, there are still Stepford Wives everywhere. The world abounds with society matrons who do nothing with their lives.

But far more frightening than the matrons engaged in make-work or pretend employment are all the young women who grew up after feminism, but have not worked since the day they married. Think of all these full-time wives—Carolyn Bessette-Kennedy, Cari Modine, Evi Quaid, Sandy Pittman, Lilly Tartikoff, Patricia Duff Medavoy Perelman, Mercedes Bass, Carolyne Roehm (and what exactly is Trudie Styler other than Mrs. Sting?)—what has happened here? When did the obligation to be your own person, to be interesting and autonomous, leave our notion of adult womanhood?

*　*　*

The bridal fantasy is the most persistent, clinging and clawing prefeminist notion, and strangely, it has achieved a veneer of importance that is such that if you asked most women if you could be Marie Curie and unmarried or be any other woman married to any other man, the Nobel Prize wouldn't stand a chance. There is something so dreamy and powerful about the idea of being a wife. And the funny thing is, most people get married, and back in the bad old days when the Brontë sisters were writing their masterpieces under the desk in the drawing room, these determined young women saw marriage as a trap, a spirit killer, a life sentence. Now, that view is no longer accurate—thanks in no small part to feminism, to birth control—but the feeling of *no man will ever want me* or *no one will ever marry me* has stepped in as the new source of dread where fear of being stuck in a miserable marriage used to loom.

It seems that feminism ought to have made being a wife as a full-time pursuit unacceptable, and yet it persists. It can be called *homemaker* or *fund-raiser* or *volunteer worker,* but the fact is that these are not career options men would choose. The feminist Big Tent, which tries to find a place for Paula Jones, is also trying to find a place for women who have chosen to just be married. This situation is as preposterous as a Harvard-trained attorney like Phyllis Schlafly posing as an antifeminist. *What you say is not as important as what you do.*

It's kind of become the party line for young feminists to talk about wanting to be sexy and wear lipstick, to wonder if they'll ever marry. I myself do this. But the whole thing has become sort of routine and obvious. Katie Roiphe talks about how she may be too independent at this point in life to marry. She wants to find a boyfriend who can pick up the check once in a while. Naomi Wolf talks about how she never thought she'd be so traditional in this and that way, she never knew she'd be so satisfied to be a mom, she never expected to get married in a white dress—actually she calls the color "dirty white." While the average age of first marriage goes steadily up (for women, it was 24.5 in 1994, up over three and a half years from 20.8 in 1970), it has become fashionable once again to marry young, to get it over with, to be safe. Of course, many of these young brides will be divorced in five years and will embrace freedom. It is amazing to see smart, sassy, competent young women rushing to the altar for fear of what will happen if they don't—there goes that Harvard-Yale study again—when what should really scare them is what will happen to them if they *do,* I mean, here's the deal: We're adults, we're people, we're vital and capable. We live with the consequences of our idiocy because we believe in our actions. If we live that way, we will never have to ask

What if? because we'll know we did what was right for us at that moment, and that's all we can do. If we, as women, have not learned to embrace this philosophy—if we cannot risk never finding the right man but having the good sense to avoid the wrong ones; if our bridal dreams and Cinderella fantasies still guide us—then feminism has not nearly completed its task. Consider this: almost everybody eventually marries, and in 1995 there were 118 unmarried men aged 18–34 for every 100 single women. Basically, a third of those of us aged 25–34 have never been married—it will take some time, but we're bound to find each other somehow. The world is big and strange and can't be trifled with.

*   *   *

I know it is the common postfeminist cant to say that the idea is choice, that women can decide to work or can opt to just marry and live a life of leisure—CHOICE, CHOICE, CHOICE. But all of us who work for a living know that this is utter bullshit. All of us can completely respect a woman who takes several years off to raise children, since motherhood is a real and honorable job, and the arrangements that couples make over time to accommodate each other's particular employment and enjoyment needs are part of fairly and gamely making their way down love's long road. But it is a corruption and bastardization and accommodation of everything feminism stands for to say that women whose identities are defined by who they marry, women who don't have careers and don't know how to take care of themselves are A-OK. With feminism, women demanded certain rights, and every woman who continues to live in a man's shadow is an affront to what few gains were made. It's not that a woman *should* be a self-sufficient person; it's that she *must*.

"Personally, I believe that a woman should put her family and her relationships—which are really at the root of who you are and how you relate to the world—at the top of your priority list," said not Marilyn Quayle or Phyllis Schlafly or Bay Buchanan, but Hillary Clinton to Gail Sheehy during the 1992 campaign. "But," she added, as the liberal caveat, "I don't believe that I, or Barbara Bush, should tell

all women that's what they have to put first . . . What we have to get away from is the idea that there's only one right choice."

This brings me back to the conundrum of the First Lady. She cannot evade her public role, even though she has no official status. And this creates an untenable situation: As long as there is a woman occupying the White House whose civic duties are too consuming for her to take a job at a law firm on her own—you cannot serve clients when you are expected to make goodwill missions to Africa and China as a matter of course—and she is not earning a salary for this service, something is wrong. And while I really want to be tolerant enough to say that whatever a woman wants to do is just fine, this abnegates feminist accomplishment: women really do need to be able to take care of themselves in order to be themselves.

Because I pay my own rent, no one would dare tell me what to do or how to be. Because I pay my own rent, no means no, yes means yes, and anyone who doesn't understand this can fuck off and die. And almost inevitably, as can be proved by file cabinets full of divorce papers that are on the public record in every county courthouse in the country, women who deny themselves the rights and freedoms of paying their own rent in the beginning end up paying further down the road in a much bigger way.

I don't know why feminism has allowed itself to be co-opted by the forces that say, *It's beautiful to be a housewife! Shopping saves! Lunch at Mortimer's!* I like doing all those things, and I feel a lot better knowing it's my own money I'm spending and I don't have to answer to anybody.

Of course, even I know that there is just one small problem with what I am saying: even I understand that the jobs available to uneducated women are considerably less remunerative than those available to men—except for stripping and whoring. Part of the reason feminism cannot hold the hard line that I wish it would is just that: better to be a wife than a hooker. People like Camille Paglia who go on about the power and glory of strippers are so stupid. This is desperate work. I don't notice *her* doing it.

However complicated women's lives seem now, feminism did not occur out of some perverse desire to upset the happy applecart: it happened because many women were stifled by their lives. Perhaps those women were only the exceptional ones who were capable of writing a book or spearheading a movement, perhaps this has been inflicted on a generally happy sisterhood. But I don't think so. Even Barbara Bush, who embraced her role as the other half of the sky so joyfully, seems to have fallen into a funk and rebelled against it at some point.

But Hillary Clinton, who was supposed to be a First Lady with a difference, seems to be taking it all lying down. The last time we saw the real Hillary was probably when she shut up some annoying reporter inquiring about her career ethics, asking whether she should have just stayed home and given teas and been a nothing. She meant what she said, and her point was fair enough: women who go out and make their way in the world may or may not be morally superior to those who don't, but they are more important and more significant people, more valued by the world. That's the way it is: women who get manicures all day are less important than women who write legal briefs.

But, perhaps chastened by the response to that remark, Hillary Clinton has been on good behavior ever since, and it is really disappointing. I would have at least thought—especially after taking on the formidable task of overhauling national health care—that Hillary would have been the first First Lady to demand a salary, to go through the congressional confirmation process when she decided to assume some pretty hefty jobs. But she didn't.

And in her embrace of the politics of virtue at the beginning of her husband's presidency, she mistook a crusade for a job. Few remember the whole moral and righteous period in the First Lady's tenure, before Whitewater made it impossible for her to be the administration's itinerant preacher, selling the religion of feeling better through the embrace of community. At the time, a profile of Mrs. Clinton by Michael Kelly featured her dressed in angelic white linen on the cover of the May 23, 1993, *New York Times Magazine*, with bold letters bannered across the bottom of the page that said, HILLARY RODHAM CLINTON AND THE POLITICS OF VIRTUE, while inside an illustration portrayed her after the article's title, "Saint Hillary." In it she spoke of her philosophical journey, of the "sleeping sickness of the soul" that afflicts many Americans; she urged us to "be willing to remold society by redefining what it means to be a human being in the twentieth century." Kelly—who is usually edgy and dubious in his approach to pols—was alarmingly reverential. This in spite of the fact that she was mostly speaking psychobabble. The reason her language in the *New York Times Magazine* article is so incoherent and touchy-feely and laughable is that it is all in the abstract, when the real way to make workers feel valued is by giving them more money. It would involve, effectively, an overthrow of the current economic system that pits the interest of employees against that of shareholders, that creates an inverse relationship between unemployment and inflation, that means a company that is doing well and profiting might still be laying off workers to make itself leaner and meaner. It would require an economy that made people feel that they are not expendable—not a psychology or a religion to make them feel better about their irrelevance. This is a capitalist country, and the way the government empowers people is by putting more money in their hands. Whatever else is wrong with this country, it has come this far on this economic system, and it is that which we can toy with—ideas are bullshit. Even American foreign policy tends to operate on the principle that our generosity is better appreciated if our own market interests are at stake. We believe we have ideology, but we don't; we have money. Every time we try to do good because we think we're being big and beneficent, we end up in Vietnam. I myself don't like this, I would like nothing more than to see love make the world go round, but just as I've come to understand the importance of paying a therapist—of attaching a specific monetary value to that hour, to making it a material thing—I appreciate the way we can mete out meaning with money, and only wish we were spreading it out a bit better.

And that's why Hillary, functioning in a salaried society, needs to demand money herself. Linda Evangelista said she doesn't get out of bed for less than $15,000 a day. Somewhere on earth there are women who don't get *into* bed for less than $15,000 a night. And I guess the rest of us have learned to settle.

PART FIVE

Used to Love Her but I Had to Kill Her

Love is a grave mental illness.

PLATO

The blonde fox in the white Ferrari.

That is how a screenwriter I know who lived in the same part of town as Nicole Brown Simpson—the poor man's Brentwood, a colony of lush little bungalows and starter condos in the flats south of Sunset—described the woman he used to see tooling around in her sporty little car, driving home after a run or a cup of coffee at Starbucks, or maybe just, as her license plate suggested, L84AD8 ("late for a date"). The point he was making in describing her this way was that he had no idea she was O.J.'s wife, no idea her romantic affiliations would eventually be the death of her, or that she would ever be world-famous for any reason other than that he, like other guys he knew around Brentwood, thought she was a real hot mama. A hot tomato, I think, was the expression he used.

And I mention this only to dispel a myth that gained some currency—in fact, rich acceptance—during the couple of years or so that constituted the O.J. trial and its prelude and aftermath. It was a dismissive belief that Nicole Brown was somehow nothing special, just another SoCal beach babe, another girl who offers to show you her tan lines, a dime a dance, a dime a dozen. To me, this was always ridiculous. As many lovely starlets and beautiful beachcombers as you may find in Los Angeles, in Hollywood, in counties like Orange and Ventura, as many women as there may be waiting for rich husbands or a lucky break in those parts, as many would-be bit players and bottle blondes as there may be lingering at the counter of Schwab's or on the corner of Hollywood and Vine, I was certain as soon as I saw those first pictures of Ms. Brown that she was never among them. She was never among the dreamy desperate Hollywood hopefuls who eventually end up with a nom de guerre like Ashley or Ashlyn or Asia or Brittany, with a wardrobe consisting of four-inch stiletto pumps and a nipple ring, with a professional life of making pay-per-view porn in stark, refrigerator-bright motel rooms in the Valley. She was also never going to marry a dentist. She was certainly never going to *be* a dentist. She looks too shielded and expensive to be bothered with such mundane things: not the genie in the bottle, but the bottle itself, the colorful ceramic case whose hieroglyphic surface is so compelling, it does not really matter if beyond and beneath the surface there is only more surface. There is something offsetting and off-putting about Nicole in photographs, something eerie and otherworldly in her exceptional, heartrending beauty—beauty of the kind that one assumes, or at least hopes, expresses a spiritual truth greater than just good looks; though, of course, it probably doesn't. Nicole's face had grace, austerity, serenity, the snobbishness of a person rich with secrets, of one who has something to tell and isn't telling.

Which turned out to be the case.

True, Nicole's taste, at least in the public photos that we all saw over and over again—the most commonly repeated one was from the opening of the Harley-Davidson Cafe in New York in the autumn of 1993—ran to ultra-sheen stretch Lycra, to the tartiest, tawdriest, tackiest mall-girl looks that never quite seem to have gotten out of the mid-eighties—and should not have been worn by any woman out of her mid-twenties. The skirts are too short, the necklines too long, the fit always seems to be inspired by a tourniquet. But forget that stuff. Because the woman was physically just blessed. Her features are so regular, so even and smooth, by physiognomic standards possibly even perfect, with a straight nose, high forehead, sloped cheeks and such fine, fine bones. And her hair has such shiny blondeness, while her expression is so blank, her eyes so far away: everything about this woman is so golden and frozen, stiff and perfect, just like a statue, a statuette, an Oscar, an Emmy, a trophy that O.J.'s acting was never going to win him. If you needed a woman to model for a mannequin mold or to pose as the face of a national statue the way Catherine Deneuve did for France's Marianne, Nicole offers the even, smooth, geometrical and unobjectionable face that would suit this purpose. She is a trophy wife, and in all her tanned bronzeness, she actually looks the part.

What I am trying to say is that it doesn't much matter to me what real refinements this woman, who was simple, would never acquire, that she wasn't educated, that to her a big goal achieved would have been owning a coffee bar in Brentwood. It doesn't matter to me that her idea of "romantic" was to create a Calgon advertisement out of her bathroom and light scented candles all around the tub—or, for that matter, to arrange the same fiery display in the living room, or bedroom, wherever. Nor does it matter that this gesture, which was once romantic and not "romantic," but has since been co-opted by the consumerist powers that be to become merely cheesy and mail-order common—in 1993, there were $569 million worth of perfumed candles sold; by 1996, it was up to $1 billion—was one Nicole bought into so completely that on the last night of her life, when the police arrived and searched her Bundy town house, they found a full tub, deflated bubbles curdling on the water's surface, the surrounding ledge covered with burnt-out votives, tapers and cylinders. It doesn't much matter to me that Nicole wore real fur and fake leather, that in the late eighties her hair was feathered, that almost all the women she knew had silicone breast implants, that she liked to have a good time, that sometimes she had a few too many margaritas and often she danced with men she didn't know very well. All these issues of taste and aspiration and desperation matter to me almost not at all. Nothing matters, at this point, but still lifes and dead images of a woman who looks so fine and dignified and full of airs. Beauty like hers is greatly powerful, especially in a place like California, because far from being just another pretty face, a slice of sunshine and good cheer, Nicole is arch and strong to appearances, suggesting all kinds of dignity, all kinds of haughtiness.

And at certain times, if she made you really mad, I am sure that you would want to punch that face and make it go away. You would just plain want to bash it in.

"For Beauty's nothing / but beginning of Terror we're still just able to bear," wrote Rainer Maria Rilke in *The Duino Elegies*. "And why we adore it so is because it serenely / disdains to destroy us."

That is how I know that O.J. is guilty. Because pretty as Paula Barbieri and Gretchen Stockdale and the combined catalogue populations of Victoria's Secret and Frederick's of Hollywood and whoever else O.J. may find himself with may be, Nicole had a quality. A quality that he discovered, she was so young, all the credit is his, he is Columbus docked at America, he feels he *owns* this quality. She is his Stepford Wife with her faraway eyes, and he is Ira Levin and every male character in the book and movie put together. Above all, she is "angel white," as he used to call her, and who can deny that Nicole Brown was one of the whitest—and, feature by feature, one of the most *Caucasian*—women he could have possibly come up with, Hellman's mayonnaise on Wonder bread with nothing else.

Everything about Nicole signified so much to O.J., so much he would not want anyone else to be privy to. And you know how it is with things that mean a lot to you. They get heavy. They drive you crazy. They make life worth living, they make life unlivable, you can't stay, you can't go, there's not enough tequila in all of Mexico to straighten out your mind, years go by and nothing ever changes. Finally, if you've got half a mind and enough of a stomach to deal with it, you might need to completely destroy this heavy thing—and she starts to be a thing, not a person—in order to ensure that you will never again be haunted by it, never again have to face this woman whose beauty captured you when she was just seventeen, whose visage has held you tight with its refinement and austerity ever since, whose loveliness, in the midst of all this Hollywood trash, and so much that is so tacky, so much that is stonewashed and marbleized and highlighted and surgically enhanced and faked in this and that way, this face is one that will make you weak forever.

Of course he killed her.

It was the obvious thing to do.

*   *   *

The day the verdict in *The People* v. *O. J. Simpson* was announced—having been delivered the day before, famously, after less than three hours of deliberation—I was preparing myself to fast for Yom Kippur. The Day of Atonement, the day of the wholly holy, would begin that evening, and like many other Jews, I found myself wondering if Robert Shapiro and Barry Scheck and Alan Dershowitz would be committing acts of contrition as well. Or would they just be talking to Larry King and Geraldo, as had been their wont until now?

At any rate, sometime that evening, the newly respectable Geraldo Rivera (how many lives had this trial changed?), now talking justice on CNBC instead of having fat from his butt transferred to his forehead on syndicated television, did an interview with Nicole's father and eldest sister, Denise. Before I get to the Browns, I must say that I cannot emphasize enough what a boon the Simpson trial has been for Geraldo—its effect on him was akin to what the Iran hostage crisis did for Ted Koppel, whose *Nightline* went from being an emergency measure during a news explosion to then become an 11:30 staple that has been on the air now for close to two decades. Of course, unlike the unknown Koppel, Geraldo was haunted by notoriety and Satan-in-suburbia documentaries. With that for a background, it made sense that *Rivera Live* became the show of record for anything O.J., attracting more viewers than *Larry King Live* did as the trial wrapped up: here was a man who liked a good media circus and was not ashamed to invoke the Dreyfus Affair at times when most people would have thought a reference to *Naked Gun 33⅓* was lofty enough. Geraldo would often remind people that he had once been an attorney himself, and he'd sometimes moralize obnoxiously or preach self-importantly, which somehow worked well for these proceedings.

The reason it worked well was that this was a trial that lacked a moral center: with the possible exception of Fred Goldman, who played the grieving parent as if this were *King Lear* (and eventually became very annoying for just that reason), no one involved with the defense, the prosecution, the jury, the police, the ever-expanding pool of witnesses, or among the friends and family of the victims has emerged from this trial unsullied. Never before have so many people looked so bad for so little. Whether it's Johnnie Cochran, who made his name as a civil rights lawyer and who so honorably defended the falsely convicted Black Panther leader Elmer "Geronimo" Pratt (and finally got him released from Pelican Bay after seventeen years), but was now race-baiting for a celebrity wife-beater; or Barry Scheck and Peter Neufeld, who have always been good lefties, founding the Innocence Project to make use of DNA to rescue indigent men from the injustice of the death chamber, but were now selling out; or both Marcia Clark and Christopher Darden, who were thought to have been incompetent with jury selection, and then with this and that thereafter; Lance Ito, who was thought to be just plain incompetent; the jurors, with their internecine squabbles over deputies and movie privileges, and who, let's just be honest here—because the color of a person's skin should not keep anyone from speaking the truth—were just plain stupid; all those witnesses who sold their stories to *Hard Copy* and thus nullified their testimony; all those producers at *Hard Copy* et al., who created a bull market for the stories of anyone who, say, drove past a white Ford Bronco anywhere in the Los Angeles area on the night of the murder; even the Brown family, grieving though they were, made the questionable move of selling the rights to a video-tape of Nicole and O.J.'s wedding.

In this motley mix, Kato Kaelin and his coif achieve the status of near-admirableness: at least he *knows* he's a slut. Kato is one person who cannot deny, standing with his hair dryer and mousse in front of his bathroom mirror, that all his life he has just been waiting for such a moment as this to arrive—even though he really does miss Nicole. This oh-wow attitude puts Kato in striking opposition to Geraldo, who believes—or at least he *believes* he believes—that he is fighting the good fight, that this is all terribly significant. And it may well be: with the amount of airtime and publication space and waking hours devoted to this trial, its various spin-offs—the TV movies and quickie books and commemorative T-shirts and the like—have earned the equivalent of the annual GNP of Romania. If ever there was an elder statesman of precisely the kind of story that the Simpson trial is, it has to be Geraldo. (And however different his approach from that of Kato, it did not keep Geraldo from having the houseguest as a guest in *his* house in Monmouth County, New Jersey; Kato's first words upon entering: "Do you have cable?") And on the night of the acquittal, he does a special two-hour broadcast that attracts two million viewers— me included; I have to go to my mom's house to watch because I don't have a television—and is the highest-rated show CNBC has ever aired.

Denise Brown is definitely the main event, the outspoken spokesperson for her otherwise guarded, even awkward clan, which includes parents Juditha and Lou, and two other surviving younger sisters, Dominique and Tanya. Maybe less than a week before, Denise had gone to some anti-domestic violence rally somewhere near Detroit and helped open up a battered women's shelter, in her new role as chairman of the Nicole Brown Simpson Charitable Foundation, which was set up to grant money to projects aimed at helping victims of spousal abuse. (The first president appointed by the Browns to head the organization, Dallas businessman Jeff C. Noebel, was forced to step down when it was found that he was awaiting sentencing on charges related to a savings-and-loan scam, and that furthermore he had been named in a domestic violence restraining order for posing "clear and present danger" to his estranged wife.) On this day on *Rivera Live* she had a prepared statement to read, which began, "The trial is over and the verdict is in . . ." She never managed to get through the rest, since Geraldo kept interrupting with questions about how they would now have to cooperate with the man thought to be Nicole's killer—after all, O.J. had the right to see his two children, who were now staying with the Browns in Dana Point, a community in Orange County, sixty miles down the coast from Los Angeles. How, Geraldo wondered, would that be? Denise, for her part, kept avoiding that question, wanting instead to talk about the lessons of Nicole's death, how we could all grow from this, how awareness of battered women's syndrome had gone up as a result of this tragedy, how it was important to take what we could from the trial and get on with our lives.

I kept thinking that this was a strangely indifferent way to talk about one's dead kid sister. Especially since the appearance of opportunism is best reserved for Kato Kaelin, not Nicole's siblings. Though

Denise's chosen conduit for public life is a charitable foundation, that does not mean that the impulse is not self-serving and self-aggrandizing. Particularly because Denise had not been doing much with her life before the murders occurred—she had even been on welfare for a time, had even been in the Huntington Beach city jail for eight days with a blood-alcohol level so high it's known as "horizontal nystagmus"—and had now chosen a cause to get involved in that she obviously knew very little about: so little, in fact, that she was unable to be at all helpful to her younger sister, unable to even see that Nicole was a battered wife. Although it was Denise herself who took the muddy-bright mug-shot-like photographs of a swollen, bruised Nicole—pictures that documented the New Year's Eve 1989 beating and were later found in her safe-deposit box—Denise still denied her sister's victimization by her ex-husband, even after her death. "She was not a battered woman," Denise insisted to *The New York Times* just ten days after the murders. "My definition of a battered woman is somebody who gets beat up all the time. I don't want people to think it was like that. I know Nicole. She was a very strong-willed person. If she was beaten up, she wouldn't have stayed with him."

Considering this grievous ignorance, it pretty much made me sick to see Denise acting as spokesperson for a cause that she failed to make herself aware of when she could have still made a difference for her own sister. In fact, in the face of such a terrible loss, it seems that quiet shame and contemplative guilt would be the correct response. I mean, I'm glad that Denise can put a whistle around her neck and yell slogans into a bullhorn and become head counselor of Camp Survive-Alive, but that's the fun part, that's the ego ride. Showing up and showing support to the people you love and helping out with the real emotional dirty work is the challenge. It's not so much that Denise failed boot camp—it's more like she never even bothered.

Thankfully, on *Rivera Live* the night of the acquittal, Denise was blocked off from reciting any agitprop when Geraldo asked her father what would happen if O.J. wanted to take custody of Sydney and Justin, the two achingly beautiful children of O.J. and Nicole's unfortunate union. Lou Brown said he wasn't much concerned with that. "O.J.'s been in prison for sixteen months," he said. "I'm sure he has a lot of wild oats to sow, a lot of women to chase after, so I don't think he'll be wanting the children all the time."

A lot of wild oats to sow.

That's where I lost it: *A lot of wild oats to sow.* Excuse me?

Is this how you talk about the man you *believe* killed your daughter and who, at the very least, *you know* beat her up repeatedly? Do you describe him as a harmless, randy teenager running on a testosterone high? Do you not show a bit more distance and disgust when talking about him on national television? Or has the trial and all its overattentions made these people crazy, Denise trying to invoke Nicole's name for a cause, which ultimately gives Denise's life a cause to latch on to, while her father speaks of O.J. as if he's some regular guy?

Is this perhaps some form of post-traumatic stress, or are these people, as I have come to believe, more than a little bit strange?

To be completely fair, in judging the Browns or any other people who have undergone a public ordeal whose glamour quotient is at best recherché and at worst schlocky, the rest of us have to bear in mind that for even those most closely involved in the spectacle, in the Greek drama's *katharsis,* life is daily. The quotidian facts of everyday routine must eventually sink in, even to those mourning the dead, and after a while, I suppose, O.J. becomes the son-in-law who set you up in business with the Hertz concession at the Ritz-Carlton and gave you a really nice Rolex watch all those years ago, and a dead sister starts to seem like the totem of domestic violence that she has become to other people, and in that lies a career opportunity, a life opportunity, even a cause opportunity.

Perhaps I sound like I'm being a bit sarcastic as I give the Browns an out, a reason for their tacky behavior while talking to Geraldo. But I'm not. I truly do believe that at the end of the day, if you remove the bloody glove and the Bruno Magli shoes—or if, say, you displace the grassy knoll and the Texas Book Depository—and if you erase any other props or scenery that have become cultural metaphors, that just scream out *somebody died tragically!,* you are left with human beings who feel tragically. And they will do strange things: she will visit her husband's killer on death row and lobby for his pardon, or he will move far away, to Micronesia or Tanzania, anywhere that there is no sign that the departed ever was. Or they may start a foundation, open an office, roll up their sleeves and get to work. Really, there's nothing wrong with that. I believe that if life gives you lemons, make lemonade, and if you run into a brick wall, sell bricks, and all that *Forrest Gump* stuff.

But for Christ sake, fucking get it together for a half hour on television with Geraldo Rivera! For goddamn less time than it took O.J. to kill the two victims, behave with a modicum of dignity!

Is that too much to ask?

It really isn't, and this inability on the part of her father and sister to project some proper degree of sorrow for the public helps illuminate what Nicole must have been up against when she was still alive. Because if these people, her first-degree relatives, cannot give her a dignified presentation on *Rivera Live* just a little over a year after her death, it is easy to believe that they must have been very inaccessible to Nicole in her life. Of course, all of this, the family's relative supportiveness or lack thereof, is impossible for an outsider to assess, and may be even more of a mystery to the people involved.

But the Browns just don't present well. The obvious thing for both press and public to do is sympathize with the mourners, but there is something so trashy and uncomfortable and itchy about the family that Marie Brenner, writing in *Vogue* in May 1995, was prompted to summarize: "Reporters who cover trials often say of witnesses that you have to take them as you find them; the same rule applies to the families of murder victims." Randall Sullivan, a far less generous observer, covered O.J. for *Rolling Stone* and was more willing to flesh out—or tease out, as the case seems to be—Brown family values as exercised in a court of law. "During O.J.'s preliminary hearing, the Brown women threw up a wall of luxuriant manes, square shoulders and trim waists against the reporters who sat behind them," Sullivan writes, his disgust, I think, more sincere than snide. "Mother and daughters groomed one another continuously, fluffing hair and smoothing eyebrows. The Brown sisters made jokes about getting fat by sitting on their butts in court all day, wondered who had fed the fish that morning and compared prices on diamond watches. Lou Brown appeared to carry nearly all of his family's emotional burden, suffering visibly . . ." This, of course, would be the same Lou Brown of the wild oats remark. Well, whatever. It isn't really fair to judge a family by a couple of journalists' courtroom notes because reporters have their own agendas, they have their own butts to sit on, they have no one to buy them diamond watches, they probably don't have much hair, and who knows how you'd behave listening to tedious testimony in a big stuffy room, and what's so great about decorum anyway?

I'd like to give the Browns the benefit of every doubt, frankly because they *seem* like a very close-knit family, taking great pains not only to spend holidays together, but even for aunts and grandparents to schlepp up to Brentwood from Orange County for Sydney's dance recital, on what turned out to be the day of Nicole's death. The daughters vacationed together, and appear to have been genuinely close, sororal. *Raging Heart: The Intimate Story of the Tragic Marriage of O. J. and Nicole Brown Simpson,* was authorized by the Brown family and written by Sheila Weller, a journalist whose previous scandalography filed on hard deadline had been *Amy Fisher: My Story.* (She has since written a book about Darien date-rapist Alex Kelly.) Because the family cooperated, Weller's book includes many photographs of all the sisters and children and various cousins and extended-family members from the Brown and Simpson clans gathered together for Thanksgiving, or celebrating Christmas in the Simpsons' New York City apartment, or New Year's Eve in a hired Cabo San Lucas villa. Even during the criminal trial, Juditha Brown walked over to O.J.'s mother to show her pictures of Justin and Sydney from a recent birthday party, lest the mother be punished for the sins of the son. Far from seeming decadent, indifferent or just plain old bad, the Browns appear to be good family-oriented folk from solidly Republican Orange County.

But still, there seems to be a missing link or some studied indifference going on here.

Somehow after insisting that Nicole was *not* a battered wife, Denise was still later able to testify in court about how O.J. would call Nicole a "big fat pig" when she was pregnant, and how a pleasant evening on the town was spoiled when "he grabbed Nicole, told her to get out of his house, picked her up, threw her against the wall, picked her up, threw her out of the house." Denise also uttered one of the trial's more grizzly sound bites when she recalled, "At one point, O.J. grabbed at

Nicole's crotch and said, 'This is where babies come from and this belongs to me.' " When Denise gave this testimony, she sat weeping on the witness stand, clearly distressed. But it does seem odd that only a few months before she could confidently tell *The New York Times* that her sister was *not* a battered wife. It also seems strange that Robert Shapiro, O.J.'s original lead attorney, told reporters that Juditha Brown said to him at her daughter's graveside, "Please take good care of [O.J.]. The children need their father." This despite the fact that he was, by then, the prime suspect. It is easy enough to drum this up to a misquote or a lie taken out of context in the press, or to Denise's more careful consideration of events over time, or to guilt and helplessness. But I'm afraid that too much just points to the fact that the Browns were at least passively in cahoots with O.J. all along. They seem to have been aware of his violent temper and tendency to tantrums, if not his outright abusive behavior.

"Nicole never told us she was battered," Denise told *Vogue*. "She would say, 'He threw me against the wine cabinet, and then we went out to lunch.' "

Juditha told Sheila Weller about a time when, shortly after Nicole had moved into O.J.'s Rockingham estate, mother and daughter had returned from dinner at a hangout called the Daisy—which seems to function as the Rick's Café Américain of this sad saga—just a little too late for O.J.'s liking, with the immediate result involving an over-wrought O.J. throwing Nicole's heirloom desk out the front door while reprimanding her tardiness. In response, all Judi Brown could do was laugh and leave. The next day, she called Nicole to ask if the desk had been moved back in.

Judi would also witness several occasions where O.J. got mad at Nicole and threw all her clothing out the window, or tore several family photographs that lined the staircase off of the walls and smashed them on the floor. "Every time they had a fight," Mrs. Brown told Weller, "he cracked those pictures and threw them down. Nicole had to keep reframing them and reglassing them. I asked Nicole, 'Why do you even bother to put them up? Why don't you just keep them down?' But she had a hard head. She said, 'No way! Those pictures are going back up!' She put them back up again and again."

Over the years there were fights that were as serious as one in which

O.J. beat Nicole, locked her in his estate's unlit wine cellar while he watched a football game, after which he beat her some more, locked her up again, resumed his television viewing (anyone who has ever lived with a football fan knows that during the season, a given Sunday can involve four games in three different time zones that are all *very important*), came back to beat her and lock her up again, until, I guess it was too dark for any more football even in Pacific time. There were other incidents that were mentioned a great deal outside the courtroom during the trial, though never admitted as evidence, like the time in 1980 that O.J. locked Nicole out of their Las Vegas hotel room wearing just a bra, or the New Year's Eve 1989 incident—which did make it to court—that involved a much-replayed 911 call to the police with descriptions of Nicole, once again, cowering for defense, wearing just a bra and, in this case at least, sweatpants.

Even after this 1989 beating, for which O.J. pleaded nolo contendere to charges of battery, Nicole's family, who could no longer have possibly found the scenes of flying photographs and dumped desks to be merely amusing bits of domestic drama, encouraged her to stay in the marriage. After Nicole showed her father the pictures Denise had taken of the wounds and bruises she'd sustained, he was still nonplused. "My parents did not take up for me," Ms. Weller reports Nicole confiding to several friends. "They blew it off. They wanted me to stay with O.J."

All of this abuse seems to have been shrugged off as just so much of the usual nonsense between O.J. and Nicole. The Browns were quite fond of O.J., he had charmed them with his personality, his gifts, his help with tuition, his beneficence in setting up Judi as a travel agent and Lou as a rent-a-car man, his kindness in employing various German émigré cousins in assorted capacities, and with his ingratiating generosity in general. With so much goodwill between O.J. and in-laws, the family naturally urged Nicole to *just work it out*. "O.J. quickly turned himself into a favorite son, setting Lou up in his Hertz dealership and helping Juditha and other family members in various enterprises," Faye Resnick, a best friend of Nicole's, explains in her best-selling tell-all as-told-to, *Nicole Brown Simpson: The Private Diary of a Life Interrupted*. By, in effect, punishing the Browns with kindness, O.J. skillfully kept the whole caravansary in his control.

"We used to be very close," Ms. Resnick claims Nicole said of her relationship with her sisters and parents sometime after her divorce. "But when I left O.J., they weren't at all supportive. They absolutely wanted me to stay with O.J. It's just like everything else, Faye. O.J. always controls everyone and everything around him." Toward the end of her life, Nicole sought counseling from Dr. Susan Forward, co-author of *Men Who Hate Women and the Women Who Love Them,* and in the few sessions she managed to get to, she made it clear she felt dangerously isolated. "Nicole's terror—her fear of this big man—was so pervasive," Dr. Forward told Sheila Weller. "She said, 'I am so alone. Where do I go? The police won't help me. My family's not supportive. They wanted me to "work it out" with him—and they're my only support system.' "

You have to understand, I don't expect parents to drag a grown woman out of her marriage unless she herself is ready and willing, which is what any battered woman must be before she is able to leave. But they let her be swept away by O. J. Simpson when she was still a teenager, at a point when my mother was still very able to voice her objections to whatever I did (dear God, she still is) and I could be dragged home, or shamed into abandoning my ridiculous course. In fact, one of the abiding mysteries in this story is what would have happened to Nicole had she never met O.J. It all seems so hard to figure: This was an upper-middle-class girl who was bright enough to be in an honors track at Rancho Alamitos High School; why, at age eighteen, was Nicole Brown not in college like most girls with her socioeconomic background? This was 1977, well beyond an era when girls waited at home for their suitors to show up—in fact, even in the fifties women went to college to look for men, and while an education was a mere perk of the more necessary marital pursuit, it happened just the same. While Nicole expressed some interest in studying photography, the possibility of art school or some other form of higher education—despite California's sprawling and variegated system of state and local colleges—does not even seem to have come up. It does not even seem to have been raised as a possibility to be rejected. After graduation, Nicole moved in with a friend in Los Angeles, took a job waitressing at the Daisy and just kind of bided her time. Although

Denise managed to get as far as New York, where she became a Ford model for a period, she found the rigors of the job too taxing, and ended up back in California. Nicole never even got as far as that. Meeting O. J. Simpson at the Daisy was her destiny.

With O.J. on the scene, it would seem that any good parent would try to get Nicole to go back to school, to at least take some courses, to do anything rather than become beholden to some flashy football player. Probably the daughter in any situation like that would rebel and complain and claim to be misunderstood and tell her parents that they don't know what love is. Still, most parents would try to do *something*. But the Browns never did, never even seemed to have batted an eyelash when at the age of eighteen she told them a much older (and still married) man she had recently started seeing was paying for her apartment in Los Angeles, putting her up so he could see her alone, so that her roommate would not be around when he wanted to be with her. Nor did they seem alarmed when they found a Porsche 914 in their driveway, left as a present for Nicole, who was spending her nineteenth birthday at home; they were never concerned about the implications of such a generous gift, even though Nicole would later say that it was to compensate for a black eye from O.J., a much less desirable present.

"My parents taught us to be gracious and to say thank you for gifts," Denise told *Vogue*. "My mother was very easygoing about that. Her attitude was that presents did not make you a kept woman. Someone pays for your apartment . . . If you're happy, what difference does it make?"

It seems that they were only too willing to allow Nicole, their second daughter, to be sold into a man's custody, they were only too happy to allow her to be kept. They seem to have designated this an acceptable life for a young woman to get herself into. And having a sense that being a man's prize object, his Maltese falcon, his Fabergé egg, is somehow a respectable role for a real live human being, an actual woman, a living doll, is the beginning of thinking that just about anything he does to her is completely fine.

Nicole was apparently bred and buttered and baked by the sun just to be a thing of beauty, more show pony than Thoroughbred. "People said somebody wealthy and famous would nab her," Valerie Rigg, a high school acquaintance, said of Nicole in one of those posthumous who-is-this-mysterious-dead-lady articles that appeared in *The New York Times*. "She just seemed bound for that. Nicole was famous to us."

"Everybody was in awe of her," added Jo Hanson, Nicole's home economics teacher in high school, where Nicole, yes, was homecoming princess (if Ms. Hanson is an aging spinster with a bit of a drinking problem, the remake of *Picnic* is already cast). "We get a lot of beautiful students, but she was the ultimate beauty. The girls liked and admired her. The guys were in love with her."

Evidently, in an era when it is assumed that women must pursue careers—or at least make a show of it—just as men do, Nicole was presumed exempt from a young age. She did not, after all, go to LA to take acting classes and go to auditions, nor did she have plans to model. She kind of went to meet her fate, to be discovered, to become somebody's baby.

As bits and pieces about the Brown family emerged over the course of the trial, it became clear that the O. J. Simpson murder story—which at first appeared to be compelling because of the elements of fame, of a fading athletic career, of a well-kept Hollywood wife—was most bizarre because of the Brown family and the prosperous Southern California dream that they represented. In the first place, one couldn't help being fascinated with the Browns simply because, though there was only a mother and four daughters, that household seemed to rage and teem with women, like a New Orleans bordello or an Old Testament desert clan or any Jane Austen novel. Beautiful women, too. Only Denise and Nicole have that Ali MacGraw arch-exotic face, in both the blonde and brunette versions, with a *Vertigo*-sharp resemblance between the two sisters—like twins born two years and twenty-two Clairol shades apart—that is so striking and jarring that little Sydney Simpson was said to have begged her aunt to bleach her hair to look just like her dead mom, as if Denise were Kim Novak and this was all just a Hitchcock movie. The yin-yang pairing of the two oldest Brown daughters (like a video version of the Beach Boys' dream of "Two Girls for Every Boy"), along with the simple profusion of femininity in the family's house of babes—the reptilian remnant of every male brain teems with the fantasy of fucking all those sisters, of rapaciously tearing through everything under the roof that wears a skirt—added a few ducats to the bride-price attached to the younger and less gorgeous girls, Dominique and Tanya. According to Faye Resnick, O.J. viewed the collective wealth of womanly charms among the Brown sisters as "the ultimate trophies"—which somehow increased Nicole's individual worth to him.

And during the trial, when the three surviving Brown girls posed for a *New Yorker* spread by Annie Leibovitz in a Laguna Beach parking lot with Nicole's Jeep Cherokee, the reverse image of that flowing femininity was writ large: instead of seeming like Sirens singing their mating song, coming out with legs spread open wide to every passerby, calling out their availability to the highest bidder, in this photograph the Browns became protective and defensive, a girl gang of three, with tough, bitter faces, expressions that said, *Don't mess with me—I've got sisters.*

"For some observers, the Brown daughters appear as if they are at an endless summer camp," Marie Brenner writes. "They are very attached to their mother and one another. When they travel, they are in and out of one another's hotel rooms, staying up late into the night."

But still, I feel certain, though these girls look hardy and hale, freckled and muscled, recovery survivors who could easily make it into *Playboy*'s "Girls of Hazelden" issue (if, heaven forbid, such a thing should ever be conjured up), though it looks as if these women are competent and in control of their own lives, something is obviously not quite right. David Margolick, the reporter who covered the trial for *The New York Times,* calls this strange feeling everybody has that the Brown girls—frankly, the mother and father too—are just a little bit off, "the *Tobacco Road* aspects of the story." In the simplest terms, even before the murder, one must have noticed that there is something rather odd about a family living in a house in Dana Point in which two of their fully grown daughters—Denise and Dominique—both live at home, each with her own illegitimate child. Now, I have no problem with women choosing to be mothers without marriage, but when not one but two daughters are in that same situation and are both forced to live with their parents as a result while another daughter is being beaten by her husband about sixty miles due north, something is just not good.

It is also strange that while the Goldman family made their presence strongly felt in court day in and day out (Who can forget Kim's wail when the verdict was announced?) and O.J.'s mother and sisters lent family support all the way through, after a while no one from the Brown family came to court at all, with the youngest sister, Tanya, being the only one to even attend intermittently. "What's happened to the Brown family?" asked Dominick Dunne in one of his monthly, morally outraged (and not for no reason) pieces of O.J. trial reportage for *Vanity Fair*. "They almost never come to court anymore. Occasionally Tanya, Nicole's youngest sister, and her fiancé, Rico, come by, but the family as a unit has not been seen for weeks in their section of reserved seats. To my way of thinking, it is a mistake for them not to come . . . On the other side of the aisle, the Simpson family are . . . constant in their attendance. You have to say this for the Simpsons, no matter how you feel about the guilt or innocence of the defendant: They're a united family in their support of O.J., and they're respected by everyone."

In his novelized account of the whole O.J. business, published in November 1997 as *Another City, Not My Own,* Dunne expanded his indictment of the Brown family, claiming that when he confronted Juditha about her clan's truancy, she simply shrugged, complaining that the courtroom was her "least favorite place to be." Even the sole sister who was present for at least part of the proceedings comported herself in a way that was no credit to the Browns: "It's unusual when an innocent victim's family is so unsympathetic," Dunne moans in *Another City.* "When Tanya, the youngest sister, who couldn't be nicer, finally came, after a little prodding from me, she brought her fiancé, a hot number called Rico, and they necked in the courtroom, right in front of the jury . . . At one time, Rico had his legs spread apart like this, and Tanya, who was in a miniskirt up to here, placed one of her legs between his two legs, and Rico had his hand on Tanya's thigh. This is not a great look for the sister of the victim, when the African-American females on the jury don't have a very high opinion of Nicole in the first place." Meanwhile, Denise justified her disappearance from the trial—glaring in the aftermath of her own dramatic testimony—because she was spending much of her time globetrotting on behalf of battered women's shelters; Geraldo Rivera's people booked her interview and speaking engagement schedule. Even Dunne, who seems genuinely fond of Denise in her girlish gutsiness and her apparent lack of guile, can't help observing that whatever nobility may be read into her fundraising activities to benefit abused wives, her inability to undergo the sedentary inactivity of sitting through a trial on behalf of her own deceased sister "makes it look like she's trying to get famous on Nicole's death."

As for the mother, who was born in Germany and had this European elegance thing going on that made you think she had real class—and was therefore presumably the last Brown bastion of propriety—was said to have been a confidante of O.J.'s until the end, which might explain why she felt uncomfortable going to the trial. "Judi had often taken O.J.'s side when Nicole complained," Sheila Weller writes in a book that, I feel compelled to keep remembering, was actually told from the Brown family's point of view, with their explicit cooperation. "[W]hen O.J. sought to win Nicole back after their divorce, Judi had told him that he was foolish to have confessed his infidelities to Nicole." In *I Want to Tell You,* O.J.'s very own book—insofar as anything with pieces of paper bound between two covers can be called a book—written, as *Mein Kampf* was, while the accused was jailed, O.J. even takes the time to say, "In the last four years I would talk to Judy more than anybody else in the Brown family. I was so close to Judy that I talked to her more than Nicole did. Through Nicole's mother, I tried to understand Nicole." This sentiment, of course, sounds completely sweet, until you recall that *the last four years* are the operative words. They mark the time after the separation and divorce, when only a deeply manipulative control freak would seek advice from his ex-mother-in-law on how to deal with his ex-wife. This is inappropriate behavior, indicating what's known as a *boundary problem.*

(By the way, you might notice that O.J. spells Judy differently from Sheila Weller; being as this is Southern California, I'm betting on Weller's version. Also, as those who've seen photographs of his suicide/ fugitive note might recall, O.J. also spells "privicy," "teammatte," "tottally," "buddie," "morr," "allways," "promblem," "murtually," "spaerate," "I'v," "futurr" and "recitly" in his own special way. Even phonetically he's way off—"recitly" doesn't even *sound* like "recently." Now, I know this is a cheap shot, that lots of bright and capable people can't spell, but the note was also grammatically incomprehensible and punctuated as if it were a work of modernist poetry, which it wasn't, I don't think. Sentences like "I wish we had spend more time together in recite years" and "Know manner what I love you" are so thoroughly subliterate that this letter ought to be used the next time they have hearings on the conflict between academics and athletics at Big Ten schools or other universities with serious spectator sports. Naturally, everyone focused on the evidentiary value of O.J.'s note—we were amused and appalled by the smiley face he made in the O of his signature, and a few people might have noticed that he spelled "battered" correctly. But, since I don't think O. J. Simpson is stupid, this missive registered with me as, more than anything, a striking blow against American education. Nobody should be able to graduate from high school—or get through *any* part of college—so pathetically unable to place words intelligibly onto paper.)

There isn't nearly enough known about the family dynamics to know exactly why the Brown sisters have this air of not having fared very well in the world, and anyway that Freudian murder mystery is never easy to solve. The simple fact that the Brown parents stayed married would seem to be reason enough for the daughters to have a better shot at mental health than many do. The only thing we know is that Juditha and Lou lived in sin before marrying, not very common back then—both Denise and Nicole were born out of wedlock because Lou's divorce took so long to go through—but once again, no real explanation for anything. There were suggestions that Lou molested or abused the girls, but that too is only speculative. It seems silly to psychoanalyze Nicole posthumously (it's hard enough to do when someone is alive), but suffice it to say that there is just something not quite right with these people. You know how some people give you the creeps, make you feel like they're keeping secrets and you ought to count yourself lucky for that—well, the Browns are just such a group.

All the beauty and quasi-California quasi-European elegance of this family's picture make it seem as if the Browns ought to invite sympathy, ought to be ones you hope and root for. But they aren't. No matter how much I came to learn about this family over time, after a while only one thing stood out: all four daughters had breast implants, but not one had a college degree.

*   *   *

I once went to an Alcoholics Anonymous meeting in Los Angeles, Hollywood to be precise, and it was there that I discovered what I call *stripper feminism*. It was a Sunday morning, and even inside this rec hall type of place it was ridiculously bright like it always is in LA. Amazingly, nobody smoked. There was a small desiccated man with thin bits of long hair—he looked to be about a hundred and two— whom everybody called "Cubby"; somebody told me he was Hubert Selby, Jr. There were a number of children of celebrities milling about the room, among them Rain Pryor, who, after the murder, had actually talked with reporters about a brief relationship she'd had with Ron Goldman. But mostly there were a lot of anonymous muscle shirts and generously splayed and displayed tattoos—on boys *and* girls—and I felt like I was stuck in a Henry Rollins monologue.

A number of young women had occasion to speak that day, either because it was an anniversary or because they were designated to give testimony about sobriety. At any rate, they all had a similar quality that I couldn't quite isolate and identify until one of them spoke for about fifteen minutes. She began by asking God to grant her humility and to help her to tell the truth so that she wouldn't fall prey to a tendency to embellish. And she used that word, "embellish," which I think of as a big word, or at the very least a glossy substitute for the more common "exaggerate." So she told her story, about her Southern California upbringing, about drinking whole jugs of her mother's Gallo Chardonnay, about getting so gone and passing out but never waking up in Brazil or any of those exotic places drunks wake up in, about waking up in her own urine and vomit, about her boyfriend the junkie who took all her money, about how she used to make a living dancing in bars. I assume she meant stripping. There are a lot of ex-strippers in recovery. Anyway, she went on to say how she'd been sober for two years, and now she has these great women friends, and she feels so lucky. And I could tell by the fact that she said *women* and not *girls* or *chicks* (as I would have) that she'd picked up some AA version of feminism, or maybe it's some bar-girl version of it, and I guess it's been a good thing for her.

Now, here's the truth about stripping or lap dancing or topless go-go dancing or whatever variation you want to make on that theme: I know that in recent years many "respectable" strip clubs have emerged—some, like Pure Platinum, are even small chains—and working in any of these places has been made to appear glamorous, with talk of girls who earn up to $1,000 a night. I have no idea how true those numbers are, though I have spent time talking to some of the girls who do this for a living, and they all say they've never taken in that much money. But I think regardless of where a woman does her stripping, any attempt to see it as "empowering" work, to pretend that men handing her money for just appearing half naked before them is a sign that she has entranced them with her beauty or her boobs or anything like that is silly. I can understand why a lot of women have stripper-for-a-night fantasies: the way Drew Barrymore did her dance at the Blue Angel in New York was probably great fun. It's something I would like to try. I think the sexually exhibitionistic high would be a real trip.

But if it's your life, your livelihood, it eventually must dehumanize you. The fact is that you're really *begging* with your body. Every last dollar you make is on the basis of some man or group of men's approval, it's based on pleasing and pleasing and pleasing some more. And that's just plain degrading.

Lots of strippers end up with drug problems, and many more just drink. There is no scientific data to support this pronouncement, but I've been to a lot of AA meetings and they are always full of women who say they bottomed out working as exotic dancers.

Well, I imagine Nicole could be one of these girls at the Hollywood AA meeting—that's where she might have ended up if she hadn't married money and if she weren't so beautiful and if she took all the wrong turns and found herself drinking to get through it all, if she found herself dancing topless at some bar on the Sunset Strip, or maybe at one of those places near LAX, if she found herself drunk and strung out all the time because she was the homecoming queen and now where had life taken her? If she found herself conscious enough just once in a while to wonder: How did life turn so ugly and wrong?

If a very different Nicole, if one she seems destined to never have been, had ever made it to recovery, she might have discovered so many things. She might have discovered the kinds of stuff I heard listening to the woman who spoke at that AA meeting, and reiterated by many of her friends who responded to her little speech. They were all pretty girls, and they were all well-spoken, and yet they all reflected on a life of partying and going to the beach and never taking themselves seriously, and never learning to take care of themselves at all. All of them seemed to have "danced in bars" on and off, or for a long stretch of time. Somehow the process of sobriety helped them learn some things that a good education, that going to school instead of beach-bumming around, might have taught them in the first place: the importance of being treated with dignity and respect, and of finding work and love and relationships of all sorts that are not shameful or degrading. They all had this reasonable brightness that was unschooled, which is certainly what the Brown girls suffer from. I wondered how these girls in AA, all intelligent enough, it seemed, to qualify for some kind of schooling in the vast state and county systems that California offers, had managed to just drift. All of them seemed to be taking courses and going back to school at last, but it seemed to me they could have avoided a lot of trouble had they just gone to college in the first place.

It's not that a college education makes a woman safe from a wife-batterer or even less likely to end up dancing topless, but, well, it does at least teach you that you've got choices, that your value is all your own, that no one can bestow it upon you or take it away. It is not for no reason that the masters don't teach the slaves to read. Just because "knowledge is power" is the annoying slogan used by every conspiracy-theory crank and every paranoid grass-roots movement doesn't make it any less true. When Nicole filed for divorce on February 25, 1992, she claimed in her statement: "By the time I was 19 years of age, we were living together most of the time. I traveled back and forth between Los Angeles and San Francisco to be with him . . . [R]espondent required me to be available to travel with him whenever his career required him to go to a new location, even if it was for a short period of time." After a brief allusion to courses she began to take at a junior college when she had some free time after hooking up with O.J.—all of which were interrupted before completion—Nicole concludes, "I have had no other college education, and I hold no college degrees. I worked as a waitress for two months. Prior to that, I was a sales clerk in a boutique. These two jobs are the sum total of my employment experience. I worked on my own as an interior decorator, mostly for respondent and his friends. I no longer have that opportunity." Of course, being denied the daily drudgery of a desk job seems a small price to pay to live in a mansion "with a full staff to assist us," including nutritionist and personal trainer, and to have residences to escape to in Laguna Beach, in San Francisco and on East 65th Street in New York. In a world in which the majority of married women work outside the home, perhaps the awesomeness of Nicole's situation was best summed up by Jeff Keller, a friend of Ron Goldman, who figured Nicole and her girlfriends enjoyed hanging out at the local Starbucks with the young men of pluck and aspiration who waited tables to pay bills because of this poverty novelty. "They had nothing to do but shop and hang out with their kids," Keller told *The New York Times* of Ms. Brown's crowd. "[Nicole] liked us."

Just the same, Nicole's doll's life is really an updated version of Henrik Ibsen's Nora—with the play's indeterminate ending recast into a bloody tabloid mess. And the door-slamming and accusations that offer such satisfaction and payback at the sloping close of *A Doll's House*'s dramatic arc provide a precise text of the kind of cool, clean break Nicole could never quite make. "You and Papa have committed a great sin against me," Nora says unequivocally to her baffled husband, adding that, as Nicole's divorce filings merely imply, "it is your fault that I have made nothing of my life." Nora claims as she walks out on Torvald that she is going to educate herself out of her hausfrau ignorance, to "try and get some sense." How much better off Nicole would have been as a curvy coed with classes to attend, how good it would have been if every time O.J. demanded she hew to his schedule, she could just tell him that she had homework, and football bored her anyway, and she wouldn't know a halfback from a half-wit, and she can see him when he gets home. Learning is emboldening. Not every educated woman is going to translate her degrees into a life in which she behaves as if she feels the principles of self-sufficiency and self-respect rule, but at least it's possible. At least when you behave like an idiot, you'll know it's your own damn fault.

*   *   *

No means no. Against her will is against the law. And all that stuff. All those slogans that all of us have heard, any of us who have gone to college in the last ten or twenty years anyway.

And of course it is all true, it is all good advice, and of course everyone I know in a healthy, happy relationship is not getting beaten and bashed around, is not living with strange forms of manipulative behavior, with the threat of abandonment and the specter of violence hanging over their love like the Sword of Damocles, always one step away from becoming a reality. I know right from wrong, I know that you shouldn't have to pay for your love with your bones and flesh, I know that, for the most part, there is no good reason ever for a man to hit a woman, I know it, I believe it, I understand that the alluring drama of sick and twisted relationships—Samson and Delilah, O.J. and Nicole, Catherine and Heathcliff—have left behind casualties, murders, suicides, overdoses, severed heads, broken bones. I know I don't want that for myself, I know I want to be involved with one of those men who've read Andrea Dworkin when even I think she's nuts and who wants to take paternity leave and even likes listening to the Indigo Girls and asks me how my day was, every day, as if he cares. I know better to love an ACLU lawyer than an Ultimate Fighter. I may even know that it's better to go for Ted Baxter than Ted Hughes. Certainly better to not be Sylvia Plath, head in the oven, better to not have despaired myself right to death with the disappointment of Ted's infidelity and inconstancy, better to never lament the instability of crazy love. "The strong, passionate, sensitive Heathcliff had turned around and now appeared to Sylvia as a massive, crude, oafish peasant, who could not protect her from herself or from the consequences of having grasped at womanhood," Plath's friend Clarissa Roche wrote, remembering the poet's state of mind shortly before her suicide, at a time when she was separated from Hughes, freezing cold from winter, feverish from hysteria. "She cursed and mocked him for his weakness, and she called him a traitor."

I read this, I think how awful to be in London in the cold winter, to be writing poetry in a house once occupied by Yeats, to have your husband somewhere else with someone else, and still, I think: *She got her Heathcliff*. She had her moment of great, big, gigantic love. And Ted Hughes, too, may have found enough drama in that relationship to satisfy the lust in his blood for the rest of his life. "He loved her and she loved him," wrote Hughes in "Lovesong," from perhaps his best-known collection, *Crow*. "Her looks nailed down his hands his wrists his elbows / He gripped her hard so that life / Should not drag her from that moment / He wanted all future to cease." As a caveat measure, telling the story of how this relationship—any of these relationships—all went wrong is worse than silence, its aphrodisiac effect on behalf of crazy love is more potent than just keeping quiet: it's like a public service announcement cautioning against heroin with pictures of River Phoenix and Kurt Cobain flashing by; it's like a lecture warning about the dangers of cigarettes, delivered while watching *Casablanca* or *To Have and Have Not*. Maybe it's boredom, maybe I read too many eighteenth-century British novels of desperate passion in distant quarters, but somehow I feel socially programmed to be drawn in and desirous of these great and disastrous romances. I mean, why would I have to be told that no means no if there weren't some reason for me to think otherwise?

And there is a reason. It's called pop culture, which is the thing I love the most, though it is a vast, totalizing machine that overwhelms everything we think, that offers us so much excitement and lawlessness and deceit on the big screen and on the jukebox and everywhere else that it might as well just scream out the subliminal messages that say *Leave your marriage! Cheat on your husband! Beat up your wife! Rape your teenage niece! Come on, give it a try!* It is pop culture that brought us the *General Hospital* story line that had Laura marry Luke even though he raped her, it is pop culture that had Elizabeth Taylor and Richard Burton duking it out in the drunken stupor and rage of a bad marriage in *Who's Afraid of Virginia Woolf?*, it is pop culture that produced *The Getaway* with its atmosphere of suspicion and persistent possibility of murder between the fugitive couple Ali MacGraw and Steve McQueen—who are somehow going to live happily ever after in Mexico just the same—and it is pop culture that gave us the Crystals' hit single, produced by alleged wife-beater Phil Spector and co-written by feminist Carole King, which had the catchy refrain "He hit me, and it felt like a kiss."

In fact, everything you need to know about the pursuit of art and commerce in postwar America—and the mass-marketing of manufactured sincerity—is contained within Mr. Spector's career. Because somehow, many of the songs written in the assembly-line atmosphere of the Brill Building and recorded by voices anonymous and unknown (Does anyone really know the difference between the Shangri-Las and the Shirelles?) against the drowning downpour of Spector's symphonic "wall of sound," are—despite a factory formula that defines them all—often alarming in their emotional evocativeness. They were also treacly and romantic, even though Spector himself was supposed to be nasty, dark, difficult and completely abusive to his wife Ronnie, lead Ronette, lead voice behind his sweetest anthem, "Be My Baby."

It is a perverse and beautiful peculiarity of American capitalism that people can profit greatly by creating products that celebrate feelings that they themselves are only marginally familiar with. And the law of unintended consequences means that many emotions are cross-referenced, or surface where they should not be: "He Hit Me (It Felt Like a Kiss)" was actually a rather sweet song until somebody noticed it wasn't; and "Be My Baby," with its bloated orchestral production, is rather more desperate, pleading and obsessive than it should be—this woman who promises "for every kiss you give me / I'll give you three," may be the girl of your dreams, but she may be an overzealous stalker in the making.

Far beyond all that is pop; in the military base that is the rest of America, there are two things that our culture reveres and romanticizes, in both cases with varying degrees of discomfort: the first is male violence and the second is female beauty. I don't even have to explain this statement very much because it is quite obvious what I mean. In movies, male machine-gun shoot-'em-up machismo is considered dopey at the hands of Steven Seagal or Jean-Claude Van Damme, family entertainment as done by Arnold Schwarzenegger, and high art and utterly respectable as executed by Sam Peckinpah, Martin Scorsese and Quentin Tarantino. But beyond the big budgets of big studios, in the mid-nineties gruesomeness enjoyed an art-house renaissance with young filmmakers and their white-trash, killing-spree road flicks doing all that they possibly could with Drew Barrymore and Ione Skye, exhausting every permutation of titles containing the words "gun" or ".45" or "doom" or "convenience store" (it was only natural for Oliver Stone to do a well-financed version like *Natural Born Killers,* where the lack of budgetary constraints allowed for a more plentiful blood flow). Even with all this independent, hipster activity, there's still a whole subset of intellectual types who actually like Jean-Claude Van Damme and Steven Seagal movies, perhaps for their comical smarminess, perhaps for the same reason that I like Merle Haggard, perhaps because, as we approach the millennium, even our guilty pleasures are as laborious and dull as acquired tastes. Of course, the really smart people were into Jackie Chan and Hong Kong martial-arts movies when they were still in Chinese, when they were still without subtitles.

Off the silver screen, where we know the red stuff isn't catsup, many otherwise sane people—even writer Joyce Carol Oates—find the unadorned brutality of boxing or the bloody violence of Ultimate Fighting rather gorgeous. In 1997, not only did *When We Were Kings,* the documentary about Muhammad Ali, win an Oscar for Best Documentary, but Mike Tyson was barred from the ring for biting off Evander Holyfield's ear (which, in all the commotion, was almost lost, until a nice young usher found the shard of cartilage and put it in a bag to be reattached) during the third round of a Las Vegas bout, with the end result of all the media attention meaning that the professional pugilists were hard to ignore, whether you were a fan or not. Meanwhile, while erstwhile Naval Academy boxer Senator John McCain was making all kinds of motions to outlaw Ultimate Fighting—where the two men go at it until somebody surrenders or a doctor intervenes, and where biting off someone's ear would be well within your rights—on the 1997 season of the sitcom *Friends,* one of the subplots involved Courtney Cox/Monica's boyfriend deciding to take up the grisly sport. But even if Ultimate Fighting is sickening enough to have been banned in several states, the respectability of the Super Bowl pretty much

proves that we don't even question the merits of gladiator-style entertainment, since, as far as I can tell, football is just so much head-
butting, justified only by the occasional requirement that the ball be
thrown around.

If the cumulative effect of this list of violent and suggestive entertainment does not convincingly indicate a strange fascination with
blood-as-fun-stuff in this country, keep in mind that the American
Medical Association now considers gunshot wounds to be an epidemic
(as opposed to a series of unrelated accidents) and that in Japan some
citizens started a gun-control movement to get weapons banned in the
United States after several Japanese nationals were shot—mostly by
mistake—while they were here.

If our love of violence is self-evident, there's even less that needs to
be said to be convincing about our outsize love of women's gorgeousness. We truly are by beauty bound. It's a truism that little girls want
to grow up to be Cindy Crawford and Christy Turlington, that
supermodels are now our superstars and role models—even before
they've made some sad attempt at acting, or whatever (what Ms.
Crawford did in *Fair Game* qualifies as *whatever*)—and that as female
movie stars have ceased to be the creatures of glamour they were back
in the forties, a strange new premium has been put on beauty and
beauty only.

Consider this: If Grace Kelly, Rita Hayworth and Audrey Hepburn
were alive and working today, they would be considered useless ornaments. Directors would think: Give her a lampshade, give her a
lightbulb, stand her on an end table, and let's ignore her like we would
any old reading light. Not because they couldn't act—they certainly
could—but confronted by reality, by the tawdriness of life without an
updo and an Hermès scarf and a Chanel suit and an Edith Head gown,
they'd have no reason to act. To them, to not be glamorous was to not
be. They wouldn't do car chases—if Grace Kelly wanted to show that
she was "game," she'd pack a complete overnight bag into a Mark
Cross pocketbook to prove that a true lady never needs more than a
toothbrush and a La Perla negligee. Kelly and these others were *cool*
with elegance. Which is why they were big stars, which is why they
could "open" a movie, which is why their male co-stars were treated
virtually as accessories, and no man got a bigger billing than they did

(well, maybe Cary Grant). *Laura* had for its star Gene Tierney, not Dana Andrews (I know it's hard to guess but Gene is the girl and Dana is the boy), *Cover Girl* is about Rita Hayworth, not Gene Kelly, *Breakfast at Tiffany's* belongs to Audrey Hepburn, and not, heaven forfend, the swishy George Peppard. Who was in *Babyface* besides Barbara Stanwyck? In *Red-Headed Woman* besides the usually platinum blonde Jean Harlow? In *Blonde Venus* besides Marlene Dietrich?

Of course, today, female movie stars (insofar as any exist) have ceded all that is foxy and fabulous to the likes of Tom Cruise and Mel Gibson and Harrison Ford. It is they who open movies, it is they whom Barbara Walters interviews—while women today can only command the occasional sitcom on NBC and the overwrought suds of nighttime soaps on Fox (none of the three original networks even have their *Dynasty*- or *Dallas*-type shows any longer; it's just all *Dateline* all the time, health insurance exposés and investigative reports on crooked diamond dealers—all this froth where there once were vamps and whores who didn't need hidden cameras to prove they meant business). Somehow women have become footmen on the silver screen. I can't figure out how we allowed this to happen: women are more naturally sex objects, we have more accessible visual allure—we were the incumbent icons! It was our seat to lose. We are like the Democrats voted out of Congress in the '94 election, we have lost a long-held advantage that is rightfully ours. Mae West, Marilyn Monroe, Bette Davis, Veronica Lake—so many Hollywood women established the Divine Right of Queens through years of aggressive casting-couch tactics and backhanded backstage backstabbing, and it surely was not so Tom Hanks could contemplate a box of chocolates on a bench in Savannah!

Nevertheless, such is the predicament we now find ourselves in, and suddenly our glamour quotient—to which we are entitled, especially those women who work, have kids, cook *coq au vin* for dinner and still find the energy for tantric sex during David Letterman—is suddenly provided by Naomi, Linda, Kate, Shalom, Claudia, the rest. Whereas at one time, I think, it was considered a limitation or a detriment that, say, Amber Valletta is this gorgeous thing without a talent, it seems now that beauty for its own sake has new virtue. How else to explain that the actress Elizabeth Hurley was only too willing to take a step backward and become a model for Estée Lauder first, and a thespian (well, of sorts) in her spare time? It seems impossible to have imagined even as recently as twenty years ago—even after *Blowup,* even after *The Eyes of Laura Mars,* even after the sexualized hipster displaced the fey fashion plate as the dominant style statement—that a girl could be an *aspiring* model, that it could be a dream you pursued while waiting on tables and mixing martinis for portfolio money. It used to be that you posed along the catwalk to pay for art school, or if you were Lauren Hutton you used Revlon to support a safari habit, and if you were Jessica Lange it was an embarrassing way to underwrite your Stanislavski Method. It was maybe even something to do until you got married, had kids and settled down. It is only the most recent phenomenon that finds being a professional beauty its own apotheosis.

But the minute actresses started calling themselves "actors" and started to think it was okay to not have plastic surgery, something like this was bound to happen, there was sure to be a greater premium placed on beauty than on talent. Obviously, Winona Ryder, Michelle Pfeiffer and many other actresses are gorgeous and elegant, but they don't carry stardom comfortably—when they claim to spend Saturday nights at home playing Pictionary with friends, I'm inclined to believe them. As the only high-style movie star at the moment, Sharon Stone, no matter how many bad movies she manages to do, will remain a star because she actually bothers to cultivate this old-fashioned fabulousness and fascination around her, and because she always looks done up in public and doesn't do this deliberately dowdy *schmattes*-and-glasses thing that Julia Roberts insists upon. Not only does Sharon Stone look great in Valentino, but she can also wear a Gap T-shirt to the Oscars and make it look like Valentino. Other than Ms. Stone, just as almost every field of endeavor has become more specific and specialized, to do beauty and beauty alone has become perfectly respectable.

Obviously, the O.J.–Nicole story has both of these guilty notional crushes in it, beauty and violence, Fay Wray and King Kong, which explains the attraction to anyone who followed this trial, and perhaps explains the attraction to the players themselves. But while we like violence and beauty in their separate spheres, the O. J. Simpson case actually asked us to look upon a situation where the brutality was applied to a good-looking woman, and where the hero of the story was not rescuing her from her torturers and tormentors, but was in fact the very one. Even if you didn't think that O.J. was the killer, it is clear that he certainly beat Nicole at least a few times—in fact, in her diaries, which were not admitted as evidence, she recorded sixty-one separate incidents of abuse—and yet somehow that element of their relationship was strangely sacrosanct, it was something no one seemed ready to assess honestly and shamelessly.

The legal aspects of domestic violence—which was referred to in court as "domestic discord," since the word "violence" was deemed prejudicial—created a rallying point for outraged feminists and social workers and women's advocates to gather around and make some noise. It gave Denise Brown a good reason to avoid going to court. But none of the spousal abuse experts making their points on CNN or *Geraldo Live* had anything enlightening to say. Even though we all knew that there must have been some kind of strange dynamic going on between O.J. and Nicole, some insulated universe that they invented and they alone understood, some kind of closed system that they had entered long ago, none of the pundits wanted to touch it, to speculate on it. The fact that the crime of wife-beating had so long been overlooked—it was only in October 1984, in the U.S. District Court decision *Thurman* v. *Torrington Police Department,* that the legal code made known "a man is not allowed to physically abuse a woman merely because he is her husband"—meant that nuanced thinking about these relationships had to be suppressed.

Meanwhile, as fired up as many people were getting about battered woman's syndrome out here in the real world, inside the courtroom none of this was getting through. One juror, interviewed after the verdict, even declared all the spousal abuse evidence "a waste of time," and left it at that. While this reaction was disingenuous and indicative of the jury's overall stupidity, it was also an understandably impatient response to a monolithic, simplistic view of what it means when a man throws his fist at a woman. Because it means many things, just as both the words "yes" and "no" mean many things, and the human condition has always been and will forever be made more complicated, exciting, fun and difficult by the misunderstandings that dog us day after day, if not hour after hour or minute by minute. And this will always be the problem when the law gets mixed up with human affairs, particularly crimes of passion or mistakes of the heart: the legal system imposes a straightforward, Manichaean set of absolutes on crooked, twisted, multimotivated human behavior. In criminal court, one can never be sort-of guilty or kind-of innocent.

And the official version of what goes on in a house of beatings has been made terrifically simple. In discussions during the trial, unless you could say that there is never a good reason for a man to raise his hand against a woman, that all domestic violence is the same as all other domestic violence, and throw in a bunch of words about "low self-esteem" and "poor self-image," there would be nothing to say. There was no way to entertain the possibility that once in a while a perfectly good man loses his temper and gets violent, surprises everyone around him—surprises himself—with what he is capable of. He acts out as if in a trance; he has no idea where all this anger and hatred is coming from. But there may be some good reason.

I mean, if you were Jackson Browne and you discovered that Daryl Hannah was leaving you for John F. Kennedy, Jr., wouldn't you be more than a little annoyed? It seems to me that when the world found out that Ms. Hannah had sustained various wounds while trying to retrieve some of her stuff out of the house she shared with Browne in the canyons of Los Angeles so that she could settle into a new love and new life in New York, there was no reason to assume that the sensitive singer-songwriter was acting as anything other than the sensitive singer-songwriter: there was no need to conjure some Jekyll-and-Hyde scenario. Sometimes people just get mad and crazy, and men in particular express pain through their fists more than their tear ducts. That doesn't make it okay or good—and that definitely does not mean that you should not leave, *flee on your donkey at godspeed,* if some guy tries to beat you up early in a relationship, when he has no reason to, when you have not yet dumped him for *People*'s "Sexiest Man Alive," when you have not yet told him that he is the worst lay in the land, his dick is too small, his head is too big, his children from the first and second marriages are all ugly brats and his breath first thing in the morning smells worse than Secaucus, New Jersey.

It may never be right for a man to strike at a woman, but it may be understandable, and the trouble that a media event like the O. J. Simpson trial creates is that just as it allows us to confront the meaning of aberrant, violent behavior, the exhaustion that everyone feels in mere anticipation of what would happen if we really tried to understand it—never mind our simple fear at discovering how great is the threat and the constancy of violence that lives in our society only very slightly below the surface of a very thin membrane—means that we categorize it, package it, put a nice big bow and some wrapping paper on it and promptly ignore it. We don't see case by case. We deny individuals. Jackson Browne and O. J. Simpson are one and the same.

*   *   *

In the *Oresteia* trilogy, the ancient Greek playwright Aeschylus describes a process of intrafamilial bloodshed and retaliation so sanguinary that it nearly tears apart Athenian society. To ensure that dangerous and destructive emotions never again boil and erupt with all the force of Mount Etna after years of dormancy, Athena decides that negative feelings must be injected into normal life, incorporated into the workaday world. The subterranean urchin-goddesses known as the Furies are therefore given status aboveground, creating a permanent place for deities who represent revenge and rebellion within the civilized city of Athens. Renamed the Eumenides, the Furies immunize Greek society against its own violent impulses, and never again are household disputes a mere preamble to civil war.

On the other hand, in the Soviet Union, where a reverse McCarthyism governed for seventy years and thought crime was always an inchoate insurrection, mental illness was used as a means to categorize subversives. Instead of incorporating negative feelings, the Soviets isolated them in a Gulag, sent them to a Siberia of the mind. Entire diseases were created around hating Stalin, you could be institutionalized for not being a part of the collective, personality variations were poison.

In the United States, where we can think whatever we want, what we want is for it all to be nice and pat. Far from being motivated by totalitarian needs, our decision making tends to come down to sheer laziness: we are tempted to pathologize all behavior just to make life easier.

While the O.J. trial brought domestic violence into the open, it may well have pushed the subtleties of personality—the simple idea that you can act as a person and not as a "syndrome"—dangerously out of view. Any curiosity about what made Nicole stay seventeen years in a relationship that was apparently violent from the start, what strange deal she'd made with the devil long ago—all that was discounted. There was never any suggestion that by documenting the abuse and leaving pictures of her injured self in her safe-deposit box—which the prosecution had to drill open as it searched for evidence—and telling her friends "O.J. is going to kill me and get away with it," Nicole might have indicated not mere resignation to her fate but a strange acceptance of it. It was never okay to conjecture that she may have believed that it was somehow the proper denouement of her star-crossed romantic life to end up stabbed outside her home, throat slit so completely that she was almost decapitated, knife slashed right across her silicone-implanted breasts, let no necrophiliac ever feel her up. ("When we heard her breasts were slashed," one friend told Sheila Weller, "we knew who killed her.") There was never any thought that this bloody crime scene was as inevitable to her as William Holden floating in the pool at the beginning and the end of *Sunset Boulevard,* a great movie about characters who always knew it would come to this, who always knew that Oedipus was a fool to fight his destined disgrace: instead of resisting fate, they get drunk with doom. Any suggestion of this kind of complicity on Nicole's part was absolutely verboten.

Somehow it was only okay to say that Nicole suffered and was murdered—never that she may have courted death or at the very least been a passive partner in her own end. That is just a far too sickening thought after years of feminism have tried to show us otherwise. While it is almost at the point where we accept our fascination with male violence on the big screen or the playing field, what I think is a bit harder to see is how much we are titillated and turned on by sexual violence, by a man turning on a woman as an act of raw desire, lustful anger, justifiable rage, sick passion. And yet, it comes at us everywhere. And not just in action movies with multimillion-dollar budgets.

I think the first crush I ever had on a literary character occurred when I read *Wuthering Heights* in high school and wondered why none of the boys in tenth grade seemed at all like Heathcliff. The insane, unfulfilled and desperate passion between Catherine and Heathcliff, one that was carried into the grave, felt like teenage angst, Brontë style. Heathcliff tended to say things like "He couldn't love as much in eighty years as I could in a day," while Catherine, lovesick and bedridden, pale and consumptive, would ask questions like "Why does my blood rush into a hell of tumult at a few words?" This book—a classic, no less—was full of hyperbole and hotheadedness, and was fueled by an emotional violence that eventually even became physical. Perhaps not intentionally, but at one point Heathcliff squeezes Catherine's arm so tight that "on his letting go [there were] four distinct impressions left, blue in the colourless skin."

The message from this always seemed clear: for a man to claim ownership of you, for him to really assure you that he wants you for his possession, he must mark you, bruise you, squeeze and imprint you, brand you with his violence. In *The Postman Always Rings Twice*, probably my favorite James M. Cain novel, violence is part of the initiation that the two young murderers make into their deep, doomed love. In Bob Rafelson's 1981 film adaptation, with Jessica Lange and Jack Nicholson, the ugly and forbidden nature of this coupling is acted out in a sexual initiation that smacks of forced entry like the kind where he'd be right to say *she wanted it* but that doesn't mean she thought she'd get it, but it also doesn't mean that the whole thing wasn't her idea in the first place. This sex-scene-as-rape-fantasy goes down on a messy kitchen table, a dirty butcher knife lying around like a stab wound waiting to happen, with a lot of cries of *no* that we all know means *yes* and a lot of pelvic pulsating and hip-to-hip contact so tight and close that people were constantly speculating on the possibility that the actors had really done it. But in the book itself, published back in 1934, Mr. Cain keeps the rococo sex surprisingly spare. "Bite me! Bite me!" Cora screams as Frank smashes his lips against hers for the first time. "I bit her. I sunk my lips into her so deep I could feel the blood spurt into my mouth. It was running down her neck when I carried her upstairs."

There is something a little too appropriate about the name James M. Cain, all his characters sinful, unrepentant outcasts and drifters, wandering nomads with the mark of Cain plainly upon them. In this pulp noir genre, I tend to think of Cain as Fitzgerald beside Jim Thompson's Hemingway, the racetrack versus the rodeo, insurance crime instead of bank robbery, California compared to Texas. Of course, both of them operate in each other's domains plenty, and both lovingly tell the story of the deep dark of the human heart, especially in sunny climates and respectable garb. In 1997, Jim Thompson's *The Killer Inside Me,* his 1952 *roman noir,* was canonized and published as part of the Library of America, although with scenes like this one between a sheriff's deputy and a local lady—not even ten pages into the book—it is unlikely to make it to any high school reading lists:

"No, baby"—my lips drew back from my teeth. "I'm not going to hurt you. I wouldn't think of hurting you. I'm just going to beat the ass plumb off of you."

I said it, and I meant it, and I damn near did.

I jerked the jersey up over her face and tied the end in a knot. I threw her down on the bed, yanked off her sleeping shorts and tied her feet together with them.

I took off my belt and raised it over my head.

I don't know how long it was before I stopped, before I came to my senses. All I know is my arm ached like hell and her rear end was one big bruise, and I was scared crazy—as scared as a man can get and go on living.

I freed her feet and hands, and pulled the jersey off her head. I soaked a towel in cold water and bathed her with it. I poured coffee between her lips. All the time I was talking, begging her to forgive me, telling her how sorry I was.

I got down on my knees by the bed, and begged and apologized . . .

"Don't talk." She brushed her lips against mine. "Don't say you're sorry."

She kissed me again. She began fumbling at my tie, my shirt; starting to undress me after I'd almost skinned her alive.

I went back the next day and the day after that. I kept going back. And it was like a wind had been turned on a dying fire . . .

The great thing about beating someone up is that then you get to make nice afterward. You get to have a private little secret about your relationship that nobody knows, your girlfriends wouldn't understand, your parents would kill you. It's almost like adultery in the sense that secrecy heightens the romance, makes the whole world of necessity disappear during those few hours in that ground-floor motel efficiency, during the afternoon on the couch in the office conference room with the door locked, hoping nobody will actually need to have a meeting or something like that in there. It always struck me as rather apposite that John F. Kennedy, who seems to have mastered the art of adultery in the White House, with wife and Secret Service and B-52 bombers so nearby, was also the President who invented the covert operation, the secret military forays into Vietnam and wherever else the CIA was misbehaving at that point. It strikes me that fascination with cloak-and-dagger intrigue in world events is not so different than needing to indulge in forbidden love and lust in private life.

But if you're not married, if you just want to feel dirty, love that starts with maiming is love that will never be clean, that will always be dangerous. Sylvia Plath's vampiric bite that draws blood from Ted Hughes' cheek the first time she meets him at a Cambridge party, the fanged kiss that leaks blood from Cora's lips in the first smooch of *The Postman Always Rings Twice*—these are pacts, promissory notes, pledges of allegiance. Because once you let someone do this to you without offering objection, you are showing yourself to be one of the wild ones, one of the willing ones: you have been initiated.

This ritual is not incomparable to gang recruits getting tattooed with the crew's emblem or puncturing a pulsing vein or somehow shedding blood as a mark of do-or-die commitment to the posse. It seems that in any situation that is a matter of life and death—and for the Crips, the Bloods and other LA street gangs that would be a fair assessment of the situation, whereas for most lovers it would not—loyalty is sealed not with a kiss, but with a fist. Suddenly the rather mundane nature of a couple's love is transubstantiated into the realm of intense, life-threatening and life-sustaining when the melodramatic element of violence is injected into the situation, whether it's appropriate or not. Since the couple in *Postman* were partners in murder, it actually made sense. For a wealthy couple with middle-class values living in Brentwood with a swimming pool and tennis court in the backyard and Michael Ovitz down the block, it makes no sense. For Nicole and O.J. it makes no sense—but it did create the intense do-or-die bond between them that could only be broken by death.

In his book *Pryor Convictions,* black comedian Richard Pryor—who seems to have exorcised these demons more effectively than O.J.—tells of precisely this effect in his marriage to white actress Jennifer Lee. "If you hit a woman she'll either run like a banshee in the opposite direction, or she's yours," Pryor writes. "The sting of violence is like voodoo. A hex. A black spell. You're possessed. Locked in a diabolic dance."

Violence in love is deeply instinctive, creating covalent bonds between sweetness and cruelty, it is the easiest way to portray intensity in romance, it is the most direct metaphor for complicated, crazy love, which is why it is used in art so much, which is why good feminists and old-fashioned moralists alike find themselves drawn into the meaning of its allure. Chrissie Hynde, the original riot grrrl, the strongest image I have of an independent punk rocker of the distaff sort, still was able to say on the first song on the Pretenders' first album, "I like the way you bruise my hip 'cause I'm precious." Later on the same album, in a song called "Tattooed Love Boys," Hynde sings about a place where girls go seeking out sexual abuse, a place where "I shot my mouth off and you showed me what that hole was for." Eventually I realized, through Chrissie Hynde's example, that there was no inconsistency in a strong woman getting bashed around by her boyfriend: in Hynde's world, girls didn't get beaten up because they were weak; rather, they got it because they were tough enough and rough enough to take it. Of course, Billie Holiday, several decades before, already made it clear that being smacked and taking it like a (wo)man was the dignified course when she sang her plaintive "Ain't Nobody's Business But My Own."

Likewise, in the film *Leaving Las Vegas,* Elisabeth Shue, playing a streetwalker on the Strip, not only willingly bends over to be spanked by her pimp but actually hands him the knife he'll need to beat her but good. In the movie *Love Games,* written and directed by feminist filmmaker Lizzie Borden, a prosecutor goes to find out why no one is willing to press charges against a serial date rapist, and finds herself similarly seduced into enjoying the experience of surrendering her body and will to this man. In *Gone With the Wind,* by many accounts the greatest romance ever made for the big screen, the most commonly replayed clip shows Rhett Butler slapping the impudent and impertinent Scarlett O'Hara in pent-up frustration and then grabbing her aloft, to head upstairs and meet her fate, whether she wants it or not.

Like most schoolgirls, I first came across the perverse sex appeal of the SS guard, the Nazi in his jackboots, in Sylvia Plath's "Daddy," the angry daughter's rant at her putatively German dead father: "Every woman adores a fascist, / The boot in the face, the brute / Brute heart of a brute like you." In Sherri Szeman's 1994 novel *The Kommandant's Mistress,* a story told alternately from the points of view of both a young Jewish woman and the concentration camp commander who takes her as his sex slave, it seems an unintended effect of this miserable coupling that it is extremely, uncomfortably erotic. In *Schindler's List,* almost the identical relationship is set up between the camp overlord played by Ralph Fiennes and the young Jewess, portrayed with sheer terror by Embeth Davidtz, whose work detail involves maid service in the commander's house. In the scenes where Fiennes contemplates just how far he wants to take his lordly prerogative to do whatever he wants with this poor chambermaid, the result was so sexy, the feelings of arousal conveyed by these two attractive young actors—no doubt, in marked contrast with what any real Nazi and any real starved and tortured concentration camp victim would look, feel and be like—that the erotic effect of her fear of him, alternated by, strangely, *his* fear of *her,* his belief that her Jew-charms are seducing him even as she cowers, shivers, frightened on the ground, the fact that this whole dynamic is powered by all the tricks that make the pornography of domination and submission such a turn-on, is almost offensive in a movie that otherwise does its best to stick with the horror of the Holocaust, to deny anyone the opportunity to indulge fantasies of captivity.

In the Broadway show (and movie) *Oliver!*, based on Charles Dickens' novel *Oliver Twist*, the kindly prostitute Nancy (in modern terms "the hooker with a heart of gold") is punched out by her boyfriend-pimp Bill Sikes, falls on the ground and then, in a showstopping ballad of devotion and heartache, pulls herself up off the floor and insists that she will stand by her man, bruises and all, "As Long As He Needs Me." *Carousel* is a musical set among Lowell's textile-mill working girls, depicting troubled lives in an atmosphere of grubby-gray tedium that is indigenous to New England, and is meant to signal a show more gritty and heart-wrenching than the usual Broadway fare (this in spite of the fact that Shirley Jones, a.k.a. Madam Milquetoast, starred in the movie version opposite the cloyingly blue-eyed Gordon MacRae). Maybe it's because the residue of hard knocks and hardships is immunity to pain, or perhaps it's because *Carousel* is just plain dated, but for whatever reason, what we would now think of as domestic violence is defined in the show as a sweet "love tap." Toward the end of the play, the teenage daughter Louise—who appears to have fallen in with a bad crowd and is heading in the wrong direction—encounters a strange man as she frolics along the road. He turns out to be the revenant of her deceased dad, Billy Bigelow, the bastard who got her mother pregnant and never got around to marrying her before getting himself killed in the manner of all bad boys who live fast and die young. Billy's purposes back on earth involve the usual reparations that, left unmended, are said to keep lost souls floating in Dante's *Purgatorio*. So in trying to impose some paternal discipline on his unruly wild child of a daughter, Billy rebukes her with a hard smack. But here's the funny part: afterward, after the pink impression of the blow has been drained of its blood rush, Louise dazedly declares that "it felt like he kissed me." She rushes home, reports this visitation to her poor beleaguered mother—who is, apparently, like most single mothers, beyond astonishment—and then asks, "Is it possible for someone to hit you hard like that—real hard and loud—and for it to not hurt at all?" To which her mom replies that something like that can happen, that it is possible, but *only if the person who hits you loves you very, very much.*

Now, let us remember that *Carousel,* whether Broadway-bound or rehashed by community-theater amateurs, is a heartland enterprise, and not some beatnik expression of alternative values. If everything about *Carousel* is solidly middle-class and middle-American, then there's nothing particularly outré about the notion that when someone you love smacks you, it doesn't hurt at all. And the party line for so many years, even in something as innocuous as a Broadway musical, was that nothing could be *more* innocuous—gentle, affectionate even—than a smash across the cheek from the man you love. Of course, a slap across the face usually does not lead to full-fledged battery, and yet, nowadays it would be impossible not to see the potential connection. And yet, the examples of glorified romantic violence that I just mentioned come from all different eras, and of them only *Carousel* seems dated—though it was revived to great fanfare and promises of true grit at Lincoln Center—and that is simply because the schmaltz and pomp and circumstance of musical theater is always atavistic.

In an essay for the *Los Angeles Times,* later republished in her collection *Life and Death,* Andrea Dworkin describes a series of rapes—by several doctors and other assorted keepers, by hands and fingers and specula—during her incarceration at the Women's House of Detention in New York City, after an arrest for attending an anti-Vietnam rally in 1965. She describes a bruised uterus and a ripped vagina and bleeding that would not stop. And she also describes how the writer Grace Paley somehow became involved in all this and encouraged Ms. Dworkin, then a Bennington College freshman, to tell her story, to take it to newspapers, to give her miserable experience a voice against the surrender of silence. So she diligently goes about the task, finding every broadsheet and tabloid listed in the Yellow Pages, she contacts them all, alerts them to her jailers' crimes, and sensational as her accusations are—*College Girl! Rape in the Lockdown! Speculum Rips Cervix!*—Ms. Dworkin gets a lot of ink. There are public hearings to follow, and eventually the prison gets torn down.

All this could ultimately read as a victory of sorts, but one of the more mesmerizing and outstanding facts of this experience for Ms. Dworkin seems to be the way so many men lavished her with pornographic letters, taking perverse and prurient delight in the detailed accounts that she gave of her rapes. "I didn't know the facts about my imprisonment were sexually arousing—to me they were an anguish," Ms. Dworkin writes. "I didn't know that in the public eye I became living pornography for men who liked to watch a frightened girl tell the story. I got hundreds of letters from men, taunting, obsessive letters. The man would say what he wanted to do to me or what he was going to do to me when he came and got me and how he masturbated to what the prison doctors had done." Now, thinking back to a time when the now thoroughly outspoken Andrea Dworkin was a young college girl in the midst of this trauma, it is plain to see that this is just awful, about the worst imaginable violation. But thirty years hence, I read her shock and I am shocked—*shocked!*—that the persistence of rape fantasies and other prison-house dreams that delight in abuse, and which are so prevalent in our society, don't inform her understanding of these wretched men and their hideous behavior. Because there are so many socially acceptable contexts in which we are allowed to indulge our icky, uncomfortable fantasies at this point—we don't even need real pornography in a world that gives us the director's cut of 9½ *Weeks* at any video store, or that shows Charlotte Rampling in the pasty, unwholesome decay and naked imprisonment of *The Night Porter*—that it seems like everyone ought to have caught on to the fact that rape might be a *crime* of power, but it is plainly a *fantasy* of sex. A man's hopeless, hapless hard-on as he feels himself aroused while reading someone describe her sexual debasement, the hot shot of something electric and filthy and exciting that the most sane and stable woman might feel while being spanked: this is the human mind doing its dirty work on the pathetically compliant human body. Just as I am certain that the creators of *Carousel* would be astonished to hear that there are elements of politically incorrect abuse in their innocent little play about the big top, Andrea Dworkin cannot come to terms with the idea that what caused her such pain to experience, when transferred onto the cold black and white of written memory, can become some other person's cheap thrills.

So while Andrea Dworkin was utterly turned off—ruined, in fact—

by her own experiences, in yet another permutation of the law of unintended consequences, she found herself with an audience of newspaper readers who were completely turned on. When you consider the kinds of things made available via middlebrow pornography outlets—that basic cable TV can lead you to 970-PEEE, that there are other fantasy phone lines where, depending on whether you press 1, 2 or 3 on the dial, you can specify incest of the brother-sister, mother-son or father-daughter variety—the idea that some men got their kicks reading about a woman's torture while incarcerated some thirty years ago seems almost quaint.

"Nobody likes to say this but we all know it's true. Sex is just so bizarre," says a detective in the novel *To Die For,* Joyce Maynard's fictionalized account of the Pam Smart case, in which a sexually overstimulated teenage boy is driven to murder his lover's husband. "Here we all are, walking around going to the supermarket, making bank deposits, shooting the breeze with someone over at the barbershop about our car. Acting like we're all normal. Everybody keeps up the act. How's it going? Just great. How about you? And the whole time we're doing this we've got this whole other life going on—the life you live behind closed doors, alone, or not alone, in the dark, when you're just a naked body burning up with animal desires. Am I the only person in the world who thinks this is strange? Am I the only one who notices?" After contemplating whether the woman who renews his license at the DMV likes being handcuffed or wears cutout panties or masturbates with Frank Sinatra records playing in the background, he concludes that you never can tell what will turn anybody on. "Let's face it, once you throw sex into the equation, anyone out there can become crazy. We're all capable of bizarre behavior. Who follows the rules? What are the rules anyway?"

Ask yourself: What turns you on? How unnerving is it to find out that sportscaster Marv Albert likes to wear garter belts and ladies' panties while biting his sex partners' backs? Wouldn't it have been preferable to have just had him be the garden-variety date rapist? Was it more lurid and damning that, during her 1982 divorce proceedings, Palm Beach housewife Roxanne Pulitzer—who was splitting up with Herbert, heir to the prize-giving family—was accused of having sex with a trumpet or alleged to be having an affair with her best friend

Jackie Kimberly, wife of the tissue man? Or is the truth that if we found out how many of our friends participated in three-ways, owned nipple clamps, played with bondage gear and had custom-fitted dildos we might all be horrified? Or comforted? Does it make you happy to know that a tacit quid pro quo apparently existed between the White House and the FBI during the Kennedy administration, an understanding that went something like: J. Edgar Hoover would keep quiet about alleged mob involvement in electing JFK—and would not be too concerned about the possibility that Judith Exner was a cervical connection of sorts between the President and Sam Giancana—so long as no one in Bobby Kennedy's Justice Department let it be known that the corpulent head of our domestic secret police liked to wear flowered ladies' dresses with ruffled sleeves? And this is only a high-level example of the mutual blackmail, the conspiracy of silence, that all of us participate in when it comes to our erotic antics. Because the strangest things do go on in people's bedrooms. It's the big unknown. Clearly there is *nothing* we can't make exciting. Sol Wachtler famously posited that a prosecutor could indict a ham sandwich if he really wanted to, and the long shelf life of books like *Portnoy's Complaint* with its forays into liver and apple halves, and *Story of the Eye* with its childhood games involving egg yolk and the cat's milk, make it plain that it would be an effort to produce a work of popular art that fails to arouse *someone*. And misogynistic violence, as Andrea Dworkin seems to have discovered, is at least as erotic as, well, any of the foodstuffs of Philip Roth's or Georges Bataille's masturbatory dreams.

In fact, offhand I can think of only two instances of movies that portrayed situations of domestic violence as absolutely miserable and painful, without any kind of redemption. The first is the New Zealand film *Once Were Warriors,* which tells of inner-city Maoris and their lives of brutal desolation and drunkenness. When the husband of the lead character gives his wife a "tanning," all the black and blue, as well as yellow and magenta, that mark the bruises on her face, along with the disfiguring flaps of loose skin and mottled flesh, make it absolutely clear that an ugly, unsexy thing has occurred. And in the Robert Altman take on Raymond Chandler's *The Long Goodbye,* the girlfriend of a gangster gets her face smashed with a Coke bottle after the guy has made a speech going on and on about how beautiful she is, how she could be a cover girl, how her features are perfection. Later in the movie, when we see her covered in bandages, with a nose cast and a mouth brace, when we see how scared she still is of the gangster, and how she has no ability to get away from him because she's so damaged: a disfigured and defaced invalid, this woman cannot escape her attacker, because he has ruined her for the rest of the world. But there is no moment of tenderness in her entrapment—if the injuries she'd sustained were mere bruises, we could envisage the standard scene of a penitent man attending to her aches, icing her black eye, making nice, begging forgiveness, begging for just one more chance. But this was clearly not a lover's quarrel highlighted by some right jabs and left hooks: this was brutal torture, the woman could not have been into what happened, and she's stuck and petrified. But these two films aside, most of the intimations of violence against women that are shown on-screen are as stylized and pretty-looking as *9½ Weeks,* infomercials for handcuffs and garter belts.

What on earth can slogans like "no means no" and "against her will is against the law" possibly mean to us, or at any rate how can they put up any sort of challenge to a society in which the most powerful cultural images are telling us that "he hit me and it felt like a kiss"? What is anyone going to say to the many of us out there who have been confronted by some version of a man's violent temper and have found ourselves excited, pulled in, taken in, turned on? How can we deny the draw, the obsessive grab of images of pain, whose force has no equal and goes unopposed in a society that has denied us the ecstasy of a god, of a religious explosion of delight, so that happiness has come to seem ho-hum and only our pain—our deep, bloody, undeniable pain—gives us the sense that we can feel at all?

It is a commonplace recounted in almost comic tones that Scandinavia—with its liberal sex education policies, its enviable public health system, its socialism of the spirit combined with a capitalism of creativity that has produced Volvo, Saab, Lego, Bang & Olufsen, Ericcsen, Ikea, Dansk, Georg Jensen and many other internationally coveted brands—is still impoverished by depression that has resulted in an astonishingly high suicide rate (although in the most recent survey New Zealand's self-inflicted death toll was highest). Meanwhile, in

Egypt and other miserable African nations and emirates and petty dictatorships with gross discrepancies between rich and poor, with—in some cases—slavery still as legal as rape and wife-burning and the like, and every kind of bad darkening life as resolutely as the Nordic winters blacken the skies in Oslo and Stockholm and Helsinki and Copenhagen, the suicide rate is always quite low.

This difference should not be seen as an indication that blonde values are bad and Third World countries are good, or even explained away by weather conditions. Even if it's true that sun makes you sunny and snow makes you sad, I'd still prefer to read this as proof that happiness is about something else, something different from life conditions, and it does have something to do with a feeling for God, an emotional connection with our Maker that is greater and deeper and bigger and fiercer than anything anyone will get from reading *The Celestine Prophecy* or from going to synagogue twice a year or to church for Christmas Mass. If any of us living in the Western world were truly able to conquer our Promethean awe at all that we *have built,* all the ways we've trumped evolution, dueled with God and apparently won—if we could transcend all this *stuff* that we live for and love so much—we might experience profound joy. But with comfort a given, it is only pain that registers as profound, as the emotion worthy of poets and painters and somber rock stars with short life expectancies. With acute lack of affect its only apparent alternative, pain has been worshipped and bound up in our sexuality in recent years as never before, as a pathetic substitute for real feelings. "I think our generation loves our pain, and if you dare take it away from us, we're going to kill you," Tori Amos said in *Rolling Stone* in late 1994. "We like our pain. And we're packaging it, and we're selling it."

Consider this: Sensory overload turns to sensory deprivation when, in 1986, David Lynch can make a movie called *Blue Velvet* and show Dennis Hopper in a gas mask sexually abusing Isabella Rossellini to the tune of a Bobby Vinton song while a thousand critics can't trip over their own feet fast enough to praise this denatured version of sexuality in suburbia, and English lit and cultural studies departments at universities are suddenly swamped by at least ten thousand dissertations that deal with that scene, Lynch's oeuvre and all kinds of other groovy postmodernist issues. For some reason, it takes this weirdness, this coldness, this incongruity to get us excited. Yes, we like our pain: it is the only thing we know.

On the other hand, most of us have never been beaten up, have no idea what broken bones, black eyes, bruised legs, anything like that imposed upon us by someone we are supposed to love would feel like. Playing with violence is all fine and good until someone gets hurt, until someone forgets that the gun is loaded. "We measure his desire by what he's willing to do to her, and we celebrate the force he's willing to show," Andrea Dworkin said of wife-batterers in a speech at a Texas conference on domestic violence. "Then, when she shows up as a pile of bleeding bones in a hospital emergency room, we say, 'Oh, that wasn't so romantic after all.' " As is often the case, Ms. Dworkin is right about the sharp divide between ravishing fantasy and ugly reality, but this is an issue that feminists have struggled with for a long time, with most of us finally accepting some sort of psychic split in the realm of desire as surely as so many monks and priests and nuns obey a vow of celibacy—looking sexless and deflated in their shapeless religious garb—though underneath they must surely quash their fleshly urges every day, every hour, every minute even. None of this was ever supposed to be easy. Whether you believe in feminism or Jesus Christ or Mary Magdalene or all of the above, you will always be forced to reconcile what you want with what you know is right. I think a lot of leading free-speech feminists who are against the censorship of pornography because they believe in the First Amendment are actually reluctant to admit that *they* like X-rated movies and dirty magazines themselves: it's not that they don't want to live in a world that *bans* pornography, but rather that they don't want to live *without* pornography, period. Even right-thinking chicks have dirty minds full of impure thoughts.

In an *Esquire* column from 1972, reprinted in her collection *Crazy Salad,* Nora Ephron admits to "this dreadful unliberated sex fantasy," one so ugly she can't share it with her consciousness-raising group (ah, the seventies) or even with her readers, except to say, "It has largely to do with being dominated by faceless males who rip my clothes off. That's just about all they have to do. Stare at me in this faceless way, go mad with desire, and rip my clothes off. It's terrific. In my sex fantasy, nobody ever loves me for my mind." Ms. Ephron doesn't elaborate much on this, though she does suggest that some harsher and rougher rape and battery follows all this ocular objectification. At any rate, I think it is a safe categorical rule—like the five years you add on to the given age of any woman over fifty, or the ten pounds you add on to the admitted weight of any woman at all—that whatever sexual fantasies someone is willing to divulge amount to maybe a tenth in degree of debauchery of what they really dream up. The only thing that we know for sure is that most of us have reveries about rape from one or another perspective, and almost none of us act on them (I shudder to think what actual rapists fantasize about).

And it's a funny thing about sexual fantasies of all kinds: unlike other types of fantasies—those flights of fancy about winning the lottery or showing the town bully who's boss or rescuing your dream girl from a car wreck—which we would love, without reservation, to experience in reality, most people really would not like their sexual desires fulfilled. It's not just that a man who wins the *Penthouse* sweepstakes and is granted command of a harem will learn the hard (and sore and not so hard) way that making love to twenty women at once is more exhausting than enjoyable—it's that most men don't even *want* to test-drive this daydream in the first place. And most women do not wish to be raped, maimed, bruised, choked, whipped or battered. But that doesn't mean the thought does not make them hot and soft and wet.

You see, many of us like a little bit of violence, or the fierce and fearsome possibilities implied by a domineering man whose touch is less than tender. Plenty of us have had some unnerving and unexpected sexual encounters where we've been hit, thrown on the floor, pushed against a wall, held down or shaken up, and many of us have found ourselves on all fours or thrown across some man's lap getting spanked like a bad, bad schoolgirl who is made to feel even naughtier as something warm shoots up between her thighs, as a tense ticklish quiver coruscates deep inside of her. The majority of us who've had such experiences can enjoy feeling dirty and debased and interested in what was happening, because despite date-rape hysteria and domestic violence media saturation, we ultimately have some sense that nothing too bad is *going* to happen. Somewhere in the apocrypha of the social compact, it is decreed that a *spanking* does not translate into a *beating*.

But I know this is slippery logic. If we condone this little bit of brute force from men—and by definition, by asking them to just be men and be different from women, we kind of do—should we not consider it part of our opportunity costs in dealing with these creatures that it will sometimes get ugly, that it will occasionally get real? If only feminism or any other philosophy or moral code could come up with something so luscious that it could conquer these base impulses that fuel heterosexual love. If only it could outsmart the will to power, he with his strength, she with her sexual snare, and both with the rape fantasy—sublimated into the push-and-pull, the resistance-yield-conquest of common courtship—that is almost a necessity in every romantic relationship, for it is only in the saying no and playing hard to get that the tease and tension and titillation is born, even for healthy people. If feminism could snuff all the dark stuff out of sex and we could all just enjoy the edenic love that has the family-entertainment feel of a trip to Disney World, then sexism will be completely eradicated. But not until then.

So it's basically never.

And that's why there is a part of me that understands why Mike Tyson or members of the Dallas Cowboys assume that if a woman comes up to their hotel room late at night, it's because she means to stay awhile. And it doesn't mean that she's crashing on the couch. Or that she'll stay for tea and crumpets, clean her hands in a finger bowl of rose water, put her white gloves back on and then go home. It's not that it ought to be assumed that a woman who joins a man in his suite at the Ritz-Carlton after 11 P.M. is there to get laid, but if you happen to be dealing with preverbal professional athletes, it's a good idea to be careful. And be prepared. And, quite frankly, before you make the trip up the elevator to one of the top-floor rooms with VIP services like delivery of *The Wall Street Journal* each morning, it might be a good idea to be willing. Because late at night, in hotel beds with their cold, crisp sheets, in front of hotel TVs with their six choices of Spectravision, what people like to do is fuck. And who can blame them?

I believe Mike Tyson committed rape on that fateful beauty-pageant night in Indianapolis, and I am glad he was convicted and incarcerated for it. But I also think Desiree Washington was an idiot to be alone with Mike Tyson in *any* room with readily available horizontal surfaces—especially a hotel, whose utilitarian value is infused with sexy implications—if she wasn't wanting to get down and dirty. Because that's what people do. And because no *does not* always mean no. It does, often enough, mean: *I'm not easy, try a little harder,* or: *I want to but don't think I'm a slut,* or: *I really do want to, but I'm uncomfortable with the enormity of my sexual desires, so only if you force me will I be able to ignore my guilt.* Now, for the sake of the law, a line must be drawn, and no must mean *no.* But the mixed messages, not just in that little two-letter word but in all the rites of dating, will not be decoded and destroyed until we raise a generation of infants in perfectly appointed little Skinner boxes so that their brains are programmed from the earliest point to enjoy clean, utopian sex, the kind we had before the serpent, before we partook of the fruit of the Tree of the Knowledge of Good and Evil and opened our eyes and saw that we were naked and felt the shame which begot suspicion which pervaded everything. And bad as this was supposed to be—the Fall, the one with a capital letter—my guess is that before that day it was all procreational sex, it was mating season activity, it was animal—and by *animal* I mean bunny rabbits, not felines. But once we tasted forbidden fruit—from the *only* tree in the whole Garden of Eden that had been proscribed—we were given the gift of vision, and instead of seeing light, we discovered darkness.

And we thought it was good

Now here we are: All these years later, and no one is exactly running to yank the string and get the lightbulb back on.

Still, no one wants to be date-raped and no one wants to be physically abused. But it is such a thin, fine line. When a rape or beating occurs between a man and woman who have just met—whether at a beauty pageant, a bar or a bar mitzvah—it's tough enough to make sense of how flirtation and a few drinks turned to aggravated assault. But with married couples, with longtime boyfriends and girlfriends: the mind boggles. A friend of mine, who is now an attorney, spent a couple of years between college and law school working for Linda Fairstein, head of the sex crimes unit at the Manhattan district attorney's office. My friend's entire job was interviewing women who had

filed rape charges—these were cases where the situation was not desperate, the lines not so clear, no one was in the hospital—just to make
sure that they hadn't then had sex the next night with the same guy
voluntarily, or they had not since married him—or if, in fact, the
woman's decision to go to the police to report the crime was not, in
the first place, part of an escalating destructive dynamic the couple
functioned in. When Pam talked to me about the women she dealt
with, she never seemed to doubt the sincerity of their claims—she was
quite sure *something* very bad must have happened; but there seemed
to be real frustration with how the situation changed from minute to
minute, how in a single conversation both the objective recall of events
and the subjective interpretation of their meaning could vary wildly,
how substance abuse blurred behavior, how love or what passed for it
had the power to mess everything until it was beyond the limits of the
law.

These situations may also be beyond the purview of psychology,
psychiatry, social work and its various subgroups. Mediation and
marriage counseling might help, but little can make the bonds between
these couples either sensible or severable. In a paper for the December
1990 volume of the journal *Family Process,* several therapists from the
Ackerman Institute in New York City wrote about their findings in
counseling couples with domestic violence problems. One of their conclusions was that it was best to approach these pairs with the assumption that their union could remain, that somehow it could be made to
work—basically, that the goal did not have to be to get the wife to
leave. This decision was partly philosophical—there was usually real
love based on some sound and long-standing ties—but it was also
practical: these couples *could not* be kept apart. They seemed to thrive
on the break-up-and-make-up process too well. "In the wake of the
irrefutable logic that compels the couple to separate, the next wave of
that logic breaks, and they are caught in the powerful tides of reaffilia-
tion. This redemptive moment in the couple's cycle . . . is as com-
plexly structured as the violent tide that produced it," the therapists
write. "The strength of this bond has the potential to defeat the most
persuasive shelter or antibattering program: The more outside forces
try to separate the couple, the more the bond binds them together
. . . Since the nature of attachment is often a mystery, even from the

protagonists themselves, they will remain caught in its grip, common-sense injunctions to separate notwithstanding."

The therapists' tolerance of these insane relationships—which is really quite smart, I think, certainly more reasonable than advocates who try to take a woman away from what she won't leave, and definitely saner than Andrea Dworkin's call for lengthy prison sentences—says as much about the times we live in, and our view of the function of all long-term relationships, as it does about domestic violence. Because it is a fact of post-sixties America that no one is ashamed of much, lots of people grew up in broken homes, in sterile suburbs, without much family, and the end product is a generation of adults who find themselves unusually willing to cling to relationships long past their point of usefulness; they find themselves wanting to *make it work* with rare determination—and with about as much methodology as a person who bangs on a television set to get the screen to stop rolling—as a corrective to the laxity of their parents, and because they just plain don't want to lose *another* person that they love. Another loss, one more loss, so many losses: *Did you say all my pretty ones? Not all?* For as long as they can remember, they've been losing parents and stepparents and Dad's live-in lover and Mom's old boyfriend, and they really want to make a stable, solid life for themselves that is not about people going away. They want to make a life about staying. So while feminism ought to make a woman feel free to leave a man who makes her unhappy in any way, these more primal forces and needs keep it going. On and on. Think about it: When in the history of human events has it ever been possible to date someone for seven years? And then finally break up.

The notion of the long battle—of: *we tried, oh how we tried,* and these are people who are not even married and don't have kids—is part of our way of thinking about love. Of course, personal dramas are patiently accepted. People who have nourished their need to stay intertwined and enmeshed can spend years in a damaging relationship, and then spend years getting out of it: divorcing, suing, seizing, whatever—basically going from the drama of the bad relationship to the melodrama of the ugly breakup. This, in our world, passes for normal. Simone de Beauvoir, who enjoyed and endured a fifty-year nonmarriage to Jean-Paul Sartre—which was, it seems, a triumph of mutual respect and separate apartments over infidelity, insanity, existentialism and Nelson Algren—has no patience for those who admire the persistence of participants in difficult relationships, dismissing them as boring and bored. "[T]he middle class in recent years has taken on an epic style of expression in which routine takes on the cast of adventure, fidelity, that of a sublime passion; ennui becomes wisdom, and family hatred is the deepest form of love," she writes, with rare disgust, in *The Second Sex*. "The truth is, however, that when two individuals detest each other, while being unable to get along without each other, it is not of all human relations the truest and most moving, but rather the most pitiable."

Just the same, as her own paramourdom with Sartre shows, all love is coded and contractual in its own particular way. Even in healthy, nonviolent and nonoppressive relationships that don't get their start in Paris between the wars, the couple lives by the laws of its own constitution, and usually it's not written out, it's not discussed, they don't know what magnetism has kept them together for so long, they probably don't want to know. After a while, it is clear that physics, Einstein's theories, his law of relativity and the way it explains how particles in the universe are drawn to each other, must surely guide human emotions as well. $E = mc^2$: I knew—really knew, could have explained it well—what the equation meant when I was in high school, when I still took science courses, before I stupidly began to think I could learn more about the world from the poets than the physicists.

*   *   *

I learned from reading a cover story on sadomasochistic sex clubs in *New York* magazine, a publication catering to the consumer habits of yuppies, that if you're into being chained and whipped or having candle wax dripped on your testicles or worse, there is an agreed-upon word you can say that means stop for real (as opposed to the random cries of "stop! stop!" that one might make at those moments as part of the fun). So in a world where they know that no doesn't always mean no, they've come up with the notion of the super-no.

Now when I think of s & m or b & d, as these practices are initialized in personal ads, I tend to think of pasty, pale men with oddly distributed body hair, women in the kind of outfits that Versace turned into dresses (could that have been his sin against humanity?), with crispy crunchy hair, dyed orange or a heavy black that looks like it may just be an oil slick. Everybody is very unclean-looking, like they don't have parents, like they were never babies who were cuddled in somebody's arms. As a result, anything that might be associated with that world—handcuffs you buy at the Pink Pussycat Boutique, a gag like the one in *Pulp Fiction*—is something I wish to avoid, and that would include the artifice of the whole situation. I am told that I am missing one of the great thrills in life, but I think if a boyfriend tied me up, I'd be more inclined to laugh at the theatrical absurdity of the situation. And then there's been so much that's been done in movies that everyone wants to try in real life, forgetting that in the privacy of your own home, there is no expert lighting and no clever camera angles. Forgetting also that there is nothing a man could do to a woman with a stick of butter that wouldn't make her think, *I hope you haven't mistaken yourself for Marlon Brando;* and there is really nothing any man could do to a woman's nipples with ice cubes that would not make her worry that she had mistakenly ended up with Mickey Rourke; and forget about gas masks and Bobby Vinton. Do you see what I'm saying? What was once the danger of sexuality has actually become a parody of itself, personified by a big fat man sitting in a Jacuzzi surrounded by runners-up from the Miss Hawaiian Tropic contest. This is not Hugh Hefner or even Larry Flynt; it's Al Goldstein.

And it's all just too damn laughable.

Sex, when dealt with as the kind of pursuit that requires regular visits to a club called the Vault; that goes from a no-equipment-necessary kind of human activity to one that involves metallic machinery which resembles nothing so much as the stuff that stocked an exercise room at a Catskills resort, circa 1953; and finally, when sex is so silly that you have fantasies about RuPaul that don't involve killing her/him or at least getting VH1 to cancel the show: if this is what sex is like when you are a thrill-seeker about it, then I am proud to be boring. I'm proud to be the most ardent proponent of the missionary position outside of turn-of-the-century China. I'd much rather live in the real world where no one needs to wear leather for the frisson of sexual heat to make itself felt, in a world that is not a game, that actually takes sex seriously, that cannot create a super-no, a word for no when you really mean it, a world where you trust the person you're with to make his own judgments or you trust yourself to leave or you trust nobody and nothing at all but go on anyway: a world where everyone knows there can be no word to stop a runaway train, where we all accept that violence just kind of erupts, that it might not stop where we want it to stop.

I remember learning in a biological anthropology class that men, left without the law to subjugate their natures, would be inclined to rape every woman that crossed their paths. (This is a difficult notion to grasp in a world where many men are too timid to ask a woman for her phone number.) But if these theories about male aggression in an antediluvian age are almost quaintly cartoonish, the emotional violence of modern love, and the potential for it to be acted out in physical ways, is not charming at all. The fact that the person you love may at any point during the fifty days or fifty years you spend together turn out to really surprise you, show himself to be quite lousy and deceitful and dishonest, may at any time abandon you with nothing, fall in love with his secretary or run off with his boss, that even the surest things in love often turn out to be just temporary shelter—this is a fact of love that makes everyone uncomfortable, and it's just too scary to contemplate. I have come to think of domestic violence as yet another of the many astonishments that may come our way, that may be a part of having chosen to love some particular man.

Just the same, this kind of fatalism comes quite close to naturalizing domestic violence, it is akin to saying that battery has its own ineluctable dynamic and because many couples in these tortured, brutal unions somehow stick together there must be a reason for it: that is the closest we come to employing Cartesian logic when explaining these relationships, and we thereby justify something bad just because it happens to be true. But how do we talk about observable uncomfortable facts—how do we talk about Nicole as responsible for her own life, and even for her death, because while she might have *finally* left him in the weeks leading up to the murder, for seventeen years she stayed? How do we say of an anonymous battered woman, a mere statistic, that she deserves the grief of her miserable marriage because she's been in it for so long, and besides, every time she leaves we spend hours at my kitchen table with legal pads planning a whole new life for her, and then the next day she goes back anyway—and I have a bad day at work because I got no sleep? How do we say to this woman something about how trying it is to be a friend in all this, that it would be easier if she just got some good pancake makeup and some large Jackie O. sunglasses and resigned herself to a life of camouflage that could very well end in murder? And more to the point, if we forget about individuals or what it is like to be party to a particular domestic violence situation, and just think about wife-beating as a public policy issue, how do we come up with a reasonable view of these relationships that allows us to admit to the ambivalent resignation that is the guiding force in most lives, to assert that just the same it's not okay to live with a man who beats you up, but still accept and understand that a woman living in this situation does not want to give up a sickness that is comfortable?

How do we simultaneously hold three states of mind that are philosophically reconcilable, but fall apart when there's another night at the kitchen table, another call to the police, another trip to the emergency room and finally a gruesome arrival at the coroner's office?

O.J. and Nicole got divorced in 1992, they attempted a reconciliation in 1993 and they split up once and for all shortly after Mother's Day in 1994. Nicole's thirty-fifth birthday was on May 19 of that year, and O.J. had presented her with a gift of diamond-drop earrings that were six carats apiece and an exquisite antique bracelet—a sparkling array of rows of diamonds and a row of sapphires in a platinum setting. By May 22, she had returned these ornaments, in an unusually scrupulous display of goodbye to all that, one that seems to have transformed a line drawn in the sand to one etched in stone. It was reported that O.J., in turn, passed his spurned offerings along to Paula Barbieri, who, in her aptly titled book *The Other Woman,* resignedly admits—echoing the words of Princess Diana in her BBC interview— that she had come to accept by that time that she "had entered a relationship not of two people, but of three."

But while Nicole spit jewelry in O.J.'s face to end it, in 1993 she was the one who had sought the reunion, actively campaigning for it, undeterred by a reluctant O.J., who apparently told her that he was happy with Paula. A five-page handwritten letter she sent to O.J. in

March of that year was omitted from the murder trial's evidence—in what seemed a rare triumph for the prosecution—but it joined a massive pile of documents that appeared to be known to everyone but the jury. "I want to be with you!" Nicole wrote. "I want to wake up with you in the morning and hold you at night. I want to hug and kiss you every day. I want us to be the way we used to be. O.J., I want to come home." She called him, and when he did not return her calls, she called again and again. She sent the videotapes of their wedding and of their children's births. She sent another note on an index card, saying, "O.J., I understand that it's probably too late but I have to do it for myself and the kids or I would never forgive myself." Since he would not return her phone calls at all, she assured him that she would only call in an emergency, and for him to please take that seriously and get back to her immediately. After that she only called his secretary, Cathy Randa, to try to get through to him, and Cathy would tell her that he didn't want to see her or talk to her, to just leave him alone. He told friends he liked his life without Nicole, he liked that there was no more screaming and yelling, he liked the way with Paula it wasn't so crazy.

And then in May, they got back together and went on vacation in Mexico.

So let's try saying these words again: *no means no*. Where did such a notion fit into the Brown-Simpson marriage? In a situation like theirs, when somebody ends up dead, it's not much different from understanding that on the nineteenth-century American frontier, when two men willingly entered a duel, they understood that it was not a matter of *if*, only of *who*. Marriages that involve a protracted history of domestic violence are basically the Wild West of relationships.

It does not matter that O.J. killed Nicole after she left, or that when a violent marriage ends in femicide, 75 percent of these murders occur after she has really severed ties: WHAT MATTERS IS THAT SHE STAYED. Blame it on battered wife syndrome, on her friends, her family, Southern California in general or Brentwood in particular: it doesn't matter. There are women who walk out on a man who punches them, and there are women who stay: that's the main difference between people who get killed and people who don't. Seventeen years later it's too late.

Nicole knew this: she wrote her will on May 8 and she was dead by June 12.

Please don't mistake any of this for a lack of sympathy for women in Nicole's situation. I'm just not sure what anyone can do besides feel bad. Feel bad and raise their own daughters as if it's possible that they will grow up to be President of the United States or CEO of Microsoft or the doctor who finds a cure for AIDS or the economist who discovers a way to end the inversely proportionate relationship between unemployment and inflation. Raise your daughters to laugh at any man who even *thinks* about throwing a punch, and raise them to be people with Filofaxes full of activities that are too fun and important and fascinating to be disturbed by a blow to the right eye. Raise your daughters to always think that any unpleasant situation—be it with a man or a manager or any of the expendable and fruitless annoyances that ruin our lives—just isn't worth it. Nobody *needs* this, *I* don't want it, I'm outta here, there are better things to do, anyone who disagrees can fuck off and die.

It's not easy to act this way, especially when it comes to love. The sanest women can become zany dingbats whenever a man shows up. I don't fancy myself to be terribly level, but I'd like to think that I would walk away from someone I loved who broke my arm, who tore at my skin, who made my eye so swollen I could not see through it. I think I would. But I know I might not. If someone came along and seemed to really understand me, to be able to touch my loneliness, to reach into me and find that very empty place and be able to make contact, to make me feel alive and loving and loved—well, I don't know how easy that would be to walk away from. And I think the violence, with its implied intensity and rawness, would be part of my belief in the strength of our connection. It is no wonder that women can find men who are violent compelling—in a world in which most of us are cut off from our physicality and willing to some extent to reason things out at times of conflict, men of fists and fisticuffs embody an urge to be done with all that chatter, to break through all the complexity and go to the raw, deep, hard emotions. Violent men can easily be romanticized and seen as frustrated, wanting to say so much but being hindered not just by the limitations of language, but also by some desire to be efficient and true, to go for immediacy and dispense with civility.

If a picture speaks a thousand words, it is easy to believe that a fist applied hard and fast to the eye, the cheek or the jaw may speak many thousand more. It is easy to forget that the only significant words in that manually made thought are probably *I hate you,* that the thousands of other unraveling ideas are too incoherent and deformed to be worth it. It is easy to forget so much about the simple diseased quality of male violence against women because it is exciting, because most of us are too numb to find very many things we especially want to argue constructively about, much less break things over.

But here is one thing I'd like to bring to any decision to stay: I'd like to accept my fate. I hope I would be able to realize that if I were choosing to believe that someone who hurt me badly could also love me, then I have accepted this dance, I have agreed to take the waltz, I am willing to engage in the games of manipulation and fear and injury that I will call love. I will accept the risk. I will sustain physical damage and I may die. But it is worth it. I finally have my Heathcliff, I finally have my mad love, my movie plot, my Tennessee Williams drama. I need this and want this, I may be sick as far as the rest of the world is concerned, but who are those people really, who are the ones who would wish to judge me? They—those people who go to couples therapy and out to dinner on double dates, they who buy food processors and ice cream makers and bread bakers and learn how to use them, they who buy the Sunday *New York Times* on Saturday night and get the puzzle done before going to sleep, they who bring picnic baskets to concerts in the park, those people who unpack everything on the day that they move and don't live surrounded by and stumbling over boxes and crates for weeks and months as if they may leave anytime, they who live in the light of day, who live always knowing, with everything around them obvious and clear: well, they don't know what love is. They don't know what I know.

I bet that's exactly what Nicole thought about life with O.J. I bet she accepted her fate and her doom—her second thoughts only surfaced and solidified at the very end. I bet she left a safe-deposit box with pictures of her bruised face in it and the diary with its record of sixty-one instances of abuse, and I bet she told her friends over and over again, "O.J.'s going to kill me," not because she was afraid it was so or that she was even trying to prevent it—I think she said it because she *knew* it was so. She was forecasting the weather, knowing full well that there's nothing you can do to stop a hurricane. Nicole did not even run for cover: she continued to live in the same neighborhood as O.J.—though she was planning a move to Malibu—and she was involved with him almost until the end. "You don't have dinner and live down the street from someone that you think is going to kill you," said one of the correspondents whose letter was included in *I Want to Tell You,* and you've got to concede the point. Even worse, for a couple of years preceding her death, Nicole had an on-and-off affair with Marcus Allen, one of O.J.'s best friends, another Heisman Trophy recipient, whom many consider the Juice's natural heir. She did this even though Marcus had gotten married in the backyard at Rockingham, she did this even though O.J.'s jealousy extended to all men walking the planet, but no one so much as this close friend and mighty symbol of who he had once been. She did this even though she knew O.J. was tailing her in his Bronco when she went to the market, the shoe store, the frame shop, everywhere (in fact, she was so aware of O.J. driving just behind her that she would wait until the last second to signal and make a turn, "just to fuck with him"). She did this even though she found O.J. hiding in the bushes outside her house. She did this in plain sight, allowing Marcus to park his car in her driveway, knowing perfectly well that O.J. was stalking her and would most certainly recognize it.

She did this, according to Faye Resnick, even after O.J. threatened to kill her if it continued, and even after numerous remonstrations from friends. "[Y]ou may be signing your death warrant," Ms. Resnick recalls telling Nicole. "How do you think this can lead to anything but O.J. blowing up and maybe carrying out his threat? Nicole, even if he doesn't kill you, what do you think he is going to do? This is even worse than before, if that's possible. Marcus just got married to Kathryn, what, six months ago? . . . Look, I'm not your mother, but you're doing something really off the wall here."

Good advice, but Nicole had become part of this pact at age seventeen, just out of high school, when she was too young to consent in any sane and reasoned manner to the life she chose—but that's the way it goes. She told people that O.J. had "molded" and "sculpted" her, that she was "his creation," a "product" of his design and desires.

Indeed, her belief that O.J. breathed the life force into the blob of clay she had once been is revealed when Nicole explains her need to keep trying with O.J. in terms of oxygen: "I'm afraid I might suffocate," she told Faye, unaware of the perversity of this metaphor, that usually one is strangled and smothered by a person's *presence,* not by his *absence.* For this woman the scary thing was not death *by* O.J.—it was death without him.

And their mutual obsession was completely Shakespearean in that their emotional lives, which should have remained essentially private, actually fueled drama and created activity around them, invited spectacle, demanded that others take sides, become accomplices. Faye Resnick makes it seem that minding this pair had become her full-time job. If theater seems more interesting to you than life, this is your kind of relationship. That somewhere in between all the craziness they managed to have children, be photographed for Christmas cards, make Hertz commercials, play golf, snort cocaine, go running, remodel a home, have Scrabble parties (my guess is that O.J. did not participate), have sex as many as five times a day and even exit a gathering at their own house, with Nicole saying by way of explanation (according to Faye), "Excuse us, please—we're going to the bedroom and fuck now": that they got anything done amid so much mess must indicate real resilience.

At times they must have believed that they could go on, back and forth, on and on like this forever. They could have continued the madness even if they remained divorced. They could have been like Burton and Taylor or Olivier and Leigh: I love you I hate you Please go No stay. With these couples, it's never really over. Vivien Leigh was too depressed and difficult for Laurence Olivier, they of course divorced, he even remarried. And still you know that she was the great love of his life, that he never got over her, that he died in her thrall, but the relationship was just impossible day by day. Same with Burton and Taylor, who surely never replaced each other—he ended with some schoolmarmish Englishwoman with all the glamour and sensuality of a scone; and Ms. Taylor, well, God knows she tried—but just the same, what they had together was completely dysfunctional.

Perhaps if it weren't for the abrupt stop to the madness that was mandated by the stab wounds that one of them inflicted on the other,

O.J. and Nicole could have been like those famous theatrical couples. They might well have aged into a situation that found them thwarting the temptation to try again, however melancholy that resignation may be, no matter how sad it is to admit that love can be corrosive like lye. "It ate their future complete it waited for them / Staring and starving," writes Ted Hughes, in "The Lovepet," another *Crow* poem. "They gave it screams it had gone too far / It ate into their brains / It ate the roof / It ate lonely stone it ate wind crying famine / It went furiously off / They wept they called it back it could have everything." The brilliance of this poem—well, one of many such aspects—is that it tells of a couple whose strife and intensity is mutually annihilating, whose love for each other is wearing when it should be fortifying; and yet, the two people who are destroying each other are presented as a unified front: they are fighting against love, they are fighting to save love, mostly they are mistaking a mess for a mission. They are very much in it together, it is their *feelings* that are the enemy—as if their love and all its attendant emotions were an external force, an interloper, even a marauding army. The one constant in all destructive relationships— for men and women both—is a tendency to privilege the couple above the individual, a style of relating which allows even people as bright and gifted as Plath and Hughes to forget that a couple is made of two *separate* people. A couple desperate to stay in their sick dynamic can blame the whole wide world for tearing them apart, they can point to El Niño, to a butterfly who flapped her wings in Japan and sent a breeze their way, they can feel under siege, as if they've been thrown into a centrifuge that's pulling at them, taking them limb for limb, turning them into amputees, diminished though they are, they are still together.

Let there be no doubt that Nicole had to be complicit in O.J.'s game or it—this relationship with a life of its own—could not have been an adolescent of age seventeen when Nicole was killed. After all, when O.J. rejected Nicole, leaving a possibility that their dynamic would be defused, she begged him to take her back. Perhaps had the murder never occurred, there might have been a few more cycles of violence and realliance, since studies do show that on average, it takes a battered woman between seven and ten failed attempts at leaving before she gets out for real. And no one seems to know whether it takes that many tries because she needs to work up the courage, or if the comings and goings are enjoyable in and of themselves.

As a low-rent cowboy-spooked version of *Who's Afraid of Virginia Woolf?*, Sam Shepard's play *Fool for Love*—which as a movie starred the author and Kim Basinger—is ninety minutes of a couple acting out their emotional violence and sexual rage in an otherwise quiet bungalow colony that is sprawled out in the middle of the Mojave Desert. While they keep getting together and breaking up, the creepy, phantom presence of Harry Dean Stanton lingers in the background as if to suggest that this might all just be a bad dream or a bad drug trip—and that's if you're lucky. In the very first scene Eddie, the couple's male half, announces that he's come 2,482 miles just to see Mae—an awful long way to go just to be yelled at. Shepard very smartly wrote both the play and its screen adaptation—I think it's probably his best work—to include all the usual lines that indicate that these two people are inextricably bound: "You know we're connected, Mae. We'll always be connected. That was decided years ago." "You'll never get rid of me. I'll track you down everywhere you go. I know how your mind works." "The second we saw each other, we knew we'd never stop being in love." These lines are written in the language of genre fiction—spoken as the clichés people resort to when fighting in love, when they are too tired to argue, when it's best to just say what's easy, because it really doesn't matter anyway, there is no chance that you will break up for real.

And Shepard's all-purpose dialogue is such that the setting might be an American desert oasis, but it could just as easily take place in Ibiza or Istanbul or Ipswich: he's provided a blueprint for conducting a sick relationship anywhere on earth. The main characteristic of these kinds of unions, which Shepard's spareness makes clear, is that they don't end, the adhesive at the heart of this heart-bond clings and sticks like bubble-gum in a knot of hair. At the end of *Fool for Love,* when the whole pathetic arrangement of cabins goes up in flames, the couple gets into a car and takes off together, understanding down deep and deep down that *we belong together,* like the refrain in a Rickie Lee Jones song.

And almost every group of friends has at least one problem couple in its midst at one time or another—usually in youth, when one has the energy for such psychodramas; by middle age, the ones who are still alive have grown bored with being driven crazy, and find they much prefer to just be bored. Usually physical brutality is not the issue. Maybe it's loud public fights, throwing wineglasses, smashing plates, spending an entire dinner party locked in the host's only bathroom caught in a screaming match that won't end, dragging near-strangers into their melee, as in *Who's Afraid of Virginia Woolf?* or, if you think about it, like Tom and Daisy Buchanan in *The Great Gatsby*, who seem to mop the floor with the people they pull through their mess. These couples end up driving everyone around them crazy, there is the tedious back-and-forth, you've spent hours talking it through, helping her find the strength to gather her belongings in some big shopping bags and just bail—and then next time you talk (maybe an hour later), they're getting married, and you feel, ridiculously enough, kind of gypped, because you have become a co-dependent accessory to their situation, and it's taking up your life and time and *you start to want to see results*. No longer do you want to be helpful: you want to get progress reports that you can live with.

"This is the part that breaks my heart," Cici Shahian, one of Nicole's best friends, told Sheila Weller, referring to the way friends aided and abetted in the reconciliation with Mr. Simpson. Cici occupies an odd position in Nicole's clique of girlfriends, as cousin of O.J. intimate Robert Kardashian (who apparently stopped speaking to O.J. after the criminal trial, and was thought to have been a snitch for Lawrence Schiller's account of the case, *An American Tragedy*), and probably the only one of these chicks who is single, and certainly the only one who holds a regular job (working at Dove Books, the notoriously cheap, reputedly sleazy-slimy Beverly Hills publisher of tabloid books like *You'll Never Make Love in This Town Again* and Faye Resnick's two memoirs). Cici, who seems to manage to live alone without too much trouble, still thought Nicole might be better off back in the mingle of marriage. "We thought that, for *all* the good reasons—the kids, the family, the relatives, the beach, the birthdays, the holidays: for all the things she loved . . . we encouraged her," Ms. Shahian explains. "We encouraged her to go back. Nobody wants to be lonely."

These friends, like Nicole herself, probably hoped things *would* get better. Certainly they could not maintain the high pitch for very much longer. Usually marriages that involve rage and infidelity and the use of household appliances and Tiffany lamps as instruments of mass destruction must necessarily burn themselves out. "It is a situation many young married couples find themselves in—one that perhaps more couples find themselves in than don't—but it is a situation that ordinarily doesn't last: the couple either reconnects or dissolves," writes Janet Malcolm in *The Silent Woman,* in reference to a marriage brought to crisis and damage by the serpentine intrusion of adultery. "Life goes on. The pain and bitterness and exciting awfulness of sexual jealousy and sexual guilt recede and disappear. People grow older. They forgive themselves and each other, and may even come to realize that what they are forgiving themselves and each other for is youth." The particular marriage whose course Malcolm was charting was the Plath–Hughes debacle, which ended, like the Brown–Simpson mess, not in a state of grace, not with acceptance of wrongs made right, not with deliverance from sorrow and sin, but with death. These women will remain, in Malcolm's words, "forever fixed in the mess . . . never reaching the age when the tumults of young adulthood can be looked upon with rueful sympathy and without anger and vengefulness." As brilliant as Sylvia Plath was and as vapid as Nicole Brown appears to have been, they are alike in that they both died emotionally intestate, guilt and blame and anger and resentment never properly willed or willed away. The last tense discussion is left at a stalemate, a confusion of feelings are stopped short, bottlenecked. Ted Hughes probably has been permanently spent, sapped of some vitality, walking around with the weight of Sylvia's suicide in 1963, which was followed, in 1969, by the suicide of his inamorata Assia Wevill, the adulteress whom Plath blamed for her marriage's decline—the new and improved replacement model who not only mimicked her predecessor by asphyxiating herself in an oven, but outdid her by gassing her two-year-old daughter to death at the same time.

And even without the added encumbrance of mental illness or poetic genius or delicate artistic temperament, Prince Charles is stuck in some moment of rift without rapprochement that he needs to live with always, with regard to Princess Diana. He will always feel there's some conversation they never had, or maybe just some lighthearted moments, when she is married to some international financier and he is married to Camilla, and they are all in attendance at William's or Harry's nuptials, and they can smile at each other and think: *It was worth it after all.* They will never have that.

And, of course, O.J. will never have that with Nicole. But he needn't feel bad. That relationship ran its course, all its possible permutations, and came to its one singular conclusion, fairly nailing down the cycle of pleasure and pain in a relationship predicated on deceit and abuse, in a partnership where the players have come to love the headache because of the relief they feel when the aspirin kicks in. So people who claim they would love the relationship they are in if only the fighting and bickering, the cheating and lying, the punches and kicks—all the pain—would just go away, if only we could begin at the beginning before it got bad, and this time we'll take a different fork in the road: all the people who want to subtract the main ingredient from something that's been cooking into its current state for months or years are just kidding themselves, failing to see how integral to the moments of joy are the hours and days of agony.

People tend to make the mistake of believing that relationships are pure personality, that left to the abstract arena of just two people who love each other, that in a world where the world disappears, all would be fine, romance would thrive like wildfire in California. People tend also to think that it is circumstances that get in the way of love, that the names Montague and Capulet killed Romeo and Juliet, that World War II separated Rick and Ilsa when she wore blue and the Germans wore gray. They even believe that paparazzi and drunk-driving killed Dodi and Diana, they believe that had the couple lived they'd be planning a wedding and moving into a house in the suburbs of Paris. But people are wrong, failing to see that everyone functions within his circumstances, that being a partisan or a princess is not a mere accident, and even if it is, it is part of you: to be born on a farm in Iowa or to a physics professor at MIT is as integral to who you are as blue eyes or a tendency to go bald in your late thirties. The fantasy of escape from external atmosphere—*Let's run away forever! Let's go to Tahiti like Gauguin and live like savages! Let's hide under the big bright sun in Baja!*—may just work out once in a while, at least for as long as the relationship remains mutually obsessive (time passes ve-e-e-e-ry slowly when you are far from civilization, in a world without clocks). But most people are stuck in the workaday world.

So let's get to the truth here: Romeo and Juliet died because histrionics and teenage love made them crazy, crazy enough to think there is nothing in a name. Rick sent Ilsa off into heroism, appearing to sacrifice his love for her to the greater causes that depended on preserving her marriage, for no better reason than that he was a commitment-phobe, plain and simple. He couldn't deal with the permanent presence of the woman he was smitten by, he couldn't deal with *what next?* For Rick, self-marooned in Morocco, it was easier to talk about a hill of beans and walk into the sunset with Claude Rains than to grapple further with love that is future, with life that goes beyond the present. And Diana died because it was as inevitable as London rain, because if you are British royalty there will, somehow, always be an ugly end if you choose to consort with a presumably overbearing, certainly nouveau riche rogue of ill-repute, a man whose machismo probably made him shout at the driver, "Faster! Lose them!" at the sight of some motorbikes and cameras. It happened because Dodi was trying to impress the princess with his imperiousness, with his power and her resulting safety, and he did this even though he knew no one has ever died of being photographed, not even the Amish—but plenty have been lost to car crashes.

But no matter what, all of these star-crossed lovers functioned in an atmosphere made to match their personalities, so that the family feud heightened the romance for Shakespeare's adolescents, the need to choose duty to the cause over a chance at true love kind of makes the sand blowing in your face and the sound of airplanes at the end of *Casablanca* feel infinitely more satisfying than any relationship that would have followed.

I hope I am not the only one who appreciated the way *The English Patient,* when adapted for film in the grand manner of an old-fashioned epic, functioned as a corrective to the *Casablanca* code, with its pretense of public duty before private desire, particularly when it's convenient, when it lets Bogey look at a girl and say, "We'll always have Paris," when it also lets him imply that we'll never have children, we'll never have in-laws, we'll never have fights about money, we'll never have to choose between tartar-control and peroxide toothpaste—and best of all, we will be able to say that it was good for the Jews. In *The English Patient,* however, Ralph Fiennes in the title role is a Hungarian count who experiences himself as a citizen of the world, his greatest loyalty is to air flight and the desert sand. Love, for him, for this weightless and careless man, is an ennobling and humbling experience, and he falls like a plane crash for a married British woman. By the end of the movie—which chooses human beings over international events—he willingly surrenders his maps to the Germans in exchange for transport to his ailing mistress, who lies dying in a desert cave.

Now, it's not like he happily helps the Nazis: a series of events, lost passports, misplaced papers, British soldiers who want to imprison him for his indeterminate nationality—it is only in the confusion and mess of war that the possibility that love can thrive, even if it is only between two people, starts to seem more significant than ever. Here, the message seems to be, is a man who knows to choose love over politics. "It's as if the Ralph Fiennes character were saying, 'I guess the outcome of the war against Hitler doesn't amount to a hill of beans in this crazy world compared to the problems of two little people,' " Rick Hertzberg complained in *The New Yorker,* sometime after the film received the Oscar for Best Picture. Now, I don't know if the fact that my reaction to the movie was diametrically opposed to Mr. Hertzberg's indicates a difference between men and women or just a difference in sensibility between me and him, but it seems to me that the reason wars have been fought is to make the world safe for love, safe for pursuit of happiness. It's not that the problems of two people matter more than Hitler, but rather that it is so unlikely that two little people will make a difference anyway, the purest protest against the Nazi hatred is to choose the personal, to refuse to let your heart be a pawn of the political.

*　　*　　*

Of course, the solution to this conundrum of male violence and female vulnerability, and one that has worked perfectly well for most people, is what's known as civilization. Whatever behaviors may have been acceptable among the Cro-Magnon men, in the world we live in it is not okay for a man to get woundingly violent with a woman. What keeps the urge in check—on those occasions when, as it is put in many a blues standard, a man has a right mind to shoot his woman down—is that most Protestant of virtues, otherwise known as self-control. In fact, this inner consciousness of the limits on physical force that a man might use against his wife or girlfriend is so inbred and instinctual at this point that most guys don't even *want* to beat the women they love. They don't even much care to beat up the men they hate. In fact, most likely they don't want to do anything more at the end of a hard working day than grab a beer from the fridge and park themselves on the sofa in front of the television set.

And there lies the perversity in this whole discussion: it is, finally, irrelevant. While the O. J. Simpson trial was the most outsize celebrity event involving spousal battery (or anything else, for that matter), many smaller-scale incidents have received intense and temporary media scrutiny before disappearing into the black hole of tabloid-TV archives; and each of these situations—because they involve taboo violence, the battle of the sexes and issues of power and control that all of us struggle with on some level—come to seem, for their moment, like Everyrelationship, like the center of the universe.

It was not so long ago that Robin Givens and Mike Tyson felt compelled to sit for an interview with Barbara Walters—in the equanimity of their Bernardsville, New Jersey, home, as if sitting in their drawing room for a society artist's portrait in oils—the small and delicate *Head of the Class* starlet complaining for all the world to know that she was afraid of her husband, she feared for her life, he drove her BMW into a tree, and what's next? At the time, *The Star* and *The Enquirer* had anointed Ms. Givens as Delilah-of-the-week, and as she began to speak in a shriekish tone, she only enhanced her shrewish reputation. In the meantime Iron Mike sat there impassive the whole time, glassy-eyed and dopey-faced, a big bear injected with some industrial-strength sedative. Between rape and jail and ear-biting in the ring, few people can remember Robin Givens as Tyson's wife—few people can remember Robin Givens at all. Nor does it seem as anything more than a mirage or a mistake that at one time Sean Penn was married to Madonna, at one time they thought it wise to make a movie together, at one time they ended up in *Shanghai Surprise*. Once it ended—as it had to, this was not exactly a Paul Newman–Joanne Woodward matchup—*People*'s cover story for the week of 14 December 1987 was headlined "Diary of a Mad Marriage," and chronicled the "jealousy, booze and brawling" that precipitated the demise of Sean and Madonna's brief union. Other, less respectable publications catalogued the various ways Sean was supposed to have abused Madonna, hints at handcuffs and ropes abounded beside images of sexual sadism and intimations of real rape (which, in fantasy free form, Madonna later seems to have reenacted in the book *Sex*).

Axl Rose and Stephanie Seymour could not have looked more in love than they did when caught in a smiling embrace on the cover of the May 1992 *Interview* magazine—with additional lovey-dovey Bruce Weber shots of lots of tongue-twisting kissing inside. But in due time both Ms. Seymour—the Victoria's Secret model who appeared as the bride who dies on her wedding night in the video for Guns n' Roses' "November Rain"—and Rose's former wife, Erin Everly, made allegations about getting badly beaten by Axl—and this too became a *People* cover, under the rubric "Battered Beauties." With unusually bad timing for a sometime professional boxer, Mickey Rourke, playing the pugilist at rest, was accused of slapping, knocking over and then kicking his model wife Carré Otis just a little over a month after O.J. killed Nicole. In the you-never-can-tell category of wife-beaters was David Soul, the blonde half of *Starsky and Hutch,* who, as the John Tesh of his day, sang "Don't Give Up on Us Baby"—a quintessentially seventies hit of the sentimental, rainbow-decal-on-faded-blue-jeans variety, an accidental and embarrassing mood that has been deliberately recast in the nineties as Lite FM. Mr. Soul (apologies to Neil Young) was exposed as physically abusive in October 1982, while he assumed the Humphrey Bogart role in an NBC miniseries version of *Casablanca.* (I'm not making this up.) After a drunk Soul returned from the set late one night, he announced his arrival at his Bel Air home by cursing and striking at his third wife, Patti (there has since been a fourth). She called the police, who charged the actor with misdemeanor battery. Patti alleged that, in his alcoholic rages, Soul's violence had resulted in broken bones in her hand and finger, and his cruelty had included sitting on her stomach for twenty minutes while she was seven months pregnant, haranguing her about her assorted flaws.

Over the years, the celebrity rap sheet of woman beaters has included Charlie Sheen's apparent pummeling of porn star Ginger Lynn, and an ugly public court case against William Hurt, with an ex-lover seeking reparations for, among other things, his brutal and bruising temper. Perhaps it is simply seeing that the expected—Axl Rose, Sean Penn—and the unexpected—William Hurt? David Soul? *Hutch?*—seem equally represented on this roster of rogues can make it seem like all the men on earth are beating up all the women on earth. It's hard not to think, though you know him not at all, that if that sweet, sensitive Jackson Browne with those gentle blue eyes and boyishly shiny hair, if that nice California guy who sings songs about girls who commit suicide can take a swing at a woman, then all bets are off. To assume the guise of public service and make us all feel connected to these sad stories of woman-beating, gossip items about domestic violence are often offered up with some version of these statistics: two thousand women per year are killed by their partners; every fifteen seconds a woman in the United States is beaten, a total of three to four million women annually; 30 percent of all female murder victims were killed by their husbands, ex-husbands or boyfriends; in 1993 alone, there were 300,000 domestic violence calls to the police in New York City; the Department of Justice, which has been keeping track of spousal abuse incidents only since 1984, reports that *most* acts of violence against women were committed by a man known to them.

The aforementioned statistics are, I would guess, as accurate and impartial as this kind of data gathering gets. On the other hand, the National Coalition Against Domestic Violence asserts that at least one incident of abuse will occur in two-thirds of all marriages: now, this is the kind of statement that is just fodder for those who think this problem has been exaggerated. My guess is that in damn near 100 percent of all marriages, at some point somebody throws an object in an intentionally hurtful direction, somebody gets smacked in the face or kicked in the balls, and thoughts of a knife to the jugular or arsenic dumped into the pot roast could be daily events, but what that has to do with *two-thirds* of couples I don't know. And then there are other statements that are more specific, and still dangerously misleading: Alana Bowman, head of the Los Angeles City Attorney's Domestic Violence Unit told *The New York Times* that "unofficial statistics from the coroner's office" show a killing as a result of spousal abuse "every day and a half." I defy anyone to tell me what that means. Why are these numbers "unofficial"? Why would the coroner know something that, say, the police officers investigating the death wouldn't know? For that matter, if the death is sufficiently suspicious so that the coroner's findings are consistent with a domestic violence homicide, why *aren't* the cops looking into it? And wouldn't it be easier to say "every thirty-six hours" than "every day and a half"? (It also seems worth noting that the coroner Ms. Bowman is referring to would be the same man, Dr. Lakshmanan Sathyavagiswaran, who forgot to get renamed on his way through Ellis Island, took eight days of direct examination and droning exegesis in O.J.'s criminal trial to say, in essence, that stab wounds were the cause of death, and was called "loony" in *The New Republic* after demonstrating a decapitation technique on one of the prosecutors, substituting a ruler for a knife.)

In this numeromania of facts and figures—and many of these are so easy to find that they were in an appendix in Faye Resnick's second book—it starts to feel like: So much gynocrime, so little time. And I don't mean to be flippant, but this barrage of percentages and fractions and decimals and likelihoods and estimates, which is meant to give all this human mess the solid, spreadsheet feel of some simple bookkeeping, actually does just that: these numbers are reductive. Some try desperately to be accurate but none are unbiased: the Justice Department errs on the side of caution, women's advocacy groups tend toward overstatement. Despite what is likely a wide margin of error, we trust statistics more than we trust anecdotal evidence, so much so that just after Nicole's murder, in the same week *Time, Newsweek,* CNN and ABC all reported—completely erroneously— that domestic violence was the leading cause of injury to women ages fifteen to forty-four. All these respected news organizations made the same mistake because someone or some group released inaccurate data, and even those who should know better salivate over statistics, repeating and reporting them without question. Anecdotal information does not have the feel of fact, does not have the integrity of integers and percentage points.

But it is particularly this kind of situation—the unaccountable cognitive dissonance of two people sharing a home, by choice, with one party committing against the other the kinds of crimes you lock the doors to avoid—that makes it essential to know the details in order to understand how something euphemistically called "spousal abuse" can be presented as flat-out wife-beating. I knew nothing about Nicole when she was a living and breathing doll-woman, but after her death, the profusion of photographs presenting her image and pictures of her life and how she lived it made it feel to me like she was absolutely, 100 percent alive. The vacant, faraway stare that characterized all the stock glossies of Ms. Brown when she was alive—she often looked like a jack-o'-lantern, as if her eyes had been injected with steroids or her brain had been replaced by a halogen bulb—became rich with anxiety and panic and precarious circumstance: the vacancy was suddenly occupied, the furniture neurotically shifted and rearranged. (It's all about: should I stay or should I go? Stay: I get Rockingham, lots of presents—though he's generous when away also—family life, parents happy, get beaten. Go: live on wrong side of Sunset, get stalked, Marcus Allen's dick, cute boys at Starbucks, get beaten.)

And just the same, however enlightening these public griefs and trials and tribulations may be, for most of us this is never going to be an issue. Whatever they are showing us on television, no matter how much blood John Woo can get into his movies, even if Wes Craven has made it into the mainstream, even if video games and comic books are red and gooey with misogyny and murder—no matter how shameless the vile display, most of us are going to go through life without ever receiving the benefit of a single violent experience on the home front. We may walk around quietly desperate, loaded up with bad and ugly thoughts about what would happen right now if I had a gun, if I had a hammer, if I could tear down that wall, if I could blow up that building. But very few women will be pulped by their spouses, and very few are even going to have hot wax dripped on their breasts—even if they ask for it. Which does not mean that domestic violence is not a problem: of course it is; even according to the most conservative statistics—if we say that "only" one and a half to two million women a year are battered—things are bad enough. But I take a look around me at most men functioning in the world, and they seem scared, more scared than women, frightened as cornered rats who can't figure why everyone is jumping on the table for fear of a puny rodent. Men, quite simply, seem so benighted and bewildered about women, they are so unconfident in their dealings with us that the discussion of male violence against women or male hatred of women is strictly academic. Of course, it is in this atmosphere of bafflement that the male advantage—physical strength—is most likely to assert itself in frustrated agony, but looking at the world outside of celebrities and criminals, it really does seem that most men, like most women, are doing the best they can, and it's tough enough without anyone wanting to toss the monkey wrench of physical violence into the brouhaha. Whatever is going on in the world where love is an extreme sport, most of us can't master the mundane. Male confusion, fear, love-hate issues, all those *Cosmopolitan* articles: that's reality for most of us.

And of course we are sick of discussing it.

All those conversations about how he won't commit, he won't move in with me, he won't marry me, he never does his share of the laundry, he doesn't spend enough time with the kids, he's too possessive, he doesn't like it when I wear short skirts, he wishes I wore sexier clothes, he hates it when I ask him if I look fat, he hates it when I flirt with other men, I hate it when he flirts with other women, I think he's having an affair, he thinks I'm having an affair, I wish he *would* have an affair, I'm not ready to marry him, he'll leave if I don't move in with him, he's too attentive, he never asks about my work, one day I just know he's going to leave me, sometimes I wonder who it is that I have been living with all these years.

There's a lot of potential for violence in all those thoughts, it is all so tenuous, all relationships, even the strong ones, have some tender and sensitive spot that can be so easily abraded, the smallest bit of rough touch and all unspoken issues threaten to explode and implode and mess up everything. Sometimes this is precisely what the relationship needs, but often enough—well, put it this way: lots of oysters are irritated by sand, but very few turn those granular intrusions into pearls. Some differences are meant to be ignored, not worked through.

Which is why people in long-term relationships that are healthy learn to be careful, learn to live with what they cannot understand. Mostly I think that works: the great calm I sense in people who have been married a long time is not just that they've stopped asking the miserable unpleasant questions, but that they aren't really curious any longer.

In "The Girls in Their Summer Dresses," Irwin Shaw's 1939 short story that is best known nowadays for lending its title to fashion spreads in May, a happy young couple bouncing about Greenwich Village on a sunny winter day suddenly hit upon a moment of truth in their marriage that would have best never surfaced. As they walk along lower Fifth Avenue, the wife becomes increasingly distressed at her husband's ogling and double-taking and just plain staring at all the women who walk by. It makes her "feel rotten inside, in my stomach," and on that note the young couple duck into a corner bar, they are deep into their brandy snifters, they are drinking Courvoisier on Sunday morning, breakfast is history. At first the husband tells her he'd never cheat, he's happily married, but after a while she insists on having him tell her why he likes checking out girls so much, and pretty soon he lists every type of woman he likes to look at: "girls in the offices," "salesgirls in stores," "famous beauties who've taken six hours to get ready," "young girls at the football games," and of course, "the girls in their summer dresses." He goes on about wandering near department stores at lunchtime to see the women shopping, he talks about women in furs, and women with strange hats, and after a while it's clear there's nothing in a skirt that he doesn't like to look at.

Most women, I think, can live with men's promiscuous eyes—partly, it is my guess, because they have no idea what kind of detailed and exaggerated visions men get just by looking—but in Shaw's story, the husband's confession, far from facilitating intimacy, creates a rupture that is going to put a permanent strain on their marriage. The husband admits that sometimes he wishes he were free to chase these girls. "Someday," she asks, in tears, "you're going to make a move . . . Aren't you? Come on, tell me. Talk. Aren't you?" The husband has no desire to go in this direction. "Maybe," he says, although any sane man would have said no. She presses him some more, says that he knows he's going to leave her someday. "Yes," he finally says. "I know."

He knows that one day when she is menopausal and undesirable, he is sure to walk out on her, one day he will no longer be able to resist the pretty young things.

After the husband's confession—or reluctant admission—the day goes on, and the marriage goes on. But we all know there's this tension, this death warrant, imposing its gloom on these people's lives, and this couple is going to live with it, at least for a while, maybe for a very long time. This truth that the husband has revealed will lie between both partners like a cocked and loaded gun that either can grab and use at any time. The stupidest part of the conversation is that it is actually in no way predictive of what will happen to this marriage: it telescopes into the future on the basis of emotions that may only be true in the present. The husband may lose interest in all the pretty girls, he may decide his happy life and wife are more important, he may be paralyzed in a car accident and find that his fantasies have backfired—he may be wheelchair-bound while it is his wife who lingers around office buildings, checking out the handsome men in their Brooks Brothers suits, men whose arms and legs and other limbs still move.

Far better never to learn certain secrets.

But the alternative requires such willful resignation. Bruce Springsteen's "Brilliant Disguise" captures the horror at the heart of intimacy like no other rock song I know of. "Now you play the loving woman / I play the faithful man / But just don't look too close / Into the palm of my hand," he sings, both advocating and despairing of the charade. "When you look at me / You better look hard and look twice / Is this me baby or just a brilliant disguise?" When you are in such close quarters with another person and still have to spend so much time just accepting all the things you can't understand, the accumulated rage must be enormous, a murder waiting to happen.

And it extends to other relationships: 70 percent of child murders are committed by one or both parents; and when a child is killed, the FBI places the odds at 12 to 1 that the slayer is not a stranger. In general, if you are going to be killed, it will probably be by someone you know. One of the reasons it was so foolish for the police who leapt over the fence at Rockingham in the initial hours after Nicole Brown's murder to claim that they were just trying to find O.J. to let him know his ex-wife had been killed before the media got there—this was their excuse for not getting a search warrant, later one of many details used to discredit the prosecution's case—is that when *anyone* is killed, the spouse or closest equivalent is *always* the first suspect.

This is, of course, a hard thing to understand. I keep trying, I try really hard, to imagine how I might snap or what might happen that would make me kill anyone, much less someone I love. Now, if you think of killing as a logical extension of any number of activities, it makes sense: I don't go around getting angry at people I don't know, I don't have any harsh feelings or feelings at all for strangers, and this is a sign that I am sane. Only the insane lash out at random. Those are the people who walk around muttering to themselves and punctuate that with the occasional outburst. So the decision, if you think of it that way, to kill someone you are close to is a sign that you are in your right mind, sort of. What is *really* weird is a guy like, say, Charles Whitman, who gets into the tower at the University of Texas and shoots at no one in particular, just a lone sniper sprinkling shots at whoever happened to be walking across the Austin campus on that particular day. Whitman's crime is just nuts, whereas O. J. Simpson behaved in a way that, to anyone who has ever been in a jealous rage, is relatively coherent.

There are so many crimes—child abuse, incest, murdering a spouse or family member—that seem incomprehensible to most of us who are not perpetrators. Incest, in particular, is a hard one to figure. Children, I suppose, can be sexy, but what kind of sick person would want to fuck an eight-year-old—especially if she were his own child? As much as this activity seems clearly demented, as does the idea of murdering a first-degree relative, the horror and disbelief most of us feel in the face of a JonBenet Ramsey or a Hedda Nussbaum, or the smug ease with which we assign the label of unmodified and unmediated evil upon Susan Smith, the South Carolina woman who drowned her two children in her car, our easy moral indignation against those who commit crimes against those they love, the ones who violate the most vulnerable, their trusting children, actually reflects how close to the surface our own feelings of rage and inappropriate desire within our own households are. How many mothers, left with a screaming and crying baby, a husband at work or out with the boys, have not wanted to throttle their own children?

As Sigmund Freud pointed out in *Totem and Taboo,* the reason incest, murder and other interpersonal offenses are taboo is not because they a priori disgust us, but precisely because they *don't*—and we need to be made to see horror in them or we will destroy ourselves. "To explain [legal and moral prohibitions against incest] by the existence of an instinctive dislike of sexual intercourse with blood relatives—that is by an appeal to the fact that there *is* a horror of incest—is clearly unsatisfactory," Freud writes, "for social experience shows that, in spite of this supposed instinct, incest is no uncommon event even in our present-day society, and history tells us of cases in which incestuous marriage between privileged persons was actually the rule." Similarly, Freud's study of the dreams of "normal people"—those who are not neurotic and doomed to become one of his case studies—shows that "we ourselves are subject, more strongly and more often than we suspect, to a temptation to kill someone and that temptation produces psychical effects even though it remains outside of our consciousness." For Freud, the man who introduced Victorian Vienna and then the whole Western world to the dark sub-rosa of the psyche, full of impulses just barely kept in check—repressed, restrained by law, inert as sticks of dynamite that have not yet been lit—many of us, without even knowing it, are just one cool remove from doing something terrible and sinful. If Johnny Cash, the original Man in Black, can boast that he "shot a man in Reno / Just to see him die," most of us, who will in the end find that there is no better reason for our behavior than the one Mr. Cash gives, will commit our misdeed against the closest and nearest person, and tell ourselves it was the right thing to do.

*   *   *

"If batterers had green dots on their heads warning women, no one would get involved with them," says Sherry Frohman, the executive director of the New York State Coalition Against Domestic Violence. "It's just a fact that so many men are shits and women just have bad luck."

I, of course, don't believe this. I feel certain people are knowing participants in their own sick dramas, and the ninety-minute telephone conversation I have with Ms. Frohman exhausts me, saddens me in a way that's tiring because it serves to underscore the great divide between advocacy and clear thinking. Which is to say, if you are going to be an advocate on behalf of victims of domestic violence—or of anything, because even crimes that don't require your complicity often receive your retroactive consent—you can't think about it too much. Like Andrea Dworkin, you have to just say, *It's the perpetrator, stupid,* and leave it at that. You really have to believe that these women would have avoided the man with the green dot on his head, though I believe that, quite the contrary, they'd have been more drawn in, more quickly.

I recall an astute moment in the movie *9½ Weeks* when Elizabeth, the female character, asks the domineering man who has so easily absorbed her into his sadomasochistic love scheme, "How did you know? How did you know I would respond to you as I have?" His response—something about seeing himself in her—does not nearly address the complexity of the question, which was, of course, the problem with the whole movie, with its depiction of sexual violence lite. But still, the screenplay knew enough to *ask*—and in a certain way, it also showed the good sense not to try to really explain *too* much in a movie that was, after all, not an art house film, but rather aimed at a popular American audience.

In the end, trying to understand a phenomenon like domestic violence is always going to be interesting and wasteful. On the one hand, it is not relevant to most of our lives except as a source of fascination, and on the other hand, if you happen to be a person who cares enough to want to help battered women, to work in a shelter or become a counselor, the best thing you can do is feel sympathy and warmth and kindness and just never ask why. I've got this strange feeling that if you try too hard to understand, you will probably end up saying, *Go back home, you belong together, don't you see you'll never escape?*

"No one can comprehend what goes on under the sun," wrote King

Solomon in Ecclesiastes 8:17. "Despite all his efforts to search it out, man cannot discover its meaning. Even if a wise man claims he knows, he cannot really comprehend it." Solomon was, of course, said to be one of the wisest men of all time—the title of smartest, which is distinct in that intelligence is not the same as wisdom, probably belongs to his father, King David—and this statement reflects his good sense. During his prosperous, productive, peaceful reign, Solomon mostly managed to keep away from trouble—the Queen of Sheba being his *bête nôire*—and to avoid examining too closely that which is clearly nuts. Solomon grew up the fair-haired, favorite son in a royal household where brothers raped sisters and siblings slaughtered siblings, and he probably perceived that much of this discord could be attributed to the overly contemplative David, who as the patriarch of this whole paradigmatically dysfunctional family, spent far too much time meditating on his sorrows and too little time just insisting that everyone behave. And sometimes it seems that with domestic violence, diplomacy is the only correct approach, because reason shall surely fail.

Trying to comprehend the illogic of accepting aching acts from or levying an attack on someone you love is like studying Scientology or the Moonies or any cult from the outside or trying to understand alcoholism or drug addiction if you've never had a taste for much more than the mild recreational high: no matter how many times you are explained by the insiders, by the experts, by the escapees and by the recovered wrecks, the emotional illness that draws people into these situations cannot be truly grasped by anyone who is not experienced. We all come so close, at one time or another, to craving what is bad for us—as teenagers, as college students, as directionless twenty-nothings—and yet it is the impulse that stops us from crossing that line, the simple survivalist instinct, which is so inborn and obvious, that makes it absolutely impossible to imagine why anyone would be so foolish as to step over that boundary. Put it this way: to a normal person, it makes sense that a Jew who has walked across the Alps into Switzerland to escape Nazi Germany may turn and look back longingly on *Deutschland,* his country, a place he still feels is home. But if that same man chooses to retread his path through the snow back to a certain death on the other side of the German border, we start to think that he deserves Dachau. In fact, even the Jews who walked around

Berlin and Frankfurt with yellow stars and the *Juden* stigmata sewn onto their clothing, but still, despite all these disasterous omens, had faith in all their atheism that reason—if nothing else—would ultimately prevail, and who refused to leave the land of Beethoven and Goethe—neglecting to remember that it was also the land of Wagner and Nietzsche—are kind of hard to sympathize with.

It is difficult to be nice when you just want to scream: *You idiot!*

Women who stay after signs of violence emerge, after they escalate, after they multiply, after they reproduce like roaches in a kitchen full of dirty dishes, are easy to despise: easier to despise than they are to defend. What was delightful, in a dingy and ugly way, about Hedda Nussbaum's victimization at the hands of Joel Steinberg was its consummate nature. Unlike Nicole, who probably did not undergo daily beatings, who had a life, who fought back, who never lost her beauty to her taste for the boot, Hedda was a mangled disaster: her nose flattened, her hair patchy and sere as an unwatered front lawn, her walk limped, her entire bone structure dislocated, rearranged as if Steinberg were some perverse Pygmalion, trying to redesign this woman into his strange notion of perfection. Hedda is so hideous that by the time we see her in police photographs we want to beat her up too, we can't blame anyone for what they might have done to a woman who allowed this to be done to her. When Hedda says of her deceased adoptive daughter Lisa that she was "glad to have known her," we lose whatever sympathy we may have had left for this fellow human who has succumbed to her own dehumanization.

We know about battered wife syndrome: we know how it makes women stay, how in their isolation and fear they lose perspective, they mistake their prison for a palace, and like hostages suffering from Stockholm Syndrome, they begin to identify with their jailers. And yet, I can say *succumbed to her own dehumanization*, because at some point, there was a moment of choice. "It's funny how you can lose your innocence all at once, without even knowing that you've passed into another existence," writes Julio Cortázar in *Hopscotch*, and that is precisely the point: a big mess happens *all at once*, it seems beyond your control if you even notice it at all, and just the same, as long as most women manage not to date or marry men who beat them, we must maintain the belief that it is perfectly possible to resist passing into that other existence.

Somehow it has to be possible to reconcile the contradictory notions that women in situations of domestic violence have made a choice, and that, at the same time, they are victims. Sherry Frohman has to *deny* the choice in order to have her agenda as an advocate and counselor taken seriously; someone like Camille Paglia, on the other hand, has to *insist* on the choice so that her brand of primally motivated and sexually liberated feminism can stand. In both perspectives, something is missing, and that something can be called complexity, but what it really is is sanity.

It's been on the docket of most reasonable, thoughtful feminists to turn all the "either/ors" of womanhood into "both/ands." The most useful lesson most of us can derive from the domestic violence model is how we might implement this delightful reading of the world into everyday life, how we might say "she wanted to get laid" without it ever implying that "she deserved to be raped." We will truly have made a breakthrough if we can accept this syllogism: 1) pornography, prostitution and stripping exploit women, but women should be free to enter these professions just the same, and more to the point, women who believe these industries are inherently misogynistic are still allowed to enjoy their products; 2) but we should still support all efforts of any women wishing to escape life as sex workers without exacting a toll in shame (which, after all, is just more exploitation) or insisting that they renounce all and accept Jesus in order to gain our sympathy; 3) and finally if we can manage and master the first two items, we will be able to judge the past without becoming judgmental in the future: we will have the right to say that certain behaviors are not okay, but we couldn't help ourselves, we like them anyway, we are human and stupid and fallible and we ought to be able to cop to our fuckups without getting arrested by the politically correct thought police, without being branded as scarlet women—we ought to grant ourselves and our fellow females just a little bit of grace. If we can find a way to accept without question the disturbing choices that some women make, if we can insist that they accept responsibility for the potentially horrible consequences, and we can still, somehow, find it within our hearts to be forgiving enough to be helpful when we can be, then there will no longer be a need for the naïveté projected by Sherry Frohman or the cantankerous and, at this point, ad hominem bravado blustered about by Camille Paglia.

And no one should mistake this for letting women off the hook too easily or babying them in any way. When I heard, in the summer of 1997, that the dismissed CEO of AT&T had been granted a $14 million golden parachute, I kept asking people—once the company began its search for a replacement—if they had any idea how I might get hired for the job, swiftly prove my incompetence and walk away with a similar deal. The gifts that men are meted out for failure—consider the fate of just about every axed studio head in Hollywood who is set up with his own production company, an office on the lot and a lucrative development deal for all his bad judgment, for green-lighting *Heaven's Gate* or *Howard the Duck* or worse—should make us feel perfectly fine about being generous with women who fuck up their lives.

The only hope we have of ever redressing the imbalances in our intimate realm is in our shameless honesty.

The alternative is to start believing in green dots.

And sometimes we will just have to recognize that nothing we can do will help, that sometimes situations are so far wrong that no amount of feminist—or any other—wisdom is going to make a damn bit of difference. The personal is *not* always political. Some women who get out of situations of domestic violence just don't do it soon enough. Sherry Frohman would say that most women murdered by their husbands are killed *after* they have moved out of the marital home, which is why it is unfair to ask, *Why doesn't she leave?* But this argument fails to account for the amount of time each woman stayed. There was a moment—it may seem as ancient as the Bronze Age to the woman in question, but there was a time—when she received the first blow. And there are people who walk away after that initial punch, or the second or third or even the tenth; and there are people who let years go by.

And when you finally get out, you will pay for the years because that is how life works. There are choices that you just can't walk away from. You do your best, but the feeling we all have that it's not fair is because, in fact, *it's not fair.*

Diana got taken in as a royal brood mare when she was too young to know better, and she too paid with her life. And I'm not sure what the police can really do for someone like Nicole—whether she leaves or stays—because the law is straightforward and the couple dynamics are anything but. Perhaps as a result of being the child of a contentious divorce, I tend to accept, perhaps too readily, that a lot of what is involved in what we tell ourselves is love is pretty damn ugly: that idea just doesn't seem so weird to me—sad, but normal. People do terrible things to each other and call it love all the time—and I'm not sure they're completely wrong. And I think when Nicole and O.J. went for it and at it and over it and under it with each other, they knew what they were doing.

*   *   *

According to Paula Barbieri, "O.J. read all the latest novels and quoted easily from Shakespeare. And not just two or three lines, like a lot of people, but three or four minutes at a stretch from *Macbeth* or *King Lear.*" There is a lot in this statement that is difficult: first of all, while I think the difficulty of Shakespeare is greatly exaggerated by circumstances—i.e., the only time anyone reads the plays is in high school, which makes us all think what is easy reading is in fact academic and tough going—I have trouble believing that O.J. reads much of anything. If he had any kind of exposure to words on paper, he could not be so orthographically challenged. So I don't even really believe he reads Dean Koontz, much less the Bard's great tragedies. Furthermore, if he were reciting soliloquies with random improvisations, who among his crowd would know to correct him? But more to the point, if we must invoke Shakespeare, two less appropriate plays are not in his repertoire. Which brings us to *Othello,* the most unmentionable of the plays that might be adjoined to O.J. since it is just too tight a fit: a black man kills his blonde wife in a fit of jealous rage. In fact, O.J.'s suicide/fugitive note, in which he claims to have loved Nicole too much, is an updated version of Othello's last speech, in which he says, "Then must you speak of one that loved not wisely but too well."

Othello's jealousy springs from his fear that Desdemona will come to her senses and go back to liking white boys. Of course, Othello could not have been worked into such a tortured, paranoid and self-loathing blather without his henchman Iago—truly one of the great creations of villainy of any era or aeon in the history of the stage, far more corrosive because he so well disguises his false intentions as friendship—but we also understand that racial prejudice is so touchy and sensitive that it is not really hard to prey upon Othello's sense of inadequacy. Long before the civil rights movement and affirmative action, Shakespeare understood how subtle manipulations involving our most superficial human traits—literally so: for what is more on the surface than skin color?—can be used to hamper and destroy the human spirit, a person's potential. To rise so high as Othello, to be so beloved of Brabantio, a senator, that he happily allows his only daughter to marry you—to have every indication that you have been accepted not as a Moor, but for yourself—and to have it all so gruesomely and murderously destroyed, to have it end in an unnecessary bloodbath, is tragic.

O.J.'s jealousy, which revolved around Nicole and would seem to have something to do with her whiteness (he was not this way about Marguerite, although in light of Nicole's murder, two complaints of abuse that she filed were unearthed), was misplaced since the only other man who satisfied her, at least according to Faye Resnick (who seems nuts, but strangely credible, her intimacy with the situation too strikingly believable), was Marcus Allen, another black all-star athlete. And Nicole was the daughter of some guy in Orange County, not a noblewoman like Desdemona. At any rate, it's fair to say that interracial romance has changed since Shakespeare's day, at least some. But O.J. married a white woman and made self-blanching a lifelong effort, and yet he is thought of as more black for having Nicole by his side than he would be if he just stuck with Marguerite.

*   *   *

Shortly before the verdict, there was a candlelight vigil held outside Nicole's home, and many people wore angel earrings and pins, as Denise Brown had been doing for all her public appearances, as some sort of sign that Nicole was now a winged spirit in heaven. One little girl interviewed on a television broadcast said that Nicole was an angel because she was dead. This really annoyed me. Nicole was not an angel, as far as anyone knew. She wasn't a bad person either, but there was no reason to think she was especially good. It was as if the means of her death bestowed upon her some honorary heroism that her life could not. I was pleased that they didn't call her a nigger lover or that the trial hadn't tried to make it seem as though her going out dancing all the time meant she was a slut who deserved to die. But just the same, it amazed me that there were only these two choices, slut or angel, that there just didn't seem any way to portray her as an overtly sexual woman who liked to party who was also a good mother.

Sometimes things have no meaning, sometimes senseless acts of violence are just that. Nicole's death, despite what are probably some well-intentioned but still fruitless attempts to make it into a clarion call for domestic-violence awareness, was just the stupid waste of a life of a woman who had not yet really learned how to live. In fact, if the people involved would accept that what happened is nothing more than senseless, they would at last begin to get the meaning after all: the meaning of cruelty and what terrible things people visit on each other for what seems to them, in the deep dark pond of narcissism and obsession that they drown in for just long enough to kill or injure someone they believe they love, to be a good reason. She cheated on me, etc. They don't realize how quickly the feeling will fade, first in the context of their own life and then into the slipstream of human history. After all, Cain and Abel taught us some kind of lesson, but how many other sibling rivals over time do we never hear about? How many pairs of people have battled to the death causing strife and misery all around them only to become among those "signifying nothing."

But everyone tries for significance, for justice, revenge, restitution, closure. Even though the death penalty has never been shown to deter murder—rather it seems to actually increase the rate where it is sanctioned, or Texas would by now be a bloodless state—people continue to call for it. Even though shelters and antibattery task forces are probably damn near useless to a woman madly in love, we go on hoping that someone may find a safe harbor. I don't mean to imply at all that nothing can be done to improve our human lot, but what would really be useful is for someone to take that little girl who thinks Nicole is an angel and tell her that isn't so: that a woman is not made heroic by her death, but by her life. Tell that little girl that *she* is the real angel here, that this is her world to invent, that history begins with her story, and she gets to write it. Tell her that she can be anything she wants to be this time around—tell her not to worry about the afterlife. You see, I believe, with the wholest hope, that we can get it right the first tine, that the urge to punish and correct and memorialize is not a way to honor the dead—who are, after all, dead—but to avoid learning how to find meaning in our own lives.

Nicole died, was killed, one spring night, because she married a sadist, because she loved him too much and then not enough, because she answered the door at the wrong moment, because the person at the door was a tall white man, because she was blonde, because she was beautiful, because her mother left her glasses at a restaurant called Mezzaluna, because the night was so still, because the moon was fat and lonely—because of so many things, not a single one of which could be construed as having been worth the trouble.

Did I Shave My Legs for This?

What he requires in his heart of hearts is that this struggle remain a game for him, while for woman it involves her very destiny. Man's true victory, whether he is liberator or conqueror, lies just in this: that woman freely recognizes him as her destiny.

SIMONE DE BEAUVOIR
The Second Sex

This is the problem for us. Remaining single is not really a choice, it's a sentence. The idea of life without a man, without children, seems impossible. This is, in fact, the law of nature, and when your parents bug you about when you will settle down—grow up, hitch up and start delivering grandchildren—they have history from time immemorial on their side: mankind is dyadic, God gave a lonely Adam a help-meet named Eve, and He made procreation a mutual and mutually exclusive experience. "Therefore shall man leave his father and his mother, and shall cleave unto his wife: and they shall be one flesh." So it is written in Genesis, as if to give us an operating manual for a two-sex planet, as if to make it simple as baking bread: you grow up in your parents' home, you are emancipated as soon as possible so that you can wed as soon as possible and become as one—in biblical times, there was no such thing as co-dependency—with your spouse (i.e., the woman assumes the man's identity).

If you believe the paleontologists and evolutionary biologists, all of us are only a collective of containers for the genes we carry: as far as the aeons leading into infinity are concerned, we are not subjects, we are not emotions and personalities and talents and SAT scores and year-end bonus figures and excellent taste in home furnishings, because we are useful only as evolving gene pools. People who don't reproduce are not really fulfilling their point and purpose as people. We belong in couples, procreating with the gusto of germs, of vermin, of climbing ivy.

And I am not willing to concede that it is all biology. I think society really and truly does not offer a supportive atmosphere to he who goes it alone. But men are granted a little bit of leeway, men are offered a few available variations: if you're John Wayne or Steve McQueen, you can gallop your horse into the sunset, if you're the Lone Ranger you chase bad guys with Tonto, if you're Don Quixote you chase windmills with Sancho Panza, if you're Butch Cassidy you chase rainbows with the Sundance Kid—and with any luck all these womenless men leave a trail of illegitimate children in their wake, genetically responsible, socially irresponsible, but always seen as solitary and solid. The female loner—a nonexistent icon, as far as I can tell—is always just lonely. Or worse: like Amelia Earhart, she simply disappears on her solo flight, as if rejected by the planet for desiring and daring the thrill of thin air, for piercing into Father Sky like a lady entering a gentleman's club back before lawsuits were filed to ensure this puny, pathetic right.

All this is just to say that single women are not societally sanctioned in their singleness. No matter what clever tricks feminism has come up with, it has not quite succeeded at truly legitimizing an unmarried woman as an autonomous being, as a person in a chosen living arrangement and not as someone whose life is in abeyance, someone who is supposed to be dreaming of playing the princess bride in her Saturday night Plaza Hotel wedding, envisioning the just-so off-the-rack Vera Wang gown, the salmon entrées and soufflé desserts from Glorious Food, the tasteful, charmingly dorky ballroom stylings of the Peter Duchin Orchestra—imagining all the floral arrangements and flower girls, seeing it all so clear, everything is there except the groom, who is basically just an accessory anyway. Even with bohemian varia-

tions—nuptials in a gothic SoHo loft, setting free five thousand butterflies after Vermont vows, the bride in black and the groom in white—
even if we try to make this Cinderella fantasy somehow more feminist
and modern and all that stuff, it still comes down to the same big bash
for what is essentially, unsentimentally, the signing of a legal contract.
I don't say this to minimize the occasion, but more to note that despite
perfunctory City Hall possibilities, every little girl grows up wanting a
wedding at the Waldorf, the persistence of puff cloud dreams of a
white dress and a train down the aisle is so deep-seated that my guess
is—no exaggeration—it would be easier to eliminate racism or end
poverty or cure illiteracy or oust Fidel Castro than it would be to
make girls stop wanting to be brides.

For some reason, the groom role, insofar as it has been implanted in
the male collective unconscious, is a nervous inevitability, with or
without tails.

And I hate the way the looming bridal vista is a prism putting
strange bends and unanticipated colors all over my perspective, all
over the social class of single women. Right now, as I write this, I am
recently turned thirty, I am by myself where it is sunny and I am happy
to be far from the madding crowd. I am happy to be single; tomorrow
or next week or next month or next year, I may not feel so sanguine in
my solitude. But any notion that I will deal with my desire to pair off
then is tacitly denied me by a societal tidal force so fierce I would think
it a conspiracy but for the fact that there's no need to plant weeds:
female anxiety flourishes in a self-perpetuating pattern that resists ra-
tional feminist analysis.

So here I am at age thirty wanting to be serenely single. It is still
okay for me to feel this way. I am still pretty. I still have time to work
out my marital status. But it's getting dicey. Clearly I am beginning to
be a misfit in my refusal/inability to settle down with someone. Now, I
have male friends who are ten or even twenty years older than I am,
and while I suppose their parents may wonder if they'll ever see some
grandchildren, it seems perfectly plausible that they will find some
twenty-five-year-old and get hitched whenever. To tell you the truth,
that seems rather plausible to me too. In five or ten years I'm sure I'll
still look great—meaning: I will still have that youthful buoyancy—
and I will still be fertile, and I can hook up with some guy half my age

or twice it, and it will all still be fine. But as much as I believe that, I don't *feel* it, because society does not want me to. Why won't the world endorse that plan? And I am so sick of so many of my friends suffering similarly. Here I am trying to live a life in which man is not my destiny, but the powers that be have done all they can to stymie any burst of joy this self-determination might give me. And though the world does not support me in my autonomy, it also does not like—or even so much as tolerate—the *Fatal Attraction*–fraught desperation that a woman is driven to by an obsessive, unuttered, oxygen-borne fear that she may find out much too late that man *is* her destiny after all. Basically, there is no acceptable, comfortable way to be a single woman.

Even worse, it seems inevitable that there will come a time when I won't look good, when men will stop flirting with me, when this freedom shit will start to feel like free-falling. Will I know? Will I become pathetic? Nothing could be more frightening than seeing the number the press did on Gloria Steinem when she got involved with Mort Zuckerman—she was accused of being girlish and frivolous and desperate to marry and have a baby after all this time. And even if none of it were true, even if she did not feel sorry for herself at all, that the idea got so much mileage was disturbing, but understandable: here was the feminist fatale, portrayed by Kirstie Alley in a television movie about her Playboy Bunny exploits; here was the woman who abandoned her fiancé after graduating from Smith because she preferred to accept her fellowship to India; here was the women's libber who would arrive late and breezing fast and frantic through the lunching crowd at the Four Seasons, her Kenneth-streaked hair trailing her like a golden halo, a speeding apparition's corona, and all the room was said to stop and stare at this gorgeous, determined creature, fabulous and leggy in her thigh-high boots and miniskirt, breathlessly setting herself down at a table with some powerful man or some wealthy man or some influential man, taking her to lunch to be convinced to contribute in one way or another to one worthy cause or another; here was the woman whose sensual appeal was such that her status as intellectual it-girl went unchallenged until the do-me feminists of the nineties played the babe card once again. If ever there was a woman who was single by choice, she was it—so what to make of this turn of events? Did she have regrets or did the media invent them? And what did this mean for me?

Who, if not Ms. Steinem—who virtually invented the word Ms.—has lived as a confirmed spinster with any kind of style? The woman of independent means, the woman who has lived through multiple marriages and picked up some inheritance, some property, or even a noble title along the way, is an age-old figure of great distinction in her old age, the deranged dowagers like Diana Vreeland, stylish ruins of royalty like Wallis Simpson, intercontinental widow Pamela Harriman—these are women who died alone but lived very much accompanied. Even Elizabeth Taylor, who is addicted to the altar, must enjoy looking back on a hotel mogul, a U.S. senator, a British thespian, a Jewish vaudeville act, a white trash construction worker—one can hardly say she did not try a little of everything. And Margaret Mead had a husband for every book she wrote. Jane Fonda appears to be taking the time-of-life approach to husbanding, getting Roger Vadim, the Svengali of sex starlets, during the breathy *Barbarella* phase; Port Huron hero Tom Hayden was the political Jane's consort-in-arms; Ted Turner gets her for the charity lunch years, the swank socialite of good stock arrives at last. Of course, the ideal is to find one that works the first time, but even these multiple marriages bespeak richness, life lived, chances taken, connections consummated, and dresses, dresses, dresses.

Doesn't Barbra Streisand seem so much better off married to James Brolin? Doesn't Madonna, after all, seem rather miserable having her baby with some random guy while Sean Penn seems so in love with Robin Wright?

But *in love* and *married* do not necessarily equate—in fact, Simone de Beauvoir once said, "The greatest success of my life is Sartre," though she chose never to make it legal with her longtime companion, her intellectual partner, her lifelong experiment in egalitarian love. "When you are married, people see you as married, and you begin to see yourselves as married," Beauvoir said in a 1972 interview with *Ms.* magazine, explaining her decision to forgo nuptial vows. "This is quite different from the relationship you have with society when you are not married. Marriage is dangerous for a woman." Whatever decisions Gloria Steinem might have made as a feminist firebrand, a true believer who, perhaps like Simone de Beauvoir, refused marriage because of her desire to deny a dated and inherently sexist institution, that choice is not the same as wishing to be alone, to live alone, to die alone. Lacking a Sartre to grow old with—which may not be the case for Ms. Steinem herself, I have no idea what her relationship status is or what it will later be—or lacking the physical fact of someone to share a bed, a house, a life with, can't have been the goal of feminism. And it is not a pretty thought for most of us, regardless.

In *The Rest of Life*, Mary Gordon writes her horrible vision of growing old alone, in an undesired, burdensome body. "Do you know what it's like when you give up the idea that you'll ever again be prized? In a way it's not so terrible. But all the songs, the stories, are about someone else. Some other kind of person," ponders a forty-eight-year-old single mother who is having an affair with a younger priest in the novella "The Immaculate Man." "You hear songs or stories, you see lovers, any age, any people, just walking arm in arm . . . Or teenagers will be kissing in the shopping mall. An old woman will help her husband across the street because the light is beginning to turn. Anything can do it. Anything you see, or read, or hear on the radio and think, 'That's not me. None of that is me. I won't have that anymore.' You feel a bit self-pitying, a little angry, but it passes, it's not terrible, many people live that way, a number of my friends. I expected to live that way the rest of my life. Living, knowing your body is of no concern to anyone except yourself. You worry that one day you might get sick, that you'll become a nuisance or a burden. No one will look at you again attentively or lovingly. No gaze will ever rest on you for anything but the merest second. Then it will move on. You grow to expect that, you give up expecting anything else."

I'd throw myself off the Brooklyn Bridge—which is actually the plan of the characters in the not-much-seen 1997 movie *If Lucy Fell,* in the event that they aren't married by age thirty—before I'd utter Mary Gordon's narrator's words so calmly. I mean, what a horrible thought. Although, I suppose having such a hysterical response to being unmarried at thirty is just as horrifying.

It seems too remarkable to be a coincidence that in 1997 at least three newly made movies besides *If Lucy Fell* explored the same theme: *My Best Friend's Wedding* had Julia Roberts distressed by being unwed at age twenty-eight, *Picture Perfect* had Jennifer Aniston faking a fiancé at thirty, and the independently released *Wedding Bell Blues* had three women—including the beautiful supermodel Paulina Porizkova—running off to Las Vegas for a weekend to get married before their thirtieth birthdays. When I consider the premise of these three films—and I am happy to note that only the Julia Roberts vehicle was a hit, which would seem to indicate that we resist indulging this kind of thinking—I am struck by what a crazy picture they paint of how women live. Our lot in life would seem to be enslavement to time—to time the avenger. To be a woman would seem to entail a denial of the present to scrounge and horde for the infinite future, which she approaches, the asymptote forever decreasing, always half the distance of the previous reach, but never quite *there:* her hand is forever extending out to this shining future finish line, but because marriage is in fact not the end but just a new beginning, a new occasion for more future planning, she never really arrives. There's always the next lifeline to anticipate—children, menopause, old age, whatever.

Meanwhile, men coast along in present perfect, watching football, a game in which four fifteen-minute quarters expand to take up hours. For a man time just kind of slipslides away, and there's always more of it. A woman has no idea what it is to live in the present tense, and a man has no idea what it is like to panic with a pounding, pumping clock embedded in your chest where your heart should be.

*   *   *

Henry Jaglom's 1987 film *Someone to Love* basically documents a gathering of still-single people, mostly in their forties, some even older, discussing how it is that life led them to an aloneness that they consider permanent. This is a project similar to the one taken on individually by Vivian Gornick, in *Approaching Eye Level*, her book of life as a somehow single woman, and perhaps more delicately and engagingly addressed by Alison Rose in a *New Yorker* essay titled simply "How I Became a Single Woman." Neither Rose nor Gornick is depressing, both just unfold events, many romantic and thrilling, many leading to all kinds of adventures overseas and underground, but none bound for the chapel of love. The message seems to be that a careless woman who craves chance and circumstance, who fails to focus on that golden ring, will find that her insouciance leads to forever singledom. The resignation of both these accounts is not presented as miserable, but considering that neither woman is dead yet—both are fiftyish, and it seems like much possibility still lies ahead—I wonder why they seem certain that their marital status is terminal. Is it just dating fatigue? Are they too tired to try? Is this what happens to you?

Will this happen to me if I'm not vigilant? Will I just disappear into the darkness and isolation of my idle, inconsequential life like all the old and infirm and unloved, whose bodies, once beautiful, perhaps graceful as ballet or strong as a buck, are now withered, wasted—corpses that are not dead—will that be my life?

And there have been long, struggling years, and my sadness at never getting it right with somebody has been huge. But I also believe in the human project I have embarked on by choosing to remain single (and it is a choice). In the abstract, when I discuss my life alone, my misadventures, my travels, whatever, people always say, "That's so interesting." Or "It's great that you do that." They marvel at the way I prefer to vacation alone, they think it's great that I'd rather provide for myself, buy luxurious and frivolous items for myself, that I love going to double features in the afternoon all alone, that there is pretty much nothing that I don't like doing by myself. But at the same time that they are impressed or intrigued, this other question looms: *Why aren't you married?* (To which my favorite reply is: *Why aren't you thin?*)

But I thought it ought to have been obvious by now that there is a real value in developing before marrying. We support this notion in men, we believe they should take their time to grow up. But there is little support for a woman going it alone through some part of her life. Partly it is just risky—women can be raped, and they can be victims of crime, and somehow they make less rugged hitchhikers. And they don't age as well, plastic surgery or no. But still, I think we owe ourselves the opportunity to be free, and in this day and age, it ought to be a given. I want to be married as much as the next person—even Courtney Love and Kurt Cobain saw fit to get hitched—but I want to do it when I am good and ready, which is all that any man has ever asked—it is all he has felt *entitled* to—and it is all I should ever want likewise.

After all, there is a point to all the mistakes, to crying on the bathroom floor searching for the last traces of cocaine. Now that I am thirty, I know for certain that there were things I did in my twenties that I needed to do. Perhaps I might have done them as a teenager or a college student, but I believe that I needed to do them as an adult, a free person, without a tour bus or a counselor or a parent or a roommate or some other guardian there to chaperone me through: There just were things I needed to do absolutely alone.

I needed to spend a week in Florence by myself, to check into the Excelsior Hotel and eat breakfast and dinner in bed with a view of the Arno, watching soccer on Italian television and be amazingly bored, I needed to walk the streets of this most romantic and recherché of cities all alone, I needed to have Italian men who could tell I was American as if I were carrying the Star-Spangled Banner harass me when I got lost in cul-de-sacs and say the only English words they knew, "aw, baby, you so pretty," I needed to find a kitten in a pretty little street and then find out his owner was a painter in an atelier just behind him, and I needed to talk to that man though somehow he spoke no English and I spoke no Italian; I needed to visit the Tower of Pisa alone and buy a cheesy souvenir replica of it alone; I needed to spend a month in Miami Beach by myself, to walk into a tattoo parlor off the main drag, get some touch-ups on a hand-done India-ink engraving some guy gave me with a needle and thread one drunken college night, and then I needed to fuck the tattoo artist—who had been working on my naked back for four hours—on the floor of the shop afterward just to make sure that the *Penthouse* "Forum" isn't all lies; I needed to walk the streets of downtown New York for hours a day, afternoons roaming by, shopping in SoHo, stopping for iced tea at the T Salon, having a manicure once a week at a Korean place in the Village, spending hours going through the sale racks at Barneys, buying lipstick I didn't need at the MAC store, basically throwing away a load of money on a lot of nothing; I suppose, in some strange way, that I needed to have the IRS seize my assets; I needed to cop heroin all by myself on Avenue C or Stanton Street, where it is always midnight, and I needed to nearly get arrested trying to score some dope in Madrid; I needed, I guess, to spend a night in a city jail in Florida; I needed to sleep with the junkie lead singer of a bad heavy metal band and then sleep with his nineteen-year-old brother the next week; I needed to write my first book with no one looking over my shoulder, and I needed to go on tour to promote it with no one special to come home to; I needed to have the best girlfriends you can possibly have on earth, to have relationships with them that have spanned through college, through moves to Ukraine and London and San Francisco and back again; I needed to believe that I would one day go to law school, that I would be the rightful heir to Clarence Darrow if I ever got into a courtroom; I needed to live, for five years, in a huge and beautifully appointed loft—that I unfortunately had to share with the psychologist who owned it, occasionally with her boyfriend, eventually with her baby and nanny, occasionally with a high colonics administrator, and sporadically with her patients, with many of my own friends who saw it as a crash pad as they passed through town, and ultimately with my roommate Jason, and most unfortunately with an inept flautist who gave flute lessons on Thursday afternoons; I needed, at age twenty-four, to be fucking a ridiculously charming man of forty-eight, so I could know I'd done it with someone twice my age; I needed to drop acid at Walden Pond and do all the ridiculous things people do on that kind of trip, which is, as far as I can tell, the only reason anyone ever goes there, and seemingly the only reason Don Henley wants to preserve it; I needed every meal I've ever eaten alone in every restaurant, I needed every waiter who insisted I read *Atlas Shrugged*, every waitress who told me what it was like to be twenty-five and a single mother going to college part-time; I needed every conversation on every airplane or Amtrak ride, every born-again Christian, every just-engaged couple who said I was the first to know about their betrothal, every vitamin salesman who gave me free samples; I needed to live alone in several different apartments, a fleabag motel, a luxe hotel and at my mother's house in Fort Lauderdale for a year and talk to almost no one I know almost never because I was so tired from all the other things I needed to do.

And still, I know I needed to do them.

I know that I would jealously hear of a vacation a friend took with her boyfriend to the Loire Valley or with her husband to Montserrat and I would think: *If only*. I would think: I want to share these adventures I have with someone. But I have had excursions with boyfriends now and then, and I have always found that I preferred the possibility and uncertainty and rank risk of being alone. I needed that, those things.

I did not want the life I have had until now, but I know I needed it.

There are other things that other women need to do: they need to have lesbian affairs; they need to drop out of medical school and become investment bankers; they need to fly with the Air Force in Iraq or work for the Peace Corps in Papua New Guinea; they need to sleep with their brothers-in-law; they need to—heaven help us—sleep with their brothers; they need to live in New Orleans for five months, in Kraków for three months and in Bangkok for two years. They *need* these things, all these things—for if they didn't, they surely would not bother, for it is so much easier to *just get married*. It is so much easier to stick with Plan A. But these are necessary tangents, and we honor the peripatetic spirit in men, we extol the wayfarer and the rickety line that his compass traces, we celebrate Odysseus on his homecoming— his *noös*—while his wife, Penelope, is praised by the Muse for her faithful looming, for her persevering and patient watchful waiting. Surely we don't want these antiquated notions of women's roles to reign on today. Women need to take their chances and be single for a while (that Odysseus could do his wandering once married is another matter to take up). No one can be sure what *will* happen, but everyone can know what they need *right now*. Men tend to respond to those calls from within with much greater certainty than women do.

A recent *New York* magazine article described a sudden spate of young brides, in which one line from one twenty-two-year-old newlywed particularly stood out: she said that she doesn't want to be thirty-five and single (which I find funny because chances are she may well be thirty-five and *divorced*). The whole notion of calculating the chances of ending up alone as a way to plan a marriage: it's like playing the odds at the track, which usually do not predict with any kind of certainty how a horse will perform, so surely this is no way to plan a partnership for life. These young marriers are trying to follow a Big Plan, as if Robert Graves had never existed. When these girls sound so sure and so organized, as if you really could plan your whole life in a Filofax, it frightens me. Disorder and mishaps are useful—or at any rate, they are inevitable. I've started to believe that the thing to do is plan for everyone else's disarray. After all, there are all these men who have told me that I am their second wife, including several who do not yet have a *first* wife, which makes me wonder: Maybe that will be my future. On the other hand, my best friend Christine thinks by now we should both be on *our* second husbands. Clearly, marriage has come to mean something other than what it's supposed to, the lifetime partnership principle seems to be preempted by some idea that this might be a fun thing to try.

Now, I will say that there is a lot of the last several years I did not need, that I would trash for just a few moments of time without them. Mostly I did not need all the heartbreaks, I did not need to learn over and over again that it is better to have loved and lost than to never have loved at all. I did not need to learn that I would have preferred the never-loved part. I did not need to devote hours to writing letters that were too short or too long to men who cared too little or too much, I did not need to obsess over will he call and will I ever see him again to the point of forgetting to eat, forgetting to wake up, forgetting to sleep. I did not need to take more than one drug overdose— accidental, deliberate, who knew after a while—to combat the hugeness of these horrible feelings, the horror of knowing for sure that I would never love or be loved again. I did not need all the time I devoted to a romantic life that I am certain now was mostly wasted and wasteful when I could have been writing, could have been reading, could have been feeding the homeless, could have been visiting with my now-dead grandfather, could have been doing almost anything else. I cannot say I see the point to any of this now, I doubt that I really saw the point of any of it then, I only know that I was driven by compulsion that seemed outside of me, like the murderer in Jim Thompson's *The Killer Inside Me,* I only know that I had a rage for this terrible pursuit and horrible disappointment that I could not stop.

And I could have lived without it. And I will do anything in my power to never have to feel it again.

And girls who marry young may either be spared that feeling or be running from it, but I just couldn't. And I hate that about myself. All the other reasons for staying single I am proud of, as proud as I am of anything else about my life; but for the freedom to throw myself at one heart failure after another, I am an idiot.

This is why, in the end, it still feels like men have all the power. They still seem to obey their impulses to run away while women are enslaved to their impulses to run toward. As long as men continually get messages about avoiding commitment while women are taught to desperately seek it out, the sexes will always be at odds with each other and nothing will work. It does not matter that men are more at the mercy of their physical and sexual temptations, that they are fools for any woman who leads them down the path to hell. "For she is the dangerous hills and many a climber will be lost on such a passage," Anne Sexton warns in "O Ye Tongues," though surely she must know that she is playing into both the fantasies and fears of men, and not much more. Because that temptation for them is akin to the need to scale Mount Everest or bungee jump or take a more calculable risk like driving over 75 on I-95: it is a risk that lives in its moment, is as real and palpable as childbirth and baking bread in its moment—but then it is gone. There is no baby or warm loaf left as a souvenir that you must suffer or savor. It does not have the constancy that my need for some man—any man—can often have.

And this is why I root for the bitch who derails the whole applecart, who throws the system off guard and makes a mess of some poor fellow's life. I cheer for her because she has broken the chain. She has taken a taste of what he has completely consumed, what has consumed him. And I would like, so much, to be the dainty sampler of the world's delights instead of the person who has need that is only satisfied with more need.

* * *

Fleetwood Mac really is the rock-and-roll band that defined being married and being single and being messed up in love both within the songs and among the group's personnel more than any other. Also, it is the band that tells the story of the prices you pay for both: Stevie Nicks is yet another tragedy of beauty aging in the wrong way. "Silver Springs," a Nicks composition from the late seventies that became a hit for the band when it reunited for a tour in 1997, celebrates the power of young attachments and the way they never quite die. But a less noticeable aspect of the song is the way Stevie understands herself to be a woman who haunts many a man. "Time casts a spell on you, but you won't forget me." Many of the best will remember her intensity and lunacy and platform shoes and witchy clothes and allusions to velvet. They will recall the blonde girl with sadsack eyes, spinning and dancing and singing with that nasal voice, veiled and revealed. "I'll follow you down till the sound of my voice will haunt you / You'll never get away from the sound of the woman that loves you." Stevie will always be the most remarkable, strange and unforgettable woman any of them was ever involved with.

But they are all married to other people now and she is not. Stevie Nicks was the girl on fire, will probably be frozen at age twenty-five forever, like publicity shots of Greta Garbo and Bette Davis that have so indelibly sealed their image at twenty-five in our minds. The world has elder statesmen and veteran actors, it has Richard Nixon and Bob Hope, but it has no use for aging starlets. All of them seem to be gone before it even becomes an issue—whether that is cause or effect, I don't know. But after playing a sex goddess, it is probably hard to play a grandmother. Male actors have less extreme transitions: rarely were they sex gods in the first place—it was not until Richard Gere in *American Gigolo* that we properly figured out how to objectify masculine beauty—and everyone knows they age more gracefully anyway. Jane Fonda has chosen to get out, so has Debra Winger, and many more have just kind of gotten lost outside the scenery, ravishing beauties who were also solid and somber actresses-actors who were still able to be pretty, often fresh-faced and freckled: Carrie Snodgress, Susan Anspach, Karen Black, Katherine Ross, Cristina Raines, Genevieve Bujold, Ronee Blakley—where are they?

Many left to raise families and never came back. But Stevie Nicks didn't do that. She has been addicted to cocaine and Klonopin, she has had silicone breast implants installed and extracted, she ballooned to 175 pounds, she was the object of derision in *Sid and Nancy* when a muumuu-clad Chloe Webb catches her reflection in a London shop window and screams aghast about looking "like fucking Stevie Nicks," she had a critic describe her as "twirling toward oblivion."

She has since recovered, or at least rehabilitated, but Fleetwood Mac took the best years of Nicks' life and she can never get them back. But whatever the price, the intensity of what went on between the couples in that band, like the very public, very impassioned and, frankly, very seventies marriage of Carly Simon and James Taylor, is something I envy greatly: at least they had that experience of really going for it. At least they dared to have a big wild love. It seems like half of my age group, grown up under the sign of divorce, are so scared of commitment that they avoid relationships altogether, and the other half is so frightened of being alone that they cling with white-knuckle grips to high school sweethearts and college romances that have long since ceased to be useful. They hang on to these lifeless, listless attachments, unwilling to go through the elementary steps, the trial and error of relating that it takes to learn to be in a *real* relationship, to be in the right one. They hide, but they don't seek. What scares me now is that fear and defensiveness guide everything, nobody meets anyone halfway anymore. In the fifties, a bad relationship meant people killing each other; now it means people avoiding each other. Stories of Edmund Wilson smacking Mary McCarthy in a drunken rage, and then telling her, as she burst into tears, to stop it or he would give her something to really cry about—awful as this sounds, the deep engagement of this sick love sounds comparatively appealing to me. For all the talk of communication these days, what that mostly amounts to is talking about a relationship rather than having one. We talk around it, above it and below it, but rarely do we just fall in and let it happen.

* * *

The world is profoundly scared of single women, they are loose cannons, the uncontrollable variable, hormones and pheromones afloat and adrift; much more frightening than the extra man at a dinner party, they are the piece that can change the status quo, upset the balance, break up families. The term "home wrecker" has somehow never been applied to a man. Today there is also the "office wrecker," the destructive female force ruining the workplace, as in the book and movie versions of Michael Crichton's *Disclosure,* whose female lead is a Silicon Valley executive who is said to think that software is just another word for her angora sweaters. But despite her putative ignorance, this rapacious bitch is crafty enough to be a menace both to family stability and to job security. Much as I wish to denigrate Crichton for inventing this misogynist's wet dream, unfortunately the hateful attitude assumed toward his character is not *pre*scriptive so much as it is *de*scriptive of postfeminist office politics. The genuine dread of the young ballbuster, brash and presumed to be hell-bent on bringing ruin on all of the men—and most of the women, who tend to divide against themselves as men never do—on her way to the top, is a genuine contemporary phenomenon, not the historical anachronism one would hope it would be.

Elaine Garzarelli, the Wall Street economist whose formulas for combining market indicators enabled her to predict the stock market crash of 1987, is maligned by her male peers regularly and with ridiculous delirium. Ms. Garzarelli is fortyish and single, and like most men who have made it big—*real* big—in the field of high finance, she has been known to be cocky and rash. Since 1987, she has made some bad calls and foolhardy predictions in a loud voice that has been duly amplified by the boys on the trading floor who wish her gone. (Of course, this is not even the usual felonious act that gets most men fired from their jobs while they do soft time, and allows them to make a gradual, respectable return to the financial world, even if, like Michael Milken, their havoc can be blamed in the main for bankrupting an entire company—in his case, Drexel Burnham Lambert.) Elaine Garzarelli now lives in a safe retreat in Florida, where she is an owner of a financial concern, and she proudly tells the press that "I can't be fired because it's my company."

Jamie Tarses, the young woman who became president of ABC Entertainment in 1996 on the strength of developing youthful, urban shows like *Friends* and *Caroline in the City* at NBC, was so beset by slander and libel from the moment her appointment was announced that it almost seemed as if she were deliberately and diabolically hired to be the straw woman if the ABC lineup did not work out. A cover story in *The New York Times Magazine* in August 1997—written by Lynn Hirschberg, who seems to specialize in nasty stories about women in complicated public positions—seemed only too happy to play into the animosity, actually describing Ms. Tarses' manner as "feline," repeatedly describing her vulnerability and male agents' belief that she takes everything personally and cries a lot, accusing her of flirting with her boss via fax to win over his favor, and just generally saying all kinds of things you would not *dare* say about a man.

With men there is no fear of the kind of sexist stereotyping journalists routinely report on without excuse or extenuation if a woman is involved: hence the Grimm-imagined shrew who is ruining a whole office because she is so favored by her boss continues to exist in press accounts of powerful women. Consider the way the obviously capable *New Yorker* editor Tina Brown still has her success tied to getting involved with husband Harold Evans when he was at the helm of *The Sunday Times* of London many years ago, and is still routinely pointed to for having special pull with her boss, S. I. Newhouse, Jr.—as if without some cache of charm (that is not apparent to most people who come in contact with Ms. Brown), this talented editor would still be an assistant fetching tea at *The Tatler.*

Women as a rule are so sexual, they are such natural erotic objects. Even after feminism, it's still hard to view men as sex objects, regardless of what any single one might do for you. Men's sexuality is tied up in one organ, while women just embody it all over. So women's unignorable sexuality makes them a threat when they aren't bonded to a particular man, and this energy isn't safely channeled. This is why there is something despicable and nightmarish about the free woman. Of course, single women are the most vulnerable class of people in our society—to crime, to poverty, to loneliness. They have, on the whole, less money, less physical strength and less status than any other group. They are not to be feared so much as to be pitied—another reaction that is not necessarily fair, but one that is more realistic than this baseless animosity.

To measure the extent to which antagonism against the single female has built up, consider this strange reversal of fortunes: in old film noir, the villainess was as likely to be married as not, but nowadays it is always a single woman that is the public menace. The bored housewives who were the classic vixens—the wretched, fleshy sexpots who preyed upon the traveling salesmen and bashful insurance brokers who darkened their doorways not knowing they were the portals to hell—have been displaced in villainy by frustrated single career women: *Double Indemnity* and *The Postman Always Rings Twice* have made way for *Fatal Attraction, Basic Instinct* and *Disclosure*. This changes the dynamics because now the predatory female is in fact nobody's wife, while the man is married: the woman's cushion of safety has been reduced if not eliminated, while the man has extensive emotional resources.

In the movie *Disclosure,* it's Demi Moore who is the deadly careerist climbing her StairMaster to nowhere, pitted against Michael Douglas, who portrays the victim of her sexual ploys. But whatever career troubles she may actually cause him, the scenes depicting the hominess of Douglas' life after hours, the appearance of wife and kids at ideally spaced intervals throughout the movie's two reels, are all meant to remind us that anything that hard-up tramp does to him is only a temporary setback because he is a good man with family values; Michael Douglas is cosseted and coddled both metaphorically and in actuality by the shelter of home and hearth. Douglas has the warmth of family, while Moore, in contrast, is alone and lonely. But we're never allowed to feel sorry for her: her role as both office wrecker and home wrecker is consummate, even though at the end she succeeds in destroying neither.

The worst insult in *Disclosure*'s despicable array of overdetermined signifiers comes at the very end of the movie, when Michael Douglas, safely and soundly resuming his happy career in his bright, sunny office, receives an e-mail from home that is signed by "A Family." Not individual names like normal people would use, or even "The Joneses," or even—what the hell?—"*Your* Family." Just "A Family," the generic brand, the type Pat Robertson ministers to, the usual kind. Like everything else in *Disclosure,* this final symbolic gesture is meant to suggest that single women are a dangerous plague preying upon family life. And of course, there's that slightly less obvious message about how they're stealing all the good jobs from men—*men who have families to support*. Never mind that it's absurd to posit that women are assuming all the powerful roles in the world of computers. Obviously Andrew Grove and Bill Gates and Steve Case prove that women are not, in any meaningful capacity, in charge of Silicon Valley.

It was Friedrich Nietzsche who said, "In revenge as in love woman is always more barbarous than man." This is the lesson of all these evil-woman movies. For the most part, the only competing alternative to the villainess in Hollywood's arsenal of Technicolor dreams is the tear-tugging high melodrama of the tragic heroine. In an interesting inversion of *Double Indemnity,* Barbara Stanwyck and Fred MacMurray team up again in *There's Always Tomorrow,* where she is a lonely widow and glamorous career gal—the stately fashion designer Norma Vale, as opposed to the bored and murderous Los Feliz houswife Phyllis Nirdlinger—and he is a lonely, unhappily married family man who falls in love with her. He invents toys and is an early innovator of robotics; she designs dresses in the manner of Edith Head. They come across as the Bill Gates and Donna Karan of their day, busy bees watching the world go by. In the end, despite the natural, refreshing rapport this pair enjoys, it of course must stop. She is left with nothing, returning to her empty life in New York, and he goes back to home life in Pasadena. But it is she who sacrifices, who insists he return to his wife and kids, who plays the virtuous role—one of the many tearjerker "women's film" roles she took after being a red-hot pistol earlier on.

Television, on the other hand, has always been more hospitable to single characters because the episodic nature of the shows requires serial relationships as plot device. Imagine if any of the *Seinfeld* characters got married: so desperate were the writers to kill off George's fiancée, Susan, that they had her die of licking envelopes for the wedding invitations. On *The Dick Van Dyke Show* of the early sixties, comedienne Rose Marie, in the role of Sally, serves as the resident spinster/tomboy, the funny chick who the guys in the office half forget is female. Mostly there's no fuss made about it—she likes to bowl and share ice cream with her cat, Henderson (back then this was strictly a boy's name)—but one episode revolves around the possibility of her going dateless on her birthday. It doesn't help when six-year-old little Richie asks how old she is and when, after she tells him she doesn't have a husband, he blurtingly asks, "Why don't you get one?"

Sally pretends not to mind, but Laura knows she must. She has to explain this to her poor benighted husband, Rob. "When a woman gets to be a certain age, every birthday is a milestone," Laura says, "and every milestone is a millstone." Sally frets as she contemplates birthday plans, tries calling her friend Fred and offering to bake lasagna, and cries in the car one night just thinking about this lonely prospect. Finally a Leo Fassbinder from her high school days shows up at the office—when at first he leaves no message, she tries all sorts of ways to figure out who it is. It's one of those things married people, people in relationships, don't understand: they don't know how important it is to take accurate messages for us single gals. Sally tells the receptionist that if the guy shows up again to tie him to a chair. He calls and they arrange a date on her birthday. The comedy in all this is that in the meantime her co-workers decide to surprise her, Fred realizes he's not busy after all, and Leo turns out to be just an insurance agent on a sales call. Anyway, it portrays the life of a single woman as rather desolate compared to happy Rob and Laura Petrie. Sally sends them away pretending to expect a date, rather than reveal that she's left alone.

The irony is that happily hitched Laura will eventually become Mary Richards, the quintessential single woman, not a swinging single gal like Marlo Thomas of *That Girl,* not a powerful media personality like the one presented on *Murphy Brown*—Mary is just middle-American Mary, an honestly overworked and underpaid woman among the alcoholic and otherwise addled men. Everyone falls in love with Mary at some point because it is just inevitable: to not believe at least for an episode or two that this dream girl is the one you ought to marry (even if you're already hitched) is to deny Manifest Destiny, the Magna Carta, the Bill of Rights, the Constitution—everything that matters would cease to be in a world where men did not fall for the hospital-corners perfectionism and goofball goodness of Mary. She just had such a certain way about her: "I'm an experienced woman; I've been around." Pregnant pause. "Well, all right, I might not have been around, but I've been . . . nearby." Mary Tyler Moore was an anti-icon. She had dates, men fell for her all the time, she turned down proposals left and right—and though she did not exactly seem single by choice, it seemed like she was not made neurotic by her situation. She seemed like she'd be all right whichever way it went, and she'd probably marry eventually, when it felt right. Or not. She was gonna make it after all.

While Mary Richards was herself childless, her show's power of parthenogenesis spawned several offshoots. *Mary Tyler Moore* was the single-woman show, and then *Rhoda* became the married version. (Do you know that I still watch *Rhoda* reruns hoping that Joe and Rhoda won't get divorced, that they'll reconcile after all, so much do I want to believe it can work? I still believe that through the power of syndication this relationship can be saved.) Now it's *Seinfeld* as the single-person paradigm, with *Mad About You* as the married version. Although TV is a much more accessible medium for actresses to find work in, somehow in all these years no network has managed to come up with a *Mary* replacement—and Mary Tyler Moore herself has been through several failed pilots. They tried to make the single-gal-next-door out of Geena Davis with a show called *Sarah,* which no one remembers, lucky for her. Now you have Brooke Shields finding her mien at last on *Suddenly Susan.* NBC has scheduled this sitcom as part of its Monday night lineup of "Must She TV"—shows centered on smart, funny women offered as counterprogramming to *Monday Night Football.* Likewise, the Fox network has come up with *Ally McBeal,* an hour-long drama about a pretty Harvard Law graduate who, between courtroom arguments and visits to her very politically correct firm's uncomfortably coed bathroom, struggles weekly to straddle the extremes of primness and promiscuity. Since Ally is meant to illustrate the issues that all young single women grapple with, this show airs in the same Monday night antispectator sports time slot. And somehow, in all this estrogen-charged TV programming, someone had the bright idea to transform swinging single gal Marlo Thomas into Jennifer Aniston's mom on *Friends* and Mary Tyler Moore into Téa Leoni's mom on *The Naked Truth.*

It's motherhood that redeems women in the Bible, with asexual, God-ordained, angel-announced reproduction the ideal. As Cheryl Exum explains in *Judges and Method,* "The immaculate conception allows motherhood to be completely separated from the sex act, dividing the virtuous mothers from the decadent swinging singles." Even now, there is a certain kind of respectability that even an *outré* outlaw like Courtney Love gets because she is, after all, a mom (never mind that anyone can get pregnant, but few can be accomplished songwriters or rock stars). Back when Debra Winger was considered a Hollywood wild thing—doing too many drugs, too many men and too much attitude on the set—*Vanity Fair* put the then-pregnant actress on the cover of its February 1987 issue in a white terry robe, her face fresh and dewy damp as if just out of a steamy hot shower, beside the headline SQUEAKY CLEAN. It was as if, married and carrying Timothy Hutton's baby, the woman who had once posed in a smooch with her dog while he pressed his paws against her tits had suddenly acquired virtue, had mysteriously been granted absolution. When I hear Chrissie Hynde singing, "I'm not the kind I used to be / I got a kid, I'm 33," I think: Good for her, especially thinking back on early interviews when she was such a mess. Motherhood is the happy ending.

Think of how much nicer everyone is to Madonna now that she is a mother—she has suddenly become more mature, more serious, more respectable, she wears chignon knots and elegant red lipstick and ladylike suits. Even the stigma of illegitimacy is smoothed by the simple grown-upness and the sexy combination of the beautiful woman with her baby-as-prop. Supermodels Stephanie Seymour, Kristin McMenamy, Beverly Peele and many others have all had children out of wedlock; actresses Jessica Lange, Patricia Arquette and Kelly Lynch are among the many movie stars who are or have been unwed moms. And nobody cares: Ingrid Bergman would still have a Hollywood career if she had embarked on parenting with Roberto Rosselini today. It has been noted that, were Harlem a country, it would have one of the highest illegitimacy rates on earth. If Hollywood and the high-fashion catwalks could unite into nationhood, I wonder what the numbers would be—and I wonder why we tolerate unwed mothers who are rich, white and beautiful and despise the ones who are black, indigent and most in need of our help.

On the other hand, dispensing with all glamour not contained in cut muscles and cut-up T-shirts, Linda Hamilton was a walking paramilitary operation in Fidel Castro's clothes in *Terminator 2*. She was an avenging mother, a lioness fiercely protecting her cubs, a woman hell-bent on making the world safe for her child. Because her martial artwork and sharp-shooting technique are all in the name of motherhood—to save, in the final analysis, Mother Earth—they assume a certain old-fashioned, primitive respectability. Hamilton's monomaniacal, presumably psychotic one-woman war with the world is portrayed as the apocalyptic equivalent of a more conventional mom insisting that the PTA purchase metal detectors.

And all these redemptive images of motherhood may even be true. It is grounding and growing to marry and mother or do one or the other. But not everyone in life has these choices. I don't mean that certain people have no one who wants to settle down with them—that too, but that's not the point—so much as life takes mysterious turns, bad decisions are made at one moment that affect us forever. If you yourself were poorly parented, it will take some time to be able to attach to someone, to find a person you might want to have kids with. And unlike men, who are given an eternity to grow up and grow out of these troubles, women age into insignificance. If they don't work out their nonsense while they are still fairly young, it is hard for them to find a mate, a partner, a spouse. Feminism wants to pretend we have forever, but we don't. Men do. And they are the ones making the rules, stigmatizing single women while at the same time making it difficult for many women to be otherwise.

*   *   *

"Years go by if I'm stripped of my beauty and the orange clouds raining in my head / Years go by will I choke on my tears until finally there is nothing left?" When Tori Amos asked that, she had a surprise hit, a commercial success, even though the question is so awful and upsetting that it is basically out of the realm of Top 40. But so many people feel the same way, like they may be disappearing, that something about life is not working out and finally they will cry themselves dead, they will be King David in Psalms, protesting and shouting out to the Lord above, begging for relief from this life of solemn sorrow: "I am weary from this groaning / all night make I my bed to swim / I water my couch with tears. / Mine eye is consumed because of grief."

But the idea is to always believe in the possibility of redemption— the day of reckoning, the time when it will all make sense. Somehow we are meant to understand that life in and of itself is the happy ending: not Dear reader, I married him, which, by the by, Charlotte Brontë never did, but that I am here, I'm my own person, I am not

Nicole Brown with faraway searching eyes, killed for—when you get right down to it—not being her own person.

Life is maybe a bit like being a vaudeville veteran singing "I'm Still Here." I've been through summer stock and dinner theater and Las Vegas revues and bad reviews and—*hah!*—I'm still here. Or what could be more perfect than the supergroup of veteran rockers that formed in the late eighties to make two hard pop albums, calling themselves the Traveling Wilburys. Among the band's membership of true rock-and-roll holdouts were Bob Dylan, Roy Orbison and George Harrison. Naturally, the Wilburys scored a big hit single with "Handle with Care," a survivor's tale of life in the trenches tracing the fickle curve of success, with allusions to days of going through Twelve Step programs and twenty different gurus, through a Christian phase, several Jewish phases, through too much pot, not enough coke, drunk beyond words, doped out of this world, divorced and in custody battles, on the Rolling Thunder Revue, made fun of on *Saturday Night Live,* and then even appearing on *Saturday Night Live*—after all that, a man can be tired. "I've been robbed and ridiculed / In day care centers and night schools / Handle me with care."

Of course men, even damaged ones, will always find someone who will handle with care.

Which is why, just once I would like to see a play or novel or memoir about an older single man who, unable to find a suitable mate, faces middle age reconciled to his aloneness, accepts as he approaches fifty that he will never marry, adopts a child, decorates his co-op as not just a bachelor pad but a permanent home. Just once I'd like to see such a portrait of a vibrant professional man who is failed by love and therefore, in most ways, by life. I want a male version of Alison Rose or Vivian Gornick.

But it could never happen. Because these men do not exist. Not that the world is not filled with unmarriable misfits among the male of the species: they are everywhere, unavoidable and unnoticeable at once. They live in rooming houses for life, they collect disability, they are marginally employed, often adrift, many of them mentally ill in a chronic way, symptoms subdued—along with most of their personality—in a permanent way by an electric-chair dose of shock meted out in a state institution in the sixties. Or they are shy and pleasant, dull and sweet, village idiots, mama's boys, gentle giants, simple men, war heroes, Vietnam veterans, dropouts and burnouts without the coping skills to interact with the world or with a woman in a meaningful, material way. They are unconscionably mean and understandably sad in a way so compelling that you wish you could be the girl who could love them as they deserve, you wish you did not have cowboy dreams of your own to chase after. They are Terry Nichols with his mail-order bride from the Philippines, and they are Timothy McVeigh with his fertilizer bombs and his middle-American paramilitary paranoia. They are Travis Bickle in *Taxi Driver* and they are Freddie, the Sylvester Stallone character in *Copland,* described by the actor to Conan O'Brien as "one of those people you take for granted, who don't make too much of a fuss, who live with a quiet dignity." They are heart-breaking and haunting.

The one thing they are not is Heidi, the heroine of *The Heidi Chronicles,* Wendy Wasserstein's Pulitzer Prize-winning play. They are not vibrant and accomplished art history professors at Barnard with personal magnetism and prominence and position to spare. They are not too good to be true. Such men do not find themselves in their forties facing single parenthood in a newly acquired apartment on the Upper West Side. Such men find wives. They just do.

*   *   *

Anger is probably the most direct emotion that human beings are capable of. "I have never felt my mind so clear and certain as tonight," Nora said as she walked out on Torvald. Anger, hate, feelings that create boundaries and barriers between us and others, that cut us off from all other ecosystems—these allow us to experience clarity.

Love ought to be an emotion with similar lucidity because it is that strong and that powerful. But let's face it, love cannot exist by itself; it requires response, it makes us porous and permeable. Unrequited love, if it does not die of its own accord, becomes obsession and sickness. The purest experience of love a human being can have is probably with infants and very young children, and with pets: all of these beings are not autonomous or capable enough to return the love we lavish upon them for no reason other than that they exist and we adore them and we can't help ourselves; we ask nothing in return—only that they let us love them without condition, that they accept this gift with grace. But grown-up love requires, in many cases, more peace treaties, both tacit and spoken, than it would take to make sense of the whole Middle East. It's about drawing lines in the sand and moving them around a million times. It is the hardest and greatest thing most of us will ever do, the challenge of finding those boundaries and watching them blow around and blur and re-form and mess up as if we were all just little specks of sand in the Tunisian desert—I mean, that's pretty much what we live for.

But I don't know what went wrong with me. I think maybe I was blown around too much as a child, but for some reason the painful clarity and righteous indignation I experience whenever I get very angry, the sense that the whole world had best stay away from me, the sense that no one else and nothing else matters—well, I've come to enjoy it. Most men, I think, find it so natural to just make certain decisions for themselves unilaterally and arbitrarily and then—gosh golly gee—find themselves lucky enough to find some woman willing to hew to their will that they cannot possibly understand why my anger is so precious to me. I'm not saying that most women will go along with men's autocratic decisions when it comes to concrete things like where to live or where to work—we have learned to fight for our rights on that front. But in emotional terms, mostly we let them do what they want and then we solve the discrepancies. I think feminism has really taken us to the point where we cannot possibly discuss who does the dishes or who folds the laundry one more time. I don't give a shit. It's all the emotional figuring, the tallying of who is more in pursuit of whom this week, and how do we keep the romance alive, and am I being a nag, and are you tired of me darling—it's all this obsessive, circular, insomnia-driven dread that is still mostly women's work, and it's fatiguing as hell.

This is how it is for me: I can't do that anymore. I am too tired. I am not selfish, but I know what's right and what's wrong, I know it with a certainty and fealty that I think is fucking awesome, and I consider this a massive feat of my own psychic system because everything in my past should only have left me blurry, muddy and confused. Mostly, I live in those gray zones, but more and more I am itched by a feeling that something isn't right, something feels wrong, I don't like it, I won't have it—and I am very, very angry. And I love it when I get to that point. Because I see clearly and nothing anyone says or does can possibly intrude.

No means no.

That's where I am. I am so angry that nothing could possibly keep me from doing what I want when I want it. I am refusing to go under, resisting arrest, denying psychic death.

I don't particularly want to be alone the rest of my life, I'm looking forward to getting married and having babies like everybody else. But if the last thirty years of my life and of the simultaneously unfolding third wave of feminism have not made that possible and it takes another thirty or thirty thousand more, then it will be my lot in life.

And I will accept it.

But whenever I am honest enough to see life as more than an academic exercise—to admit it matters for how it feels daily, that the cosmic outlook is not really worth shit—I feel terrible longings. Whenever I hear songs like Jimmy Webb's "If These Old Walls Could Speak" or Neil Young's "Harvest Moon," I really feel deeply and viscerally the awe and wonder of matrimony, and I am certain it is not something I want to miss out on. Especially the lines: "Here's someone who really loves you / Don't ever go away." Or: "Because I'm still in love with you / I want to see you dancing on this harvest moon."

After all these years, still dancing by the dark light of the moon.

*   *   *

At the end of the movie *Heartburn*—underrated in the Nora Ephron oeuvre—Meryl Streep leaves Washington, D.C., as a refugee from marriage to the inconstant journalist played by Jack Nicholson. As she boards the Eastern shuttle to New York—that old standby which has since been morphed multiple times into the Trump shuttle then the Delta shuttle with a few other carriers holding forth in between, a long sturdy marriage displaced by a pattern of serial monogamy with interim affairs—the credits roll and Carly Simon's "Coming Around Again" starts to play. The song seems to both celebrate and derogate the movie's theme, its depiction of the triumph of hope over experience that allows us to love again and again, against the idiotic odds. As Rachel, Streep's character, sits down on the plane with her two children, she starts to sing "The Itsy-Bitsy Spider" with them, their little fingers pantomiming the creeping upward crawl. Now, as far as I'm concerned, Simon's song is the worst in Lite-FM, but on an alternate version that includes a group of kids who sing "The Itsy-Bitsy Spider" as counterpoint to her very adult lament, it is just so sad. Because by teaching that ditty to little kids, we are basically preparing them early on for disappointment—over and over and over again. And because, after all, we are all of us just spiders climbing up a drainpipe.

But there is some part of me that wants to believe that at some point it ends, that somewhere along the way life settles into some kind of comfort, into something more than just free-falling down the side of K2 and then picking up my pitons and rope and clambering right back up, in pursuit of my next notion of a nirvana that does not exist. I mean, I have been fighting the good fight long enough. I'd like quiet, I'd like to think I'm more than just a spider.

But maybe I'm less than one. And maybe persistence is a virtue, plain and simple and not just Sisyphean idiocy.

I don't know.

I don't know if I can stand to fuck up one more time and have one more, as people politely put it, *experience*.

"Experience," which is just a euphemism for heartache and heartbreak, failed love and false promises, for every time you told yourself *This is the real thing* and *Finally I've found my way home* only to end up lost in a muck or lying across rickety train tracks, praying for deliverance and not knowing if that would mean getting run over or being spared; "experience," which is a neutral word that most people know only means something good on a résumé, a term that in the rest of life is more like a criminal rap sheet full of mishaps that cannot be expunged, this indelible quality made more frightening because there are no authorities keeping track, no one is forcing you to remember these things, it is all your own fault, it is *only you who cannot forget*; "experience," which is supposed to be the playground and peep show and life-size labyrinth of adolescence, which can, when it occurs at the right time in life, if it is meted out by the proper source, if it is delivered in moderate and judicious measure—if it is the fender bender you suffer as a teenage driver that reminds you to keep your hands on the wheel and your eyes on the road—can make you a more capable lover and friend, spouse and partner. But for me and many my age, it's been head-on collisions and near-death experiences, trauma, sustained damage, bruises to the brain, permanently hemorrhaging hearts. None of us are getting better at loving: we are getting more scared of it. We were not given good skills to begin with, and the choices we make have tended only to reinforce our sense that it is hopeless and useless. So years go by, and everything that happens only makes what has already happened more painful.

"Experience," Oscar Wilde wrote in *Lady Windermere's Fan,* "is the name everybody gives to their mistakes." How nice to know that one word covers an assortment of items that are so plentiful.

＊　＊　＊

In the end, with so many reasons to be bitter and exhausted, it sometimes feels like embracing life and love is the only answer. In the movie *Blue,* part of Krzysztof Kieslowski's trilogy of films inspired by the colors of the French flag, Juliette Binoche plays a contained, carefully composed woman who loses her husband and child in an auto accident, and she is once again a single woman. Julie, as Binoche's character is called, is austere and cautious with her emotions, carrying the grief and strength of young widowhood with great elegance, saving her unruly tears for private—and yet, this apparent dignity is a bit frosty, even a little warped: she is the kind of person that you would describe as perfect and mean it as an observation, not a compliment. The role of bereft woman is one she takes to naturally, which is why it is so dangerous for her: left alone, she will just stay that way, she will be reduced to the minimal self she once was. Her only sense of life was in her immediate family, and without them, every gesture and thought is all Julie can do to keep her loneliness from turning to terror and rage. Her alienation is symbolized by the cat she brings home to kill the mice in her apartment: as if to say, it's a cruel world, and I can only add to the cruelty, turning small creatures on smaller ones (they are newborn mice).

Then Julie finds out that her husband had a mistress and that the woman, an attorney, is pregnant. The mistress admits that he loved her.

This discovery leaves Julie with many choices. It retroactively re-writes the story of her storybook marriage—although, this being France, it does not necessarily mean their life together was a sham. But it might mean that her chilliness left her husband lonely. In the process of trying to integrate with the world, to dispense with her gorgeous but miserable mystique, Julie slowly determines to be charitable and compassionate, even with predicaments that ought to bring her des-perate pain. She chooses to give the mistress a house she owned with her husband to live in with the baby when it is born. While being shown around the house, the mistress says that the dead husband had told her a lot about his wife. "He said that you are good and that you are generous. That you want to be good and generous. Even to me." In all the sorrow and death and discovered deceit, Julie chooses to be kind and loving and embrace life, to show decency and largesse to those around her.

After dealing with the mother of her deceased husband's future offspring, Julie next takes up the task of completing his last work as a classical composer, a symphony commissioned to celebrate the unifica-tion of Europe. Of course, it soon becomes clear that Julie was the one who really wrote the beginning of this composition, that she has al-ways been the true creative force, hiding herself and her talent behind her husband's name. This will be the first time that she takes credit. Into this large orchestra piece, Julie weaves the lines spoken by Paul in the Book of Corinthians, the words about how all is nothing without love: "Although I speak in tongues of men and angels, I'm just sound-ing brass and tinkling symbols without love. Love suffers long. Love is kind. Enduring all things. Hoping all things. Love has no evil in mind." And in using these verses—the lines frequently read from at wedding ceremonies, the Bible's aptest address on the matter of the union of souls and the glory of human communion—Julie gives the passage a new context and makes for herself a new understanding of what love is: it is not about romance or marriage; it is about living in a world without pity, with little sense of community, and choosing to reach out and show love to people who one might expect her to hate.

"I continued to love despite all the traffic light difficulties," writes Bob Kaufman in "Song of the Broken Giraffe," which about says it all.

And every day, despite an unforgiving and rapacious employment of the death penalty in our country, particularly in Texas and Florida, there are people who choose to be forgiving, who choose to be loving when no one would ever deny them the bitterness and horror that tragedy has given them the right to. I will never forget the man who lost his daughter in the Oklahoma City bombing and, despite dissent from every sector of the community of survivors, he parted company from all the victims' rights fanatics to say that he did not want Timothy McVeigh to get the lethal injection because, he explained, "If I am ever going to forgive him, I need him to be alive." And I will never forget SueZann Bosler, a hairdresser in Opa-Locka, Florida, who in 1986 watched a man stab her clergyman father to death in the church where he ministered. The murderer also stabbed SueZann once in the back and twice in the head, leaving her with a fractured skull that required six hours of surgery to repair. Nevertheless, at her assailant's sentencing hearing, Ms. Bosler spoke out, entreating the court not to give him the death penalty, passionately passing along the simple message: "Why kill people to show that killing is wrong?"

She has chosen forgiveness over vengeance.

And that has to be the guiding principle, it is the only chance any of us has for happiness. It is so hard to be more and better than the terrible things that happened to you, but it helps to start seeing bad people as more and better than the worst things they've done. We may never be so near to the Lord in our capacity for joy that we would find ourselves, like the Hasidim in war-torn Europe, able to dance and celebrate our last bits of life when the Holocaust would destroy us. We may never be the African slaves who tapped out music with their feet when their instruments were denied them, making a noise of protest and ecstasy and existence when the day had been too long, with too much cotton, too many acres, too much sun, too many lashes, too much hunger. We may never, in the mundane monotony of our daily lives, know what it's like to be cut down to so little, to be reduced to such a slight fragment of our own humanity that we are forced to use all that we have, to find the liveliest life force within what little is left—and to accept that the only choice that has still been granted us is whether to be bitter or gracious.

All I would like in my life, what I wish for so very much, is to someday have the strength and be free of the resentment and anger that I carry around with me like Linus' blanket for just long enough to become one of those people who is better than the worst thing that happens to her.

How I would love to be that woman.

Bibliography

Aeschylus. Richard Lattimore, tr. *The Oresteia*. Chicago: University of Chicago Press, 1953.

Alexander, Shana. *Anyone's Daughter: The Times and Trials of Patty Hearst*. New York: Viking Press, 1979.

———. *Very Much a Lady: The Untold Story of Jean Harris and Dr. Herman Tarnower*. Boston: Little, Brown, 1983.

———. *When She Was Bad: The Story of Bess, Hortense, Sukhreet & Nancy*. New York: Random House, 1990.

Allen, Woody. *Four Films by Woody Allen*. New York: Random House, 1982.

Amis, Martin. *London Fields*. New York: Vintage, 1991.

———. *The Moronic Inferno*. New York: Penguin, 1995.

———. *Visiting Mrs. Nabokov and Other Excursions*. New York: Harmony Books, 1993.

Anderson, Christopher. *Madonna, Unauthorized*. New York: Simon & Schuster, 1991.

Andreyev, Leonid. Herman Bernstein, tr. *Samson in Chains: Posthumous Tragedy*. New York: Brentano's Publishers, 1923.

Anonymous. *Go Ask Alice*. Englewood Cliffs, N.J.: Prentice Hall, 1971.

Anonymous. *Primary Colors: A Novel of Politics*. New York: Random House, 1996.

Atwood, Margaret. *Bluebeard's Egg*. New York: Bantam, 1997.

Bal, Mieke. *Death & Dissymetry: The Politics of Coherence in the Book of Judges*. Chicago: University of Chicago Press, 1988.

———. *Lethal Love: Feminist Literary Readings of Biblical Love Stories*. Bloomington: Indiana University Press, 1987.

Barbieri, Paula. *The Other Woman: My Years with O. J. Simpson*. Boston: Little, Brown, 1997.

Barrymore, Drew, with Todd Gold. *Little Lost Girl*. New York: Pocket Books, 1991.

Basinger, Jeanine. *A Woman's View: How Hollywood Spoke to Women 1930–1960*. New York: Alfred A. Knopf, 1993.

Beauvoir, Simone de. H. M Parshley, tr. and ed. *The Second Sex,* New York: Alfred A. Knopf, 1953.

Benedict, Helen. *Virgin or Vamp: How the Press Covers Sex Crimes*. Oxford: Oxford University Press, 1992.

Berquist, Jon L. *Reclaiming Her Story: The Witness of Women in the Old Testament*. St. Louis: Chalice Press, 1992.

Blair, Gwenda. *Almost Golden: Jessica Savitch and the Selling of Television News*. New York: Simon & Schuster, 1988.

Bloom, Claire. *Leaving a Doll's House: A Memoir*. Boston: Little, Brown, 1996.

Bradlee, Ben. *A Good Life: Newspapering and Other Adventures*. New York: Simon & Schuster, 1995.

Brock, David. *The Seduction of Hillary Rodham*. New York: The Free Press, 1996.

Brontë, Emily. *Wuthering Heights*. New York: Bantam, 1983.

Broumas, Olga. *Beginning with O*. New Haven: Yale University Press, 1977.

Brown, Lyn Mikel, and Carol Gillian. *Meeting at the Crossroads: Women's Psychology and Girls' Development*. New York: Ballantine Books, 1992.

Brownmiller, Susan. *Against Our Will: Men, Women and Rape*. New York: Simon & Schuster, 1975.

———. *Femininity*. New York: Simon & Schuster, 1984.

Buchmann, Christina, and Celina Speigel, eds. *Out of the Garden: Women Writers on the Bible*. New York: Ballantine Books, 1994.

Bundesen, Lynne. *The Woman's Guide to the Bible*. New York: Crossroad Publishing Company, 1993.

Burchill, Julie. *Girls on Film*. New York: Pantheon, 1986.

Cain, James M. *Double Indemnity*. New York: Vintage Books. Vintage Crime/Black Lizard, 1992.

———. *The Postman Always Rings Twice*. New York: Vintage Books, Vintage Crime/Black Lizard, 1992.

Carus, Paul. *The Story of Samson: And Its Place in the Development of Mankind*. Chicago: The Open Court Publishing Company, 1907.

Chace, Susan. *Intimacy: A Novel*. New York: Random House, 1987.

Chodorow, Nancy. *The Reproduction of Mothering: Psychoanalysis and the Sociology of Gender*. Berkeley, Calif.: University of California Press, 1978.

Clark, Marcia, with Teresa Carpenter. *Without a Doubt*. New York: Viking Press, 1997.

Clines, David J. A., and Tamara C. Eskenazi, eds. *Telling Queen Michal's Story: An Experiment in Comparative Interpretation*. Sheffield, England: Sheffield Academic Press, 1991.

Cohen, Coleen Ballerino, Beverly Stoeltje, and Richard Wilk, eds. *Beauty Queens on the Global Stage*. New York: Routledge, 1996.

Corso, Gregory. *The Happy Birthday of Death*. New York: New Directions Publishing, 1960.

Cortázar, Julio. Gregory Rabassa, tr. *Hopscotch*. New York: Pantheon Books, 1966.

Cose, Ellis. *A Man's World: How Real Is Male Privilege—and How High Is Its Price?* New York: HarperCollins, 1995.

Darden, Christopher, with Jess Walter. *In Contempt.* New York: HarperCollins, 1996.

Davidson, Peter. *The Fading Smile: Poets in Boston from Robert Lowell to Sylvia Plath.* New York: W. W. Norton, 1994.

Deen, Edith. *All of the Women of the Bible.* New York: Harper & Brothers, 1955.

Des Barres, Pamela. *I'm with the Band: Confessions of a Groupie.* New York: William Morrow, 1987.

———. *Take Another Little Piece of My Heart: A Groupie Grows Up.* New York: William Morrow, 1992.

Didion, Joan. *Play It As It Lays: A Novel.* New York: Farrar, Straus & Giroux, 1970.

———. *Slouching Towards Bethlehem: Essays.* New York: Farrar, Straus & Giroux, 1961.

———. *White Album.* New York: Farrar, Straus & Giroux, 1990.

Dunne, Dominick. *Another City, Not My Own: A Novel in the Form of a Memoir.* New York: Crown, 1997.

Dunne, John Gregory. *Monster: Living Off the Big Screen.* New York: Random House, 1997.

Dworkin, Andrea. *Life and Death: Unapologetic Writings on the Continuing War Against Women.* New York: Free Press, 1997.

Eftimiades, Maria. *Lethal Lolita.* New York: St. Martin's Press, 1992.

Ehrenreich, Barbara. *The Hearts of Men: American Dreams and the Flight from Commitment.* New York: Anchor Books, 1983.

Eliot, T. S. *Selected Poems.* New York: Harcourt, Brace, 1936.

Englade, Ken. *Deadly Lessons: The True Story of the Seductress, the Student, and a Cold-Blooded Murder in New England.* New York: St. Martin's Press, 1991.

Ephron, Nora. *Crazy Salad: Some Things About Women.* New York: Alfred A. Knopf, 1975.

————. *Scribble Scribble: Notes on the Media*. New York: Bantam Books, 1979.

Erickson, Steve. *Leap Year: A Political Journey*. New York: Poseidon Press, 1989.

————. *Arc d'X*. New York: Poseidon Press, 1993.

Euripides. Rex Wagner, tr. *Medea*. Chicago: University of Chicago Press, 1955.

————. Emily Townsend Vermeule, tr. *Electra*. Elizabeth Wyckoff, tr. *The Phoenician Women*. William Arrowsmith, tr. *The Bacchae*. Chicago: University of Chicago Press, 1959.

Exum, Cheryl J. *Fragmented Women: Feminist (Sub)versions of Biblical Narrative*. Sheffield, England: Sheffield Academic, 1993.

————. *Literary Patterns in the Samson Saga: An Investigation of Rhetorical Style in Biblical Prose*. Ann Arbor: University Microfilms, 1976.

Faithfull, Marianne, with David Dalton. *Faithfull: An Autobiography*. Boston: Little, Brown, 1994.

Faludi, Susan. *Backlash: The Undeclared War Against American Women*. New York: Crown, 1991.

Farrow, Mia. *What Falls Away: A Memoir*. New York: Doubleday, 1997.

Fein, Ellen, and Sherrie Schneider. *The Rules: Time-Tested Secrets for Capturing the Heart of Mr. Right*. New York: Warner Books, 1995.

Ferguson, Sarah, with Jeff Coplon. *Sarah the Duchess of York: My Story*. New York: Simon & Schuster, 1996.

Fisher, Amy, with Sheila Weller. *Amy Fisher: My Story*. New York: Pocket Books, 1993.

Flowers, Gennifer. *Passion & Betrayal*. Del Mar, Calif.: Emery Dalton Books, 1995.

Flynn, Elizabeth A., and Patrocinio P. Schweickart, eds. *Gender and Reading: Essays on Readers, Texts, and Contexts*. Baltimore: Johns Hopkins University Press, 1986.

Fox, Paula. *Desperate Characters*. New York: Harcourt, Brace & World, 1970.

French, Marilyn. *The Women's Room*. New York: Simon & Schuster, 1977.

Freud, Sigmund. James Strachey, tr. *Totem and Taboo*. New York: W. W. Norton, 1950.

Friday, Nancy. *The Power of Beauty*. New York: HarperCollins, 1996.

Fried, Stephen. *Thing of Beauty: The Tragedy of Supermodel Gia*. New York: Pocket Books, 1994.

Friedan, Betty. *The Feminine Mystique*. New York: W. W. Norton, 1963.

Friedman, Myra. *Buried Alive: The Biography of Janis Joplin*. New York: William Morrow, 1973.

Gaar, Gillian G. *She's a Rebel: The History of Women in Rock & Roll*. Seattle: Seal Press, 1992.

Gaitskill, Mary. *Bad Behavior*. New York: Poseidon Press, 1988.

———. *Because They Wanted To: Stories*. New York: Simon & Schuster, 1997.

Garner, Shirley Nelson, Claire Kahane, and Madelon Sprengnether, eds. *The (M)other Tongue: Essays in Feminist Psychoanalytic Interpretation*. Ithaca: Cornell University Press, 1985.

Gilbert, Sandra M., and Susan Gubar. *The Madwoman in the Attic: The Woman Writer and the Nineteenth Century Literary Imagination*. New Haven: Yale University Press, 1979.

Gilligan, Carol. *In a Different Voice: Psychological Theory and Women's Development*. Cambridge: Harvard University Press, 1982.

Gilman, Charlotte Perkins. *The Yellow Wallpaper*. New York: Feminist Press, 1973.

Goldin, Nan. *The Ballad of Sexual Dependency*. New York: An Aperture Book. 1986.

Goldman, Shalom. *The Wiles of Women/The Wiles of Men: Joseph and Potiphar's Wife in Ancient Near Eastern Jewish and Islamic Folklore*. Albany: State University of New York, 1995.

Goodman, Jonathan. *The Passing of Starr Faithfull*. Kent, Ohio: Kent State University Press, 1996.

Goodwin, Richard N. *Remembering America: A Voice from the Sixties*. Boston: Little, Brown, 1988.

Gordon, Mary. *The Rest of Life: Three Novellas.* New York: Viking Penguin, 1993.

Greene, Graham. *The Third Man.* London: Faber & Faber, 1988.

Greer, Germaine. *The Madwoman's Underclothes: Essays & Occasional Writings.* New York: Atlantic Monthly Press, 1986.

Gregory, André, and Wallace Shawn. *My Dinner with André.* New York: Grove Press, 1981.

Gross, Michael. *Model: The Ugly Business of Beautiful Women.* New York: William Morrow, 1995.

Guare, John. *Six Degrees of Separation.* New York: Vintage Books, 1990.

Gur-Arieh, Michal. *It Was Turned to the Contrary.* Tel Aviv: Sifrait Poalim Publishing House, 1984.

Harris, Jean. *Stranger in Two Worlds.* New York: Macmillan, 1986.

Harrison, Colin. *Manhattan Nocturne.* New York: Crown, 1996.

Harrison, Jim. *Wolf: A False Memoir.* New York: Dell, 1971.

Haskins, Susan. *Mary Magdalene: Myth and Metaphor.* New York: Harcourt, Brace, 1993.

Heilbrun, Carolyn G. *The Education of a Woman: The Life of Gloria Steinem.* New York: Dial Press, 1995.

Hillel, O. *Joseph and the Wife of Potiphar.* Jerusalem: Hotzaat Hakibbutz Hameuhad, 1983.

Holmes, A. M. *The End of Alice.* New York: Scribner, 1996.

Howe, Florence, ed. *No More Masks!: An Anthology of Twentieth Century American Women Poets.* New York: HarperCollins, 1993.

Hubbard, David Allan. *Strange Heroes.* New York: Trumpet Books, A. J. Holman Company, a division of J. B. Lippincott Company, 1977.

Hughes, Ted. *New Selected Poems.* New York: Harper & Row, 1982.

James, Henry. *Portrait of a Lady.* New York: New American Library, 1963.

Jamieson, Kathleen Hall. *Beyond the Double Bind: Women and Leadership.* New York: Oxford University Press, 1995.

Johnson, Joyce. *What Lisa Knew: The Truth & Lies About the Steinberg Case*. New York: G. P. Putnam's Sons, 1990.

Kam, Rose Sallberg. *Women of the Bible*. New York: Continuum Publishing Co., 1995.

Kates, Judith A., and Gail Twersky Reiner, eds. *Reading Ruth: Contemporary Women Reclaim a Sacred Story*. New York: Ballantine Books, 1996.

Katz, Jon. *Virtuous Reality: How America Surrendered Discussion of the Moral Values to Opportunists, Nitwits & Blockheads Like William Bennett*. New York: Random House, 1997.

Kestenbaum, Wayne. *Jackie Under My Skin: Interpreting an Icon*. New York: Farrar, Straus & Giroux, 1995.

———. *The Queen's Throat: Opera, Homosexuality and the Mystery of Desire*. New York: Poseidon Press, 1993.

Kugel, James. *In Potiphar's House: The Interpretive Life of Biblical Texts*. San Francisco: Harper San Francisco, 1990.

Kundera, Milan. *The Unbearable Lightness of Being*. New York: Harper & Row, 1984.

Larue, Gerard. *Sex and the Bible*. Buffalo: Prometheus Books, 1983.

Lessing, Doris. *The Golden Notebook*. New York: Simon & Schuster, 1962.

Linda, Liza, Robin, and Tiffany (as told to Joanne Parrent). *You'll Never Make Love in This Town Again*. Los Angeles: Dove Books, 1996.

Linklater, Eric. *Husband of Delilah*. New York: Harcourt, Brace & World, 1962.

Livingston, Jane. *Lee Miller*. New York: The California/International Arts Foundation and Thames & Hudson, 1989.

Malcolm, Janet. *The Silent Woman / Sylvia Plath and Ted Hughes*. New York: Alfred A. Knopf, 1994.

Mankowitz, Wolf. *The Samson Riddle*. London: Valentine Mitchell, 1972.

Marcus, Greil. *Lipstick Traces: A Secret History of the Twentieth Century*. Cambridge: Harvard University Press, 1989.

Marks, Elaine, and Isabelle de Courtivron, eds. *New French Feminisms: An Anthology*. New York: Schocken Books, 1981.

Maynard, Joyce. *To Die For*. New York: Dalton Publishers, 1992.

McCain, Gillian, and Legs McNeil. *Please Kill Me: The Uncensored Oral History of Punk*. New York: Grove Press, 1996.

McDonnell, Evelyn, and Ann Powers, eds. *Rock She Wrote: Women Write About Rock, Pop, and Rap*. New York: Dell, 1995.

McNally, Terrence. *Master Class*. New York: Plume, 1995.

Merkin, Daphne. *Dreaming of Hitler: Passions & Provocations*. New York: Crown, 1997.

Middlebrook, Diane Wood. *Anne Sexton: A Biography*. Boston: Houghton Mifflin, 1991.

Milford, Nancy. *Zelda: A Biography*. New York: Harper & Row, 1970.

Millett, Kate. *Sexual Politics*. New York: Doubleday, 1969.

Milton, John. *The Portable Milton*. New York: Viking Press, 1949.

Minot, Susan. *Lust & Other Stories*. Boston: Houghton Mifflin/Seymour Lawrence, 1989.

Morgan, Robin, ed. *Sisterhood Is Powerful: An Anthology of Writing from the Women's Liberation Movement*. New York: Vintage Books, 1970.

Morton, Andrew. *Diana: Her True Story*. New York: Pocket Books, 1992.

Nabokov, Vladimir. *Lolita*. New York: Alfred A. Knopf, 1955.

Ogden, Christopher. *Life of the Party: The Biography of Pamela Digby Churchill Hayward Harriman*. Boston: Little, Brown, 1994.

O'Hara, John. *Butterfield 8*. New York: Random House, 1994.

Paglia, Camille. *Sex, Art and American Culture*. New York: Vintage Books, 1992.

———. *Sexual Personae: Art and Decadence from Nefertiti to Emily Dickinson*. New Haven: Yale University Press, 1990.

———. *Vamps & Tramps: New Essays*. New York: Vintage Books, 1994.

Palladino, Grace. *Teenagers*. New York: Basic Books, 1996.

Palmer, Abram Smythe. *The Samson Saga: And Its Place in Comparative Religion*. New York: Arno Press, 1977.

Parker, Dorothy. *The Portable Dorothy Parker*. Brendan Gill, ed. New York: Viking, 1991.

Penrose, Antony. *The Lives of Lee Miller*. London: Thames & Hudson, 1985.

Plath, Sylvia. *Ariel*. New York: HarperCollins, 1981.

———. *The Bell Jar*. New York: Harper & Row, 1971.

———. *Collected Poems*. New York: HarperCollins, 1986.

———. *The Journals of Sylvia Plath*. New York: Ballantine Books, 1991.

Pollitt, Katha. *Reasonable Creatures: Essays on Women and Feminism*. New York: Alfred A. Knopf, 1994.

Radakovich, Anka. *The Wild Girls Club: Tales from Below the Belt*. New York: Crown, 1994.

Renoir, Jean, John McGrath, and Maureen Teitelbaum, tr. *Rules of the Game*. New York: Simon & Schuster, 1970.

Resnick, Faye D. *Nicole Brown Simpson: The Private Diary of a Life Interrupted*. Beverly Hills, Calif.: Dove Books, 1995.

———. *Shattered: In the Eyes of the Storm*. Beverly Hills, Calif.: Dove Books, 1996.

Rilke, Rainer Maria. Leishman, J.B., J. B. Leishman, and Stephen Spender, tr. *Poems*. New York: Alfred A. Knopf, 1996.

Rosenbaum, Ron. *Travels with Doctor Death and Other Unusual Investigations*. New York: Viking Penguin, 1991.

Rotter, Pat, ed. *Bitches and Sad Ladies: An Anthropology of Fiction by and About Women*. New York: Harper's Magazine Press, published in association with Harper & Row, 1975.

Schneir, Miriam, ed. *Feminism: The Essential Historical Writings*. New York: Random House, 1972.

———. *Feminism in Our Time: The Essential Writings—World War II to the Present*. New York: Vintage Books, 1994.

Seagren, Daniel R. *Couples in the Bible*. Berkeley, Calif.: Baker Book House, 1972.

Sexton, Anne. *Selected Poems of Anne Sexton*. Boston: Houghton Mifflin, 1988.

Sexton, Linda Gray. *Searching for Mercy Street: My Journey Back to My Mother, Anne Sexton*. Boston: Little, Brown, 1994.

Shakespeare, William. *Macbeth*. New York: Oxford University Press, 1990.

———. *Othello, the Moor of Venice*. London: Penguin, 1970.

shange, ntozake. *for colored girls who have considered suicide/when the rainbow is enuf*. New York: Macmillan, 1975.

Shaw, Irwin. *Short Stories of Irwin Shaw*. New York: Random House, 1937.

Shepard, Sam. *Fool for Love*. San Francisco: City Lights Books, 1983.

Sheres, Ita. *Dinah's Rebellion: A Biblical Parable for Our Time*. New York: Crossword, 1990.

Simpson, O. J. *I Want To Tell You: My Response to Your Letters, Your Messages, Your Questions*. Boston: Little, Brown, 1995.

Sinclair, Marianne. *Hollywood Lolita: The Nymphet Syndrome in the Movies*. London: Plexus, 1988.

Smith, David. *Beyond All Reason: My Life with Susan Smith*. New York: Pinnacle Books, 1995.

Smith, Patti. *Babel*. New York: G. P. Putnam's Sons, 1978.

———. *Early Work 1970–1979*. New York: W. W. Norton, 1994.

———. *Seventh Heaven*. San Francisco: Telegraph Books, 1972.

Soderberg, Steven. *Sex, Lies, and Videotape*. New York: HarperCollins, 1990.

Sophocles. David Green, tr. *Oedipus the King*. Robert Fitzgerald, tr. *Oedipus at Colonus*. Elizabeth Wyckoff, tr. *Antigone*. Chicago: University of Chicago Press, 1954.

Spungen, Deborah. *And I Don't Want To Live This Life*. New York: Villard Books, 1983.

Stein, Jean, with George Plimpton. *Edie: An American Biography*. New York: Alfred A. Knopf, 1982.

Steinem, Gloria. *Outrageous Acts and Everyday Rebellions*. New York: Holt, Rinehart and Winston, 1983.

Stoppard, Tom. *Arcadia*. London: Faber & Faber, 1993.

Thernstrom, Melanie. *The Dead Girl: A True Story*. New York: Pocket Books, 1991.

Thompson, Jim. *The Getaway*. New York: Vintage Books, Vintage Crime/ Black Lizard, 1958.

―――. *The Killer Inside Me*. New York: Vintage Books, Vintage Crime/Black Lizard, 1952.

Tisdale, Sallie. *Talk Dirty to Me: An Intimate Philosophy of Sex*. New York: Doubleday, 1994.

Toobin, Jeffrey. *The Run of His Life: The People Versus O. J. Simpson*. New York: Random House, 1996.

Trow, George W. S. *Within the Context of No Context*. New York: Atlantic Monthly Press, 1980.

Vadim, Roger. Melinda Chamber Porter, tr. *Bardot Deneuve Fonda: My Life with the Three Most Beautiful Women in the World*. New York: Simon & Schuster, 1986.

Van Doren, Mark, and Maurice Samuel. *In the Beginning, Love: Dialogues on the Bible*. New York: John Day, 1973.

Vanderbilt, Gloria. *The Memory Book of Starr Faithfull: A Novel*. New York: Alfred A. Knopf, 1994.

Wachtler, Sol. *After the Madness: A Judge's Own Prison Memoir*. New York: Random House, 1997.

Wakoski, Diane. *The Motorcycle Betrayal Poems*. New York: Simon & Schuster, 1971.

Washington, Mary Helen, ed. *Black Eyed Susans: Stories by and About Black Women*. New York: Anchor Press, 1975.

―――. *Midnight Birds: Stories by and About Black Women*. New York: Anchor Press, 1980.

Wasserstein, Wendy. *The Heidi Chronicles, Uncommon Women and Others & Isn't it Romantic*. New York: Vintage Books, 1991.

Weil, Grete. John Barrett, tr. *The Bride Price*. Boston: David R. Godine, 1988.

Weiss, Rabbi Gershon, with Rabbi Aryeh Kaplan. *Samson's Struggle: The Life and Legacy of Samson—Reflecting 2,000 Years of Jewish Thought*. Jerusalem, New York: Feldheim Publishers, 1984.

Weller, Sheila. *Raging Heart: The Intimate Story of the Tragic Marriage of O. J. and Nicole Brown Simpson*. New York: Pocket Books, 1995.

Welles, Orson. *Touch of Evil*. New Brunswick, N.J., 1985.

Wharton, Edith. *The House of Mirth*. New York: Bantam Books, 1984.

Wilde, Oscar. *The Picture of Dorian Gray*. New York: Dell, 1960.

Witchel, Alex. *Girls Only: Sleepovers, Squabbles, Tuna Fish and Other Facts of Family*. New York: Random House, 1996.

Wolf, Naomi. *The Beauty Myth: How Images of Beauty Are Used Against Women*. New York: William Morrow, 1991.

———. *Fire with Fire: the New Female Power and How It Will Change the 21st Century*. New York: Random House, 1993.

———. *Promiscuities*. New York: Random House, 1997.

Wolfe, Linda. *Double Life: The Shattering Affair Between Chief Judge Sol Wachtler and Socialite Joy Silverman*. New York: Pocket Books, 1994.

Wollstonecraft, Mary. *Vindication of the Rights of Women*. New York: W. W. Norton & Company, 1988.

Woolf, Virginia. *A Room of One's Own*. New York: Harcourt Brace, 1990.

Wyden, Peter. *Stella: One Woman's True Tale of Evil, Betrayal, and Survival in Hitler's Germany*. New York: Simon & Schuster, 1992.

Yeats, W. B., Richard J. Finneran, ed. *The Collected Poems of W. B. Yeats*. New York: Scribner, 1996.

Young, James. *Nico: The End*. Woodstock, New York: The Overlook Press, 1993.

Acknowledgments

This book was written over the course of about a year, during which I lived in four different apartments, three hotels, one seamy residential motel and two different houses. When life becomes unstrung and peripatetic at a time when you are also working on something you care about more than anything else on earth—which is to say, in my case, this book—if you are lucky you will discover that love comes from surprising sources, that kindness and generosity can be the lingua franca and common currency of people all over the place.

I must first thank my mother, who is relentlessly supportive of me even when she does not understand or like what I am doing. I lived in her apartment in Florida for a long while, and without the time and peace that haven provided me with, I could not have gotten this work done. For some reason, my mom is never quite able to see—or feel—how much I appreciate her, that I like her just fine as is, that if I had the opportunity I would not choose another mother—for some reason my mom has never quite understood that I love her so, different as we are, but I really do. Her generosity and bafflement and affection are written into the best and worst of everything I am.

I must also thank my Florida relatives, who became the family I never had while I was camped out in their neighborhood. Lewis and Wandy Wang Druss and their awesomely adorable daughters Meredith and Samantha were kind enough to look after me, keep me company, and include me in all kinds of familial outings that I had only known about from watching *Eight Is Enough* and *The Brady Bunch*. Perhaps someday Skunky will become the dog they deserve. Sadly, we never made it to the state fair, or even the county fair, but maybe next time. Aunt Zena and Uncle Bill Druss are the coolest eighty-somethings I know of, and I will gladly eat the early bird special or visit Sawgrass Mills with them anytime. In fact, I will happily do just about anything with or for them anytime because they are such genuine gems.

I never intended to establish any ties while down in Florida, but after some confusion about parking spaces, I ended up befriending my downstairs neighbor, Laura Breuer, while trying to apologize. As soon as I discovered that she had both a VCR and a cat to play with, I knew she was worth cultivating, and when she understood that I needed to cash a check so I could buy the Gucci horsehair slides that I had been coveting forever right that moment, I knew I was right. Eventually we became like Mary and Rhoda—which never happens in New York—and I came to adore her and count on her advice and patience and fun-lovingness, and when I left, I found myself missing her terribly. I must also thank Jim Bennett for suffering through tirades against the death penalty and rants against renting videos from the new release section, for helping me move (albeit in an un-air-conditioned truck) and being a pal.

I owe much more than the usual authorial respect and gratitude and servitude to my Doubleday family—and after I basically lived in their offices for part of the autumn of my discontent, promising each day that the next day the manuscript would finally be done, I feel safe calling these long-forgiving souls "family." Matt Ellis, assistant *par excellence*: let's bury the hatchet over permissions, printing problems, and whatever other hassles I created for you during your first day, followed by your first week, followed by your first month, and soon to be your first year on the job—thank you awesomely and massively for all. I owe you dinner at Aquavit (Betsy will pay?). Laura Hodes: thank you for all your help early on, for always going out of your way, and for that most appropriate pillow. John Pitts: thank you for the wonderful job so far with the advance excerpt and your early-on enthusiasm for this project—and for teaching me how to use e-mail. Mario Pulice: thank you for making the book look so alarmingly amazing—and for the promise of pizza in Fort Lee anytime. David Vance: you are a photographer of such talent and skill that I fear—actually, I *know*—I will only disappoint anyone who sees your pictures before they meet me; thank you so much for doing such a wonderful job with the cover, and for, in spite of what I just said, managing to capture some essential piece of me in the images that you created. Special thanks go to Kathy Trager for saving me from the legal wrath of the women herein. Lawrence Krauser: thank you so very much for being there while I was looming at the Bertelsmann building late into the night, and thank you especially for having that extra bit of kindness that kept you waiting longer than you should have when I was more strung out than I could have explained; and for whatever part you had in the copy editing process—I appreciate that too. Harold Grabau: I don't believe we've ever really met, and I'm sure the copy editing of this book was such a pain in the ass that you never want to meet me, but nevertheless, thanks for the bang-up job with a mess of a text; thanks also to Maureen Cullen, Bob Daniels, Mark Hurst, and Jack Lynch for working overtime and holidays to catch my sloppiness and errors before anyone else did. Alison Cherwin: consider this an early thank you for attending to nightmares yet to come and disasters yet to accumulate—and for doing a fantastic job. Janet Hill: thanks for conversation and Chinese food after I'd gone fifty hours without sleep on a Saturday afternoon, and thank you for hiring Mayuri Reddy, a woman with the good sense to have a physician boyfriend to call when I was strangled by a panic attack in the office next door. Harriet Rubin: I don't know you, but I love your office, especially the daybed. Pat Mulcahy and Michael ("Pencils down!") Palgon somehow got used to my addled presence in the office long past the point when it could possibly be justified—thank you for running such a warm and wonderful company that allowed me to work in my hopelessly inefficient way—I hope you will somehow forgive all the inconvenience I created. In the meantime, Jaguars all around. Finally, Arlene Friedman was brave and committed enough to this book to keep it on an accelerated track when there was scant evidence that I could deliver—and she understood that her confidence in this project would *make* me do the work. Besides being a great publisher, she's also completely haimish. The belief Arlene and everyone at Doubleday has had in this project from the get-go has been, for me, a force of nature.

Thank you to Maria Verheij, an extraordinary researcher, a true pal and an amazing aid for any household crisis—let's just say that I'll hold the nail if she's doing the hammering. Maria is also a natural blonde whose command of the English language is far superior to that of most Americans. Her return to Holland was made bearable only by Emma Cobb, who unearthed some truly apocryphal material. There are many women whose secrets are not safe because Emma has discovered them.

Thank you also to the publishers of the foreign editions of *Prozac Nation* who did so much to make my idiomatic Americanese comprehensible in the most exotic places. Like England, a country, as they say, separated from ours only by an ocean and a language: thanks to Stella Kane and all at Quartet for bridging that gap to the point where I feel at home in London. Maarten Asscher at J. M. Meulenhoff must be singled out for gallantry, Kajsa Leander and Ernst Malmsten at Leander Malmsten must be praised for their style and substance, and Sylvia Querini and Miguel Martinez-Lage at Ediciones B for, quite literally, thinking of everything (especially ways to avoid getting arrested in Madrid).

How have I been blessed with such incredible friends? In the last couple of years, I have been so lucky to have people in my life whose loyalty was deeper and stronger than my ability to indulge in destructiveness and drama, or my insistence on withdrawing from life—or from the active duties that friendship demands—for more than just a little while. I am proud and humbled by the presence of these people in my life. Christine Fasano put aside her own misgivings about what I was doing to myself and was a friend in need and in deed: somewhere along the way, Christine made a leap of love and kindness that was much greater than I think either of us expected, and it was through her exertions that we both discovered how strong the bonds of friendship are in a world that is otherwise truly without pity—I mean, it is not just anyone who will stop in Fort Lauderdale for a day to check in on me en route to New York from Brazil. Jody Friedman looks like a Bond girl and writes scholarly papers on missile deployment and takes business trips to Zimbabwe and takes phone calls from Oscar Arias—and in all this glamour and genius, she still finds time for me. Jody and I together have watched a lot of strange and difficult things happen in the last few years, and I thank God every day that our relationship is intact, that we can still rent movies and get our highlights done together—and that things have worked out so much more happily in the end. Sharon Meers thought there was hope for me when there really was none—which is why eventually there *was* hope. Sharon has been my bedrock over the years: she is surely the only woman who has ever moved to San Francisco and met a *straight* man almost as soon as she deplaned, deciding to marry him within a matter of months. She also completed the New York City marathon and became a member of the Council on Foreign Relations in the same year; when I grow up, I want to be just like Sharon. Roberta Feldman: I hope you are swingingly single and making it safe for a market economy somewhere in Moscow or Lvov or Warsaw, but wherever you are, please know that your presence permeates this book. There are lessons I learned from Roberta freshman year that still ring true many years of maturity since. Mark McGurl wins huge points with me for driving four hours each way through Florida's dull, flat terrain just to see what had happened to me. Jason Bagdade has been out of touch, but still, love never dies. Elizabeth Ackerman, Kera Bolonik, Tom Campbell, Amanda Filipacchi, Jonathan Glickman, Emily Jenkins, Steven Johnson, Jamie Linville, Peter Robles, Betsey Schmidt, Stefanie Syman—though I've been away and out of touch for quite a while, and though lifestyle changes and long hours have kept us more apart than I like, all of them should know that they mean a lot to me and I miss them much. I am grateful to Rachel Brodie and Naomi Shechter for remaining a part of who I am after all this time.

Mare Winningham: what a gift it was to get to know you late at night by telephone, for all those months of girl talk and movie talk and music talk and book talk and just general cross-country gab. I am ready for my close up—in person, I hope. In the meantime, you should know that your friendship was a sustaining force while I was hiding in the swampland and trying to write. You are truly a woman of heart and mind.

Great gratitude must be extended to Silver Hill and Wilton House. I especially thank Ellyn Shander, M.D., for being such a grandly innovative, daring, and eccentric therapist and Joanne Waters for patience and wisdom. Most of all I must thank Sue Carroll, Roberta Green and Gregory Blake at the Cottage for having far greater faith in me than I did in myself, for being forbearing with all my brattiness, and for showing untold kindness and caring when I really did not deserve it—and teaching me how to be a person who did. Residents at the Cottage—whose anonymity shall be respected—probably affected me and meant more to me than they'll ever know or I'll ever be able to say; I wish them all long life. On the home front, much appreciation to Paula Eagle, M.D., for enduring with such calm what must surely be a very frustrating task—I hope it will be easier from here on; I'm looking forward to it.

I feel obligated to thank the entire hospitality industry—God bless whoever invented room service—but especially the staffs of the Riverside Hotel in Fort Lauderdale and the Millennium and Peninsula hotels in New York City. Caroline Kim, a housesitter of great reliability, allowed me to leave home and be accommodated at these places. Thanks to her for caring for Zap, my cat, who is such a fine and gentle creature that only someone as sweet and caring as Caroline would possibly do.

How lucky I am to occupy the same planet as Bruce Springsteen and Bob Dylan. *Nebraska* and *The Ghost of Tom Joad, Highway 61 Revisited* and *Blonde on Blonde*—those albums, the voices they carried, reached me when nothing and no one else did. Without them I might still have been able to write this book, but without the small fix of God's presence that I could hear in Springsteen and Dylan, I can't imagine why I'd have bothered.

Chris—what can I say? Thank you so much for being the sweet, adorable voice on the other end of the phone when I was a thousand miles away, thank you for every Nexus inquiry you ever ran for me, thank you for more information on Pamela Anderson than even Tommy Lee would care to know, thank you for your care and kindness, for the safety and sanity of your presence. To paraphrase a mutual favorite, when I was at my most impoverished, thank you for teaching me how to give. Most of all, thank you for reminding me. You drew seven circles around my soul. I think you already know I could not have done this without you.

With regard to my editor, Betsy Lerner, and my agent, Lydia Wills, to whom this book is dedicated: to enumerate their contributions to this work and to my life would be an attempt to delimit what has been for me an unlimited wellspring of generosity, advice, insight, and (because I can think of no other word) love over the last few years. Suffice it to say that this book is as much theirs as it is mine, that their blood, sweat, and tears are in the ink of every page, that their contribution to everything that is here is such that, as Pablo Neruda wrote at the end of one of his odes, they have "lived half my life, and will die half my death."

In memoriam:

Gunnar O'Neill 1968–1995

Jeff Buckley 1966–1997

Athan Alton 1968–1998

Rejoice, O young man, in thy youth

Ecclesiastes 11:9

Permissions

Reprinted with the permission of Scribner, a division of Simon & Schuster from *for colored girls who have considered suicide when the rainbow is enuf* by Ntozake Shange. Copyright © 1975, 1976, 1977 by Ntozake Shange.

"I'm On Fire" by Bruce Springsteen. Copyright © by Bruce Springsteen. Reprinted by permission.

"Beginning With O" by Olga Broumas. Copyright © 1977. Reprinted with permission of Yale University Press.

"Handy Man" by Otis Blackwell and Jimmy Jones. Copyright © Warner Bros. Publications. Reprinted by permission.

"Doll Parts" by Courtney Love. Copyright © Mother May I Music 1992. Reprinted by permission.

"Lady Lazarus" by Sylvia Plath. Copyright © 1982. Reprinted by permission of HarperCollins Publishers, Inc.

Excerpts from *Selected Poems of Anne Sexton.* Copyright © 1988 by Linda Gray Sexton, as Literary Executor of the Estate of Anne Sexton. Reprinted by permission of Houghton Mifflin Company. All rights reserved. Previously published in *Live Or Die* (1966).

"The Edge" by Sylvia Plath. Copyright © 1982. Reprinted by permission of HarperCollins Publishers, Inc.

"Daddy" by Sylvia Plath. Copyright © 1982. Reprinted by permission of HarperCollins Publishers, Inc.

Excerpts from *The Journals of Sylvia Plath,* Copyright © 1982 reprinted by permission of Doubleday.

From *The Selected Poetry of Rainer Maria Rilke* by Rainer Maria Rilke, edited & translated by Stephen Mitchell. Reprinted by permission of Random House, Inc.

"Marlene on the Wall" by Suzanne Vega. Copyright © 1985 Warner Bros. Publications. Reprinted by permission.

"T' Ain't Nobody's Business (If I Do)" words and music by Porter Grainger and Everett Robbins. Permission granted by MCA Music Publishing.

"The Lovepet" by Ted Hughes. Copyright © 1982. Reprinted by permission of HarperCollins Publishers, Inc.

"Love Song" by Ted Hughes. Copyright © 1982. Reprinted by permission of HarperCollins Publishers, Inc.

"Brilliant Disguise" by Bruce Springsteen. Copyright © 1987 by Bruce Springsteen. Reprinted by permission.